THE CHURCH

AND

THE TWENTIETH CENTURY

THE CHURCH

AND

THE TWENTIETH CENTURY

BY

NORMAN SYKES   H. D. A. MAJOR

PERCY DEARMER   T. G. ROGERS

C. E. RAVEN   A. T. WILSON

DOUGLAS WHITE   F. L. CROSS

L. ELLIOTT-BINNS

AND

G. L. H. HARVEY (Editor)

Essay Index Reprint Series

BOOKS FOR LIBRARIES PRESS, INC.

FREEPORT, NEW YORK

First Published 1936
Reprinted 1967

LIBRARY OF CONGRESS CATALOG CARD NUMBER:

67-26747

PRINTED IN THE UNITED STATES OF AMERICA

PREFACE

The contributors to this volume have not met for discussion or conference, and each contributor is responsible for his own paper only. In view of the character of the general subject, it has seemed well to include papers written from different points of view, even at the cost of some loss of homogeneity. No attempt has been made to suppress such divergencies as naturally appeared.

G. L. H. Harvey

CONTENTS

FOREWORD

By

The Bishop of Birmingham

Here is a volume of essays written by men exceptionally vigorous alike in thought and feeling. They are all members of the Church of England. All but two are ordained ministers of the Church and one of the exceptions is the son of a clergyman of great distinction. For the most part they are liberal churchmen, heirs of a tradition which can be traced through some of the greatest of Victorian divines to the Cambridge Platonists and so to those who, in the spirit of Erasmus, broke with mediaeval superstitions at the Reformation. When the essayists discuss various phases of their common topic, "The Church and the Twentieth Century", they naturally have in mind the Church of England; and they consider its problems in the light of its history during that first third of the century which is already past. With their analysis of the existing situation I find myself largely in agreement: with the type of reform in doctrine, liturgy, and policy on which the hopes of most are fixed, I am in complete sympathy.

After reading the volume I asked myself whether its quiet good sense afforded any certainty that the Church of England would pursue the path so persuasively marked out; and, as I have reflected upon the world in which we find ourselves, grave doubts have arisen. It is not that I think that the two alternative forms of faith persisting in the Church are more likely to endure. Religion must, of course, give man a satisfying sense of union with a Goodness that spreads its power throughout the

Universe. Thus in some way or another the fact of the Atonement must be preserved and evil must be explained. But we can no longer maintain the Evangelical tradition which uses for the Atonement a substitutionary theory of the death of Christ and rejects biological evolution because it puts an end to the belief that sin came through Adam's fall. Similarly, every religion into which the notion of the Divine enters must be sacramental. God must be revealed in the normal life of man. But what is commonly called Catholicism emphasizes a superstitious sacramentalism: it is the transformation of the Gospel of Palestine under the influence of the ancient Mystery Religions. Since all religions are tough, such Catholicism will die but slowly. But clearly it is already fighting a losing battle, its adherents an aggressive—and tiresome—minority in modern European civilization.

Liberalism, then, ought to triumph in the Church of England. Its sweet reasonableness ought to commend that Church to the English people, and so gradually ought to spread throughout the world such re-formulation of the religion of Christ as is in harmony alike with the knowledge and with the finest spiritual striving of our time. Yet he would be a bold man who would prophesy such a triumph. There is an element of unreason in man, as inexplicable as the existence of evil. Such unreason shews itself wherever emotion is strong and therefore commonly appears as a factor of triumphant religious propaganda. Moreover, successful exponents of established forms of faith, under the influence of popular approval, often emphasize the unreasonable elements of those forms though, as a concession to sound sense, they may use a thin veneer of apparently good argument. The observer who doubts the power of unreason in religion may mournfully reflect that the great halls in our industrial cities would be wellnigh empty for a lecture by a master of philosophical theology: they are filled to overflowing by the preaching of the Four Square Gospel or of Christian Science.

The historian will not forget that Christianity arose in a decaying civilization and flourished as the decay grew worse. Those elements in the Gospels and Acts of the Apostles which scholars assign to the myth-making fancy of the first two or three Christian generations and of which we would fain be rid, were especially the elements beloved by Christians when the standard creeds were framed. Dr. Dearmer and others in the volume before us plead persuasively that the burden of the Creeds should no longer oppress those who use the Prayer Book. But behind the Creeds lies the New Testament—a collection of books deservedly held sacred and yet containing not a little which we cannot accept as a record of fact.

A generation ago—at the turn of the century— many enthusiasts hoped that Christianity, free from sectarian irrelevances, might conquer the world. Christianity had at the time wonderful success in attracting the sympathy of, if it did not actually convert, some of the best representatives of the great Asiatic civilizations. To Asia it went, backed by the prestige of European culture, a culture which obviously, by its insight into the nature of things and its consequent material power, was stronger than any competitor. But the tide has since ebbed. Our scientific culture has been almost completely absorbed by Japan; and other Eastern races are more slowly accepting and using its methods and results. None the less, Asiatic peoples are turning from the Christian faith to their own religious instincts and traditions. Their more thoughtful representatives say: Is the contention wholly fanciful?—that in every culture religion in its formal aspects is a survival from more primitive times. Facts, beliefs, arguments are preserved by religious conservatism when they have really ceased to be credible. Thus the actual religion of a people differs from its formal faith. Until recently the religion of Western Europe was not the Christianity of creeds and articles of faith drawn up by official councils but an indefinite theism coloured by the ethical teaching of Christ. What it will be in the future is for Eastern observers a problem of great complexity: for ourselves it is a question of supreme importance.

I doubt whether in the present volume our essay-ists, as a whole, have adequately allowed for the disintegrating effect on all forms of belief, Christianity included, which is caused by the increasingly close juxtaposition of the rival creeds of mankind. It is well known that, for several generations, the thought of men and women returning from a prolonged stay in India has been permeated by pantheism. At the present time the influence of that metaphysical outlook increasingly colours Western philosophical thought. Furthermore, no one can reflect upon modern Germany and ignore the fact that not in Japan alone can flourish the cult of the divine State and its semi-divine leader. And the atheism which is at the root of much Chinese religion finds its counterpart in Europe in ethical and social enthusiasm which, though religious, has no apparent need of the idea of God. From an amalgam of religious notions and from the mutually destructive criticism of competing forms of faith, the religion of the future may ultimately emerge. But he would be a bold man who would confidently prophesy the nature of the evolution of Christianity during the present century.

Much depends on the course of civilization in Europe. If religion be a divine revelation, we must allow that that revelation is profoundly affected by social conditions. Our civilization was grievously hurt by the Great War. In consequence, Christianity, as we could observe it in the great countries of Europe before the war, has been deplorably injured. The Christian faith, albeit in a corrupt form, has vanished from Russia: and the Christian student of affairs will observe without compensatory satisfaction that simultaneously the religion of Mohammed has vanished from Turkey, another participant in the conflict. A host of recent pronouncements by obsequious clerics, excited by the Abyssinian campaign, shews how Catholicism has been barbarized in Italy. In France derelict parishes and crumbling churches shew the decline of religious belief—the devout have ceased to be a menace to the secular State: and it is lamentable that Barthianism, which for most of us conceals its irrationality by evasion, should be the one form of Christianity to raise its head in Germany against the prevailing cult of the State and its leader.

If such are some of the consequences of the war of 1914–18, we may well be apprehensive as to the future of religion in Europe if a like conflagration should again break out. I confess that personally I view the future with grave misgiving. The international rivalries, jealousies, and suspicions that lead to war are growing in strength. A vast conflict becomes yearly less improbable. If it comes, it will coarsen all the nations which take part in it. There will be an appalling aftermath of political and social disorder and decay. Religion will not perhaps be exterminated; but all the finer elements in Christianity, and possibly even nominal allegiance to Christ, will be destroyed. At the present time a surprising number of philosophical thinkers—among them some of repute—will argue against belief alike in God, human freedom, and personal immortality. After a further great war with its consequent spiritual sickness it is probable that such negations would be generally accepted. Moreover, demoralization would be evident even in coteries among whom theistic beliefs were maintained: they would combine such beliefs with superstitions arising like a miasma from ground impregnated with blood and poison-gas.

It is, however, wellnigh useless to speculate as to the future of religion in the political, social, and moral chaos that would virtually end European civilization as we have known it. We must pray that such a suicide of Europe will be averted: that, though other civilizations have proved fragile, our own will survive for some centuries, at any rate, owing to the amazing progress in the conquest of Nature which its men of science and inventors have made. But, even if we can assume a continuity unbroken by catastrophe, I doubt whether we can expect Christianity as we know it in this country to flourish little changed. For fully two generations elementary education has now been universal in Great Britain: secondary education is of more recent development and the size and influence of the universities is still increasing. In this process of change conditions have only gradually become such that the religious beliefs of most of the teachers are no longer the result of what we may term systematic Christian influence. The teachers and, in consequence, the children whom they train are increasingly critical of traditional beliefs. The teachers may, it is true, have no expert knowledge of philosophical speculation or of literary and historical criticism of the New Testament. But they absorb methods, conclusions, and, above all, atmosphere. In consequence of such almost unconscious activity of mind and spirit, a new *Zeit-geist* is being created. The historic churches —the Church of England included—must adapt themselves to this *Zeit-geist* or become sectarian minorities, struggling, highly organized, probably waspish, groups.

In the present volume repeated reference is made to Prayer Book revision and to the rejection of the proposals brought before the House of Commons in 1927 and 1928. The actual cause of the rejection was the fact that the Revision gave legal status to an ecclesiastical revolution which sought to re-establish a sacramental superstition rejected at the Reformation. Archbishop Davidson, distressed by the liturgical chaos that developed during the war, was persuaded to allow in the projected revision the permanent "reservation" of the consecrated elements of bread and wine. In practice such permission meant the cult of the consecrated wafer: encouragement of the belief that in consecration any priest could associate the spiritual presence of Christ with the elements. The modern world rejects such priestly pretensions as an absurdity; and the House of Commons, in spite of pertinacious lobbying, surely unparalleled in our recent history, remained true to the modern outlook.

That Davidson acted contrary to his instinctive judgement I have no doubt. His refusal to support the re-presentation of the 1927 Book unless its rubrics were changed—a bad blunder tactically—was significant of his deep uneasiness. Most certainly some of us left him in no doubt that, when the revision sanctioned permanent reservation, public controversy became inevitable. I myself asked that, as the decision was of such fundamental importance, the names of Bishops voting for and against permanent reservation should be taken and entered on the minutes of the revision proceedings. When my request was declined I sat back and reflected upon a story—whether true or apocryphal I know not—told me shortly after I went to administer the diocese of Birmingham. Small Heath is an industrial suburb of the city, a centre of so-called "rebel" churches. According to the story, two ill-dressed lads were observed arguing in one of its streets. One of them ended the discussion by saying decisively: "It isn't Jesus: it ain't nothing but a piece of bread. Jesus wants yer to be good." The onlooker's eye passed from this Erasmus of the gutter to his background—and saw the great Waverley Road Secondary School of the City of Birmingham.

But a defect of the revised Prayer Book, even more radical than the concession of reservation, was the almost complete refusal of the revisers to accept any results of modern critical study of the origins of Christianity. For instance, a proposal was made to sanction an alternative collect to that set for Christmas Day with its words, an offence to many who regard marriage as holy, "born of a pure Virgin". The proposal was rejected. Again, it is well established that the original and rightful text of St. Luke's Gospel did not in its account of the Last Supper contain the words "Do this in remembrance of me". In fact, there is no command in the Gospels that the Eucharist should be continued. I therefore proposed, when we were revising the Communion Office, that in the consecration prayer the words "and in his holy Gospel commanded us to continue" should be replaced by "and according to St. Paul commanded . . .": the proposal was rejected. At intervals during the tedious process of revision similar test resolutions were moved. None had any chance of acceptance. The revision, in fact, from the standpoint of modern scholarship was worthless.

We may doubt whether the proposals suggested at intervals in the present volume for incorporating sound and progressive scholarship are adequate. There is no question that they indicate the character of the revision which ought to be made. But, while we wait for an adequate revision, such Continental scholarship as is represented by Loisy's *La Naissance du christianisme* and by Guignebert's *Jésus* will permeate the teaching profession of England: and the situation will grow worse. With increasing emphasis the Prayer Book will seem to maintain beliefs which the intellectual leaders of England have discarded. Doubtless reply will be made—it might be made by one or two writers in the present volume—that, if such Continental scholarship as I have mentioned prevails, Christianity as we have known it will be radically changed. To that I answer that we are living in an epoch of radical change. Religious belief cannot remain unaltered in an era when our understanding of the Universe and of human history has been vastly enlarged.

Much that our fathers believed must perish. Let it perish. Look to the future. Religion, I am certain, is indestructible. I have personally no doubt but that an empirically reached theism will ultimately maintain itself as the most reasonable explanation of man and his world that can be set forth. The ethics most naturally in harmony with such theism are, I am convinced, to be found in the teaching of Jesus. In words of Tennant, whose *Philosophical Theology* I commend to all stimulated by the present volume of essays, "Christ revealed God in that he understood him and has enabled us, not to see what he saw without using the same means, but to see as he saw by our own 'personally' aided insight and assimilation".

Many an ecclesiastical partisan — conservative Evangelical joining hands with Anglo-Catholic—will say that, in so far as the point of view which I have set forth is that of the essayists in the present volume, it destroys the Christian faith. It does nothing of the kind. Christ's ethics give an edge to theism, which make it not a philosophical cushion but a spiritual sword. Such ethics create not merely men who are clean-living and trustworthy, honourable and honoured. They create the social reformer, eager to destroy social injustice: the eugenist, quietly confident that as knowledge increases we can eliminate unsound racial stocks: the pacifist, ready at the cost of his own life to preach peace between the nations. Such men are the salt of the earth: and, so long as such are salted by Christ, he will remain God's witness to mankind.

E. W. B.

April 20, 1936

I

THE IDEAL OF A NATIONAL CHURCH

by

REV. NORMAN SYKES, M.A., D.Phil.

Professor of History in the University of London
Examining Chaplain to the Bishop of Chichester and to the
Bishop of Exeter
Author of *Church and State in England in the Eighteenth Century*
(The Birkbeck Lectures in Ecclesiastical History, 1931–33)

SYNOPSIS

MODERN European tendencies are not favourable to the ideal of a free church in a free state. Moreover, the evils associated with the nationalism of Totalitarian states have bred distrust of the religious nationalism expressed in national churches. But it is significant that the states which to-day are most Totalitarian are those states whose development and history have been most affected by association with the great mediaeval international corporations, the Holy Roman Empire and the Papacy.

ECCLESIASTICAL INTERNATIONALISM

The Roman Papacy is the ecclesiastical counterpart of the Holy Roman Empire. Its title-deeds are the Donation of Constantine and the Pseudo-Isidorian Decretals rather than the Petrine texts of the Gospels. The incompatibility of Roman claims with the forces of nationality and freedom caused the revolt which led to the formation of national churches.

THE TOTALITARIAN STATE

The absolutist claims of the Totalitarian state constitute a grave challenge to the Christian belief in the intrinsic value and sovereign status of individual, family, and church. They are the more dangerous because of the power of the machinery at the disposal of a modern government for purposes of propaganda. Though Totalitarian states may differ in their economic and religious creeds, they all use the same means, the suppression of freedom, in order to secure their ends. The mediaeval Church was, in principle, a Totalitarian state, and its Totalitarian pretensions were not abandoned after the Reformation, when Rome still continued to denounce liberty of conscience, speech, and of the press. The suppression of freedom is incompatible with Christian principles.

RESPUBLICA CHRISTIANA

The threat of modern Paganism constitutes a strong reason for an alliance between Church and State; but

Totalitarian methods must be forsworn and each partner must recognize the rights of the other. The State must not advance absolutist claims, and the Church militant and imperfect must not demand rights which only befit the Church triumphant and perfected. Where, as in Italy, the Church has made the most extravagant claims to supremacy, its influence on secular life has been least effective. If a state dissociates itself from religious profession or adopts an anti-religious policy, the ideal of a national church ceases to be practicable.

Ecclesia Anglicana

The sixteenth-century ideal of a national Church of England envisaged a complete identity of personnel in Church and nation. The methods used by Henry VIII and Elizabeth with the object of suppressing dissentient opinion illustrate the dangers implicit in this conception. Presbyterianism, no less than Episcopalianism, was eager to impose religious uniformity. After 1689 the principle of toleration was accepted. It is an error to regard the Nonjuror schism as a protest against Erastianism. The Nonjurors protested, not against the authority of the State in matters of religion, but against the exercise of that authority by a king whom they regarded as a usurper. The propounder of the doctrine of the complete and inherent sovereignty of the Church was the Latitudinarian divine, William Warburton, who regarded establishment as a free alliance between two sovereign and independent bodies. Nearly two centuries later the Enabling Act was based on his principles. After his time the progress of liberalism brought about an increasing secularization of Parliament. It was this which inspired Keble's denunciation of "national apostasy".

The Tractarian demand for recognition of the freedom of the Church was accompanied by the development of ceremonial extravagances and extreme and exclusive claims on behalf of episcopacy and apostolic succession.

Establishment and Comprehensiveness

A national Church must needs be a comprehensive church, and comprehensiveness demands a wide spirit of tolerance within the church. On the other side, the continuance of establishment depends upon the retention of the goodwill of the separated churches. The traditional attitude of the Church of England to reformed churches at home and abroad has been one of friendly association. To a national established church the duty of striving for the fullest union with non-episcopal churches at home is paramount.

The Episcopate in a National Church

There is a danger that immersion in diocesan activities may lead the Bishops to neglect their functions as religious leaders of the nation, a danger which is increased by the formation of additional dioceses. The conditions of the day demand the creation of an episcopal cabinet or standing inner council, which should not limit itself to the consideration of specifically ecclesiastical matters.

The traditional English method of appointing Bishops is consonant with Catholic historic tradition, and secures the appointment of Bishops who are competent to perform the functions of the episcopal office in its wider national aspects.

Parliament and Ecclesiastical Affairs

The development of the sovereignty of Parliament over all rival authorities converted the royal supremacy into a parliamentary supremacy, an anomalous position for which the Enabling Act of 1919 sought to provide a remedy. In general the procedure laid down in the Act has worked well, though the rejection of the Revise Prayer Book measure caused deep dissatisfaction in ecclesiastical circles. It should, however, be borne in mind that, as Archbishop Davidson admitted, the House of Commons reflected the opinion of the majority of churchmen on the more controversial points in dispute. Nevertheless, the Archbishops' Commission on the Relations between Church and State has in its Report advocated the abolition of the parliamentary veto upon spiritual measures, and this despite the fact that since the passing of the Enabling Act there has been no real violation by Parliament of the spiritual independence of the Church of England. It is important in the present situation to remember that abstract principle should be adapted to concrete circumstance, and that theoretical anomalies do not in themselves justify revolutionary changes.

CHURCH AND NATION

It has been asserted that the Church has been so organized and clericalized as to lose its national character, and that a kind of moral disestablishment has resulted. The remedy for this is not actual disestablishment, but the development of such a sense of the responsibility of the Church of England towards the nation as will lead to a sustained effort to recapture the lost association of the religion of the English people with the established church. Especially urgent is the duty of providing for secondary religious education, a task which can only be fulfilled in co-operation with the Free Churches. No less urgent is the need of securing a better intellectual training for ordinands. The Church should seek "a universal blessed union of all reformed churches, both at home and abroad". With this in view, the restrictive clause in the declaration required from applicants for inclusion in the Electoral Roll should be removed, and Nonconformists welcomed as occasional communicants. Along such lines churchmen should seek, in accordance with the traditions of the sixteenth and seventeenth centuries, to recover the national character of the Church of England.

I

THE IDEAL OF A NATIONAL CHURCH

"*Libera Chiesa in Libero Stato.* Such is the aphorism in which the maker of Italian unity summed up the ideal of statesmanship for the solution of the perennial problem of the two powers. Whether or no this ideal can be attained is doubtful; that it never has been attained is certain."[1] During the twenty-three years which have elapsed since Figgis prefaced these words to his study of *Churches in the Modern State*, the ideal of a free church in a free state has counted unhappily few victories to its credit, whilst the intellectual climate over large parts of Christian Europe has become definitely hostile to the conception of ecclesiastical freedom. It may seem indeed that Figgis' confident assertion that the ideal "never has been attained" needs modification in the light of the legislative recognition of the position of the Church of Scotland in 1921; but this solitary achievement in North Britain stands out the more conspicuously amidst the receding tide of spiritual liberty on the continent of Europe. Moreover, the association of the Totalitarian states of contemporary Europe with fervent aspirations of political nationalism has tended not unnaturally to cast a dark shadow of suspicion and disfavour upon the principle of nationality, and especially upon its religious expression in the form of national churches which were the result of the Reformation movement.

---

[1] J. N. Figgis, *Churches in the Modern State*, p. 3 (1913). The general position adopted in this essay owes much to the lecture of Dr. Ernest Barker, "Christianity and Nationality" (1927), reprinted in *Church, State, and Study* (1930), to which reference should be made.

Writers are not lacking, therefore, who, in the interests of the Roman Catholic Church, urge that "Protestantism, Liberalism, and Communism are the three successive stages by which our civilization has passed from Catholicism to complete secularism",[1] and argue that only by reversal of the process and restoration of the papal authority can Europe hope to save itself from destruction.

But if the apologist for national churches may no longer assume even in England a predisposition to accept the principle of his cause, he has no occasion to dread exchange of argument with his adversary. It is pertinent at the outset to observe that those European countries which are victims of Totalitarian despotisms—and the exclusion from this purview of Russia and Turkey may be justified by the evident fact that they have remained throughout the centuries alien neighbours rather than naturalized members of the European community of nations—are precisely those whose destinies have been affected by their association with the international corporations of the Middle Ages, the Holy Roman Empire and the Holy Roman Papacy. For whilst the pursuit of the phantom-authority of Holy Roman Emperor defeated all attempts until Bismarck towards a unified German nation, the resolute determination of the Papacy to preserve its temporal principality at the price of a protracted disunity of Italy prevented the rise of a united Italian kingdom until the *annus mirabilis* of modern Europe, 1870.

ECCLESIASTICAL INTERNATIONALISM

Nor if the survey is transferred from the sphere of civil polity to that of ecclesiastical, does the cause of national churches suffer from comparison with the pretensions of an international society. The Roman

[1] C. Dawson, *Religion and the Modern State*, p. 148 (1935).

Papacy belongs to the same order of ideas and to the same political organization of society as the Holy Roman Empire. Its title-deeds are the Donation of Constantine and the Pseudo-Isidorian Decretals rather than the Petrine texts of the Gospels, and its *milieu* the imperial city of Rome rather than the provincial atmosphere of Jerusalem. For even as the Council of Constantinople decreed that the Bishop of that see should have "the primacy of honour next after the Bishop of Rome, because Constantinople is new Rome", so the Council of Chalcedon, confirming its decree, accepted the argument that "the Fathers properly gave the primacy to the throne of the elder Rome, because that was the imperial city", and deduced from it the propriety of giving "equal privileges to the most holy throne of New Rome".[1] So late as the age of Bede, in the early eighth century, "the claim that the authority of Rome is different in kind from that of the other patriarchates had not been made; in fact, stress was laid at Rome on imperial grants as the source of its prerogatives, and soon after Bede's death the famous fiction of the Donation of Constantine was to be invented in support of the same claim".[2] By this forgery the supremacy of the see of Peter "as well over the four chief seats, Antioch, Alexandria, Constantinople, and Jerusalem, as also over all the churches of God in the whole world," was explicitly based upon imperial decree; and the bestowal upon the popes of the further donation of "the imperial power, and dignity of glory, and vigour and honour",[3] together with the right to wear the imperial diadem and tiara,

---

[1] B. J. Kidd, *Documents Illustrative of the History of the Church*, vol. ii. p. 98 (3rd Canon of Council of Constantinople), p. 300 (28th Canon of Council of Chalcedon) (2 vols., 1923).

[2] E. W. Watson, "The Age of Bede" in *Bede, His Life, Times and Writings* (ed. A. Hamilton Thompson), p. 40.

[3] E. F. Henderson, *Select Historical Documents of the Middle Ages*, p. 325 (the Donation of Constantine).

justifies the contention of Hobbes that "if a man consider the original of this great ecclesiastical dominion he will easily perceive that the papacy is no other than the ghost of the deceased Roman Empire sitting crowned upon the grave thereof". Against such claims to universal dominion national kingdoms and churches might revolt with no more compunction or need of apology than national monarchs felt in rebutting the pretensions of the Holy Roman Emperor.

The actual causes of the revolt which led in England and elsewhere to the establishment of national churches are writ large in the history of the papacy during the later Middle Ages.

> The idea of a national church can only be judged by comparison with its alternative. The idea of a church universal in its organisation has been tried, and as a matter of fact has failed, because it could not make room for two forces which have been most powerful in shaping the modern world—the forces of nationality and freedom.[1]

Attention has been drawn already to the circumstance that the two chief European countries in which to-day nationality is pressed to the extremes of an aggressive nationalism are those which were the main victims of the mediaeval experiments in internationalism by the Holy Roman Papacy and Empire. Since the Reformation, moreover, the chair of Peter has become the monopoly of Italian ecclesiastics, whose policy in temporal affairs at least has effectively nationalized the Roman Church despite its professed super-national character. Nor would it be unduly boastful to affirm that the measure of freedom, intellectual and spiritual, enjoyed within such national churches as those of England and Sweden will challenge favourable comparison with the ecclesiastical tradition of the post-Tridentine papal communion. If the appeal be to history, national

[1] Mandell Creighton, "The Idea of a National Church", in *The Church and the Nation*, p. 214.

churches need not fear its judgement in relation to the international Church of Rome.

The Totalitarian State

At the present juncture, however, it may seem that all problems which relate to the differences separating the several Christian churches from each other sink into relative unimportance in face of the challenge to Christianity created by the advent of the Totalitarian state. Of the gravity of the emergence of the Totalitarian state—a phenomenon so widespread as Russia, Turkey, Austria, Germany, and Italy—no doubt may be entertained; nor of the incompatibility of its claims, as expressed typically in the Italian doctrine that "Fascism conceives of the state as an absolute, in comparison with which all individuals or groups are relative, only to be conceived of in their relation to the state", with those of Christianity. Christianity indeed must be insistent and emphatic in its affirmation that the individual, the family, and the Church have an intrinsic value and existence apart from the State and its recognition of their rights. Their status is as sovereign and essential as that of the State. In so far as the causes of this new order of political society are economic, their investigation lies beyond the purview of this essay; though it may not be impertinent to observe that in Germany, Italy, and Turkey economic considerations are subordinated to the demands of a rabid nationalism, which is itself a product of the Great War, from which source sprang also the revolution in Russia. Further, the portent of the Totalitarian state has assumed a new gravity by reason of the unprecedented power at the service of modern government for the propagation and inculcation of its claims. In face of the potential danger that the contemporary state may at any moment "use all the agencies at its command to impose on the whole community a philosophy of life and a pattern of living which are wholly, or in important respects, contrary to the Christian understanding of the meaning and ends of human existence", it is urged by critical observers that "it would be folly to allow the highly important difference between authoritarian and democratic forms of government to blind us to the fact that this menace may be present even where there is no dictatorship".[1]

The warning will be pertinent if it persuades Christians of all denominations to survey carefully the characteristics of Totalitarian states. But this scrutiny should be extended no less to their underlying similarities than to their apparent differences. It is easy to perceive the incompatibility of Christianity with the materialistic communism of Russia or with the Aryan racialism of Germany. Greater difficulty arises in the cases of Italy and Austria, on behalf of which it is pleaded that "the Fascist state as such is not consciously or intentionally hostile to religion", since it has in fact "given a much fuller recognition to the place of religion in national life than did the democratic régime which it replaced".[2] By comparison with Russia it is indeed claimed for the Roman Catholic Totalitarian experiments that "a dictatorship which deprives us of our political liberty would be preferable to an order which denies those fundamental spiritual rights without which human life loses its *raison d'être*".[3]

The crucial question, however, remains as to the definition of "those fundamental spiritual rights without which human life loses its *raison d'être*"; and in this connexion it is imperative to recollect the vital differences which distinguish authoritarian from

[1] J. H. Oldham, *Church, Community, and State*, pp. 14-15.
[2] C. Dawson, *Religion and the Modern State*, p. 135.
[3] *Ibid.* p. 132.

democratic states. Such recollection would seem to have deserted the memory of writers who find it possible to see in England, for example,

> how all the apparatus of the social services—universal secondary education, birth-control clinics, ante-natal clinics, welfare centres, and the rest—may become instruments of a collective despotism which destroys human liberty and spiritual initiative as effectively as any Communist or Nazi terrorism.[1]

Such a transformation would be possible only by the extinction of the freedom and liberty which are the outstanding differentiae between Totalitarian and democratic states. In fact it would be necessary for the press, instead of offering free criticism of the policy of the existing government, to present only official expositions of desiccated news; for the universal secondary education to be directed to the exclusive inculcation of some equivalent of communism or racialism or caesaro-papism (such as might perhaps be offered by the theory of British Israelism); for attendance at birth-control clinics to be compulsory, and for the benefits of the medical services to be restricted to persons officially enrolled as members of the single-party in control of the administration; and for the government to adopt "the phial of castor oil, the dungeon, or exile to an island" in order to convert public opinion to uniformity and servitude. In this process indeed the collective despotism would have been accomplished; but democracy would thereby have disappeared to give place to a unitary régime based upon that denial and forcible suppression of freedom of thought, conscience, and writing which constitute the fundamental common characteristic of dictatorships whatever their economic or religious creed.

The challenge presented to Christianity by the Totalitarian state is not simple but complex, em-

---

[1] C. Dawson, *op. cit.* p. 106.

bracing not only ends but means; and all attempts to concentrate attention upon the goal pursued without examination of the means employed serve but to darken counsel. If a Totalitarian state should offer to any chosen denomination of Christianity the tempting prospect of an alliance, wherein temporal and spiritual authority should be combined for the forcible suppression of atheism, secularism, and even dissent from the established church, is such an acceptance of the agents of persecution compatible with the principles of Christianity? It is necessary to remember that the Holy Roman Church of the Middle Ages was in its claims essentially a Totalitarian state, demanding the suppression of heresy and the extirpation of heretics by the civil power, controlling education both in respect of curricula and the personnel of teachers, affirming the right of the papacy to wield both spiritual and temporal power, and asserting the necessity to salvation of the subjection of all souls to the government of the Roman pontiff. Nor did the principles of such pretensions disappear with the Reformation, though they suffered a change of form. The *Index Librorum Prohibitorum* preserves the principle of denial of the freedom of writing and printing; whilst during the last century Gregory XVI, in his bull *Mirari Vos*, denounced liberty of conscience as *"absurda illa . . . ac erronea sententia, seu potius deliramentum"*, and liberty of the press as *"deterrima illa, ac numquam satis exsecranda et detestabilis libertas artis librariae ad scripta quaelibet edenda in vulgus"*.[1] The *Syllabus Errorum* of Pius IX likewise included amongst the *Errores qui ad liberalismum hodiernum referentur*, religious toleration in every form; denouncing on the one hand the contention that *"Aetate hac nostra non amplius expedit, religionem catholicam haberi tan-*

---

[1] C. Mirbt, *Quellen zur Geschichte des Papsttums*, p. 439 ll. 30-31 and ll. 42-3.

quam unicam status religionem, caeteris quibuscumque cultibus exclusis" (lxxvii), and on the other hand the argument that "*Hinc laudabiliter in quibusdam catholici nominis regionibus lege cautum est, ut hominibus illuc immigrantibus publicum proprii cujusque cultus exercitium habere*" (lxxviii).[1]

Such official pronouncements make plain the continued claim of the Roman Church to be a Totalitarian society, and its evident affinity with the methods of contemporary authoritarian states for the suppression of freedom of conscience, speech, and writing, provided only that they are applied to the protection, not the persecution, of the Roman Catholic faith. But it may be doubted, notwithstanding, whether this acceptance of the agents of oppression is compatible with the essential genius of Christianity: *Ubi Spiritus Domini, ibi libertas.*

> No educator can discharge his task unless he encourages frankness, outspokenness, and sincerity amongst those whom he undertakes to teach. The Church, as the divinely appointed educator of mankind, must cherish these qualities. Tolerance is needful to the individual; for it is the expression of that reverence for others, which forms a great part of the lesson which Christ came to teach him.[2]

The fundamental principle of the Totalitarian state in its creation of a unitary society from which all freedom has been ruthlessly banished by exile and terrorism is the plain contradiction of the spirit of Christianity: *Non tali auxilio, nec defensoribus istis.*

> Liberty is a tender plant and needs jealous watching. It is always unsafe in the world, and is only secure under the guardianship of the Church; for the Church possesses the knowledge of man's eternal destiny, which alone can justify his claim to freedom.[3]

---

[1] Mirbt, *Quellen*, p. 454, ll. 23-7.
[2] M. Creighton, *Persecution and Tolerance* (Hulsean Lectures), p. 137.
[3] *Ibid.* p. 140.

On this account, therefore, it is impossible to exaggerate from the Christian standpoint the importance of the differences dividing democratic from Totalitarian régimes, or to doubt in which political and intellectual climate the Christian Church may be more at home in its stewardship of the true doctrine of human freedom and responsibility.

RESPUBLICA CHRISTIANA

The essential truth of the present situation, however, is that "the life-and-death struggle of the Christian Church is not with the State as such but with modern paganism";[1] and provided the methods of the unitary state are rigidly forsworn, an alliance of Church and State is laudable and desirable. Unless the ideal of a *respublica Christiana* is to be dismissed as itself anti-Christian, there is no inherent incompatibility in the alliance of Church and State for the mutual succour and aid which the one may afford to the other according to the several capacities and functions of each. A primary condition of such partnership is that neither partner should think more highly of itself than is becoming, but that each should be at pains to recognize the rights of the other. If the State advances such claims to an absolute character as constitute the keystone of Totalitarian régimes, the Church must needs offer an unequivocal denial. But the natural tendency to reply to these assertions by equal claims on behalf of the spiritual society in order to depress the status and authority of the civil power must be resisted. Ecclesiastical claims couched in the mediaeval phraseology of the superiority of the sun to the moon or in the modern form of contrast between the order of creation and that of redemption fail in their purpose, since their exaggerations recoil upon the head of their expon-

[1] J. H. Oldham, *op. cit.* p. 15.

ents. It may be true that the coercive power of civil government to "restrain with the civil sword the stubborn and evildoers" is the result of the imperfections of fallen human nature, whence arises the organization of the State as distinct from the institution of society. But is it otherwise with the Church? History records no authentic evidence of either the ecclesiastical or civil polity of a society of perfect men, enjoying the idyllic conditions of Rousseau's imagined noble savage. For though Jerusalem which is above is free and is the mother of us all, that Church of Christ which is without spot or wrinkle is the Church triumphant, being the pattern laid up in the heavens, towards which the whole state of Christ's Church militant here in earth looks as to its final consummation. History knows only this Church militant composed not of the spirits of just men made perfect already, but of peccable and peccant pilgrims towards eternity.

> The theologian may indulge the pleasing task of describing Religion as she descended from heaven, arrayed in her native purity. A more melancholy duty is imposed on the historian. He must discover the inevitable mixture of error and corruption which she contracted in a long residence upon earth, among a weak and degenerate race of beings.[1]

Claims correspondent with the virtues of the Church triumphant may not be advanced in behalf of the Church militant; nor may the State be relegated to the ignominy of Augustine's *grande latrocinium* and the Church identified with the *civitas Dei*; rather both Church and State are equally means towards the realization of the *regnum Dei, sicut in caelo et in terra.*

The warning against advancing exaggerated claims on behalf of the visible Church in relation to

---

[1] E. Gibbon, *The Decline and Fall of the Roman Empire*, cxv. (ed. Bury), ii. p. 2.

temporal society is emphasized unmistakably by the evidence of history. It is not accidental that Italy, the seat of the papacy in whose behalf the most extravagant of all claims to supremacy over civil government have been consistently made, has been of Western countries throughout history the most secular. During the Middle Ages, it is significant to note that the universities of Italy were founded by secular agencies and were mainly, though not exclusively, concerned with the prosecution of secular studies, in contradistinction to the universities of north European countries, which grew up out of cathedral schools and developed their principal activities in the sphere of philosophical theology. Whilst Salerno was famous for medicine and Bologna for law, Paris became the home of theology. In the Renaissance likewise, Italy embraced its pagan and secular aspects, whilst its religious and theological characteristics were emphasized north of the Alps.

The ideal of a national Church rests upon persuasion of the validity of the conception of a *respublica Christiana*, expressed through the unit of political organization, the nation.   For the Christian prince it claims "that only prerogative which we see to have been given always to all godly princes in Holy Scriptures by God himself; that is, that they should rule all estates and degrees committed to their charge by God, whether they be ecclesiastical or temporal". It affirms that the State neither transgresses its boundaries nor mistakes its function in adopting the profession of Christianity as the rule of its civil ordering of life. As with Christian princes so with their parliaments, which it believes to be not "so merely temporal, as if they might meddle with nothing but only leather and wool". Such affirmations do not exclude the possibility that in any nation the modern State may either dissociate itself from all religious profession or even adopt an anti-religious policy. In such circumstances the ideal of a national Church ceases to be practicable. But it does not lose thereby its value as an ideal nor disavow the advantages of an alliance of Church and State alike to the nation and the Church.

A national Church stands in close relation to the life of a particular nation, and tries to lead it into a recognition of its eternal destiny, not to force it into a common mould. It persuades rather than commands, its weapon is influence, not power.[1]

ECCLESIA ANGLICANA

It follows from the close relationship of national churches to the political societies with which they are associated that generalization concerning their common characteristics is beset with more than usual difficulties. It is better to abandon the endeavour to obtain a universal formula, and to concentrate attention upon the ideals of that particular national church known to history as the *Ecclesia Anglicana*. According to the mind of the sixteenth-century reformers, the Church of England was to be truly *Ecclesia Anglorum*. Stated in its most attractive form by the persuasive eloquence of Hooker, this theory envisaged a complete identity of personnel in Church and nation:

> Seeing there is not any man of the Church of England but the same is also a member of the Commonwealth, nor any man a member of the Commonwealth which is not also of the Church of England ... so albeit properties and actions of one kind do cause the name of a Commonwealth, qualities and functions of another sort the name of a Church to be given unto a multitude, yet one and the selfsame multitude may in such sort be both, and is so with us, that no person appertaining to the one can be denied to be also of the other.[2]

[1] M. Creighton, "The Idea of a National Church", in *The Church and the Nation*, pp. 214-5.
[2] R. Hooker, *Ecclesiastical Polity*, Book VIII. c. i. 2.

Likewise it was affirmed in the preamble to the Act of Appeals of 1533 "that this realm of England is an empire . . . governed by one supreme head and king . . . unto whom a body-politic, compact of all sorts and degrees of people divided in terms and by names of spiritualty and temporalty, be bounden and ought to bear, next to God, a natural and humble obedience".[1] The principle of this conception was truly that of *ein Reich, ein Volk, eine Kirche*; and the methods used by both Henry VIII and Elizabeth for the suppression of all dissentient opinion, whether Puritan or Papist, indicated the perils of a nationalism so compacted and maintained. Nor was the danger removed by the establishment of a presbyterian national church in North Britain. In the seventeenth century, when the tide of fortune brought down episcopacy with the monarchy in England, the presbyterian party were as eager for a national church without toleration of dissent as the episcopalians had been. It was to the work of Cromwell during the Commonwealth in behalf of Independency and to the failure of the Savoy Conference that the Toleration Act of 1689 was due; and historically the gain from the collapse of the Tudor ideal was great beyond the benefits which might have ensued from its success. For the enactment of a legal toleration, even restricted to orthodox Protestant Dissenters, established the principle of the lawfulness of repudiation of the established church, and prevented the tyranny of a unitary state based upon an enforced religious uniformity in agreement with Louis XIV's revocation of the Edict of Nantes in France.

After the Revolution settlement of 1689 the maintenance of an established church was accompanied by admission of the principle of toleration of dissenters. Moreover, the problem of dissidence was

---

[1] Gee and Hardy, *Documents Illustrative of English Church History*, p. 187.

emphasized at this juncture by the schism of the Anglican Non-jurors, in whose secession some modern writers have seen a pioneer protest against Erastianism. The endeavour to set up the non-juring dissenters as champions of the spiritual freedom and independence of the Church against Erastian encroachment, though attractive and possessing an indubitable sentimental appeal, is lacking in historical basis. It was not against the authority of the State in religion that they protested, but against the exercise of the prerogatives of the Lord's Anointed by an usurping king whose title was that of conquest, not hereditary right. How otherwise had the Non-jurors accepted James II's revival of the Court of High Commission, an illegal act, or his use of this court to secure the suspension of Bishop Compton of London from his episcopal functions? And why should the non-juring church continue to apply to the exiled papist Stuart prince at St. Germains for nominations to replenish its episcopal succession? "The real interest of the non-juring schism was political rather than religious; and its roots go out to vital events of the past. At the bottom it is the obverse side of the Divine Right of kings that they represent."[1] It is not to the Non-jurors that recourse must be had for the enunciation of the doctrine of the inherent sovereignty and independence of the Church within its proper sphere, but to a Latitudinarian ecclesiastic, William Warburton.

The genesis of Warburton's treatise *The Alliance between Church and State* lay in the practical necessity created by the Revolution settlement of evolving some new defence of the establishment of the Church of England in face of the legal recognition of cor-

---

[1] H. J. Laski, *Political Thought in England from Locke to Bentham*, p. 66. See also N. Sykes, *Church and State in England in the Eighteenth Century*, pp. 285-90. The *Report* of the Commission on Church and State (vol. i. p. 19) dissents from this view, though without giving reasons.

porate dissent from its communion. With the Toleration Act had disappeared even the theoretical and legal fiction of the identity of Church and State upon which Hooker's apology had been built. How, then, was the privileged position of the Church of England to be justified against the increasing demands of the Protestant Dissenters for full civil and religious equality? Beneath an admitted artificiality and eccentricity of argument, which has detracted from the importance of his apologia, Warburton laid down in unequivocal terms the doctrine of the complete and inherent sovereignty of the Church, which some Anglican historians have supposed to be the peculiar discovery of the Tractarians. Abandoning completely the assumption of an identity of personnel between Church and State and with it the conception of the *respublica Christiana* as a single society governed by two hierarchies of officers, spiritual and temporal, which had lain at the basis equally of mediaeval theories and those of Hooker, Warburton conceived of establishment as an alliance, freely entered into for mutual advantage, between two originally sovereign and independent societies, Church and State.

> Having found that each society is sovereign and independent of the other, it as necessarily follows that such union can be produced only by free convention and mutual compact. But nothing can give birth to a free convention but a sense of mutual wants that may be thereby supplied, or a view of mutual advantages to be thereby gained. Such then is the nature of that famous union which produces a church established, and which is indeed no other than a political league and alliance for mutual support and defence.[1]

In making such an alliance the State in no wise assumed the character of judge between the rival

---

[1] W. Warburton, *The Alliance of Church and State* (1736), Part II. Section I. p. 53.

churches in regard to purity of faith, worship, or doctrine. Its sole interest was to secure the support of the religious body representing the largest single aggregate of citizens.

> Hence we may see the reason and equity of the episcopal church being the established church in England, the presbyterian the established church in Scotland, an absurdity in point of right which our adversaries imagined the friends of an establishment could never get clear of. From hence we may discover the duration of this alliance. It is perpetual, but not irrevocable, *i.e.* it subsists so long as the church thereby established maintains its superiority of extent; which, when it loses to any considerable degree, the union is dissolved.[1]

Within this framework of establishment Warburton further marked his originality of thought by enunciating the theory of corporate personality and will,[2] by which could be justified the creation within the State of an inexhaustible series of social groups, each with its independent and sovereign authority within the proper sphere of its competence; a condition of society representing the exact antithesis to the totalitarian conception of the State.

> It is strange indeed [commented Figgis] that Dr. Gierke and Professor Maitland should have their counterpart in a Latitudinarian ecclesiastic, writing at a time when political and theological thought was essentially atomistic; yet it can hardly be denied that Warburton was what they would have called a "realist", even if the realism be imperfect.[3]

For the Church Warburton, consistently with his principles of alliance, claimed a proper freedom in the initiation of legislation concerning its internal affairs, provided that the sovereignty of the State

---

[1] *Ibid.* Part III. Section I. p. 111.
[2] *Ibid.* Part II. Section V. p. 102.
[3] J. N. Figgis, "William Warburton" in *Typical English Church-men from Parker to Maurice* (ed. W. E. Collins), p. 231.

were safeguarded by giving to Parliament the right
of assent or rejection.

> There is reason that propositions for such laws should
> sometimes come from the Church; which we must sup-
> pose well-skilled (as in her proper business) in forming
> and digesting such new regulations, before they come
> before the legislature. . . . For to have laws framed and
> modelled solely by the State, and (without previous com-
> munication) imposed upon the Church, is making of it
> the meanest and most abject of the State's creatures.[1]

Warburton wrote more than a century and three-
quarters before the Enabling Act of 1919, but the
principles of that statute were expounded in his
treatise, with its insistence that the presence of the
episcopate in the House of Lords was "too few to
deliver the sense of so large a society" as the entire
Church of England.

But although more credit than is usually given is
due to Warburton for his unequivocal exposition of
the inherent independence and sovereignty of the
Church, of the contractual nature of the alliance
between Church and State which is the basic condition of an established church, and of the necessity
for the Church to have the right of initiation of
ecclesiastical legislation, his case was rested avowedly
upon the necessity of a test-law, the effect of which
would be to exclude from the national legislature
religious dissenters from the established church lest
they should endeavour to overthrow its privileged
position. Even so early as 1736, the date of publication of Warburton's treatise, the provisions of the
Test Act were being rendered inoperative by the
passing of an annual Indemnity Act, and the principle of his argument was challenged by the presence
of representatives of Scotland in the Westminster
Parliament with freedom to speak and vote upon bills
concerning the internal administration of the Church

[1] Warburton, *op. cit.* Part II. Section III. p. 87.

of England albeit their country had an established presbyterian church. During the century which divided Warburton's essay from Keble's Assize Sermon the Test and Corporation Acts were repealed and Roman Catholic emancipation granted; and with the further advance of liberal principles during the nineteenth century, all religious tests were abolished in favour of Jews, agnostics, and persons of any or no religious persuasion. It was this circumstance of the progressive secularization of Parliament which provoked the impassioned denunciation by Keble of national apostasy when a Whig Administration ventured to reduce the admittedly superfluous Irish sees to a more modest and reasonable number and thus to lay profane hands upon the ecclesiastical ark of the Covenant.

Many Anglican chroniclers of the Tractarian Movement have done both it and themselves less than justice by writings in which

> the ritualistic development plays a greater part than the extensive moulding of Church conception and Church practice which has affected the whole Church, and not merely a part of it as ritualism has done, and which alone can assure to the Oxford Movement its place of honour in English Church history.[1]

The most important characteristic of the new ecclesiastical movement was its doctrine of the Church; and especially its conception of the Church of England as the local expression of the Catholic Church of Christ. Keble added little to the essential argument of Warburton concerning the inherent sovereignty of the Church, and his protest against the Irish Bishoprics Bill was almost grotesque in its irrelevance (for the Irish Church stood in greater need of temporal reform than its English counterpart and little evidence was to be found of any

---

[1] Y. Brilioth, *The Anglican Revival*, pp. 337-8, and the examples there cited.

attempt at self-reformation); but he applied the principle of the independence of the Church to a new set of conditions both in Church and State. In the sphere of temporal reform indeed the activities of Blomfield and of the ecclesiastical commission were far more effective in clearing away a host of obsolete mediaeval survivals which hampered the freedom of the Church to adapt itself to the new age than the mere denunciation of national apostasy; and it is to be regretted that the Tractarian leaders looked coldly upon such efforts instead of according to them their cordial co-operation. But together with the assertion of the spiritual authority and autonomy of the Church, the Oxford reformers set forth novel claims on behalf of episcopacy and the apostolic succession, and looked away from Warburton's complacent pride in the national established Church of England to the Catholic Church of the epoch of the oecumenical councils. Furthermore, in the debate which naturally followed concerning the relationship of the reformed English Church to the Tridentine Church of Rome, an accumulation of prejudice and passion prevented the impartial examination of such arguments as those put forward in Newman's famous Tract XC:

> In it he argued that the XXXIX Articles, strictly construed, did not contradict the official teaching of the Roman Church as formulated in the sixteenth century and therefore were not a barrier against union, which he desired. His argument as we now see was valid. The Articles were carefully drawn so as not to exclude the moderate majority of their period; those whom they alienated were the zealots of the Roman and Puritan extremes. But they had come in popular esteem to be regarded as a proclamation of principles hostile to Rome. Men were prejudiced, and had not the knowledge of history needed to counteract the prejudice.[1]

Faulty historical argument, however, was not

[1] E. W. Watson, *The Church of England*, p. 226.

wholly on one side. Although much prejudice was raised against Tractarian views which were entirely consonant with those of the Caroline divines, extreme claims were advanced on behalf of episcopacy and the apostolic succession accompanied by a consequent unchurching of all non-episcopal churches, in striking contradiction to the opinions of those seventeenth-century Anglicans to whom the Tractarians were wont to appeal in support of their general position. The protracted episode of disputes concerning ceremonial was particularly unfortunate. For the

> coldness of the Tractarians towards Catholic ceremony had the unfortunate effect of throwing the leadership of the ceremonial revival into the hands of men with more zeal than scholarship. In the absence of authoritative guidance each clergyman was inclined to make his own law. He consulted contemporary Continental use rather than the older traditions of the Church of England; and sometimes he fell into extravagances for which no warrant, either contemporary or historical, could be found.[1]

The association of the Tractarian demand for recognition of the freedom of the church with extreme opinions concerning episcopacy introduced a new bitterness into the relations of Church and Dissent; nor has the Church of England recovered even in the twentieth century from the ill-effects of the like association of the ideal of ecclesiastical independence with extravagances of ceremonial eccentricity. Notwithstanding, the Tractarian conception of the Church has won a striking victory, not only within the borders of the Church of England, but also in the sphere of the relations of Church and State in England. The complete defeat of the Public Worship Regulation Act of 1874 by the passive resistance of

---

[1] J. G. Lockhart, *Charles Lindley, Viscount Halifax*, Part I. pp. 185-6.

churchmen inspired by Tractarian ideals stands as a remarkable testimony of the impotence of the temporal power to impose its will upon the Church of England. With the memory of this statute and also of the Ecclesiastical Titles Act of 1851 which related to the Roman hierarchy in England,[1] it may be averred that no British government will easily embark upon any *Kulturkampf* nor advance Totalitarian claims in respect of the Christian churches within its dominions. Within the Church of England the spread of high views of ecclesiastical autonomy has been noteworthy. It cannot be doubted that the Tractarians rendered a most notable service to the Church in recalling it to visions of its catholic and apostolic heritage at a time when the secularization of parliamentary personnel had made that assembly no longer even predominantly an Anglican lay synod. The task which awaits the contemporary Church is to dissociate this ideal from the heritage of suspicion created in the public mind by the customs and extreme tenets of pro-papal zealots within its ranks.

Establishment and Comprehensiveness

The past history of the Church of England has moulded and fashioned both its character and claims as the national established church. At the outset it is evident that a national church must necessarily be comprehensive. "The more general the terms of communion are, and the wider the bottom is made (consistent with the well-being of a society), the wiser and juster is that institution." Warburton's words remain true of the character of a national church. But the implications of this are often overlooked.

[1] H. J. Laski, *The Problem of Sovereignty*, chaps. iii. and iv. The victory of the doctrine of the spiritual independence of the Church is officially written in the *Report* of the Church and State Commission (1935).

Within its communion, the several schools of church-manship must exhibit a ready toleration towards each other, agreeing to differ in emphasis and interpretation of matters of belief and practice, seeking to preserve an essential unity in the bond of peace, and not claiming exclusive authority to represent the Church in the interests of a particular standpoint. Without, it must be recognized that the liturgy and articles of the Church of England cannot be expected to satisfy the mutually exclusive and contradictory demands of all the separated churches. Neither Romanists nor Nonconformists can wholly approve the Book of Common Prayer. Otherwise their state of separation would be ended. Nor when legislative projects are presented to Parliament dealing with matters of faith and liturgy, should representatives of dissenting churches ask the right to judge of them in accordance with their own ecclesiastical standards. The only lawful standard is their consistency with the official formularies of the Church of England. The claim of that church to justify its continuance as a national and established church lies in its larger comprehensiveness. On the other hand, it is evident that the continuance of its establishment depends upon the goodwill of the separated churches. Since the legal recognition of toleration in 1689 it has been always theoretically possible for a parliamentary majority to effect the disestablishment of the episcopal Church of England. Such a measure has been carried in relation to the episcopal Churches of Ireland and Wales; and its extension to England is possible at any time when popular opinion as reflected in Parliament, or even in the House of Commons alone under the provisions of the Parliament Act of 1911, is sufficiently strong to maintain a majority in favour of such legislative proposals.

The historical tradition of the Church of England affords ample precedent for an attitude of friendly association with reformed churches, both at home and abroad. Towards adherents of the Roman Church indeed sentiments of amity cannot be translated into act, so long as the papacy maintains its policy of unchurching Canterbury and of prohibiting its members from common acts of worship. But with the non-episcopal churches the situation is otherwise; and appeal may be made to the Caroline Anglo-Catholic divines in support of the attempt to restore acts of fellowship. To so erudite and cautious a scholar as Dr. Claude Jenkins it seems "impossible to deny that the English Bishops recognized the foreign churches as churches", and also "that there are probably isolated cases of men not episcopally ordained having ministered in the Church of England".[1] After the Prayer Book revision of 1662 and the requirement of episcopal ordination as a condition of ministration in the Church of England, the practice continued for more than half a century on the part of leading presbyterian ministers and laity to communicate at the altars of the established church from purely religious motives as a "healing custom" and a symbol of amity without any political reference. A presbyterian deputation, waiting upon Bishop Burnet in 1702,

> told his lordship that the communicating with the Church of England was no new practice among the Dissenters, nor of a late date, but had been used by some of the most eminent of their ministers ever since 1662, with a desire to shew their charity towards that Church, notwithstanding they apprehended themselves bound in conscience ordinarily to separate from it; and that it had been also practised by a number of the most understanding people among them, before the doing so was necessary to qualify for a place.[2]

[1] C. Jenkins, in *The Anglican Communion* (ed. H. A. Wilson), pp. 56-7.
[2] E. Calamy, *An Historical Account of My Own Life*, vol. i. p. 473 (ed. J. T. Rutt).

On the Anglican side the custom was welcomed not only by low-church prelates such as Burnet and Tenison, but by so impeccable a high-churchman as Archbishop John Sharp of York, who expressly commended the conduct of Ralph Thoresby, the eminent antiquarian, in communicating monthly at Leeds parish church whilst attending a Dissenting congregation otherwise. Sharp indeed placed Thoresby in correspondence with a learned presbyterian divine in order to remove any scruples by his testimony to the widespread presbyterian usage.[1] Likewise Sancroft issued to the bishops of his province in 1688 for transmission to the clergy articles in which the latter were required to approach Protestant dissenters, and to

> exhort them to join with us in daily fervent prayer to the God of peace, for an universal blessed union of all reformed churches, both at home and abroad, against our common enemies; that all they who do confess the holy name of our dear Lord, and do agree in the truth of his holy word, may also meet in one holy communion, and live in perfect unity and godly love.[2]

The custom of occasional communion persisted amongst individual Methodists long after the formal severance of the Methodist Churches from the parent Church; and a piquant evidence of the survival of interdenominational Christianity is afforded by the account given by Archbishop Davidson of his father:

> My father absolutely declined to limit himself to one denomination. I remember the eagerness with which he answered someone who made the remark that a man must be surely either a Presbyterian or an Episcopalian, by saying emphatically: "I am both; and if I were one or other only I should be false to my deepest beliefs".[3]

[1] Letters of Eminent Men addressed to Ralph Thoresby, vol. i. pp. 320-26.

[2] E. Cardwell, *Documentary Annals of the Reformed Church of England*, vol. ii. p. 376.

[3] G. K. A. Bell, *Randall Davidson*, vol. i. p. 9.

The duty of the Church of England to strive for the fullest union with non-episcopal churches at home has been recognized by the Lambeth Conferences of 1920 and 1930; and as a national established church this task is of paramount importance.

The Episcopate in a National Church

"A state which possesses an established church obviously does not have to create its own spiritual ideals or its own moral standards, for these things are already given in the church".[1] The provenance of such a tribute may perhaps be surprising, but so persuasive a statement of the ideal and function of an established church may be welcomed. In an episcopal church its realization must depend of necessity to a very considerable degree upon the character of the episcopate, alike in personnel and in the prevalent conception of the office and work of a Bishop. It is of the utmost importance at the present time that the comprehensive ideal of the episcopal office fashioned by the secular tradition of English religious and political development should be maintained. Of the primary function of the Bishop as father-in-God no doubt exists; nor may criticism be fairly levelled at the contemporary Anglican episcopate in respect of its standards of devotion to duty in the spiritual oversight and ecclesiastical administration committed to its charge. But the very success and ubiquity of the episcopal father-in-God presents a danger lest other and wider aspects of the office and work of a Bishop may be forgotten and neglected in favour of its local habitation and name.

The bishops of England will soon be a name without a meaning. They are bishops of dioceses, and make an immense fuss about their business and their letters, so that people groan over their lamentations about their

[1] C. Dawson, *op. cit.* p. 43.

work—they are good diocesan bishops, but bishops of England, no![1]

The letters of Archbishop Benson are full of recurrent complaints of similar character, the vigour and vehemence of which fall sometimes upon the reader's ear with surprise. With the considerable increase in the number of dioceses since his primacy the danger has become much greater. Almost inevitably "the diocese is much more than the Church", especially in face of the financial and administrative problems of newly created sees, and the function of the Bishop to give counsel concerning the wider affairs of Church and nation is increasingly forgotten. Yet of the vital importance of these wider duties no doubt can exist. Benson was insistent upon "the claims of the English Church and of the English nation upon the fullest exercise of his mature judgement";[2] Creighton entertained

> a strong feeling that a bishop ought not to be merely an ecclesiastical official, but a link between various classes and various activities; he ought to try and make all sorts of things converge, so that the standard and efficiency of each is heightened;[3]

and Davidson in a Charge delivered whilst Bishop of Winchester affirmed that the English tradition rightly expected that the Bishop should

> be giving time and thought to a whole multitude of central things in the life of the nation or the church, things quite other than diocesan. . . . Unless I am strangely mistaken [he concluded] it is not the wish of contemporary churchmen, whether lay or clerical, that their bishops should now for the first time in our history be so exclusively local officers as to have neither time nor opportunity for interests which are larger still.[4]

---

[1] A. C. Benson, *Life of E. W. Benson*, vol. ii. p. 260.
[2] *Ibid.* vol. ii. p. 697.
[3] *Life of Mandell Creighton*, vol. ii. pp. 201-2.
[4] Bell, *Randall Davidson*, vol. i. p. 317.

The realization of these wider duties involves certain adjustments of the ecclesiastical constitution to modern circumstances. Certainly a stop must be placed to the multiplication of dioceses, as Davidson stated to Queen Victoria so long ago as 1888, urging "the encouragement of suffragans rather than the multiplication of sees".[1] For the creation of more dioceses leads ultimately to the reduction of diocesan episcopacy, as Benson satirically prophesied, to the level of diocesan inspectorship,[2] and to the reluctance of clergy of eminence to accept nomination to the episcopal office. Observers of the Protestant Episcopal Church of America, even those with a natural predilection to emphasize the pastoral aspect of the episcopal office, voice the opinion "that there are altogether too many bishops in the American Church", adding the pungent criticism that their ubiquity ministers chiefly to "the satisfaction of local pride and vainglory", and concluding that "the American Church likes its bishops more plentiful than powerful".[3] Further, for the efficient discharge of the duty of *consilium* to the Archbishop of Canterbury, there is urgent need of the establishment of an English episcopal cabinet. This reform was urged by Benson, who advocated "a cardinalate in some form" and "a standing inner council".[4] The Bishops composing this council, which should include the occupants of the two primatial sees, and those of London, Durham, and Winchester at the least, should be freed to a sufficient degree from diocesan administration by the further provision of suffragans, and should reside for a sufficient period of each year in London. Nor should their counsel be confined to purely ecclesiastical matters. The English tradition

---

[1] Bell, *op. cit.* vol. i. p. 120.
[2] *Life of Benson*, vol. ii. p. 203.
[3] *The Church Times* (American Correspondent), October 25, 1935.
[4] *Life of Benson*, vol. ii. pp. 126, 130.

has recognized the importance of the episcopal office by a liberal representation of the episcopate in the upper House of Parliament. In the present generation unfortunately attendance in Parliament tends to be regarded as an unprofitable and obsolete burden, a sentiment not unnatural in view of the demands for the presence of the Bishop always in his diocese. But the entire episcopate of Davidson presents an impressive and convincing testimony of the real importance and value both to Church and nation of his participation in parliamentary debates. The list of his interventions is sufficient evidence of the breadth of his interests and of his conviction that the episcopate "was entrusted with a place in the legislature not only for what are technically called ecclesiastical questions but for whatever things directly concern the moral life and social well-being of the nation". Moreover, his speeches shew a freedom of criticism of the policy of governments which indicate that the bench is not under bondage; for no archbishop in a Totalitarian state would have ventured upon the independent line taken by Davidson during the General Strike of 1926. For this commerce in affairs of State he deemed no apology necessary.

> It means a good deal in my judgment for the Church's good that the man who holds the archbishop's position should have this kind of natural and friendly access to the men to whom is given the responsibility for the nation's affairs. It places not the archbishop only, but the Church, in quite a different relation to public life in its religious and secular aspects.[1]

Such intimate and confident association typifies the ideal relationship between Church and nation upheld by the principle of a national church. Furthermore, episcopal participation in debate in the upper House of Parliament affords the best occasion for the

---

[1] Bell, *op. cit.* vol. i. p. 710.

enunciation of opinions upon statecraft, since there prelates speak to their peers in an atmosphere more conducive to criticism and rejoinder than that of diocesan conferences or of the Church Assembly.

Both the situation of the episcopate in national affairs, and the suggestion of an episcopal *curia* with its consequent need of a careful selection of the prelates to occupy such positions of responsibility, bring forward the question of the method of nomination to the episcopate. It is a matter for profound congratulation that the Archbishops' Commission on the Relations of Church and State has recommended no change in the traditional English procedure in this respect. The Commission indeed has recognized the weight of historical precedent behind it, and its formal ecclesiastical correctness since the spiritual authority of the Bishop is derived from consecration, and the responsibility for consecration rests with the Archbishop, whose co-operation is indispensable to this final step.[1] Certainly the English procedure is fully consonant with historic Catholic tradition, and, it may be added, especially with papal procedure, as may be illustrated from concordats concluded by the Vatican with republican no less than monarchical governments and with states of the New World, such as Chili, as well as of the Old, such as France and Austria.[2] In England the influence of the sovereign in episcopal appointments has been paramount since the first establishment of Christianity amongst the Anglo-Saxon kingdoms. The year 1215 is an important date in English history because of the acceptance by King John of the Great Charter; it is of equal importance in that of Europe because it witnessed the assembly under the reforming zeal of

---

[1] *Church and State: Report of the Archbishops' Commission on the Relations between Church and State*, vol. i. pp. 90-92.
[2] E. W. Watson, "The Continuity of the Church of England", in *The Church of England* (ed. W. R. Matthews), pp. 37-8.

Innocent III of the fourth Lateran Council. Magna Carta contained the famous royal promise *quod Anglicana ecclesia libera sit*; and the council at the Lateran laid down careful rules for the proper conduct of elections to the episcopate. It is therefore of the greatest interest to observe that during the period from 1215 to 1273 in England, immediately after the two assemblies above-mentioned, out of 76 successful episcopal elections 15 "were not only formally canonical but actually free".[1] The real effect of the Reformation in this regard was to exclude the pretensions of the Pope and thereby to put an end to squabbles and intrigues between Crown and papacy for the control of episcopal elections by concentrating the right of nomination in the Crown.

Much criticism in the present generation has been directed against the practice of nomination on the recommendation of a Prime Minister who need not be a member of the Church of England or of any Christian church. But the Bishop of Chichester's recent biography of Archbishop Davidson has supplied convincing evidence of the predominant influence of the primate in episcopal appointments.

> Never, in the many instances of episcopal nominations during twenty-five years, did the prime ministers make a single appointment which they knew to be fundamentally objectionable to the archbishop. This does not mean that they always took the archbishop's advice about fitness for a particular see, but that, if the archbishop insisted that a particular person was wholly unsuitable for the office of bishop, no prime minister ever during these twenty-five years persevered with his name. . . . In every case the merits of the person ultimately chosen were carefully and conscientiously considered; and there was no instance whatever of what could be fairly called a mere political job".[2]

Davidson himself was emphatic upon the practical

---

[1] M. Gibbs and J. Lang, *Bishops and Reforms*, 1215–72, pp. 69, 92.
[2] Bell, *op. cit.* vol. ii. p. 1237.

wisdom of allowing to the Prime Minister a real independence of choice; for his standpoint might be regarded as representing that of the educated laity. The result of the informal consultation of Primate and Prime Minister has been to secure a degree of regard for the wider aspects of the episcopal office which it would be difficult to ensure by any other method, and to maintain the presence on the bench of an element representative of scholarship and administrative experience. Mr. Asquith sent to Davidson in April 1913 a list of thirteen Bishops of 1895 (comprising Benson, Temple, Westcott, Ellicott, Durnford, Ridding, Stubbs, Creighton, Wordsworth, Talbot, Basil Jones, Jayne, and Percival) with the comment that, "without any wish to disparage the scholarship of the present bench, it is to be observed that the whole of these (except perhaps Durnford) were headmasters, professors, or dons".[1] The continuance of this succession of Bishops is vital to the influence and standing of the episcopate in the esteem of the nation and especially of the educated laity. Nor is this fact stressed only by Anglicans. It was the presence of such an element on the bench which evoked the admiration and envy of Gallican churchmen, as in the desire expressed by Grandmaison and Battifol that Davidson would make more Bishops like Lightfoot, Chase, or Gore,[2] and in the counsel of the abbé Firmin recorded in Dr. Lacey's essay to "tell your lord Halifax to cultivate the Broad church, not to quarrel with them; they are the really characteristic Anglicans whom we need in the Catholic Church".[3] For the constitution of a Canterbury *curia* the nomination of bishops qualified by knowledge and experience to deal with affairs of sacred learning and of administration is essential.

---

[1] Bell, *op. cit.* vol. ii. pp. 1240-41 (footnote 3).
[2] *Ibid.* p. 1248 (footnote).
[3] T. A. Lacey, *Wayfarer's Essays*, No. 21, p. 143.

Alike in theory as judged by the evidence of history and, in practice the English method of episcopal nomination stands approved.

Parliament and Ecclesiastical Affairs

Peculiar to the English tradition is the position of the British Parliament in ecclesiastical affairs; and the process by which the royal supremacy has been converted into a parliamentary, and the convocations have lost their position of parity with the Parliament constitutes the *differentia* of English constitutional history, namely, the development of the sovereignty of Parliament over all rival authorities. Into the several stages of this historical evolution it is unnecessary here to enter. But it is evident that with the progressive removal of all religious tests upon Members of Parliament during the nineteenth century, a gravely anomalous situation was created by the continued monopoly of the right of initiating ecclesiastica llegislation in an assembly without any assured affiliation to the Church of England. The passing of the Enabling Act of 1919 therefore was a matter for great congratulation; for by its terms the National Assembly of the Church received a wide delegation of powers for the discussion and preparation of measures to be submitted to Parliament for the approval of both Houses. Parliament indeed has not abandoned in theory its right to initiate ecclesiastical legislation; [1] but the attempt to introduce such legislation without consultation and co-operation with the Church Assembly would be so serious a step, if ever made, as to call for reconsideration of the terms of the Enabling Act. Apart from the retention of this theoretic right, the power of Parliament in respect of measures presented by the Church

[1] The *Report* of the Church and State Commission is insistent upon this point, vol. i. p. 34.

Assembly formally to the two Houses for their assent, is limited to that of final acceptance or rejection without authority to amend. Such a final power retained by the Parliament might indeed conceivably be so exercised as to render nugatory the concessions made by the statute of 1919, and calling in such case for its reconsideration. In point of fact, of 63 measures presented by the Church Assembly to Parliament, 59 have been enacted, a sufficient testimony to the general desire of Parliament to help, and not to hinder, the work of the Assembly and of the national Church.

Two of the rejected measures, however, outweighed most of those accepted in importance and gravity; and the situation arising out of the dual rejection of the Prayer Book revision projects of 1927–8 produced the appointment of a Commission to review the relations of Church and State, the *Report* of which is concerned to a considerable extent with this specific issue. The series of events culminating in the rejection of the revised Prayer Book is complex, and incapable of explanation in terms of any one of its constituent elements. It is possible, for example, to regret the attitude of opposition officially adopted by some of the Nonconformist churches of the realm, or to point out the anomaly by which members representing Welsh and Scottish constituencies in Parliament exercised a right of speech and suffrage upon a measure which could not affect the episcopal churches of those countries; and it is certainly possible to regret the rejection of the projects without thereby desiring any change in the constitutional relations of the Church Assembly and the Parliament.

It is evident, however, that the chief cause of the rejection lay in the disagreement amongst churchmen, clerical and lay, concerning the alternative Communion Office and the provisions for Reservation of the consecrated elements of the Holy Communion. This disagreement proceeded from the Anglo-Catholic school as well as from the Evangelical, and both dissentient elements were represented in the parliamentary debates on the question. Of the truth of this circumstance the Bishop of Chichester's biography of Archbishop Davidson affords evidence from the Archbishop's private diaries as emphatic as surprising.

> I have found it very difficult to know what, speaking generally, ought to be my own line in regard to proposals for changing the Communion Office. On the one hand my own instinct would have been for leaving that Office alone and adhering to what has satisfied people for more than three centuries. And I am certain that such is the view of the overwhelming majority of English churchmen throughout the country. The average M.P. or County Councillor, or local squire, or man of business, says emphatically, "Let it alone". Ought it to be one's policy to fall in with that wish or give leadership in that direction, and practically refuse what ecclesiastically-minded folk want in the way of change or reform or reversion to older usage? The answer is not easy. . . . The majority of churchmen want no change. But the people who do want the change are the people who have studied the subject and care about it most.[1]

The biographer does not challenge the accuracy of the late primate's estimate of lay indifference or antipathy to change; indeed, by granting that Davidson's own lack of interest in the subject sprang from his 'taking a lay point of view', he admits its justice. The question is pertinent, then, as to whether any change in the constitutional relations of Church Assembly and Parliament is justified on the ground of the rejection of a measure, the controversial parts

---

[1] Bell, *op. cit.* vol. ii. pp. 1331-2. The antipathy of the laity was emphasized in even stronger terms in a review of Bell's *Randall Davidson,* in *The Manchester Guardian* of November 11, 1935, by Canon Peter Green.

of which were not desired by "the majority of church-men". It is difficult indeed to substantiate an indictment against the House of Commons as violator of the spiritual independence of the Church, when, according to Davidson's assertion, its action prevented the enactment of a project which had not commended itself to "the overwhelming majority of English churchmen".

The justice of such a contention is allowed by the Commission itself in the recommendation of its *Report*, which emphasizes the necessity of agreement amongst the several schools of thought within the Church prior to any appeal to Parliament for further grant of spiritual freedom. Upon the imperative character of the need for unity on such controverted questions as the Holy Communion and Reservation, and in the approach to Parliament for constitutional changes, the *Report* is emphatic.[1] Unfortunately, it attempts no answer to the convinced judgement of Davidson that the majority of lay churchmen throughout the country remained undesirous of these controversial sections of the revised Prayer Book of 1927–8; and therefore its proposal to replace the vote of Parliament by those of the Church Assembly and of the diocesan conferences fails to carry conviction. Fundamentally its demand for the abolition of the parliamentary veto upon spiritual measures (that is, measures relating to "the doctrinal formulae and services and ceremonies of the Church of England, and the administration of the Sacraments or sacred rites thereof")[2] rests upon the *a priori* theory that the determination of such matters can only belong to an assembly claiming to represent the worshipping laity of the Church, and not to a body "which might consist largely of non-Christians and does consist largely of persons who are not mem-

[1] *Report*, vol. i. pp. 57, 64, 96.
[2] *Ibid.* p. 62.

bers of the Church of England".[1] In reply to this, it must be reiterated that no case has yet been established of any real, as distinct from apparent, violation of the spiritual independence of the English Church by the Parliament since the passing of the Enabling Act. When such a case is proven, then suitable action may be taken; but constitutional changes should be advocated in respect of actual abuses, not of hypothetical possibilities. It may be pertinent to remind the Commissioners further that historically the *Ecclesia Anglicana* has often preferred to adopt its own means towards an agreed end; and that it is the province of statesmanship, in Church as well as State, to have regard to practical conditions, and if the desired ends are being attained by methods which are practically efficacious though not theoretically impeccable, to adapt abstract principle to concrete circumstance. In support of this standpoint the august authority of Pope Gregory VII himself may be invoked; for that great champion of the spiritual independence of the Church allowed William the Conqueror and Lanfranc in England to continue the practices of royal nomination to the episcopate and of lay investiture despite his own formal prohibitions of such customs.

> To a king who, by being just and righteous, by caring for the welfare of the church, showed that he belonged to the kingdom of God, much could be forgiven. Even the laws against appointment and investiture by laymen need not be pressed over far.[2]

Modern students contend indeed that Hildebrand's true policy is to be found in this mediating and compromising attitude towards England rather than in his defiant opposition towards the emperor Henry IV of Germany. In like manner it may be confidently

---

[1] *Ibid.* p. 41.
[2] J. P. Whitney, *Hildebrandine Essays*, p. 90.

affirmed that, despite the theoretical anomaly of an assembly bound by no religious tests possessing a right of final negative upon measures relating to the doctrine and liturgy of a particular Christian church, in point of fact in England the present constitutional relations between the Parliament and the Church Assembly do not hinder the work of the Church of England nor violate its spiritual independence. Indeed the revelation of deep-seated religious feeling in the English nation vouchsafed during a twelvemonth which has witnessed both a royal jubilee and a royal death should give pause to critics who deride the national character and vocation of the established church.

Church and Nation

It is upon the need to reaffirm and fulfil this national vocation that attention needs rather to be concentrated, in correction of some contemporary tendencies. For, as R. A. Knox in *Barchester Pilgrimage* has piquantly observed,

> in Barchester, as elsewhere, the Church of England has had a price to pay for its Life and Liberty. Organized and clericalized, it does not seem national any longer; it passes, in the public eye, simply as one among a multitude of sects. . . . In Barchester, as elsewhere, English people have not lost their religion, but they no longer feel that they have any right or need to go to church. When I asked Mr. Bunce how modern congregations in the cathedral compared with those of his youth, he said, "There's fewer goes, and oftener". And this, it seems, is what has happened since the war; a rallying of forces within the Church, accompanied by, and producing, a kind of moral disestablishment.[1]

This attitude of spiritual defeatism is writ large in the Commission's *Report*. It is true indeed that the *Report* pronounces against disestablishment, but

---

[1] R. A. Knox, *Barchester Pilgrimage*, pp. 184-5.

very half-heartedly, and only after a confession that the seductions of disestablishment are so strong that some of the Commissioners definitely prefer it to the present situation. Amongst this number stands the Archbishop of York by his own confession.[1] It is strange that actual disestablishment should be thought a remedy for the spiritual malady of moral disestablishment; and that the Church should not rather deem it a primary duty to recapture the lost association of the religion of the English people with the established church. For it is certain that if the Church of England declines the responsibility, no other Christian church can even attempt it. To the advocates of disestablishment may be commended the counsel of Stubbs, who, whilst holding that the Church could recover from its effects after half a century, added that

> the risk could only be run on the jeopardy of the millions of souls that would be left to ruin in the first stages of the experiment; and it cannot be incurred by us who are in trust, without a certain desertion of our duty, and disloyalty to the cause that we are sworn to serve. If the change is forced on us from without, we will face it manfully, and in faith continue our work on new conditions; but it is no true honesty and it cannot be true policy to betray the citadel because our forces can possibly be better handled in the field.[2]

The fundamental weakness of the *Report* lies precisely in the lack of any evidence of appreciation of the responsibility and duty of the Church of England towards the nation. The preoccupation with the problems of an alternative Communion Office and perpetual Reservation (although in the opinion of Davidson they were themselves not desired by the majority of English churchmen), and

---

[1] *Report*, vol. i. p. 49, and *The Times*, February 6, 1936.
[2] *Letters of William Stubbs, Bishop of Oxford*, pp. 311-12 (ed. W. H. Hutton).

the demand for spiritual independence in order to enact such measures, are symptoms of blindness towards the urgent problems facing the contemporary Church. Of this circumstance Davidson was well aware; and the warning has been echoed by Dr. Oldham that "it may well be that the conflict between Christian faith and the secular interpretation of life will have to be waged in the field of public education". In which case "the Church will have won little in obtaining liberty to preach and to conduct its own worship and services", if it fails to provide an efficient modern system of divinity for use in secondary schools.[1] Here lies the most vital issue of this generation; and in this field the Church of England can only advance in co-operation with the Free Churches. What is urgently needed is a national scheme of religious instruction based upon modern methods of Biblical study which will furnish all secondary schools with a systematic divinity curriculum resting upon the same basis of intellectual integrity and professional competence on the part of the teacher as the secular subjects there taught. To this end Anglicans and Free Churchmen can and should join forces; and upon the foundation of sound knowledge thus laid each separate church can construct privately its own superstructure of church polity and credal confession according to the desires of its own members. Equally urgent from the standpoint of the Church of England is the provision of a better intellectual training for its ordinands, which can only be attained by the concentration of theological teaching in the faculties of theology of the English universities, leaving to the rural theological colleges pastoral and homiletic instruction. Compared

---

[1] J. H. Oldham, *Church, Community, and State*, pp. 17-18; Bell, *Randall Davidson*, vol. ii. p. 1335, where Davidson regretted that liturgical questions, not being themselves "of supreme deep-down importance" yet, absorbed clerical interest "to the detriment of wider things".

with the problems existing in the field of public education, matters of liturgical reform and abolition of the parliamentary veto are unimportant and secondary.

The Church of England should set itself to solve the question of spiritual independence by realizing its character and vocation as the national church of the English people. Its ideal should be that avowed by Sancroft of "an universal blessed union of all reformed churches, both at home and abroad, against our common enemies". And like Sancroft, who embarked upon the consideration of measures for the comprehension of moderate Protestant Dissenters at home within the national church in addition to shewing "greater friendship to members of the foreign Reformed churches than perhaps any other archbishop of Canterbury",[1] disciples of this ideal should advocate practical steps towards its realization. In the first place, the restrictive clause in the declaration required of the laity desirous to be enrolled upon the parochial electoral rolls (that "they do not belong to any religious body which is not in communion with the Church of England") should be removed; and the way thereby made open for the co-operation of Nonconformists in a fuller parochial fellowship. Further steps might be taken in conformity with the precedents set by seventeenth-century bishops, since from their practice the Church of England has inherited a tradition of recognition of foreign Reformed churches as churches, and a welcome at home of Nonconformists as occasional communicants at its altars as an eirenical and religious custom. By steadfastly following such a pattern the Church of England may be rescued from Tractarian departures from Anglican traditions; as when Keble in his Assize Sermon described Nonconformist

[1] C. Jenkins in *The Anglican Communion*, p. 57; D'Oyly, *Life of Sancroft*, vol. i. pp. 327-30.

churches as "houses upon which Apostolical authority would . . . set a mark as unfit to be entered by a faithful servant of Christ", and Newman in Tract I asserted of episcopal ordination that "we must necessarily consider none to be *really* ordained who have not *thus* been ordained".[1] Modern Anglo-Catholicism in its following of the Tractarians in this regard betrays a sense of uneasiness in relation to the seventeenth-century church, which is reflected in *Anglicanism*, an extensive anthology purporting to illustrate the thought and practice of the Church of England in that epoch. For its editors have deemed it fitting to omit all reference to and evidence of the custom of occasional conformity; to include only a meagre trinity of references to the recognition of foreign reformed churches, to one of which, taken from Cosin, there is prefixed an apologetic editorial comment that "the isolation of the Anglican exiles on the Continent naturally led them to look as favourably as they could upon the Protestant churches with which they were brought into con-tact";[2] and to excise from an extract indicative of Hooker's doctrine of the Eucharistic presence his conclusion that "the real presence of Christ's most blessed body and blood is not therefore to be sought for in the Sacrament but in the worthy receiver of the Sacrament".

From such aberrations the Church of England may hope to free itself in pursuit of Sancroft's goal. In the proclamation of such an ideal, moreover, English churchmen who seek to stand in the traditions of their sixteenth and seventeenth-century pre-decessors (and amongst these Evangelical and Broad churchmen may claim a foremost place) may unite towards the recovery of the national character

[1] J. Keble, *Assize Sermon* (Centenary Edition, p. 13), Tract I in *Tracts for the Times*, vol. i. p. 3 (edition 1840).
[2] P. E. More and F. L. Cross, *Anglicanism*, p. 398.

of the *Ecclesia Anglicana.* Nor need they be ashamed of that vision of its vocation which Creighton set forth as

> a church, not existing in indefinite space, and founding claims to universality on the ground that it has no particular home, but a church rooted in the minds and hearts of the English people. . . . A church fitted for free men, training them in knowledge and reverence alike; disentangling the spirit from the form, because of its close contact with sons who love their mother and frankly speak out their minds; not wandering among formulae, however beautiful, which have lost their meaning; finding room increasingly for every form of devotional life, but training its graces into close connexion with men's endeavours and aspirations; having no objects of its own which it cannot make plain and manifest as being for the highest good of all; afraid of nothing, receptive of new impulses, quick, watchful, alert; proving all things, and ever ready to give a reason for its principles and their application; exhorting, persuading, and convincing; so rooted in the past that it is strong in the present, and ever more hopeful of the future. . . . Is this only a dream to be realized—for assuredly it must be—at some future time and under some other name? Or shall we enter upon the possession which is really ours, did we but know it? Our difficulties and differences arise because we have not a sufficiently lofty conception of the destiny of the English Church. If any disaster befalls it, the record that will be written hereafter will be that English churchmen of this our day were not sufficiently large-hearted and high-minded to recognize the greatness of the heritage which was theirs.[1]

[1] M. Creighton, *The Church and the Nation*, pp. 284-5.

II

TOWARDS PRAYER BOOK REVISION

by

H. D. A. MAJOR, M.A., D.D.

Vicar of Merton
Principal of Ripon Hall
Editor of *The Modern Churchman*

SYNOPSIS

IN Elizabethan days Public Worship was regarded as conducive to national welfare. This conception of Public Worship has largely died away, but it is reviving in the form of a conviction that Public Worship creates values which exhibit themselves in national conduct and character. It produces a spirit of optimism based on confidence in Divine government of the world, and bears the fruit of a brotherly love which manifests itself practically in social righteousness and social service. It inspires to self-discipline and provides a spiritual background for mundane life. In view of this conception of the function of Public Worship as creative of values, the test of our services will be the result produced, and elements within them which do not produce something real precious and comprehensible will be rejected by the modern reviser. Though in the past the Prayer Book has been an important creative factor in national life, to many who neglect Public Worship to-day it seems to have nothing to contribute to human welfare, though there are other factors which conduce to this neglect. One of these factors, especially in rural parishes, is the arbitrary introduction of changes. Changes should not be made without the whole-hearted consent of the parishioners. Modern experience has taught that in every parish there should be three or more types of Public Worship. Revision may be by way of expansion, or of revival of mediaeval elements which were abandoned at the Reformation or by development and emendation along modern lines.

PRAYER BOOK EXPANSION

New needs, interests, and problems should be dealt with in Public Worship. Much is being done to-day in this direction without legal authorization, though many of the new prayers which are used are of poor quality.

CATHOLIC REVISION

The Reformers showed great courage and faced great risks in purging Public Worship of things which they considered untrue, uncertain, meaningless, idolatrous, superstitious, and blasphemous. Some, who think that they went too far, have illegally restored things which the Reformers rejected. Others wish to revise the Prayer Book in such a way as to assimilate Anglican Public Worship to Roman or Eastern types. In centres where this kind of Public Worship is really desired authority should not attempt to suppress it; but revision of the Prayer Book along such lines would alienate the great mass of English people.

A Modern Revision

In view of advancing knowledge, the growth of experience, and a changed outlook, some wish that there should be a modern revision which would do for the present age what the revision of the Reformers did for their age. There are beautiful and moving passages in the Prayer Book which have lost the devotional cogency which they possessed for Tudor Englishmen and conflict with our profoundest moral and social convictions. There is to-day a serious doctrinal crisis. Prayer Book revision should reflect the points in which the New Faith differs from the Old, and should be based on loyalty to the Holy Spirit speaking here and now. It is the duty of Church authorities to purge our Services of expressions of belief in outworn doctrines which are to-day rightly discredited. Unless this is done people will increasingly be driven into Scepticism or Superstition.

Obsolete and Detrimental Dogmas

Among obsolete and detrimental dogmas which should be eliminated from a revised Public Worship are the doctrines of everlasting punishment, the inherited guilt of infants, the expiatory sacrifice on the Cross, the instrumentality of a Virgin Birth in the Incarnation, the direct interference by prayer with the order of nature, a temporal and spatial judgement, a corporeal resurrection. Only essential doctrines should find expression in Public Worship; but at the same time those who still hold other doctrines should not be deprived of full fellowship in the Christian Church or of the right to use an unrevised Liturgy.

MORNING PRAYER

Praying in the Name of Jesus.—Prayer in the name of Jesus is not prayer in reliance on the merits of Christ's propitiatory sacrifice, but prayer to God in the light of the revelation through Christ of the Divine Nature and Will. Revision should omit the pleading of Christ's merits in prayer to the Divine Father.

Order of Public Worship.—In Public Worship there is a fixed element, constituting the Order of Service, and a variable element. Even those who may hold that the Order of Morning Prayer is liturgically perfect may feel that the penitential element is over-stressed. In the Primitive Church there were penitential and festal seasons, but except during the penitential seasons the typical attitude of the worshipper was not penitential but one expressive of filial joy. Repetitions are better discarded. In the variable element consisting of Opening Sentences, Psalms, Lessons, Collects, Hymns, large freedom and judicious selection are desirable.

THE LITANY

The undue length of the Litany should be remedied by dividing it into two portions. Revision should secure the elimination of archaic theology. Only one who was at the same time a modern theologian and a master of literary form could produce an adequate Revision of the Litany.

EVENING PRAYER

The Order of Evening Prayer should be different from that of Morning Prayer, or, alternatively, Evening Prayer should be of an entirely free character.

THE TREATMENT OF SCRIPTURE

Modern Biblical study has rendered untenable the Tudor view that Scripture is uniformly and in all its parts "the very pure word of God". Only the most significant portions should be included in the Lectionary, and these should be arranged in series each of which should deal with a definite theme. Though they may be appropriately used elsewhere, passages from sources other than the Old and New Testaments and the Apocrypha should not be included in the Lectionary

Christian Sacraments

Though Sacraments are an important element in Public Worship, Church History teaches that they are liable to a mechanical, magical, and materialistic interpretation. They should not be compulsory on those to whom they are not congenial. New Testament criticism makes it doubtful whether Jesus made Baptism or the Eucharist institutions of his Church, and they should therefore not be imposed as essential to Church membership.

The Holy Communion Service

Of all services that of Holy Communion is the least in need of revision. Revision would be difficult and its accomplishment might be attended with grave disadvantages. Modern Churchmen would welcome the substitution of the original form for the later form of the Decalogue, the permissive substitution of the two Great Commandments or the Beatitudes, the excision from the General Confession of the more excessive expressions of penitential grief, the omission of the last two Comfortable Words and the insertion of one from John vi. 37, the omission of all Proper Prefaces, the omission of the opening paragraph of the Prayer of Consecration, the permissive use of the second Post-Communion Thanksgiving as an addition instead of as an alternative to the first, the substitution of the Oecumenical Creed for the so-called "Nicene Creed". There should also be an Alternative Simple Office of Holy Communion which would be primarily a Service of Commemoration and Self-consecration and omit references to disputable and difficult theological dogmas.

Holy Baptism

The Service of Holy Baptism, which ought to be a public service, has largely become a private service, partly because of its length, and partly because it expresses beliefs which are not those of most educated Church people, such as the belief in the washing away of the guilt of an infant by the baptismal water. None of these beliefs is essential to Baptism nor required by the Christian Faith. The ablutionary symbolism of Baptism is pre-Christian and sub-Christian. St. Paul interprets the water as symbolical of the death and resurrection of Christ, while the Fourth Gospel emphasizes the contrast between Baptism with the Spirit and Jewish baptisms, or the baptism of John the Baptist. These apostolic interpretations of baptismal symbolism were replaced by cruder interpretations. The doctrine that baptism delivers the infant from the wrath of God is morally and theologically objectionable. The sponsors should not be required to affirm in the name of the infant beliefs which exceed a general affirmation of the Christian faith, but they should be required to make an explicit engagement to see that the child receives a Christian education. Archaisms can easily be removed. The word *regeneration* is too technical for use in a popular Service. The Baptismal Service should primarily stress the Divine sonship of the child and its second birth into God's Family on earth. The gift of the Holy Spirit is not transmitted by manual acts nor by material elements nor by uttered formularies. Some alterations in the Catechism would be consequent on a revision of the Baptismal Service.

Baptism of Adults

The Service of Adult Baptism would differ from that of Infant Baptism in the absence of sponsors and a fuller stress on the distinction between the old life and the new.

Confirmation

Little revision of the authorized Service of Confirmation is necessary. There should be no suggestion of transmission of the Holy Spirit by the imposition of the episcopal hand. There is need for a service of admission into the Church of England of members of other Christian denominations.

The Marriage Service

Certain inappropriate passages and references should be omitted. The demand that the vows of husband and wife should be identical has much to commend it. The vows taken cannot be too plain and too literal. For the concluding address a brief and simple exhortation should be substituted, and the Service should contain a reference to the conditions which ought to determine the size and welfare of the family.

THE VISITATION OF THE SICK

The Service for the Visitation of the Sick, having largely fallen into disuetude, a succinct body of rubrics giving directions and advice would be of value. The humble sick room is singularly appropriate for the celebration of Holy Communion.

THE CHURCHING OF WOMEN

Though the Service of the Churching of Women is a service of thanksgiving for deliverance from the peril of childbirth, behind it lie superstitions created by pagan taboos. It should include a thanksgiving for the birth of the child, prayers for the Divine Blessing on the home, and should lay stress on the responsibility of parentage. It ought to be a Family Service.

SERVICE FOR THE BURIAL OF THE DEAD

In the Service for the Burial of the Dead blended with the Christian belief in immortality and the Fatherly Providence of God are a number of beliefs derived from Jewish eschatology. To-day such beliefs as those of the Grand Assize and the Resurrection of the Flesh have been replaced by more spiritual conceptions of Judgement, Heaven, and Hell, while among educated Christians the dominant faith is faith in the love and wisdom of God. This healthy change in outlook should be reflected in the Service, and the older views, so far as they conflict with the more spiritual view, should be purged out.

THE COMMINATION SERVICE

For the Commination Service should be substituted an Ash Wednesday Evening Service in which expression should be given to a sense of corporate as well as personal guilt and the need for reform and betterment.

The Ordinal

The Ordinal requires little revision except in such points as the question put to deacons about the Holy Scripture. For this question might be substituted the question put to priests on this point. More stress should be laid on the doctrine of the Spirit-bearing Church.

The attempt at Prayer Book Revision which had its origin in the Report of the Royal Commission on Church Discipline took too long and reflected ill on the statesmanship of the ecclesiastical leaders. The impression was given that in the name of revision the Church authorities were going back behind the Reformation, and it was to this that the rejection of the proposals by the House of Commons was due. The interest of Parliament testified to the extent to which the people of England care for their Church. The bishops sometimes forgot the nation in their preoccupation with small groups of partisans in the Church. The result was a Book which was unsatisfactory from both the literary and the liturgical standpoint. It is to be hoped that the bishops will take up the task of revision again, and, altering fundamentally the method of procedure, aim at a revision marked by sincerity, simplicity, and spirituality. The example of the creators of our Prayer Book should be followed, and all that is doubtful, whether historically or doctrinally, should be omitted.

II

TOWARDS PRAYER BOOK REVISION

IF in the spacious times of Great Elizabeth we had asked one of the statesmen or prelates of the period, What is the purpose of Public Worship in a National Church? he would have replied, The due honouring of Almighty God, without whose blessing the nation cannot possess enduring success and prosperity. For those great Englishmen, the Public Worship of Almighty God was an essentially practical affair: it was something which all "who wished well unto our Zion" must be sedulous to promote and maintain.

That is why in those days the laws of Church and State punished all who absented themselves from Public Worship.

It would, however, be unjust to our authorized Prayer Book to suggest that it is either solely or predominantly national in its objective. It is certainly not neglectful of personal needs on the one hand and is also strongly conscious of international needs on the other. It prays for the whole state of Christ's Church, for all sorts and conditions of men, that God will grant to all nations, unity, peace, and concord, and fetch home to his flock all Jews, Turks, infidels, and heretics.

Nevertheless, the dependence of national welfare upon Public Worship was strongly in men's minds in those days although such a conviction is now almost non-existent. "Things begun religiously are ended prosperously"; so the "judicious Hooker" affirmed, and all responsible national feeling was convinced of the truth of his statement. The welfare of the

Commonwealth depended upon the Public Worship of Almighty God with reverence, fervour, and purity.

To-day there is no such conviction. Men and women go to church to save their own souls; to receive Sacramental Grace; to calm their troubled hearts; to listen to an attractive preacher; to hear good music; to come away feeling happy. This is true of the bulk of those who go. There are still a few perhaps who go in order to maintain an institution which they regard as a valuable conservative element in our national life and to set a good example to those less enlightened and dutiful than themselves. But, speaking broadly, the promotion and maintenance of Public Worship, as a necessity of national welfare, has very largely died away. I believe, however, that we have reached a point where it will begin to revive. Patriots are beginning to recognize that religion can perform invaluable services in our national life. They do not think of the way in which it does this, as did the Elizabethans. They think of it rather as creative of values which exhibit themselves in national conduct and character. The public worship of God they regard as a potentially important factor in the creation of these values.

Values Created by Divine Worship

The first of these Values created by Divine Worship is Faith in a God of infinite love, wisdom, and power. Such a faith creates a spirit of optimism, confidence in the essential goodness of the Universe, and the essential righteousness of the Divine government: the conviction, to use St. Paul's phrase, that all things work together for good to them that love God. Such a faith is bound to reflect itself, not only in the character and conduct of the individual who has it, but also in the whole life of a community composed of such faith-possessing individuals. Such a faith will not only make for social well-being but also for mental and physical health.

An increase in suicide and insanity, nervous breakdowns, and anarchic pessimism, is one of the evil results of the decline of such a faith in God. Its gift is "the peace which passeth all understanding", the calm which enables us to face life's evils and dangers without despair and trepidation.

Another supremely important value which Public Worship should create is the obligation of brotherly love, which shews itself in the practical form of social righteousness and personal service to our fellows, where they are in need of such service.

Public Worship can do much to create the value of self-discipline; the realization that there is a higher life which is achieved by the consecration of this lower life to ideal ends instead of yielding to the temptation to dissipate it in self-indulgence.

> Whene'er a noble deed is wrought,
> Whene'er is spoken a noble thought,
> Our hearts in glad surprise
> To higher levels rise.
> The tidal wave of deeper souls
> Into our inmost being rolls
> And lifts us unawares
> Out of all meaner cares.

Public Worship provides a spiritual background for mundane life. It gives it meaning and worth. For brief seasons, at any rate, it lifts us above sordid cares and interests.

In Public Worship of the right kind we find ourselves at times walking with our fellows, like Bunyan's pilgrim, upon the Delectable Mountains, from whence, on a clear day, we may discern the Celestial City.

These and many such like values Public Worship should create and foster. If it does so in any community, it is conferring upon that community "the purest treasure mortal times afford" upon the possession of which and the propagation and development of which, human welfare, personal and social, economic and political, depend. It is the duty of the National Church to teach that all these moral and spiritual values exist primarily in God and that it is only by human communion with God, prayer to God, reliance upon God, obedience to God, that these moral and spiritual values can be possessed by human beings. Hence our Public Worship will be tested by its power to do this. All in our Public Worship which does not contribute to this end will be discarded. As a result of this ideal of creative worship we shall be led to eliminate much in our present services which to-day does not contribute to this end.

When in the light of this ideal we study our services our test will be: not, Has this scriptural precedent? or Is it a Catholic practice? but, What is it achieving? What good is it producing? What real result, if any, is it accomplishing?

All in our Church services that does not create, and create something real and precious and comprehensible, our modern reviser will reject.

Of course there is for the purpose of creative worship a large amount of immensely valuable material in our present Prayer Book. Its services had not a little to do in creating that character and temperament which is so essentially "English" in the best sense of that term. The fact that the Church of England could be described as "the Conservative Party at prayer" indicates this.

The serious student of English social life can hardly fail to observe that the English Church is the most English of all our institutions. Even in the United States of America, the Englishman who attends the worship of the Protestant Episcopal Church and associates with its clergy and leading laity forgets for the time that he is in America.

It is plain that our Prayer Book has been for four

centuries an important creative factor in our national and personal life. Nevertheless, owing to a number of causes which we cannot deal with here at length, it is ceasing to be creative: indeed has ceased to be creative, so far as large numbers of our population are concerned. This is partly due to the Continent-alizing of the English Sunday. This English institution, which in less pleasure-loving days formed a restful interlude, not divorced from cheerfulness and pleasant human intercourse, was primarily devoted to Public Worship. Now, every form of recreation is cultivated over "the week-end", except the recreation that comes from "a Sabbath well-spent", to use the phrase of the seventeenth-century judge, Sir Matthew Hales.

One reason at least for this growing neglect of Public Worship is, not simply that it is unable to compete in attractiveness with many forms of sport and pleasure, but, that it has seemed to have nothing to contribute to human welfare. Such an attitude is unsound, and mistaken, but the Church authorities cannot be absolved from blame in the matter. The Church's Public Worship has become unpopular for a number of reasons. The parochial clergy have insisted on giving their parishioners what they think is good for them, but which the parishioners, in many cases, do not want, and feel they do not need. The substitution at eleven o'clock on Sunday morning of a sung Eucharist, instead of the accustomed Morning Prayer and Sermon has emptied the churches in rural England and dealt a very serious blow to the practice of Public Worship.

Changes in Public Worship must have very large popular local support or they cannot be profitably made. It is much better that a community should attend a form of Public Worship which is not the very best form, than that it should attend no form of worship at all. All reformers of Public Worship must bear this in mind; that if changes are to be made, they must receive the whole-hearted consent of the parishioners. To introduce unpopular reforms into Public Worship which drive away the congregation, is to throw out the babe with the bath water. We stress this here because, although we believe that important changes are needful and desirable in our Public Worship, we would have no such changes made in any church if there is not a whole-hearted acceptance of them by the great bulk of the parishioners. Of course such whole-hearted acceptance can only follow on wise and attractive educational preparation.

Another lesson which our modern experience should have taught us is, that in every parish there ought to be three or more types of Public Worship. It greatly strengthened Public Worship when the Holy Communion service was transferred to an earlier hour and celebrated apart from Morning Prayer and Sermon. Again, it greatly strengthened Public Worship when, after the example of Bishop Dupanloup, children's services were made a part of our English liturgical practice. Again, special Sunday afternoon services for groups of men or women, united perhaps in some particular parochial organization, have led to a further strengthening of Public Worship, especially where this has been combined with definite religious education. Again, the giving of the Evening Service on Sunday a more popular form than the eleven o'clock service has also led to a strengthening of Public Worship. The great proportion of English Church people who attend Sunday Public Worship are "oncers", and by this variation in the type of Sunday services, a larger proportion of the parishioners are induced to attend. It will be noticed that it was not the Church authorities that initiated these variations, but the pastoral wisdom and enterprise of parish priests.

F

Notwithstanding these efforts, Public Worship is ceasing to be creative of moral and spiritual values in English life. This is because the services themselves have less creative value than they ought to have. To secure more of this creative value they need revision.

The word revision is ambiguous when used in this connexion. Churchmen who speak of Prayer Book revision seem to have at least three different ideals of it.

(1) Prayer Book Expansion

First there are those who recognize that there are a number of things in our modern life which had no existence when our authorized Prayer Book was composed—ranging from aeroplanes to the League of Nations. Public Worship which is concerned, among other things, with human needs and human interests and human problems, and above all with human welfare, ought to deal with them in Public Worship. Harvest Festivals and Armistice Days ought to have special services, and of course, so they have. But these services are not contained in the Prayer Book.

To-day we are much concerned nationally with problems of education, employment, slum abolition, preservation of natural beauty, youth movements, and so on, and a Public Worship which neglects these many-sided national interests will lose creative power. For in, and through, these interests, moral and spiritual ideals may be created and developed. Perhaps this aspect of Prayer Book revision should be more properly styled Prayer Book expansion. All interested churchmen desire this expansion of our Liturgy. It is only right to add that most parish clergymen, encouraged by those in authority, have, even though it be illegally, done much in this direction. It is also only right to add that much of it has been of very poor quality compared with the work of our sixteenth- and seventeenth-century Prayer Book makers.

(2) "Catholic" Revision

Secondly, there are those who feel that our English reformers in dealing with Public Worship were much too drastic in their purgation of the mediaeval services. There were many things in those services which our Reformers regarded as idolatrous, superstitious, and blasphemous. And they shewed extraordinary courage in eliminating them from Public Worship. In these tolerant days, it is difficult to realize the greatness of their courage and the intensity and detestation which their efforts at purgation excited. The fact that the Archbishop of Canterbury and four Diocesan Bishops in his province were burned to death at the stake for the part they played in this reformation of Public Worship is an unforgettable reminder of the risks which attended it. The Reformers not only, of set purpose, purged out everything which they regarded as untrue, they went even further than this, although it has not been so generally recognized; they purged out all that seemed to them to be uncertain. They also purged out all that seemed to them to be meaningless. "Dark and dumb ceremonies", although not so evil as superstitions and idolatries, had to be done away with. They went even further. Things in themselves unobjectionable, but which experience had taught the Reformers could be misunderstood and misused, were also better removed. We sometimes have our Tudor Reformers of Public Worship presented to us as timid opportunists. They were nothing of the kind. They were judicious and statesmanlike. Undoubtedly they knew how to handle men and the occasions in which to advance their cause, but in the embodiment of their ideals, they do not seem to have flinched. Nothing which they thought wrong or unworthy was permitted by them in the national Public Worship.

There are churchmen to-day who think that our Reformers went much too far in their purgation of Public Worship. That they eliminated much that was devout, ancient, beautiful; things which good men and good women in the past used and loved; these things, and how many they be, they desire to have restored to our Public Worship. Many of these things they have restored, although illegally, to the great dissatisfaction of vast multitudes of English Church people. With the best of intentions they have caused men to "abhor the offering of the Lord". This process is spoken of as the "catholicizing" of our English Public Worship. For these lovers of the Christian worship of the past, or for Christian worship as it is to-day in the Church of Rome, or in some cases in the Orthodox Churches of the East, Prayer Book revision means the assimilation of our English Public Worship to these Continental forms.

We are convinced that Prayer Book revision of this kind will not strengthen Public Worship in this country. It has secured, and will secure, many converts for the Church of Rome. It will raise hopes for the conversion of England in the minds of the less understanding Roman Catholics, but it will lead to the increasing desertion of our churches by the great mass of English people. In Parish Churches where this kind of Public Worship is really popular and desired, as is undoubtedly the case in some centres, wise and tolerant authorities will not attempt to suppress or penalise it, but revision of our Prayer Book services on these lines would be a profound mistake.

(3) A Modern Revision

Thirdly, there are those who desire a revision of our Public Worship on modern lines. They have no desire to go behind the principles and liturgical practices of the English Reformation. They revere the creators of our Prayer Book. All that they desire is that what those great Englishmen did for their age, modern revisers may be enabled to do, in some measure, for the present age. One of the reasons which has greatly reduced the creative power of our authorized Public Worship to-day is that our services in many cases are out of date. That is why they seem dull to some people, or mechanical or meaningless or palpably insincere to others. This is no fault of the great men, religious geniuses, and intellectual giants who composed those services. It is due to so much water having flowed under the arches since those services were composed. In other words, the advancing knowledge, the growth of experience, the changed outlook have rendered some of the noblest compositions of our Reformers uncouth and ineffective.

> By the mystery of thy holy Incarnation;
> By thy holy Nativity and Circumcision;
> By thy Baptism, Fasting, and Temptation;
> By thine Agony and bloody Sweat;
> By thy Cross and Passion;
> By thy precious Death and Burial;
> By thy glorious Resurrection and Ascension;
> And by the coming of the Holy Ghost,
>   Good Lord, deliver us.

This suffrage from our English Litany has a literary quality for modern ears which is dependent upon something more than the collocation and arrangement of vowels and consonants. It is the utterance of a human soul, as it contemplates the mystery of salvation and the stages of its accomplishment, imploring the Soul of All Things for deliverance from sin and death.

We can find nothing among the vast number of modern liturgical compositions comparable to it.

Amazingly beautiful as it is, and we write what follows with extreme hesitation, it lacks to-day the devotional cogency and creative power which it possessed for Tudor Englishmen. The reason for its lack of virtue is that, deep down, we feel that it is approaching the Divine Father in a way which is not sanctioned by our conviction that he is the God of Love. Moving as the appeal is, it is based upon a belief in the efficacy of the expiatory sufferings of Christ. We, however, are unable to bring ourselves to believe that God needs our pleading of such an expiatory sacrifice in order to forgive us our sins and to deliver us from evil. What the modern mind believes, if it believes anything at all about the matter, is the teaching of Jesus in the parable of the prodigal son.

Out-of-datedness in thought, in other words, conflict with our profoundest moral and spiritual convictions, can render and does render some of the most majestic portions of the Prayer Book services ineffective for modern creative worship. The problem for the modern reviser is no easy one. It is to capture for modern men the extraordinary literary and devotional quality which the Prayer Book services had for Tudor Englishmen. Yet these modern men have a conception of the Universe, of the creative process, of the Creator himself, which differs greatly from Tudor conceptions. This alteration in view is by no means detrimental or to be condemned. It is an immense advance, intellectually, morally, and spiritually, upon the *Weltanschauung* of those who produced our incomparable liturgy.

Archbishop Davidson strove to persuade both Church and State to accept the Deposited Book by affirming that it made no departure from the doctrinal position of the authorized Prayer Book. Whether it did, or did not do so, is arguable, but that its chief promoter claimed that it ought to be received and sanctioned because it did not do so, must seem to modern students of contemporary religious thought a reason for justifying its rejection.

If the revised Prayer Book is to reflect and maintain the old theology, then there is no need for a revised Prayer Book at all for it can never express that old theology in liturgical forms with the devotional cogency and creative power of our authorized Prayer Book.

It is needful to stress at the outset—and this is the *crux* of revision for our traditionalists—that modern English men and women who need and demand a revised Prayer Book are those who need and demand that it shall reflect the convictions of the New Faith in those very points in which that New Faith differs from the Old. If this is not done, Public Worship must lack creative power.

What our Church authorities have to realize and face is that there is a doctrinal crisis in our Church and to comprehend what is the nature of this crisis. If it were a political crisis, it would be vocal; if it were an economic crisis, it would be vocal; if it were a purely ritualistic crisis, it would be vocal; but being a doctrinal crisis, it is very largely silent. It shews itself, not by the indignant protests of the laity, but by their silent desertion of a Church which adheres to an outworn dogmatic system. They feel that what she is teaching is incredible. With rare exceptions they are convinced that it is of no use to tell the Church authorities that this is the case. Doing so can do no good—they are convinced that the authorities will not change. They cannot: they dare not. Moreover, these modern-minded people feel that by open protest they might disturb "the simple faith" of many Church people, whose faith they have no desire to disturb. As for doctrinal controversy, they loathe it, and realize from what they read of it that they have neither the ingenuity nor the erudition required for successful participation in it; and so without any form of protest they withdraw from attending Church services and supporting Church activities, save where those activities are social and philanthropic. We do not wish to be understood as saying that the doctrinal crisis is the only crisis the Church is faced with; there are a number of others, but the most serious crisis, because the most fundamental and difficult, is the doctrinal crisis. It is much the most dangerous crisis because so many of the Church authorities dare not face it, or if they face it, face it only in defiance, which is a perfectly hopeless way of facing it.

There is only one way in which it can be faced and that is by faith in the Holy Spirit. That Spirit which, if we yield rightly to his teaching, can and will guide us into all the truth. If our Church authorities regard Holy Scripture or the authorized dogmatic system or some inherited apostolic tradition as their supreme authority and not the Holy Spirit speaking to them here and now, they will be unable to cope with the situation. It is the Holy Spirit who created the Christian Church and inspired, in accordance with that Church's needs at particular stages in its evolution, the creation of the various institutions which it possesses. But the supreme possession of the Christian Church is the Spirit of truth, freedom, love, manifest in the life of Jesus himself.

"With freedom has Christ set us free." "Where the Spirit of the Lord is, there is liberty." "It is the letter which killeth but it is the Spirit which giveth life." Possessed of this Spirit, the Church authorities can face the doctrinal crisis. Without faith in the present inspiration of the Spirit, they must fail, as the slaves of tradition and dogma.

The Divine revelation given through the Holy Spirit to-day must be supreme over all preceding Divine revelations. This is the Gospel of Divine

Creative evolution. We ought not to fear for one moment that this reliance upon the Holy Spirit to-day, for insight and guidance, will cause us to depart from the heart of the Gospel of Jesus. The things in our traditional theology which are doing so much to weaken the message of the Christian Church to the largely unheeding world are not to be found in the Gospel of Jesus. The doctrine of the Fall, which is the corner-stone of our traditional theology, the original Gospel of Jesus neither teaches nor pre-supposes. The Revelation of the Holy Spirit to-day is rendering "uncouth" much of the structure of the Pauline theology, and that of St. Augustine, and St. Thomas Aquinas, and Calvin; but not the heart of the Gospel of Jesus. It is a creative worship, based on the principles of that Gospel, developed and applied in the light of our modern knowledge and experience which we need, if our Public Worship is to be real for modern men and women and if the Church itself is to become the moral and spiritual power station of our national life.

I write these words on Easter Monday when the Proper Preface for the Office of Holy Communion runs thus:

> But chiefly are we bound to praise thee for the glorious Resurrection of thy Son Jesus Christ our Lord; for he is the very Paschal Lamb, which was offered for us, and hath taken away the sin of the world; who by his death hath destroyed death, and by his rising to life again hath restored to us everlasting life.

What does this Thanksgiving for the Resurrection of Jesus presuppose? It requires those who utter it to unite the essential Christian belief in the Resurrection with the Jewish legend of the origin of Israel's Passover festival. It identifies Jesus with the Paschal Lamb—a very primitive Christian identification it is true, but to-day an identification as obscure as it is incredible.

The Proper Preface also presupposes the possession by the first man of original immortality. This original immortality he forfeited by the Fall. Jesus, by his propitiatory sacrifice and by his Resurrection, has restored to mankind what had been lost by the Fall. Can such theories, though St. Paul held them, be held to-day by people of education?

It is doubtful even if those who profess to believe in propitiatory sacrifice really do believe in it; and how rapidly they are diminishing in numbers. Why, then, should our Easter Thanksgiving in our Public Worship be specifically united to these old-world beliefs and modern unbeliefs?

We are bidden to keep our Easter feast "not with the old leaven, nor with the leaven of malice and wickedness: but with the unleavened bread of sincerity and truth".

It is the duty of our Church authorities to purge out from our services these expressions of outworn belief and so render possible sincerity and truth in our Public Worship for the nation at large.

The Christian religion is either true or it is nothing: it is concerned with essential reality. Our conviction is that the fundamentals of its theology are sound but they are intermixed with beliefs which are to-day rightly discredited. Moreover, these fundamental truths themselves are expressed in language which is archaic and in certain cases misleading.

We must have a reformulation of our theology even though a number of our clerics and ecclesiastical laymen who do not number one in fifty of our population, forbid, or implore, us not to undertake this difficult and dangerous task.

It is painfully manifest that organized Christian religion is slowly but steadily losing its hold on the English people. The nation is becoming divided into two camps—the sceptics and the superstitious—and each of these camps seems to constitute an increasing necessity for the existence of the other: and so the evil grows. Those who like neither of these camps are fast becoming as sheep without a shepherd, or rather as sheep without a fold.

The Theology, not we hope the Religion, of England has changed: liturgical revision must take account of this difficult and disconcerting fact.

Obsolete and Detrimental Dogmas

We have to say it, not only in the interests of truth, but in the interests of the Christian religion and the human race which it exists to bless, that our traditional Christianity contains a number of obsolete and detrimental dogmas which are enshrined in parts of our public services, and which do much to discredit those services in the estimation of large numbers of people of good-will and good life.

We cannot indicate here explicitly why such doctrines are rightly disbelieved and rejected by many. All we would plead for is that they should be eliminated from our revised Public Worship.

The doctrine of everlasting punishment in the *Quicunque Vult*; the doctrine of original guilt inherited by infants which appears in our Baptismal service; the doctrine that Jesus offered to God an expiatory sacrifice on the Cross, by faith in which human sins are forgiven; the doctrine that the Divine Incarnation was accomplished by a Virgin Birth; the doctrine that the order of nature and the operation of physical laws can be directly affected by prayer; the doctrine that the history of this world may be terminated at any moment by Christ's descent from heaven and the advent of the Day of Judgement; the doctrine that the bodies of the dead will on that occasion rise from their graves—ought not to find a place in our revised public services.

Even those of our fellow-churchmen who believe

that any or all of these doctrines are true could perhaps bring themselves to consent to their elimination from our public services on the ground that it is not necessary for the salvation of any individual that he should hold them.

All that is necessary in Public Worship is that faith in the essential doctrines of the Christian religion should inspire that worship and be developed by it. If, therefore, not one of the doctrines named above can be shown to be an essential doctrine of the Christian religion, it can claim no absolute right to find a place in our public worship. Therefore those in authority, recognizing the cogency of this plea, ought to assent, as a basic principle of revision, that these doctrines should be allowed to disappear from our revised liturgy. This does not mean either that those who wish to believe these doctrines should be deprived of their full fellowship in the Church, or that they should be deprived of the right to use the unrevised liturgy which contains them.

If, however, our Church authorities are to sanction forms of Public Worship which deliberately omit these ancient traditional doctrines, it can only be on the ground that they believe in the evolution of Christian theology, or in other words that they recognize that the Christian religion is the religion, not primarily of the letter, either of creed or scripture, but the religion of the Spirit, and that as the Spirit is leading the Church into fuller knowledge of the truth, it is also shewing the Church the imperfection of many of the old forms in which the truth was expressed and also the errors to which that truth was in certain cases united. If the Church is resolved to be the Church of a tradition, the Church of a Creed, the Church of a sacred Book, in the sense that it regards any or all of these things as having more authority than the ever-present, ever-inspiring Spirit of freedom, truth, and love, then of course dogmatic reformation is out of the question and effective liturgical revision. But if the Church is not going to be first and foremost the Spirit-bearing Church, its leadership of the human race has been surrendered.

Yet, if this be so, we have no doubt that the Spirit will create a new *organon* through which to carry on the education and salvation of mankind.

Morning Prayer

(*a*) praying in the name of jesus

The first question to be clearly answered by all revisers of Public Worship is: What is Christian Prayer? It is prayer in Christ's name. Here is a fertile cause of misunderstanding and malpractice. Many have supposed that praying in Christ's name means pleading before the Divine Father the merits of Christ's propitiatory sacrifice as a ground for hearing our prayers and granting them. Hence the name of Jesus is inserted in nearly every prayer addressed to the Divine Father. The older form was "through Jesus Christ our Lord". Later forms, much favoured by the Protestant Reformers, have "for the sake of Jesus Christ our Lord" or "for the merits of Jesus Christ our Lord". This was regarded as praying in the Name of Christ. It is not, however, what the New Testament means by praying in the Name of Christ. Jesus never taught that the Divine Father either heard or granted prayer on account of the merits or the sacrifice of his Son. The Divine Father is ever ready to hear prayer and to answer prayer. The Divine Father is ever ready to forgive sinners where the sinners themselves, in a spirit of penitence and love, are exercising forgiveness towards their fellow-men.

Praying in Christ's name is praying to God in the light of Christ's unveiling to men of the Divine Nature and the Divine Will. Or to put it in another way: It is praying to the Divine Father as Christ himself would pray were he in our circumstances.

The Lord's Prayer, our pattern prayer, presents us with the principles and methods of effective prayer. That prayer is truly in Christ's name, though it does not conclude with the formula, "through Jesus Christ our Lord". The revisers of our Public Worship would do well to take this into consideration and omit the pleading of Christ's merits in our petition to the Divine Father.

(*b*) ORDER OF PUBLIC WORSHIP

In all public services, and herein they differ from private and family devotions, it is extremely important to have a fixed element and also a variable element. The fixed element should consist of the *order* of the service. The *order* of any particular public service should always be the same. This principle is, in our experience, often detrimentally neglected by the composers of, or officiants at, modern services. As a result, the congregation do not know what to expect or what to do next: the sense of continuity and method is lost and also the sense of calm and restfulness. A public liturgical service should proceed definitely from point to point. This is its action.

The *order* of our Morning Prayer seems to us liturgically perfect.

Those who would assent to this view feel that there are two weaknesses in our order for Morning Prayer: its penitential opening and its repetitions.

(*c*) PENITENTIAL ELEMENT

They feel that the penitential element is too largely stressed. They hold it unnatural that our services should always open with a confession of sin and petitions for forgiveness. Is this the right way for a child to approach his father on every occasion?

Ought man to be always conscious that he is a sinner when entering the Divine Presence?

There is much historic support for those who protest against the penitential character of our normal Public Worship.

There are great differences in human beings, even Christian human beings. Religious psychology has stressed the difference between the once-born and the twice-born. It is the twice-born for whom the consciousness of sin and the need for Divine Forgiveness will immediately arise when entering the Divine Presence. For the first-born it is not so.

Are we to have separate types of Public Worship for each of these classes? The Primitive Church faced the situation, possibly unconsciously, by having festal and penitential seasons. The festal represented the normal ideal of Christian worship. On every Lord's Day and in the period from Easter to Whitsunday Christians were required to stand for Public Worship. Only penitents, under ecclesiastical censure, were required to kneel. At penitential seasons, which were rare in the Primitive Church, presumably all knelt, but the typical attitude of the early Christian engaged in worship was non-penitential. He neither knelt nor bowed his head. He stood upright with uplifted face and uplifted hands—a son of God, without fear and without doubting. Hence standing, not kneeling, was the normal Christian posture at Holy Communion.

It should not be forgotten that Morning, as well as Evening Prayer, in the First Prayer Book of King Edward VI, began with the Lord's Prayer and had no public confession and absolution. To return to this practice for normal occasions might be a good thing. After all there is a penitential element in the Lord's Prayer: "Forgive us our trespasses". On special occasions, the penitential seasons, Morning Prayer might suitably begin with confession.

Yet the very fact that in the Second Prayer Book of Edward VI the public confession and absolution were inserted before the Lord's Prayer, indicates that a serious need must have been felt for them. It may be replied that the Reformers thus stressed public confession and absolution in order to abolish the practice of private confession and absolution, and in doing so departed detrimentally from the joyous filial note of Primitive Christian worship.

It ought to be remembered that it is not simply personal sin, or sin of the individual, that is confessed in the General Confession, but the sin of the Church.

There is great need to-day for the quickening of the conscience, whether ecclesiastical, personal, social, national or international. If it be true, as Sir Oliver Lodge said, that nothing troubles the modern man less than the thought of his sins—so much the worse for the modern man and the modern world. It is upon the development of the consciousness of sin that personal and social reformation and progress depend in a very large measure, and therefore it is important that Public Worship should not ignore it, but develop it and direct it into effective practical efforts.

(d) REPETITIONS

All repetitions—we need not argue whether or not they be *vain* repetitions—are better discarded, and for this amongst other reasons that a reasonable brevity in Public Worship is desirable in order to secure the better attendance and attention of congregations.

When the Holy Communion is united with and follows on Morning Prayer, Matins should stop with the *Benedictus*, used as an Introit, and the celebrant should omit the recitation of the opening Lord's Prayer. This custom has become very general to-day and is much appreciated, and should certainly be authorized. Perhaps on these occasions

Morning Prayer had better begin at the Lord's Prayer.

(e) THE VARIABLE ELEMENT

Of the *variable* element in Morning Prayer which consists of Opening Sentences, Canticles, Psalms, Lessons, Collects, Hymns, Sermons—all that need be said is, that the largest freedom of selection should be granted and the most judicious selection made. Particular care should be exercised that no sub-Christian elements should be admitted into the Prayer and Praise of the Congregation. The case of the Lessons is different for they do not form part of the congregation's worship.

The recitation of the Baptismal Creed, commonly called the Apostles' Creed and the *Quicunque Vult*, although something of a liturgical innovation and a national peculiarity, but not to be condemned on either of those accounts, is treated by another essayist in this volume.

THE LITANY

The Litany, a liturgical composition of unparalleled quality, loses in effectiveness, partly because of the archaic character of its theology, and partly because of its great length. To omit the recitation of the Litany on these accounts would be a very serious liturgical loss. The objection to its length can be remedied either by having it as a special service alone or by dividing it into two—the division taking place at the end of the Litany proper.

The objection to its archaic theology is much harder to deal with, because it demands the knowledge of a thoroughly competent modern theologian combined with the gifts of a master of literary form, and where is such a combination to be found? The late Bishop Ridding of Southwell, by patient devotion and unusual liturgical skill, shewed in our own days what could be accomplished in this form of composition and we may hope that some modern Cranmer may yet arise to give us an English Litany which is modern in its theology and as perfect in literary form and devotional fervour as its Tudor predecessor.

We do not think that it would be possible for any committee, however large and however learned, to produce a Litany of first-rate quality. It must be the work of an inspired individual.

EVENING PRAYER

It would certainly be better that Evening Prayer should have a different order from Morning Prayer or perhaps it might be a good thing that there should be no fixed order at all in this case. To have one of our public services of a free, not of a fixed character and to have this freedom exercised at a service most likely to be attended by non-regular church-goers, has much to commend it. Such freedom would facilitate its adaptation to local and temporal religious needs.

THE TREATMENT OF SCRIPTURE IN A REVISED LITURGY

One great purpose of the Tudor churchmen who composed our Liturgy was to scripturalize it; that is to say, to bring it into harmony with the teaching of Holy Scripture so that it should contain nothing that was contrary to Holy Scripture. One way of scripturalization was to secure the regular reading of large portions of Holy Scripture in the Church services. For these churchmen, the Scriptures were "the very pure Word of God"; they believed in the plenary inspiration of Scripture and that nothing was necessary to salvation which is not contained in the Scriptures or can be proved by them.

Modern Biblical study precludes our being able to regard all Scripture as "the very pure word of God". We value the Scriptures because they contain the account of a Divine revelation culminating in the personality and teaching of Jesus Christ. This progressive Divine revelation we believe to be essentially true and the highest religious revelation received by man. But a great deal of the Bible is like a vein of auriferous quartz—gold-bearing it is true, but only containing little particles of gold here and there. The quartz has to be mined and be subjected to a series of processes before the pure gold can be secured. Much of the Bible contains very little of the Divine revelation in its purest and most precious form, and we doubt whether in our Church services any except the very richest portions of the Scriptures should be read or at any rate any except the most significant portions.

If this principle be accepted, then a new lectionary is required, and one in which the Scriptural readings will be so selected and arranged as to present and teach the various stages of the Divine moral and spiritual revelation contained in Scripture.

Of course, to do this, those making the Scriptural selections would have to have definite themes in mind and arrange the readings in series in elucidation of these themes, *e.g.* such a series as the messages of the prophets; the visions of the apocalyptists; main principles of Israelite legislation; Jewish ideals of character; the lessons of the wise; the beatitudes of Jesus; the questions of Jesus; the parables of Jesus; the allegories of Jesus; the exhortations of St. Paul; the affirmations of St. John; the patience of St. Peter; the wisdom of St. James.

This would mean that much less Scripture would be read in Church but it would be much more significant and educative. This applies, not only to our lessons from the Old and New Testaments but also to our Epistles and Gospels at the Eucharist. In certain cases our present Epistles and Gospels have been admirably selected, as for instance, the Gospel and Epistle for Christmas Day. But in many other cases a much more valuable and impressive selection could be made.

The modern use of the Psalter at our Sunday services which ignores the method of using the Psalms as prescribed in our authorized Prayer Book has set a good example—but even this selection could be bettered if those who made it had felt free on occasions to use only portions of the Psalms. In that case it would be best to have in our Prayer Book a Psalter consisting only of those Psalms and portions of Psalms selected for Public Worship.

Before the era of modern Biblical criticism we did not feel free to handle the Scriptures in this way, but the knowledge of the Truth has made us free.

In connexion with the revised use of Holy Scripture, it will be asked: Would you restrict the reading of sacred writings to the Old and New Testaments and the Apocrypha? Ought not noble passages to be read from the Greek philosophers and the sacred books of other religions and also from later Christian literature, *e.g.* St. Augustine's *Confessions*, the *Imitatio Christi*, William Law's *Serious Call*, and the *Ad Diognetum?*

I do not doubt the value of such readings but I do doubt the advisability of substituting them for passages from our Bible in the Sunday services. We have little enough time for the public reading of Holy Scripture even if a very exacting selection from it be made. Besides the opportunities provided by week-day services for extra Scriptural reading, we have also the pulpit, and the pulpit is probably the best place for these extra Scriptural lections as they can there be commented on and compared with Scriptural parallels.

It is generally agreed that all Scriptural lections in Church should be introduced by a brief sentence or two indicating their significance.

We shall never be able to hear or read our Bible aright unless we are taught to recognize that two religions, the old and the new, are to be seen struggling for supremacy in its pages and at times even in the teaching and life of the same individual. This is one of the many things which distinguishes the outlook of the modern Biblical student from his predecessors. The conflict witnessed is not so much between the diabolical and the Divine, the bad and the good, but between the lower and the higher, the old and the new; that which was good in its day, but which has been rendered uncouth by the advent of a greater good.

CHRISTIAN SACRAMENTS

Sacraments are a most important element in the public worship and constitution of the Church, but their use is beset by two dangers. (1) First, so Church History teaches, they are always liable to, and seem indeed to invite, a magical, mechanical, and materialistic interpretation. This is natural enough, as in primitive religious ritual they are always interpreted in this way.

All the Christian Sacraments are capable of a spiritual, moral, and rational interpretation, and great care should be taken to guard against their being given any other interpretation.

(2) The authorities of the Christian Church have from apostolic times made the acceptance of certain Sacraments compulsory for full membership. As a consequence, the Eucharist has been used as a powerful instrument of Church discipline. Although Sacraments are of great use to many Christian worshippers, they ought not to be made compulsory for all. Some natures, be they rationalist or mystical,

are repelled, or at least, not attracted by Sacraments, and to make Sacraments compulsory increases the aversion of these natures and goes beyond the teaching of Jesus Christ.

New Testament criticism makes it extremely doubtful whether Jesus made Baptism, or the Eucharist, institutions of his Church. Though it may be held that the Eucharist originated with Jesus, we cannot feel sure that he intended to make it a permanent and essential institution for his Church. Had Jesus instituted Baptism and commanded it to his apostles, it is unlikely that St. Paul could have written to the Corinthians: "Christ sent me not to baptize, but to preach the Gospel" (1 Cor. i. 17).

Though what these Sacraments symbolize is essential to salvation, yet these Sacraments themselves are not essential. Hence, the Church ought not to make these Sacraments compulsory for Church membership.

The Church of the future must include in its fellowship the sacramentally minded and non-sacramentally minded Christians.

THE HOLY COMMUNION SERVICE

In many respects our Order for the Administration of the Holy Communion is the least in need of revision of any of our services, and that perhaps mainly because very few of those who attend it desire it to be revised, and even those who, on theological grounds, desire its revision, recognize the extreme difficulty of such a task and the grave disadvantages which may attend its accomplishment. If the present service were to be revised Modern Churchmen would welcome the following changes:

(*a*) The substitution of the original form of the Decalogue for the later and expanded form (see the

Warburtonian Lectures of Dr. R. H. Charles). This substitution would eliminate such statements as that God is a jealous God, and that he made the world in six days, and that we should honour our parents in order that we may live to a good old age.

(*b*) The permission at any time to substitute the two Great Commandments for the Decalogue.

(*c*) The permission to substitute the eight Beatitudes from St. Matthew's Sermon on the Mount.

(*d*) The excision from the General Confession of the more excessive expressions of penitential grief, *e.g.* "provoking most justly thy wrath and indignation against us", "the burden of them is intolerable". The confession from the literary point of view would lose nothing by these omissions and our sense of scrupulous veracity would gain much.

(*e*) The omission of the last two Comfortable Words and the insertion between the first and second Comfortable Words from John vi. 37, "Him that cometh unto me I will in no wise cast out".

(*f*) The omission of all Proper Prefaces.

(*g*) The omission of the opening paragraph of the Prayer of Consecration, which is fraught with great difficulties—doctrinal and critical—for the modern student of the Gospels. The prayer might begin thus: "Almighty God, our heavenly Father, grant that we receiving these thy creatures of bread and wine in remembrance of the death and passion of thy Son, Jesus Christ our Lord, may be made partakers of his most precious Body and Blood. . . ."

(*h*) The alteration of the rubric so as to permit the second Post-Communion Thanksgiving to be said in addition to the first. These thanksgivings are complementary, not alternative.

(*i*) The substitution of the ancient form of the Oecumenical Creed for the present so-called "Nicene Creed". This would mean (1) that the creed would begin "we believe" and continue throughout in the first person plural; (2) that the virgin birth clause (which was not in the original creed of Nicaea) would be excised; (3) that the Filioque clause ("the Son"), which was only added in the sixth century and has needlessly affronted the Eastern Church, would disappear.

We think that modern-minded churchmen would be entirely satisfied with this revision as it would stress, more than does the Prayer Book form of our Oecumenical Creed, that the communicants as a body are affirming the faith of the Church in its historic form.

Were it granted we cannot see why members of the Anglo-Catholic and Evangelical parties should feel any real sense of loss. But here we should not wish them to be deprived of the authorized form provided they were willing to grant congregations who desired it permission to use the revised form.

AN ALTERNATIVE SIMPLE OFFICE FOR THE HOLY COMMUNION

There is, as those know who have travelled through the British Empire and have lived in its backwoods as well as in its industrial centres, a real need for a very simple modern service of Holy Communion. This need is in some measure recognized in our Prayer Book by its service for the Communion of the Sick: but our Prayer Book also needs a service for the Communion of the Simple.

Such a service would commemorate the Captain of our Salvation and what his Passion has meant and should mean for mankind. This would be a service primarily of Commemoration on the one hand and of Self-consecration on the other. It would omit all references to disputable and difficult theological dogmas. This would not prohibit those who took part in it from believing in the expiatory sacrifice of

Christ nor on the other hand would it compel them to do so. What is a "very comfortable" doctrine for some men is a most uncomfortable and incredible and impossible and unchristian doctrine for other men, and these other men are as much entitled to the ministrations of the Church in this modern world as are the former class, who are a diminishing company.

The English Church authorities must recognize this need and this right if they are to draw into closer union those who are "god-fearers" but who remain all their lives on the fringe of the Church or outside it, and never enter into the warmth and light and fellowship of the Upper Room. They are not to be judged by our modern Pharisees for the things which they cannot believe; still less are they to be practically excommunicated for this supposed defect in their faith. It is the duty of the English Church authorities to provide a Communion Office in which these people can whole-heartedly share, if they will. They probably possess as much in the way of doctrinal dogmatic equipment as did many of the primitive apostles.

Holy Baptism

It is most important that Holy Baptism, which was *the* great Sacrament of the Church of the first four centuries, should be, as far as possible, a public service. Yet, in the Church of England it has largely become a private service, and this is mainly due to the character of our present office for public Baptism. It is much too long and it reflects convictions and beliefs which are not those of most educated church-people to-day.

(*a*) The 1662 service asks at the outset whether the infant has been baptized. This question, if necessary, should be put privately before the service.

(*b*) The service then proceeds to state that all men

are "conceived and born in sin". There is no doubt that this was the conviction of St. Augustine of Hippo, but it is not the conviction of Christian people to-day. Moreover, the statement itself casts a needless aspersion upon Holy Wedlock and the married life of Christian people.

(*c*) The service teaches that the infant's sins are mystically washed away by the baptismal water.

(*d*) It also teaches that by Baptism the infant is delivered from God's wrath.

(*e*) It also requires the sponsors to affirm specifically their faith in a number of statements in the Baptismal Creed which they do not really believe.

(*f*) It also, by its references to Noah's ark and the Israelite passage of the Red Sea, increases the sense of remoteness from reality.

Not one of these things to which exception has been taken is really an essential of the Sacrament of infant Baptism. No one is required by the Christian Faith to believe in the guilt of original sin being inherited by infants, nor to believe that this guilt is actually washed away by the baptismal water. It is indeed open to question whether the baptismal water should be interpreted in this way.

St. Peter, in his First Epistle, asserts that Baptism is not absterging—the washing away of the filth of the flesh—but the response of a good conscience unto God (1 Peter iii. 21).

The washing or ablutionary symbolism of Baptism is pre-Christian and indeed sub-Christian. Pagan baptizings and Jewish baptizings and possibly the baptism practised by John the Baptist were of this character. They washed away uncleanness: in primitive times, the uncleanness of taboos; in a later period, the uncleanness of moral defilement.

This primitive magical or mechanical view of Baptism was protested against by the more enlightened pagans themselves, ranging from Euripides to Ovid. The Roman poet, himself no moral paragon, protested that too easily his superstitious and criminal contemporaries believed that the guilt of foul crimes was removed by ceremonial washings:

> Ah! nimium faciles, qui tristia crimina caedis
> Fluminea tolli posse putatis aqua![1]

The conviction of the Greek dramatist is expressed in the Pythian Response addressed to pilgrims to Delphi approaching the Castalian Spring:

> To the pure precincts of Apollo's portal
> Come, pure in heart, and touch the lustral wave;
> One drop sufficeth for the guiltless mortal;
> All else, e'en Ocean's billows cannot lave.

In the New Testament the baptismal water is variously interpreted. St. Paul interpreted the water into which the baptized had been plunged or submerged as symbolical of a burial with Christ which terminated his old pre-Christian life; and his emergence from the baptismal water as symbolizing his resurrection with Christ to newness of life (Romans vi. 4; cf. Col. ii. 12).

The writer of the Fourth Gospel is at considerable pains to distinguish essentially Christian Baptism from Jewish baptizings and even from the baptism practised by John the Baptist. These were baptizings with water; but the essentially Christian Baptism is baptizing with the Spirit. It has even been maintained that the passage in Christ's dialogue with Nicodemus has had the phrase "and of water" (John iii. 5) inserted into it in order to bring it into harmony with contemporary Christian practice and belief; and that what our Lord said in the uninterpolated text was: "Except a man be born of the Spirit he cannot enter into the Kingdom of God! That which is born of the flesh is flesh and that which

---

[1] Ovid, *Fasti*, Book II. 45.

is born of the Spirit is Spirit. Marvel not that I said unto you: ye must be born from above" (John iii. 6). The whole discourse of Jesus with Nicodemus is concerned with the New Birth: Birth from above, Birth by the agency of the Spirit. Other passages in the Fourth Gospel indicate that water for this writer is the symbol of the Spirit. "He that believeth on me, as the Scripture hath saith, out of his belly shall flow rivers of living water. (But this spake he of the Spirit, which they that believe on him should receive . . .)" (John vii. 38).

There is little doubt that the water which flowed from Christ's side, when pierced with the spear (John xix. 34), symbolized for this writer the gift of the Spirit. But religion is the most conservative of all institutions, and these more profound and inspiring ideals of the symbolism of Baptism seem quite quickly, notwithstanding their apostolic authority, to have succumbed to the earlier magical, and mechanical, conception of baptismal symbolism. It was so much easier to understand, and so much more comfortable to believe, that sins were washed away by this ceremonial, than to realize what was meant by the ideals of the New Birth from above, the New Life in the Spirit. There is therefore no need that the water used at the Baptism of infants should be interpreted as the instrument of ablution, especially since in the modern mind, the infant is sinless, and so has no sins to be washed away.

It is equally needless to insist that Baptism delivers the infant from the wrath of God. Such teaching is not only needless, because no modern person really believes that unbaptized infants are the objects of God's wrath, but it is utterly repulsive, because it presents the Divine Father, the God of Love, as if he were some barbarously savage deity who has to be propitiated by magical rites from venting his wrath upon human beings.

The part played by the sponsors in the service lacks effectiveness. This is partly due to the sponsors being required to affirm in the name of the infant (a very artificial proceeding), that it believes more than they believe themselves.

It is of course necessary that the baptizing minister should have evidence that those who bring the child to be baptized, and are responsible for its nurture and education, are Christians. But if verbal professions are to be taken as sufficient evidence of this, it would be better that a general affirmation of Christian faith, which they can honestly make, should be demanded from the sponsors.

Another weakness in the part played by the sponsors is, that the promises made by them do not explicitly bind them to do that for the child which is of the first importance. The sponsors do not promise explicitly to bring the child up as a Christian. It is true that they are charged in the service to bring the child up as a Christian but the Church, through its minister, has received no explicit promise that this will be done. Yet if Christian Baptism is to be a reality for the infant, it must be followed by Christian education. This promise, that Christian education shall be given to the infant, ought to be most explicitly made, before the rite of Baptism is administered.

As for the archaisms of our present authorized service, they can very easily be excised, as they were in the revised baptismal service of the Deposited Book.

The word *regeneration*, although essentially sound, as a statement of what Baptism does, is too technical a term to be used in what ought to be a popular and very simple service.

We may well admire the way in which, in the Second Prayer Book of King Edward VI, our English baptismal service received a second purgation when Exorcism, the Chrism, and the Chrysom were removed from the baptismal service of the First Book of King Edward VI.[1]

But our baptismal service needs a third purgation, which will not only deprive it of nothing essential, but will liberate the Christian truth in it from pre-Christian and sub-Christian imperfections.

What the baptismal service needs to do primarily is to stress the fact that the infant brought to be baptized is not simply the child of its parents to do what they like with, but the child of God, who has entrusted them with the responsible care of the infant, which they must bring up as his child.

Baptism does not make the child a child of God, for he is a child of God already, as the result of the possession of human nature, made in "the image of God". It is the possession of his rational, moral, and spiritual consciousness which constitutes him God's child. Baptism should affirm this divine sonship impressively, clearly indicating the responsibility which it involves for the child's guardians. Secondly, Baptism should stress the doctrine of the New Birth and its privilege. The child's first birth is into a human family with its human relationships, affections, and duties. The child's second birth is into the Family of God on earth—the Divine Society—the Church, which Christ founded, and for which he died on the Cross. Membership in this society grants to the child greater privileges, nobler and wider affections, more exalted duties than membership in his earthly human home.

This new status is symbolized by the minister holding the child in his arms and saying as he signs him with the cross:

---

[1] The first Prayer Book of King Edward VI exorcised the infant to be baptized by bidding the evil spirit to come out of him. The infant was anointed with oil (the Chrism) symbolizing the gift of the Holy Spirit. He was clad in a white robe (the Chrysom) symbolizing the innocency with which by Baptism he was endowed.

We receive this child into the congregation of Christ's flock, and do sign him with the sign of the Cross, in token that hereafter he shall not be ashamed of Christ crucified, but manfully to fight under his banner against sin, the world and the Devil, and to continue Christ's faithful soldier and servant unto his life's end.

The gift of the Holy Spirit vouchsafed in Baptism is neither magical nor mechanical. It is not transmitted by manual acts nor by material elements nor by uttered formularies. The Holy Spirit, given in and through Baptism, is the necessary, concurrent, and cumulative possession of a human being progressively realizing in his consciousness, conduct, and character the supreme truth which Baptism affirms, and the reality of those relations into which he enters, whose life develops in accordance with those convictions and relationships. Thus understood and practised, Baptism becomes the initiation of the child into the higher and the wider life of sonship to God, and fellowship with man in a Divine Society.

Such a revised service of infant Baptism would demand some alteration in the doctrine of Baptism as set forth in that admirable document our Church Catechism.

Baptism of Adults

The service for adult Baptism would only differ from that of infant Baptism in that the baptismal promises are made by the individual baptized and no sponsors are required to be responsible for him.

The service for adult Baptism may rightly stress and develop more fully than can be appropriately done in the service of infant Baptism the distinction in the principles and practice between the old life and the new.

Confirmation

Our authorized service of confirmation is not in need of revision and can be and is most helpfully supplemented by addresses, hymns, and additional prayers.

Any revision of the Confirmation Service, and there is a danger of such, which implies that the gift of the Holy Spirit is actually transmitted by the imposition of the episcopal hand, which is certainly not taught in our present service, would be retrogressive.

And here it ought to be stressed that there is serious need for a service for the admission into the membership of the Church of England of those who have been members of other Christian denominations. The use of our present Confirmation Service in such cases is incongruous. Our Confirmation Service is plainly intended for young persons who have been baptized with the English rite, and is not suitable to the circumstance of those who have lived for years as Christian communicants and even ministers of other denominations.

The Marriage Service

Our Marriage Service is one of great moral and spiritual value, but it does stand very definitely in need of modernization. The reference to the dreadful day of judgement at the beginning of the service; to Adam and Eve and the Divine institution of marriage in the time of man's innocency; to the example of the Hebrew patriarchs and their wives, are all better omitted.

The strong demand that the vows of husband to wife and wife to husband should be identical has much to commend it. Even if it be urged that it is the duty of a wife to obey, yet it ought to be conceded that her obedience should be entirely voluntary and not as the outcome of a compulsory vow taken at marriage. The modern doctrine of the equality of the sexes has created a prejudice against the wife taking any such vow. The reference to the endowment of the wife with all the worldly goods of her husband, even although the word "endow" be interpreted as "entrust", is in most cases palpably fictitious.

Again, the phrase "with my body I thee worship", though the word "worship" here plainly means "honour", is perhaps better omitted as being generally misunderstood. Vows taken on such an occasion, as they are binding for life, cannot be too plain and too literal. Even when the services were in Latin, the marriage vows were made in the vulgar tongue.

The statement of the triple purpose of marriage contained in the opening address would lose nothing by a modern substitute which at any rate omitted "a remedy against sin" as one of the purposes of marriage.

It is generally recognized that the concluding address, which consists almost entirely of a catena of Scriptural passages, is best omitted, and some very brief and simple exhortation substituted for it, which stresses the value of the institution of marriage— personally and socially—and the lifelong obligation of the marriage vow.

In view of our modern knowledge of eugenic principles, the marriage service should contain some specific reference to conditions which ought to determine the size and welfare of the family. This advice could be given either in a rubric or in some general statement in the service itself.

The Visitation of the Sick

The service of the Visitation of the Sick is so much in need of simplification and modernization that it has very largely ceased to be used in the pastoral care of the sick.

Probably modern pastoral needs would be sufficiently met by a succinct body of rubrics giving directions and advice for such occasions.

A commonly expressed view that the sick-room of some poor person in very humble circumstances is not suitable for the celebration of the Holy Communion is one which the writer's experience contradicts decisively. It has seemed to him to be the essentially right service if the moral and spiritual conditions are there: the temporal conditions, by contrast, enhance the awe and solemnity of the service and its essentially spiritual quality.

THE CHURCHING OF WOMEN

The Churching of Women is a service which stands in very serious need of revision. At present it is a thanksgiving by a mother for deliverance from the great peril and pain of childbirth. But this is not all. Behind it lie feelings or rather superstitions created by pagan taboos. Country clergymen know from their experience that it has no specifically Christian significance for not a few of those taking part in it. It is used for reasons of traditional respectability, even by those who are not at all respectable. Although the Baptism of the infant may be deferred, the churching of the mother in some localities may not be deferred without the greatest personal inconvenience, because she may not go out until she has been churched.

A mother will come to Church to be churched who will come on no other occasion, except it be for the Baptism of the infant. When the child has been "done" she has, as far as she is concerned, no further use for the Church's services.

Whilst containing a thanksgiving for the mother's safe deliverance, the service of Churching ought to contain a thanksgiving for the birth of the child, and stress ought to be laid on the responsibility which the gift of the child involves. The service should also contain prayers for the Divine Blessing not only on mother and child but also on the home. The service ought to provide for the attendance of the father of the child and other members of the family. In conservative parishes, among the less educated classes, there is very little prospect that such provision will be taken advantage of, but in suburban localities, and among the educated classes, there might be many who would be very glad of this domestic service in Church—the bringing of the family into the House of God.

SERVICE FOR THE BURIAL OF THE DEAD

Owing to its circumstances, there is no service which is more solemn than the service for the Burial of the Dead. Its fine literary quality impresses many who listen to it, but find themselves quite at a loss to believe what it affirms.

In it the Christian belief in human immortality and in the Fatherly Providence of God is blended with a number of outworn beliefs, derived from Jewish eschatology. Of these beliefs the most difficult of acceptance is the resurrection of the body.

Plain people understand the Burial Service to affirm that the dead will be raised from their graves at the Last Day, when the "trumpet shall sound and the dead shall be raised incorruptible".

There is no doubt that this particular belief has been the possession of the Christian Church from primitive times, but to-day it is not held either by plain people or by Christian theologians. The general belief is, that the soul at death passes into the spiritual world, and never again has anything to do with its fleshly integument, which has been deposited in the grave.

For the traditional belief in the Great Assize at the end of the world (derived originally from Zoroastrianism), when all humanity shall appear for judgement before the Great White Throne, a conviction has grown up that Divine judgement takes place immediately on the death of the individual, and that that judgement determines his state in the next stage of his existence. The judgement is not a legal sentence but is the result of the individual's character, which determines his woe or bliss in his new environment. The man himself becomes his own heaven or hell. Hence, heaven and hell are thought of not as localities but as personal states, and there is every degree of purgatory between them. The soul of the departed is not thought of as discarnate, or bodiless, but as being clad in a spiritual body—the house which is from heaven, of which St. Paul writes (2 Cor. v. 1 f.).

Conversation with modern educated Christian people indicates that their beliefs about death and the inscrutable future assume this form; but in their minds, above all that is mysterious and much that is sad, there is a strong faith in the love and wisdom of God; and that he, notwithstanding all appearances to the contrary, does all things well, and that the innumerable dead, our own dear ones and the dear ones of others, are in his wise and gracious keeping.

Now, convictions of this kind are of the greatest value in the creation and maintenance of our moral and spiritual ideals, and it is immensely important that our Burial Service, or other services of commemoration of the dead, should present them clearly and cogently. The older views, which conflict with them, ought to be purged out of our Burial Service, and these modern Christian convictions given sole and supreme place.

THE COMMINATION SERVICE

The Commination Service, which is seldom used as it stands in our Prayer Book, ought to be replaced by an Evening Ash Wednesday service, setting forth the need for self-examination and self-discipline. But the service, besides stressing these things, ought also to stress the need for social, national, and international betterment.

It is important that to the consciousness of personal sinfulness should be united the sense of corporate guilt, and the need for serious, judicious, and effective reforms. Such a service could of course be used on many other occasions.

THE ORDINAL

Our Ordinal is in very little need of revision save where it implies beliefs which are not really held by those taking part in the service. This refers particularly to the question put to deacons about the Holy Scriptures: Do you unfeignedly believe all the Canonical Scriptures of the Old and New Testament?

To this question, the ordinand is required to reply, "I do believe them".

Yet there is no bishop in the English Church who does not know that there is not one in a hundred of our ordinands who does believe them. It is impossible, as the result of our modern Biblical studies, for any intelligent educated clergyman to make this affirmation literally, and it suggests a certain moral callousness on the part of our ecclesiastical authorities, that this declaration should still be required from our ordinands. The subject has been debated for years, and various amendments of the question, or substitutes for it, have been suggested. Perhaps the solution least open to objection is that the question about the Scriptures put to priests should be substituted for the present question put to deacons. The question and answer run as follows:

Are you persuaded that the Holy Scriptures contain sufficiently all Doctrine required of necessity for eternal salvation through faith in Jesus Christ? and are you determined out of the said Scriptures to instruct the people committed to your charge, and to teach nothing, as required of necessity to eternal salvation, but that which you shall be persuaded may be concluded and proved by the Scripture?

Answer. I am so persuaded, and have so determined by God's grace.

The Ordinal would gain in strength and value if the doctrine of the Spirit-bearing Church were more definitely expressed in it. If the truth were emphasized that the ministries of the Christian Church are essentially the ministries of the Spirit, and that the supreme authority in the Christian Church is not custom, creed, or Scripture but the authority of the Spirit of freedom, truth, and love, ever present to inspire, strengthen, and guide all in proportion as they yield themselves to him.

When we contemplate the great advantages to be derived from a judicious and enlightened revision of the Prayer Book we are perhaps amazed that such a revision has not been accomplished long ago in a Spirit-guided Church.

The story of Prayer Book revision in the twentieth century is depressing reading. If it does nothing worse it at least points to a dire lack of statesmanship in our ecclesiastical leaders.

The Earl of Clarendon, over two centuries ago, complained that of all classes of educated men the clergy were the worst judges of affairs, by which he meant they were lacking in the gift of practical statesmanship; and the historian of the Great Rebellion had no little experience, as his own record proves he was himself no mean judge of affairs.

The demand for Prayer Book revision in the twentieth century sprang out of the Report of the Royal Commission on Church Discipline. Compared with Tudor revisions of the Liturgy, our twentieth-century revisers were extraordinarily dilatory. The late Archbishop Davidson, however, had enunciated the comfortable *dictum*: the longer it takes the better it will be.

It proved possible, however, to take too long. For the longer the revision took, the larger became the demands of those who desired that the revision should take on a reactionary form. The crisis was reached when the bishops conceded to them their demand that the revised Prayer Book should provide for the Reservation of the consecrated elements at the Holy Communion. It was felt to be certain that this must lead to the practice of the adoration of the reserved elements in the Church of England as in the Church of Rome. This would mean that, in the name of revision, the Church authorities were going back behind the Reformation, and were yielding to a skilfully organized campaign to "undo the work of the Reformation".

Large numbers of Church people, many of whom had become disgruntled with the Romanizing practices illegally introduced into their parish churches, influenced the House of Commons to reject, on two successive occasions, the revised Prayer Book which contained this provision.

In 1933 Dr. Dearmer, an English churchman of great liturgical learning and strongly catholic in his sympathies, looking back on what happened, wrote thus of the episode:

> In 1927, after many years of discussion, a new revised Prayer Book, called "The Deposited Book", was approved by the National Church Assembly by 517 votes to 133. The Measure was passed by the House of Lords, but rejected by a small majority in the House of Commons. The Book was then slightly amended and embodied in a new Measure; the vote in the Church Assembly now sank to 396 in favour of the Book, and it was defeated in the House of Commons by an increased majority of 266 to 220. It therefore did not receive the

assent of the Crown, nor was it submitted to the Convocations for final ratification. It has thus no authority, and cannot be regarded as a new English Prayer Book; but most bishops have stated that they will not proceed against any incumbent who, with the approval of his Church Council, confines his deviations from the Prayer Book of 1662 to those allowed in the Deposited Book of 1928. Thus in practice the Deposited Book allows a good deal of elasticity under the Ordinary, which is necessary and indeed inevitable; and much experience is accumulating which will be valuable in a future revision. It is very generally felt that, together with a great deal of admirable new material, there is a certain amount that needs alteration, and few perhaps now would wish to see a new Prayer Book for the coming generation laid down in exactly the form of the Deposited Book.

What seemed at first to many a blow to the Church of England, and to the Establishment that has brought so much good both to Church and State, may well prove to have been a blessing in disguise. It was of enormous significance that the Houses of Parliament should have devoted so many days to the discussion of public worship, and "with such sincerity that cavilling was silenced". Continental observers were astonished, and it was well said among them, "We envy you your controversies". The people of England care about their Church and are profoundly interested in its ways of worship. Indeed it may be said that the failure of the book was really due to the Bishops having sometimes forgotten the Nation in their preoccupation with small groups of partisans in the Church.

A Member of Parliament who took a leading part in supporting the Measure said the last word upon the subject: "The House of Commons will pass anything that the whole Church wants; but it will pass nothing about which the Church itself is divided". The statesmanship indeed of the leaders of the Church at that time was in fault; agreement should have been obtained; and matters against which there were substantial minorities in the Assembly (and much larger opposition in the country) should have been dropped.

It is now generally acknowledged that, desirable

as Prayer Book revision is, it would have been a mistake, for which all parties in the Church would have been very sorry to-day, if the House of Commons had passed the Deposited Book.

The twentieth-century revision was not, judged either by liturgical standards or by literary standards, up to the level of previous revisions. A great deal of good material had been brought together, but the actual work of revision was a poor production. Obviously the wrong men were employed to do it. As a result, we had our greatest liturgical authority, Dr. Brightman, subjecting the revision to drastic criticism; and Professor Saintsbury, as eminent in literature as Brightman in liturgiology, publicly deploring its poor literary quality.

It is said that Dr. Bridges, the Poet Laureate, whose services might have been secured to the immense betterment of the undertaking, was not invited to help. The Church authorities, who were at the time deeply incensed with the action of the House of Commons, dropped the task of Prayer Book revision, and have done nothing in that direction since.

It is to be hoped, however, now that it is becoming generally recognized that the House of Commons was right in its judgement, that the bishops will take up the task of revision again, but will, as the result of painful experience, alter fundamentally the method of procedure which helped to wreck the former effort.

It may be hard for the Church Assembly to forgive the House of Commons for knowing better about Church affairs than did the Assembly itself. Nevertheless it is a Christian duty to forgive, and we hope that this forgiveness will be achieved as soon as possible, and the work of Prayer Book revision resumed with a good grace.

As modern-minded churchmen we do hope that the new revision will be inspired by enlightened and comprehensive principles—the principles of Jesus.

A revision which is not the outcome of these principles can serve no useful purpose at all. Sincerity, simplicity, and spirituality should be the marks of the new revision.

It is sometimes forgotten that the creators of our Prayer Book at immense risk to themselves, and with a moral courage that it is hard to estimate in these days, refused unflinchingly not only to authorize anything in their revised liturgy which was untrue but even anything which was doubtful. They thus commended their effort to the Church of their day: "Here are left out many things whereof some are untrue, some uncertain, some vain and superstitious".[1]

We hope that our new revisers will adopt this principle. Doubtful doctrines, doubtful historic facts, are far better omitted from our public liturgy. It is folly to obtrude them to-day when our prevalent scientific education is making us increasingly sensitive to the claims of truth.

Bishop Lightfoot asserted that in the sphere of religious faith, provided only a few things were right and tight, it would suffice.

"The plague of the Church for above a thousand years", wrote the saint of English Puritanism, Richard Baxter, "has been the enlarging our creed and making more fundamentals than God ever made".

To those who would plead that in view of our unhappy party differences in the Church we had better postpone Prayer Book revision, we would cite the saying of an Anglican saint, Francis Paget: "To do nothing when you ought to be doing something is the height of rashness".

---

[1] Concerning the Service in the Church in the First Prayer Book of King Edward VI.

III

PUBLIC WORSHIP AND THE CREEDS

by

PERCY DEARMER, D.D.

Canon of Westminster
Professor and Fellow, King's College, University of London

SYNOPSIS

Our Debt to the Creeds

THE Creeds saved the Church during the Dark Ages from being submerged by heresies, repulsive eccentricities, and the still surviving tendency to polytheism. Amid the mythologies of the Middle Ages the insistence in the Creeds on fundamental simplicities saved Christianity from becoming a welter of superstitions. It is possible that a small company of scholars might produce a good modern creed, but we cannot be sure that it would not be out of date at a not distant future, and it would not carry the authority of the ancient creeds. Even so recent a statement of orthodox non-Roman faith as the Lambeth Quadrilateral of 1886 is passing out of date. Other comparatively modern attempts at credal formulation are now entirely unacceptable. A new oecumenical creed would not be as good as the old.

The Fundamental Change

The Creeds belong to a different world from ours, and stand within an obsolete framework of philosophical, historical, and scientific presuppositions. Neither Creed can be accepted in the sense it was intended to bear. This makes the Creeds unsuitable for Public Worship.

Common Difficulties

To the enquiring layman the Creeds bristle with difficulties. Some can be met by explanation and some by retranslation. But an honest retranslation would involve an assertion of belief in the resurrection of the flesh, a belief which has been widely abandoned during our lifetime, though it was generally held until quite recent years. The enquirer must not only realize that "Hell" is not the Hell of conversational usage, but must also forget whatever he may happen to know about limbo and the harrowing of hell. Then he must be informed that the Ascent and Session on God's Right Hand are not to be taken in a spatial sense, nor is the Parousia to be taken in the temporal sense which it certainly had for the framers of the Creed and, until recent times, for those who used it. It would be impossible to provide an agreed translation of *communio sanctorum*. There are other reinterpretations, explanations, and retranslations which are necessary.

When we come to the Nicene Creed (and still more does this apply to the Athanasian Creed), the specialized technical phraseology used renders it unsuitable for recitation in church. In fact, to those who are not scholars its language seems to assert tritheism. The underlying assertion in the Creeds of the Divine Unity is easily missed. The tritheistic heresy has been and is widely prevalent. Apart from the Athanasian Creed, little has been done to counteract it. It is further suggested to the non-theological worshipper by the continual use in the services of the *Gloria Patri* and the illegal but common practice of using the "ascription" before the Sermon.

The Difficulty with Non-Christians

The difficulties which the use of the Creeds presents to missionaries who are working among people who have not our background and take the Creeds at the hard face value of their words is very grave. Especially is this so in Muslim countries. Too much explanation is required. It is not enough to say that the Creeds take the unity of God for granted. The Creeds were drawn up to meet a different position from that of our own day.

Even at home there is an increasing multitude of people who think that Christians are tied to the face value of the Creeds which, when they go to church, they hear recited with ceremonial emphasis. It would be well if the apologist at home could point to an official statement in modern terms.

The Distortion of Values

The Creeds have been and are of great value; but their proper position as theological statements has been upset by their inclusion in the services of the Church. With the decline of belief in the inerrancy of the Bible, they have usurped the throne of Scripture and been invested with infallibility. Their constant repetition has produced an exaggerated impression of their authority. A fourth-century complex has been engendered. The Church should be content with Christianity, and men should be able to belong to it on Christ's own terms. Credal fixity was an accident caused by the breaking up of civilization after the fifth century. As Dr. Adrian Fortescue has pointed out, it is "a very naïve mistake to think that all Christendom ever agreed in recognizing one, or two, or three creeds as final, authoritative, and quasi-inspired documents".

THE THREE USES OF CREEDS

I. AT BAPTISM

From the beginning creeds, as affirmations of faith, have had a natural place in Christian baptism. The distinction between religious faith and assent to a theological declaration is important. Originally only an act of faith in Jesus Christ was required at Baptism, and baptism was in the name of Jesus. In the course of the second century it became the rule to baptize in the name of the Trinity. We have no actual baptismal creed earlier than the third century. The Apostles' Creed is a typical fourth-century document. The creeds of the second and third century were much shorter. The expansion was due to the need of combatting the errors of Gnosticism and Montanism. A late second-century creed is found in the *Epistola Apostolorum* and a third-century creed in the *Egyptian Church Order*. The legend ascribing the composition of the Apostles' Creed to the twelve apostles helped in the fourth century to preserve it from further change.

The ideal baptismal creed is the Scriptural one: "I believe in Jesus Christ". In the Baptismal Service this might be printed first, followed by the words "Then may the minister say", and the Apostles' Creed.

II. AS TESTS

The second stage of credal development is marked by the use of creeds as tests of orthodox belief. An example of a creed used for this purpose is the Creed of the Council of Nicaea.

(1) From this point of view the creeds should be printed in the Prayer Book as venerable and valuable documents. The Creed of Nicaea, the Creed called Nicene, the Creed

called the Apostles', and the Canticle commonly called the Athanasian Creed might be printed in a section by themselves with a note as to their date. In the Catechism the Short Creed with the Apostles' Creed might be included, with a new Explanation. It would be undesirable to include in the Catechism an ethical creed. The Two Duties provide all that is needed.

(2) The Churches all desire to maintain "The Faith behind the Creeds" and a historic creed is therefore useful in working out the means of Reunion. Though the Creeds can no longer be accepted at their face value and have therefore lost their use as real tests of orthodoxy, they remain valuable as pointers to the common belief. No test which excludes true disciples of Christ is satisfactory. In spite of the value of the Creeds, in various ways they act as a hindrance to the spread of Christianity at home and abroad, and their continual use in public worship creates the impression that the Church is static.

III. IN PUBLIC WORSHIP

The third stage was reached when, as a liturgical afterthought, the Creeds came to be used as protests against heresy, made in Public Worship. This development began locally about the year 500, and did not become general till about 1000 and then only in an incomplete manner. It was not till 1552 that, in the Second English Prayer Book, the Nicene Creed became an invariable part of our Communion Service. The Apostles' Creed has a similar halting liturgical history. Never used in the East, it was in the West introduced into the monastic service of Rome in the ninth century. In the First English Prayer Book it was appointed to be said by the priest alone, and in the 1552 Prayer Book it was appointed to be said by the people. The Athanasian Creed, which was the only profession of faith in the Sarum Breviary to be said aloud, was substituted on certain days. A further innovation was the nineteenth-century custom of emphasizing the recitation of the creeds by turning to the east, an unauthorized and inappropriate custom. The recitation of creeds in Public Worship is an act not of worship but of policy.

FAITH AND BELIEF

Belief is cognitive, faith is conative. Worship is the expression of faith, and to introduce into it a statement of belief is to lower its tone. Worship is directed not to the Christ of the christologists but to the Christ of the Gospels. The Lord's Prayer, being a looking forward, a surrender to God, is an act of faith and therefore appropriate to Public Worship. It has been said in defence of the liturgical use of creeds that it is like the waving of flags; but the waving of flags in Public Worship would be barbarously inappropriate.

New Creeds for Old

It has been suggested that alternative creeds less inappropriate to Public Worship might be substituted for the Apostles' Creed and Nicene Creed. But we should remember the tendency for any credal form to acquire an undesirable finality. In practice those of a conservative disposition would take less exception to omission than to substitution. It might be possible to get them to realize that omission is real conservatism, besides being a liturgical and psychological improvement.

Liturgical Use of Creeds To-day

The rubrics being as they are, the choir might sing the Apostles' Creed as an anthem, thus treating it as in some measure an act of worship. Though the Deposited Book did not touch the Apostles' Creed it moved in the right direction by allowing the shortening and omission of the Athanasian Creed and by allowing the omission of the Nicene Creed on days other than Sundays and Holy Days.

The Danger of being Static

Scientists are believed because they make no claim to finality. Theologians are suspect because of the fixity which is unjustly attributed to them. The result of reciting creeds in church is that they are regarded as *mantras*. They become static and lose their vitality. There are Church leaders who would prefer to see the religion of Christ dwindle into nothingness rather than abate one jot of the Nicene interpretation of his person. The justification of the long reluctance of the Church to use creeds in worship is the ever-present danger of burying the future in the past.

III

PUBLIC WORSHIP AND THE CREEDS

OUR DEBT TO THE CREEDS[1]

WITHOUT the Creeds the Church would probably not have got through the Dark Ages—men being what they are, and God's method of not overruling human freedom being what history shows it to be. Indeed, even with the iron safeguarding of what is called the Athanasian Creed popular religion (and much theological religion also) did manage to continue the ancient polytheism, and is still very largely a belief in three separate Gods, to which the generous fancy of the Mediterranean mind has added two or three others. But this only shows that forms of words fail after a time to do the work intended of them if they are not kept alive by reconsideration or revision. At the time the Creeds saved the Church from slipping permanently into one or other of the heresies. And the heresies really were wrong. In the maddeningly complicated and often unreal controversies of the age, when even the orthodox found it hard to keep the narrow path of metaphysical sanity (and even Athanasius became Apollinarian in opposing the mistaken theory of Arius), the gradual formulation of the two Creeds saved the Church from many repulsive eccentricities. Their restraint, their simplicity are wholly admirable; and they are rightly regarded with a gratitude amounting to tenderness by theologians.

[1] For convenience I am including the Athanasian Canticle when I speak of the Creeds in this paper, and the Apostles' and Nicene only when I speak of the two Creeds.

The Creeds deserve indeed our highest reverence, esteem, and gratitude. Their value is permanent. They are a magnificent testimony, clear, concise, and beautiful, to the wisdom of the Church in a period of extreme difficulty and confusion, when the civilization and the sanities of the ancient world were crumbling, when there was no science—and no Universe—when Greek philosophy was in its last decadence. Their insistence on fundamental simplicities brought the Church through the Barbarian invasions, when every country outside the Byzantine Empire was conquered and looted; they provided a core of essential Christianity amid the mythology of the Middle Ages, when the established system of persecution prevented men from saying what they thought. If we are impressed with the absurdities and idolatries that grew up in spite of the Creeds, we may take comfort in the reflection that those old formularies saved the Christian religion from becoming a mere welter of confused superstitions.

If the Church had been faithful to their spirit, and had observed their basic principle of requiring as little dogmatic speculation as possible, of recording essentials and sticking to history, the crimes and blunders of the past and the present failures might have been avoided. For indeed the existence of false forms of Christianity is undisputed, and the failure also to supply what the world needs to-day. People only differ as to which forms are false and to whom the failure is due.

Let those therefore who may read these lines differ as they may among themselves, they will all agree that the controversies which divide Christendom have been mainly about matters as to which the Creeds are silent, and that the doctrines which have alienated vast numbers from the religion of their fathers are not in the Creeds at all. The inerrancy of the Bible, for instance, the theories (some of them very repulsive) about the atonement, damnation, and eternal torment; all the diverse doctrines about orders and episcopacy and the character of the true Church; the endless and exacerbating disputes about the sacraments. We hardly need to remind the reader of the long-established growth in some Churches of the cultus of saints, images, and ikons, nor of transubstantiation, purgatory, penance, compulsory confession, indulgences, and the treasury of merits, nor of the Papacy itself, nor of the continued activity of the Vatican in adding a huge body of required beliefs to the Creeds, a collection so complex and so large that only specialists can keep it in mind, and ordinary folk substitute for it all, and for all the Creeds, the simple and touching article of belief, "I believe in the Pope".

All this is strong evidence of the wisdom of the Great Church in confining its requirements to the Nicene Creed. Some may think that we should make better creeds at the present day. Certainly we should not, if *all* Christendom could be miraculously assembled to make a new creed. A small company of scholars who happened to be in agreement could doubtless produce a very good creed; but it would carry no weight because it would have no authority. And would it hold good in fifty years' time? We are so sure that what is modern in 1935 will be modern and obviously true in 1985 that it is well to look back. We need not go as far as that prolific age of confessions, the seventeenth century, when the divines of the Westminster Assembly regarded it as obvious that some are destined by the mere pleasure of God to "unspeakable torments, both of body and soul, with the devil and his angels for ever", and that these include all non-Christians, "be they never so diligent to frame their lives according to the light of nature".[1]

---

[1] *The Larger Catechism, Westminster Assembly,* Edinburgh, 1865, ans. 89, 60.

Even the Lambeth Quadrilateral, which has been regarded from 1886 to the present day as establishing common ground for all the orthodox non-Roman Churches, is already passing out of date in its third article (as in others), since there are now few scholars left who could subscribe to the statement, "The two Sacraments ordained by Christ himself—Baptism and the Supper of the Lord—ministered with unfailing use of Christ's words of Institution and of the Elements ordained by him", without grave mental reservations.

The truth is that human ways of expressing spiritual or any other form of truth lose their validity with time and become a stumbling-block. It seemed obvious a hundred years ago to a very representative body of Protestants that certain things were true; and the Evangelical Alliance made a creed of nine articles in 1846, which declared "The utter depravity of human nature in consequence of the Fall" in its 4th article, and the "eternal punishment of the wicked" in its 8th. One could multiply instances indefinitely; but we may safely conclude that a new oecumenical creed would be not so good as the old, and that if Christendom had been content with the old Creeds the principal causes of superstition, persecution, schism, alienation, and unbelief would not have come into existence.

The Fundamental Change

But if the statements of the Vatican Council or the Westminster Assembly or the others are subject to the general law of human thinking and cease to have the validity which once they seemed for many minds to possess, can we hope that the ancient Creeds are miraculously immune? Has the changed world we live in made no difference in their orthology?

To ask the question is to answer it. The Creeds

stand within a framework of historical, scientific, and philosophical suppositions which are obsolete. The proof of their world-view was in an infallible volume, every part of the Old Testament providing evidence for a theology of the Incarnation, which rested upon the exact contemporary evidence of the younger son of Zebedee. Within the Ptolemaic universe their description of the Christian religion is coherent and complete. The universe is in three storeys, and the earth is its centre. Below the earth is hell, into which Christ descended: above is heaven, so concrete that it is sometimes called the firmament, into which he returned. God, who is up in heaven, made the world by his fiat, and he intervenes miraculously sometimes when it is necessary. The chief intervention was that which is summarized in the brief statement of the birth, death, and resurrection of his Son. From heaven the Son will return to hold a judgement of all who have died, together with those who are alive at the time.

Everyone therefore takes the Creeds in an anagogic sense and not literally. It is not a matter of one clause or another. Each Creed, whichever we take, is a consistent whole: and that whole belongs to a different world from ours, and can only be accepted to-day by not taking it in the sense that it was intended to bear.

The Creeds are therefore unsuited to Public Worship; for you cannot in an act of worship preface them with a statement that they do not mean what they seem to mean; and if you do not, either they will be recited with indifference to their meaning (which is what normally happens), or their meaning will be misunderstood (except by an occasional theologian), or it will be resented by thoughtful Christian people who will in increasing numbers abstain from coming to church altogether.

Candid minds and tender consciences! And do not

these exist among the thoughtful clergy as well as among the laity?

COMMON DIFFICULTIES

For the enquiring layman indeed the Creeds bristle with difficulties. At the very outset he has to note that the Apostles' Creed has nothing to do with the apostles, and does not in fact state their belief; that the Nicene Creed is not the creed of Nicaea; and that the Athanasian Creed is not by Athanasius, and is not indeed a creed at all, but a canticle, and a Latin one at that.

A little shaken, he may go on to say that at least he can accept the first part of the Apostles' Creed. The theologian, however, being a scrupulously honest man, has to point out that there is a difficulty in every vocable. The use of "I" instead of "we" can indeed be readily explained, and so can the difference between to "believe" and "believe in", though in fact it very seldom is explained to or understood by the average intelligent man. The expert has to go on to shew that *Deus* is not satisfactory as a rendering of *Theos*, and that the whole of religion turns on the question, What do we mean by the word "God"? In the word "Father" we have the true use of a creed; for it is a summary of the Gospel teaching; yet even that great word is inadequate, unless we add the whole content of the word "Mother" to it, and acknowledge that one word must be as near the Reality as the other. We have next to admit that "almighty" is a mistranslation altogether, and a heavy obstacle to the philosophically-minded enquirer—or even to the plain man who asks, "Why does an almighty God allow war"?—unless he knows that *omnipotens* is a clumsy Latin translation of *pantokrator*, and should be rendered into English as "all-ruling".

But can we really help him by retranslation? If we are to provide an accurate translation, we must be honest about it; and then we have to alter "resurrection of the body" into "resurrection of the flesh" (as it is correctly rendered in the service of Baptism): for the Latin reads *"carnis resurrectionem"*, and this in Greek is *"sarkos anastasin"*. There is no getting over the fact that the authors of these words meant what they said, and that nearly all Christians down to quite recent times have believed that at the Last Day people would climb out of their graves with new flesh on their bones, as is illustrated by many pictures painted for ecclesiastical authorities and by hymns such as "On the Resurrection morning", which was added to *Hymns Ancient and Modern* as late as 1889, and was described by Julian in 1891 as "the exquisite Easter hymn".[1] It is no question of a horrible crude meaning being forced on to what was originally a spiritual conception. The idea which has been given up only during our lifetime is that which the Apostles' Creed was meant to enforce as a condition of orthodoxy; and when we say that it means the survival of personal identity with capacity for expression in a spiritual body, we have indeed St. Paul on our side, but we are "restating" the Creed not less drastically—perhaps more so—than those to whom "Born of the Virgin Mary" means that Jesus was the son of a woman generally known as the Virgin Mary (as the most unsaintly Cyril of Alexandria is commonly called "Saint Cyril"); for those who thus interpret are at least using the phrase in a possible sense, though it is certainly not the sense which its original users intended.

But if we insist on the full value of the words being given to this clause, what right have we to allow new meanings to other clauses? "Descended into hell" does admit of some defence: we can explain it in its

---

[1] *Dictionary of Hymnology* (J. Murray), 1897 ed., p. 114.

most restricted sense by saying that originally it meant only that Jesus shared the common human experience after death, whatever that may be; and that "hell" only means the hidden existence of the intermediate state, so that *"descendit ad inferna"* really means "he passed into Hades". But our unfortunate layman then has to strip "hell" of all its modern associations, and of all its meaning in conversational use; he also has to forget whatever he may happen to know from literature and art about limbo and the harrowing of hell; and if he happens to remember that the Devil was often represented as parading in that mysterious place, and that it was once and for long the general belief that Christ found the Devil there and vanquished him, a murmur of protest may well emerge and he may ask, "Why retain an article which needs so much explanation and has been, and by a vast number still is, so entirely misunderstood? Would not the Creed be better without it? Whatever truth may now be inferred from it is already implied in the mention of the three days' interval between the death and resurrection. I could", he may conclude, "believe more securely in the Resurrection if it were not made to lie between two clauses which cannot be taken at their face value in plain English." The American Prayer Book indeed already allows its omission, and has thus taken an important step out of the old static philosophy.

For he will probably have remembered something while we were explaining that "Ascended into heaven" and "Sitteth on the right hand of God" are statements which no one takes literally as a spatial movement and position—even in Europe (in China a further difficulty occurs, because there the left hand is the post of honour, and missionaries have to resort to a kind of looking-glass explanation). He knows that in Europe and America no one who considers the matter is likely to be unaware that those who contend most strenuously for nearly all the other articles of the Creeds do yet accept these two clauses in a purely "symbolical" way—though that is not the right word, since a symbol is something concrete. For us indeed they are the expression in metaphorical language of a great truth, and they lead up in noble language to the culmination of the second section of the Creed. But there are few who now take those culminating words, spatial and temporal as they are, about Christ's coming from heaven to judge the living and the dead in the sense which they certainly had for those who framed them, and for those also who have recited them until recent times. They have to be explained—away. And that is painful for the candid mind and tender conscience of the conservative advocate.

In the last section we should have to agree that *Spiritum sanctum, sanctorum communionem*, and (unfortunately, as we have said) *carnis resurrectionem* all need retranslation or restatement. But we should point out the high value of the phrase "Holy Catholic Church" in preserving us from the error of those who think that their own Church is the whole Church; and of the words "the forgiveness of sins", in preserving us from the fear that besets those millions who are taught that some sins are "mortal" and that these are punished by endless torment unless they have been absolved by a priest. We might well dwell upon that, because the whole life of man is involved in it: we might shew that this article means that God forgives all sins, and that both in the Greek and the Latin the word for "forgive" means the absolute putting away of sin and the complete reinstatement of the sinner, so that the consequences of his sin are not reckoned against him. It is wholly admirable; but then it is Scriptural.

It is, however, impossible to provide an agreed

translation of *communio sanctorum*, because experts differ widely about the meaning of the words. If we could translate them "the fellowship of Christians", no doubt our enquiring layman would be pleased; but Greek and Latin have their linguistic defects, and the translation may be "communion in holy things", like the *communio sacramentorum* of Augustine. The reasons for thinking this to be the real meaning are very strong.[1] Some think that the words are but a synonym for the Church; but this is most unlikely: the more common idea is that they refer to intercourse between the living and the departed; but this has now little support: and the idea that the clause refers to the glorified Saints in heaven or to their cultus is not, I believe, held by responsible theologians of any school. It would be only by using the phrase in so vague a sense that it might mean almost any kind of union or communion that agreement could be reached; for even the broad idea of fellowship in a great tradition, inspiring as it is, would involve a complete restatement of the article.

Our intelligent laymen may retort, "But what is the use of reciting a belief at all your services which the learned disagree about, and which does not seem to mean what we were told at our Confirmation?"

After dealing with this we should have to conclude by pointing out that the last word, "everlasting", though so fine to end with, is another that needs re-translation. For it has a meaning quite different from "eternal", and is misleading as a rendering of *aeternum*, while *aeternum* itself does not express the meaning of *aiônios*, though it conveys the mind of the Fourth Gospel less inadequately than "everlasting".

At this point it would be wise to stop, since that is the end of the simpler part of the problem. If our

---

[1] See, *e.g.*, the whole chapter in F. J. Badcock, *The History of the Creeds* (S.P.C.K., 1930), pp. 213-41.

intelligent layman insists on going on to the subtle matters which are dealt with in the Nicene Creed, we shall find it difficult to prevent him feeling still more strongly that no creeds are suitable for recitation by people who for the most part do not even know the meaning of "quick" in the simpler creed, still less of the august phrases with which the Nicene guards the mystery of the Holy Trinity.

And as for the Athanasian Creed, invaluable as it is to the trained student,[1] who has some acquaintance with its highly specialized phraseology, laymen, who cannot be expected to know the technical meaning of words like "incomprehensible", and who dislike the whole document because some of its statements are plainly unethical (a fact which the clergy still sometimes condone), may be pardoned for saying that it is entirely unsuited for use in church, and ought never to be used in any service whatever. To that most of us would agree, now that Dr. Pusey's great campaign is forgotten; though we should add with a sigh that, if it had been understood, or had been written in a shorter and more intelligible form, it might have saved the Church from that tritheism which has in practice been the dominant creed.

For we must frankly admit that, though the two Creeds were formed in order to safeguard the unity of God, they appear on the face of it to be tritheistic, to state a belief in three Gods—in fact to favour polytheism. A handful of scholars are well aware that this is the opposite to the truth, but one has to know something about the history to understand how that is.

No attempt (outside the Athanasian Canticle) is made to state that, in spite of the three apparently

---

[1] Less so perhaps to the younger generation. A young lecturer in philosophy has lately written that she can believe in the Father, in Christ, and in the Holy Spirit, but "cannot think of them metaphysically in terms of the Athanasian Creed".

separate sections of the Nicene and Apostles' Creeds, there underlies them the firm conviction that God is one: indeed where the word "one" occurs at the opening of the Nicene Creed, it conveys the impression that "one" refers to the Father, and that two and three are to follow; and though the great phrases of the second section do correct that impression, their fundamental testimony to the Divine Unity is easily missed. That it has been generally forgotten, and that most Christians, most people thinking of themselves as particularly orthodox, have been tritheists, will not, I believe, be denied. Indeed, few theologians have been immune from the heresy; as is shewn by the once dominant doctrines of the Atonement, which assume a transaction between two different Persons, a third Person being also involved, and in the theories of the first thousand years the Devil coming in as a very active fourth party. The constant recitation of the two Creeds in church keeps this tritheism alive, and perhaps aggravates it in the popular mind. It is not, I think, unfair to say that the horror of unitarianism has been balanced by no active objection to tritheism, and that apart from the Athanasian Creed no serious effort has been made to correct it. The continual repetition of the *Gloria Patri* in the services increases the impression, because so far from anything being done to restore the balance, the clergy love adding new triadic formulas like the "ascription" before the Sermon, though this is illegal in the Church of England. The cumulative effect on the minds of all except a few metaphysicians is enormous; and it is not to be wondered at that many sermons unconsciously assume this form of polytheism—as in the case of a preacher whom a friend of mine recently heard extolling the importance of his Order with the words, "Now God only had one son, and he was a clergyman". The Blessing in the Communion Service is indeed one of the few liturgical instances in which the orthodox doctrine is made clear. How little the universal danger impressed our ancestors is shewn by the explanation of the Apostles' Creed in the Catechism:

Question. What dost thou chiefly learn in these Articles of thy Belief?

Answer. First, I learn to believe in God the Father, who hath made me, and all the world.

Secondly, in God the Son, who hath redeemed me, and all mankind.

Thirdly, in God the Holy Ghost, who sanctifieth me, and all the elect people of God.

And it never occurred, even here, to anyone that it would be a good thing to say also, "And yet they are not three Gods, but one God".

The Difficulty with Non-Christians

We have drawn attention to the difficulties of a normal educated layman. Those which confront the missionary in some countries are even more serious. We have alluded to one small obstacle in China: let us now leave that great country on one side, and leave the problems of Buddhism and of Hinduism also, for the simpler issue of Islam. This we can suggest in a short dialogue. Those who like myself have lived among Muslim as well as Hindu students cannot help wishing that our friends at home had some experience of enquirers who are without our background, our knowledge of the Gospels, our softening tradition, and to whom the Creeds have the hard face value of their words, and no more. A Muslim will often say something like this: "We believe in one God; but you Christians, according to your Creed, which you are always repeating, believe in a God whom you call the Almighty Father; you then say that he had only one son, and the son you call a second God: but then you go on to say that this Son had another father, for he was generated by a third God, whom you call the Holy Ghost". Criticisms of this sort are being constantly made, and their ultimate result is that Islam continues to be a great rival missionary power. We of course may answer by explaining first that "only" is a mistranslation (mistranslations again!), and that "only-begotten" is nearer the mark, but that what is really meant is "unique". We may proceed to explain that we also believe strictly in one God; though in the rich personality of God there are three Activities; and that the two Creeds take the unity of God for granted, indeed that they were made expressly to prevent tritheistic ideas.

By this time the attention of our polite Muslim student has probably begun to wander, and he is vaguely thinking how much better is his own simple creed: "There is one God, and Muhammad is his prophet". But if he is in a brisker frame of mind, he may very naturally reply: "Then why don't you say so? Why does your creed omit all reference to the supreme fact which our creed states—that there is one God? You take it for granted? Yet both your Creeds consist of three separate parts, each of which deals with a different Divine person. And if by 'conceived by the Holy Ghost' you really mean that Jesus is the Son of God (which many of us would agree with), then why don't you say so, or why aren't you content with saying 'his unique Son, our Lord'?"

Well, we have our answers ready of course; but there is an enormous amount to explain; and he is thinking all the time that Hindus also have all their answers ready. He does not see—and many of our own clergy at home do not see—that the Creeds were drawn up to meet quite a different set of objections and of errors, and belong to a world of thought quite different from that of the present day.

And at the present day there are millions in

Christian lands, their numbers always increasing, whose presuppositions have little more of the Christian tradition in them than have those of India—millions who do know that we take the unity of God for granted, and who do not care, millions now who think that Christians are tied to the face value of the Creeds and to the cosmogony in which they are framed. They do not use words like that, for the most part, and they do not mention Hellenistic philosophy; but they shrug their shoulders; they find that, if ever they go to church, one or other of the Creeds is being recited, with a special ceremonial emphasis. A few take refuge in the worship afforded by Christian Science or one of the other Churches that seem to be less tied; the great majority have given up public worship altogether.

How much more powerful would be the work both of the Christian apologist at home and of the missionary abroad if he could point to an official creed in modern terms, such as that drafted by Dr. Douglas White:

A Short Creed

I believe in God, the Father of all; and in Jesus Christ, revealer of God and saviour of men; and in the Spirit of Holiness which is the Spirit of God and of Jesus: by which Spirit man is made divine: I acknowledge the communion of all faithful people, in beauty, goodness and truth: and I believe in the forgiveness of sins, the glory of righteousness, the victory of love, and the life eternal.

For that is what we really mean.

Yet no creed should be printed without its date; and surely every creed ought to come up once in a century for revision.

THE DISTORTION OF VALUES

The three Creeds have done inestimable service in preserving essential verities, and those two which are more properly called by the name distil their great subject into a small compass, serving religion still to-day almost as much by what they omit as by what they include. But their proper position as theological statements has been upset by their inclusion in the services of the Church, especially since the invention of printing. They have come to be taken as holy scriptures of unique quality and supreme authority. Indeed, the decay of belief in the inerrancy of the Old and New Testaments has caused many to ascribe to the Creeds an authority which they can no longer ascribe to the Bible, and to find in them the satisfaction for their natural yearning after infallibility. This has been especially the case with the deservedly honoured school of Dr. Gore, who himself put aside such stories of the Nativity as that of the Magi by giving them the Hebrew name of *midrash*, which caused the minimum of shock, but strove with all his power for that part of the Nativity stories which support an article of the two Creeds, as we have them, the virgin birth.[1] The Creeds were set on the throne which the Scriptures had formerly occupied; they were the voice of the Church, and possessed an infallibility which kept the Christian religion safe. This was strengthened by the idea, common during the last

[1] The virgin birth is mentioned in our present forms of the Nicene and Apostles' Creeds. It is not, however, in the original Nicene Creed (see p. 139), nor in the baptismal creed quoted by Eusebius of Caesarea at the Council of Nicaea in 325.

The supposition that it is to be found in some earlier baptismal creeds seems to be failing for lack of evidence. At first the birth of Jesus is not mentioned; then the words "*natus est*" begin to occur before the word "*passus*" or "*crucifixus*". The virgin birth is, however, of course an early belief; and is stated, for instance, by Tertullian. It is first mentioned in the Creed of Marcellus of Ancyra (though here the text is not above suspicion) *c.* 340, and in that of Niceta of Remesiana, 370–375. The formulas of the Council of Antioch against Paul of Samosata, 341–5, have "born of a virgin", "of the virgin", and "of the holy virgin". The Creed of Eunomius, 383, has "of a woman" (*gunaikos*); but the virgin formula is usual, and it seems to have become fairly common by the last quarter of the fourth century. The Athanasian Creed, however, which is probably of the fifth century, does not mention the virgin birth.

generation, that the Bible was "the Church's book", beneath which lay the fallacy of forgetting that the Church was the Bible's child.

Thus the constant repetition of two particular creeds in the services of the Church has produced a greatly exaggerated impression of their authority. Some of our Bishops have recently shewn how serious a loss of proportion may develop from breathing a too exclusively Nicene atmosphere. Statements have been made which provoke the retort, "Nicaea or Nazareth?" Indeed there are those who assert that they would rather see the Church reduced to a few hundred members (in other words, destroyed) than that it should cease to insist on the Nicene Creed for all who would belong to it. This is an unfortunate position, and is rendered worse by the fact that even the most Nicene amongst us admit that there are, after all, some clauses which cannot be taken literally.

The future existence of religion in this sorely tried world depends on whether the Church will be content with Christianity.

If Christianity is to survive as a religion of fellowship, still more if it is to triumph, it must be free from theological entanglements, and men must be able to belong to the Christian Church on Christ's own terms. To set up any other standard is to act in opposition to the Gospel and to deprive the Shepherd of his flock.

Because people have continually recited the Creeds in their worship they have come to think of them as the infallible core of Christianity; and the very existence of the Church and of the Christian religion is in danger because of the exclusiveness thus engendered. Yet these two Creeds have no special authority, and are only two among many, owing their prominence to the fact that they came to be recited in so many of the Church services, more especially in the Church of England.

There was no intention of fixing any creed upon the Church. In her earlier and most vigorous centuries she had no creeds. When formal statements grew up, they were documents drafted in order to arrive at common agreement. The Council of Nicaea, for instance, did not make a creed as we have come to understand the word, but drafted a set of short definitions to exclude the very serious danger of Arianism—the pagan worship of a demi-god. Other councils, and many Bishops, added clauses or made new creeds, with no idea that the process would ever come to an end. That fixity was merely an accident, caused by the breaking up of civilization after the fifth century; so that when thought and theology began to revive, as the Dark Ages passed in the eleventh century, the surviving creeds had acquired a position of unassailable prestige. This they mainly owed to the new custom of using them in Public Worship.

Dozens of creeds were issued with authority, and no one can have thought that any of them would come to be regarded as the last word and beyond the reach of further improvement. Though indeed, when one thinks what additions might have been made in subsequent ages, one cannot but be glad that they reached a state of arrested development.

All this has been so little understood that the reader may perhaps think he is being offered new and strange ideas. The facts, however, are almost a commonplace, though they are seldom brought forward. In illustration of this it is worth while quoting from a Roman Catholic book with the official imprimatur, where they are stated with frankness:

> It is also a very naïve mistake to think that all Christendom ever agreed in recognizing one, or two, or three creeds as final, authoritative, and quasi-inspired documents. A creed is simply a statement of certain chief points of the faith, drawn up by some council, bishop,

or even private person for use at baptism or (later) other function. There have been scores of creeds made by all kinds of people; their authority is just that of the people who made and use them. No creed contains the whole faith, from any point of view. No creed even pretends to be inspired; none is a final standard in itself, but must rather be measured by its conformity to another standard, like any other ecclesiastical document. To appeal to "the creeds" is almost as futile as to appeal to introits or collects.[1]

The Three Uses of Creeds

I. AT BAPTISM

A creed of some sort is a natural part of the Christian initiation, a preliminary to the baptismal act; and in this way creeds began. But even here they began as a profession of faith, not as a mere declaration of theological assent. "Sirs, what must I do to be saved?" said the jailor to Paul and Silas; and their answer was, *"Believe on the Lord Jesus*, and thou shalt be saved". This is the true spirit of the Gospels: "If thou canst do anything, have compassion on us, and help us", said the father of the afflicted boy; and the answer of Jesus was, "if thou canst! All things are possible to him that believeth."[2]

That is faith, not mere belief. But in the very language we have to use we bear witness to the confusion of the two things. When Christendom has failed to hold the meaning of a Christian virtue, the failure is shewn by the debasement of the original terms.

[1] Adrian Fortescue, *The Mass*, The Westminster Library, ed. Bernard Ward and H. Thurston (Longmans, 1912), p. 286. There was, however, one creed compiled (though not for use in the services, but as a test of orthodoxy among Bishops) by a General Council—the *genuine creed of Nicaea*, which we print on p. 139.
[2] Acts xvi. 30-31; Mark ix. 22-3; R.V.

Charity, for instance, was a specifically Christian virtue, a cultivation of widespread care and affection, which is quite different from love; but it has not proved strong enough to develop a verb—we have to say that we "love" the unemployed, just as if it was the same emotion as our love for our children, or as falling in love: thus charity came to mean alms-giving, so that a society had to be formed for its Organization. Faith, in the same way, proved too weakly held to develop a proper verb of its own; and we have to read, "All things are possible to him that believeth", which as it stands might almost be mis-interpreted, "A man can perform miracles, if only he will assent to the creeds". So faith degenerated into belief; and belief degenerated into credality and often into credulity. This was intensified during centuries of oppression; for in the Middle Ages if a man was insufficiently credulous, he was liable to be taken by the Inquisition or other organizations, tortured, and burnt alive—indeed Spain has only just celebrated the first centenary of the abolishment of the In-quisition.

Paul and Silas thought that only faith in Jesus Christ was necessary for Baptism; but there is in Acts viii. 38 a verse, interpolated by later copyists and relegated to the margin in the Revised Version, which shews the stage arrived at in the second century when belief in a doctrinal proposition has taken the place of faith   though the creed is a very simple one: In the original text the eunuch says to Philip, "Behold here is water; what doth hinder me to be baptized? And he commanded the chariot to stand still: and they both went down into the water, both Philip and the eunuch; and he baptized him." This did not conform to later usage; so the copyists make Philip require a declaration of assent, which, short as it is, yet shews the transition from the act of faith in Christ which Paul and Silas had required to a belief in something about Christ—"I believe that Jesus Christ is the Son of God".

Baptism was at first a baptizing into the name of Christ, or into that of the Father and the Son. Whether the Trinitarian fórmula in Matthew xxviii. 19 is editorial or whether it also is an addition made by the copyists is still a matter of debate among experts in early Church history: if it be due to the author, then Loisy's drastic transference of the whole book to about the year 125[1] is not without some justification. But the triple formula occurs in the *Didache* (7), which was probably written before the close of the first century; and indeed the connexion between joining the Church and receiving the Spirit —that intensely felt reality—made natural the mention of holy spirit, or of the Holy Spirit, at baptism. So Acts ii. 38 reports Peter as saying, "Repent ye, and be baptized every one of you in the name of Jesus Christ unto the remission of your sins; and ye shall receive the gift of holy spirit", or "of the Holy Ghost", as it is rendered in our Bibles. Indeed, the Spirit of God, or of Christ, occurs constantly in the Epistles in connexion with the names of God and of Christ, though such expressions cannot be called a trinitarian formula, and few would now claim that character even for the familiar "Grace" of 2 Cor. xiii. 14, "The grace of the Lord Jesus Christ, and the love of God, and the participation in the holy spirit be with you all"—whether we use capital letters or not.

Baptism in the New Testament is simply baptism into Christ, and if we can use the word "formula" at all, it is a single formula of which we must speak. There are four definite instances of such baptism, and these are supported by many other phrases: two of baptism "in the name of Jesus Christ",[2] and two

---

[1] In *La Naissance du christianisme* (Paris, Nourry), 1933.

[2] Acts ii. 38 (already quoted above); Acts x. 48 ("He commanded them to be baptized in the name of Jesus Christ").

"into the name of the Lord Jesus".[1] The challenging question of St. Paul in 1 Cor. i. 13, "Was Paul crucified for you? or were ye baptized in the name of Paul?" also points to the simple form of baptism into Christ.

In the middle of the second century we find, not indeed a creed, but a baptismal formula in the name of the Trinity, when Justin Martyr writes, "In the name of God the Father and Lord of the universe, and of our saviour Jesus Christ, and of the Holy Spirit, do they then receive the washing in water" (*Apol.* i. 61). About the year 200 Tertullian provides evidence of the then established custom, when he says that "we are immersed thrice into the three persons at each several mention of their names" (*Adv. Prax.* 26); though the formula even in the third century was not fixed, as the mention by Origen (in his commentary on 1 Cor. vii. 5) of "invocation of holy Spirit and of Christ and of the Father" illustrates.

Until recently the whole matter was in profound confusion owing to the theory, supported by the learning of Kattenbusch and Harnack, that the Apostles' Creed as we have it, the old Roman Creed, came into existence early in the second century, with only a word or two lacking. Dr. F. J. Badcock[2] has conclusively shewn that the Apostles' Creed is a typical fourth-century document. The creeds of the second and third centuries were much shorter; and their gradual enlargement can be traced. There is just enough extant material to give secure guidance, though we have no actual baptismal creed earlier than the third century.

Briefly, all the evidence goes to shew that late

---

[1] Acts viii. 16 (Moffat's translation, "They had simply been baptized in the name of the Lord Jesus"); Acts xix. 5 ("When they heard this, they were baptized into the name of the Lord Jesus").

[2] In *The History of the Creeds* (S.P.C.K., 1930), cap. I, etc.

in the first century the candidate for baptism was asked,

"Dost thou believe in Jesus Christ our Lord?"

or "the Son of God?" the words varying in different places and at different times; that in the second century the question was expanded, mainly because the being and character of God could not be taken for granted among pagans as it could among Jews, into such words as "Dost thou believe in God the Father? In Jesus Christ our Lord? in the Holy Spirit?" The spread of gnosticism would lead to the addition of the two words, "suffered", "born", and also of the "resurrection of the flesh": "his Son" would be a safeguard against Marcionism. The clause about "the forgiveness of sins" guarded a vital principle, when the Montanists and many others taught that grave sins involved exclusion and eternal damnation without possibility of remission. Before the middle of the third century the baptismal interrogation, which was still short, must have run in most places much in the following words:

> Dost thou believe in God the Father almighty? Dost thou believe in Jesus Christ, his unique Son, our Lord, who was born and who suffered? Dost thou believe in the Holy Spirit, in the holy Church, in the remission of sins, and in the resurrection of the flesh?

A little before this we have the earliest creed exactly known, which happens to be a personal and not a baptismal one. But let us quote Dr. Badcock: "The earliest Creed known word for word which can be dated with reasonable certainty is contained in the so-called Letter of the Apostles, *Epistola Apostolorum*. This is a pseudonymous treatise originally written in Greek and now extant in full in Ethiopic, but there is a small portion of it in Coptic, and a fragment in Latin. It is probably to be assigned to Asia Minor before 180." Here is the text:

[Belief] In God the Father almighty,
> In Jesus Christ our Saviour,
> And in the Spirit, the holy, the Paraclete,
> Holy Church,
> Forgiveness of sins.[1]

The so-called Egyptian Church Order with its kindred documents provides us with a creed definitely baptismal, and was, in its original form of the third century, as follows in the Coptic version, with a few variants in the Ethiopic and Arabic:

> I believe in the one true God, the Father almighty,
> And in his only Son, our Lord and our Saviour Jesus Christ,
> And the Holy Spirit, giver of life to the universe,
> The Trinity of the same substance, One Godhead,
> One Lord, one kingdom, one faith, one baptism,
> In the catholic holy Church,
> And in life eternal.[2]

Thus very slowly and for intelligible reasons the creed gathered new clauses, till in the fourth century it had reached in some places the form of our Apostles' Creed, still preserving a restrained and balanced character which gives it high value to-day. The legend was then invented and accepted that each of its twelve articles had been contributed by one of the apostles; and this helped to preserve it from further change.

What then would be the ideal arrangement for a revised Order of Holy Baptism at the present day?

The ideal baptismal creed is the Scriptural one, "I believe in Jesus Christ". Most will prefer to con-

---

[1] *Ibid.* pp. 25, 24, and p. 25 for references. It may be as early as 150, or as late as the early third century.

[2] *Ibid.* p. 27. For the Egyptian Church Order and its relation to the Canons of Hippolytus, etc., see E. Hauler, *Didascaliae Apostolorum Fragmenta*, 1900; F. X. Funk, *Didascalia*, 1905; E. Schwartz, *Ueber die pseudoapostolischen Kirchenordnungen*, 1910; R. H. Conolly, *The So-called Egyptian Church Order*, 1916 (Cambridge Texts and Studies, vol. viii. no. 4).

tinue using the Apostles' Creed at Baptism, some wish it to begin in the earlier way, "We believe": but I cannot think we have any right to put barriers in the way of a thoughtful man who wishes to join the Christian Church. The Founder of that Church made no barriers whatever, but welcomed the faith of those who were not Christians in any sense of the term as it is now used, and many of whom doubtless never became Christians in any sense, except that they remembered their healer with love. To belong to the Christian Church to-day it is indeed necessary for a man to be a Christian, but if we wish all the followers of Christ to be one fellowship, as they were at first, if we have any belief in the Catholic Church as a reality, and desire to save it from being a mere phrase connoting isolation, exclusion, and sectarian-ism, then surely we must be content to take our stand with Christ, with St. Paul, and with the whole New Testament, and to require no more as of necessity than "I believe in Jesus Christ".

The subject of the Baptismal Service is, I believe, being dealt with in another paper in this book. My own suggestion would be that the Scriptural form should be printed first in the service, and should be followed by "Then may the minister say" and the Apostles' Creed. This would remove the difficulties, moral and intellectual, which we have noticed, and would make the Church as free as the Jerusalem which is above. The educational value of the service would be increased if the "Short Creed" on page 111 were added.

II. AS TESTS

The full development of the various creeds, especially in the Nicene form, belongs to the second stage, when they became tests of orthodox belief. They defined the then Modernist View, as against the still prevalent old-fashioned binitarianism. The student can explore this subject in the ample literature which has been provided by Hort, Heurtley, Kattenbusch, Hahn, Swete, Harnack, Brightman, C. H. Turner, Bethune Baker, A. E. Burn, Elmer More, Major, Badcock, and others. Here in this small space we will be content with reproducing the text of the real Creed of Nicaea, so that the reader can compare it with the developed form now in use:

The Original Nicene Creed

We believe in one God the Father all-ruling, maker of heaven and earth and of all things visible and invisible.

And in one lord Jesus Christ, the son of God, begotten of the father, only-begotten, that is of the substance of the father. God out of God, light out of light, very God out of very God, begotten not made, being of one substance with the father, through whom all things were made, both in the heaven and in the earth, who for us men and for our salvation came down and was incarnate was made man, suffered and rose on the third day, ascended into the heavens, is coming to judge the living and the dead.

And in the holy spirit.

Then follows an anathema against all those who may deny the eternal pre-existence and deity of the second Person of the Trinity.

At the present day there are two ways in which this second use of the Creeds confronts us as a practical problem.

(1) They are needed as official documents, both venerable and valuable, in the Prayer Book. They could no more be removed than could our ancient architecture or the ancient poetry which forms the chief substance of Divine service.

I would venture to suggest that in the ideal Prayer Book they would be printed together in a section by themselves—the Creed of Nicaea, the Creed called Nicene, the Creed called the Apostles', the Canticle commonly called the Athanasian Creed —properly described in some such way as this, and

with sub-headings denoting their respective centuries, so that they should not convey a misleading
impression to the people.

In the Catechism, where intelligible simplicity is
specially needed, some form of the Short Creed on
page 111 seems to be the most ideally suitable, but,
since most people would wish to have the Creed
called the Apostles' Creed, this also would doubtless
be given as well. A new explanation would be essential. Here is one, based on a form already sanctioned
in one Diocese as a basis for teaching, which may
serve to suggest a possible line of development:

> *Question.* What do you chiefly learn by these state-
> ments of the Christian faith?
> *Answer.* I learn to believe in God, who has made him-
> self known to us—
> Firstly, through his work of creation, wherein he
> forms us for the knowledge of himself, and is the
> Father of all men.
> Secondly, through the life of Jesus Christ our
> Saviour, who has unveiled to men the character and
> will of God.
> Thirdly, through the Holy Spirit, the giver of life,
> who sanctifies us in his freedom, truth, and love; and
> inspires us in the fellowship of Christ, that we may do
> our duty in this life and fit ourselves for the life of the
> world to come.

As to the proposal that an ethical creed should be
provided in the Church Catechism, I think we may
be profoundly grateful that no such attempt was made
in the past. For instance: Cruelty was not thought
wrong; it is not among the Seven Deadly Sins, nor
is it mentioned in any moral code that I have read.
On any day in the Middle Ages thousands of innocent people were rotting in dungeons and hundreds
were being tortured in ways that are beyond the
powers of description: books in great number for the
guidance of confessors were issued, in which (contrary to the way of Christ) the minute analysis of sin

takes the place of the love of goodness; yet in books like *The Agenbite of Inwit*, among all the classes, divisions, and subdivisions, cruelty is not mentioned even as a venial sin.

The Two Duties in Church Catechism are a great monument of the modern era; and they have impressed upon the English mind, not only the sense of duty, not only the Golden Rule, but also the central truth of the Christian religion, that man has a binding duty not only to God but also to his brother man.[1] What else do we need?

(2) A historic creed is useful also at the present day in working out the means of reunion between the Churches. Although some, like the Church of Czechoslovakia, are shewing signs of impatience with the Nicene Creed, they all desire to maintain *"The Faith behind the Creeds"*, and the Eastern Orthodox Churches hold rigidly to the Nicene Creed, and to no other—though it is not *our* Nicene Creed, since they will not have the *filioque* clause.

Thus the reconciling phrase in the road to reunion is that of the Lausanne Conference on Faith and Order (where, however, it would be more exact to read "Belief" instead of "Faith")—"The Faith which is witnessed to and safeguarded by the Creeds".

But the very fact that such a reservation is needed, because we can no longer get theologians to accept the actual words of the Creeds at their face value, and in the sense which was meant by those who framed them, shews that they have lost their use as real tests of orthodoxy. They remain invaluable, but as pointers to the common belief, not as precise statements of what all hold to be true. The most conservative theologians admit that some of the articles,

---

[1] Still current misunderstandings suggest a few verbal alterations—"to order myself lowly and reverently to all", for instance, and "to do my duty wherever I shall be".

even in the simple Apostles' Creed, must be taken metaphorically; and the Roman Church, by its dogma of papal infallibility, having replaced all the Creeds by something quite different, its members could be compelled to drop them altogether, as they are already compelled to smother them under incredible articles of belief, including that in endless torment, with many later additions. At the other extreme are Churches of no small learning and piety, which shew their respect for the Creeds by keeping them at a respectful distance, neither applying them as tests nor using them in their services. Many to-day who are orthodox hold themselves free of the Creeds; many cannot accept them at all, and yet are true disciples of Christ. A test which excludes such people has ceased to perform any useful function. Therefore the Creeds are becoming pointers to the common faith in Christ, in order that they may be used as means of reconciliation.

The Creeds remain then an indispensable agent for Christian reunion, a subject of grateful study for the theologian, a source of inspiration, a treasured means of teaching. But they do not help the thoughtful layman to-day, nor that always large body of the clergy who are laymen in theology; they are not of use to the missionary, whose life is spent in preaching Christ; they do not help to commend the Christian religion to the world at large; and they are a serious obstacle in the countries nominally Christian, where few educated people accept them now with any conviction.

And their continual use in Public Worship has created the impression that the Church is static, not in the sense that it is sprung from Christ and grows in the habit of his Gospel—for that is to be dynamic; but in the sense that it cannot either reach back to the Gospel or forward out of the fifth century to the twentieth.

III. IN PUBLIC WORSHIP

The third stage was reached when the Creeds, from being tests, became protests, made in Public Worship (in the positive sense that belongs properly to the word Protestant), and as such passed from the theologians who understood them to the laity who did not.

They are a liturgical afterthought. We are so used in the Church of England to hearing creeds on every occasion that it needs an effort to remember that they are not an integral part of Public Worship, and that their public recitation cannot be called a Catholic custom, even in the looser sense of that epithet. The use of the Creeds in the services is in fact an accretion which began locally about the year 500, and did not become general till about 1000, and then only in an incomplete manner.

Creeds came to be introduced as a protest against heresy, as in the first instance at Antioch (between 476 and 488), and at Constantinople (between 512 and 517), when Arianism was the danger: for the same reason the Nicene Creed was in 589 introduced into Spain, where the Visigoths had but recently renounced that error. In the ninth century it was used in Gaul by some but not by all. Rome did not add it to the Liturgy till the eleventh century, when the Emperor Henry II noticed that there was no creed at his coronation in 1014, and asked the Pope to add the creed, as was the custom in his native Germany. This was done; but only for Sundays and the greater festivals, as is still the rule in the Latin service to-day. This was also the rule in our own country, and was continued in the First Prayer Book of Edward VI, by a rubric allowing the omission of the Creed "on workdays and in private houses", a statement which shews that the creed being a festival *addition* was by then forgotten. It was not till 1552, the date of the Second English Prayer Book, that the Creed became an invariable part of our Communion Service.

In the Roman Church it still counts for little. At low mass it is inaudible. At high mass it is a musical performance, during which everyone sits down.

The Apostles' Creed has a similar halting liturgical history. Never used in the East, it had no place in the original Hour Services, Mattins, and Evensong, nor in the late fourth century additions of Terce, Sext, and None. Somewhere about the beginning of the seventh century, Prime and Compline were further added to the monastic services; and in the ninth century the Apostles' Creed was inserted into Prime, and somewhat later it appeared in Compline also, and in the introduction to Mattins. It was, however, recited privately, only the last two clauses being said aloud, as a versicle and response. Curiously enough the only profession of faith in the Sarum Breviary to be said aloud was the Athanasian Creed, which was ordered to be sung daily at Prime after the Psalms. In the First English Prayer Book, the Apostles' Creed is appointed to be said by the priest alone, the Athanasian Creed being substituted for it on the six greater festivals. In the Prayer Book of 1552, the Apostles' Creed was ordered to be said by the people, as at present, and the Athanasian Creed was given seven more occasions, on Saints' days. It was in fact the Modernists of the time who last made the recitation of the Creeds congregational and constant.

A further stage was reached by the unauthorized introduction during the nineteenth century of the custom of emphasizing the recitation of the Creeds by turning to the east. There is no word about this in the Prayer Book or in the service books of any other Church, and no precedent in any pre-Reformation custom, though there is an analogous custom in Islam. It was first attempted by some of the Laudian

School; but I do not know of any evidence for its continuance. That such a custom should have become almost general by the end of the Victorian era (accompanied often by the equally unauthorized habit of making the sign of the cross) shews how the sense of true proportion in worship had been lost. The old rules had preserved the right principle, by directing the choir to turn to the altar at acts of worship only—*Gloria Patri*, *Gloria tibi Domine*, *Gloria in excelsis*, and the Canon.

To say that the use of creeds in Public Worship was a mediaeval abuse which was not removed at the Reformation, but intensified, would be too sharp a way of putting it; but such a statement would not be altogether untrue to the facts. There was a slow process of accretion during the Dark and Middle Ages, which remained incomplete and as it were tentative, until the accusations of heresy against the Reformers and their desire to assert the Conciliar orthodoxy led them to complete the process in the Second English Prayer Book.

The recitation of creeds, in fact, is not an act of worship, but of policy. This is true of the first steps as well as of the last; and the Church would never have begun to introduce them into Public Worship if the mentality of its members had not been distorted by the maddening controversies of earlier times. Faith had dwindled into belief.

Faith and Belief

A liturgical error! Belief is cognitive, faith is conative: belief is the acceptance of statements, the assent to propositions; faith is personal activity, love breaking into vision. Worship is the activity of prayer and praise, the ascent of the soul to God, the casting of our love upon him; it therefore depends on faith and is the expression of faith. To introduce a statement of belief is to lower the tone of worship, because worship is communion with God and not with theology. And to make Public Worship an occasion for mutual reassurance in terms of theology is to lower the mental integrity as well as emotional power of the worshipper.

It is precisely when belief is taken for granted that worship is real. For faith then comes into play: and faith is dynamic. This is sometimes obscured by the common use of the phrase "the Christian Faith" as a romantic substitute for "the Christian Belief", a confusion which the Church Catechism wisely avoids in the demand, "Rehearse the Articles of thy Belief". For the Christian faith is really faith in Christ, a personal relationship with a person.

And this is the teaching of the New Testament, where faith is a venture, something that reaches beyond the actual to the eternal, which, as it succeeds, is described with psychological accuracy in the Epistle to the Hebrews as "the substance of things hoped for, the evidence of things not seen" (a translation which has not been improved by the Revised Version or by Dr. Moffat)—the substantiation or "realization", as Dr. Tennant says, of things hoped for and unseen; for faith, when it is truly directed, results in realization.[1] It is truly directed when it is directed to the true Christ, the Christ not of the christologists but of the Gospels.

So with St. Paul. All his argumentation is to clear the way for the stretching forth to Christ; faith for him is freedom, the glorious liberty through which he can press forward to the goal. He abounds in fervent affirmations, but gives no formulated creed. The very strength of his christology (if one may use the word here at all) is that it is without definition. Indeed, as Dr. James Mackinnon has remarked, he

---

[1] F. R. Tennant, *Philosophical Theology*, Cambridge University Press, 1928, vol. i. p. 297.

"would evidently not have subscribed the Nicene and later creeds", and "would probably have been denounced as a heretic".[1] "Christ must reign" is his substance of things hoped for; "Jesus is Lord" is his evidence of things not seen.

As to the mind of Jesus himself there is no doubt. Belief in God he takes for granted. Faith is for him a thing so dynamic that to possess it is to be cured in body and soul. "Thy faith hath made thee whole", he says to those who came to him; and they were Christians in no other sense than they reached out to him for help.

There has been from the beginning something much better than a creed in all Christian forms of worship, a short poem—a rhymed hymn, they tell us, it must have been in the Aramaic original— which is a real act of faith, a looking forward, and a surrender to God—the Lord's Prayer.

That which our Saviour Christ himself has taught us is indeed true worship. For the cry of worship is "Thou and we"; but the way of the Creeds we use is "I and him"—to many, alas, it is really "I and them". There are eloquent defences of the liturgical use of creeds;[2] but they amount to little more than the suggestion that such use is like the waving of flags. But the waving of flags in worship would be barbarous.

Therefore I would dare suggest that the words "may be said or sung" should be prefixed to the Creeds in our services, with the view to dropping them ultimately from this position altogether.

New Creeds for Old

There are some who wish to be allowed to use as an alternative to the Apostles' Creed and the Nicene

[1] J. Mackinnon, *The Gospel in the Early Church*, Longmans, 1933, p. 87.
[2] *E.g.* in E. S. Drown, *The Apostles' Creed To-day* (New York, The Macmillan Co., 1917), pp. 124-9.

Creed some other affirmation of faith which will be less open to objection for use in Public Worship. I myself do not think that they go far enough. Such a permissive alternative would be the Johannine Creed which is reprinted in *Songs of Praise* (no. 433).[1] It is there printed as a canticle, and (perhaps without the words "We believe") it is admirable for such a purpose, and will, I hope, be more and more used as an anthem. And the place for the anthem is not in a section devoted to praise and prayer, but, like the Lessons and the Sermon, during an interval. The advocates of the permissive use of alternative creeds will need to bear always in mind the strong tendency for any credal form to acquire an undesirable finality. We may feel sure at this moment that the beautiful Johannine Creed expresses the belief which will be that of all future ages; but we may be mistaken. The unhistorical element in the acts as well as in the discourses of the wonderful original may cause the next generation to take a different view, and another philosophy may be in fashion. There is also a clear practical advantage in the omission of creeds from Public Worship as compared with the permissive use of alternative creeds. Those who wish to go on using the old creeds will do so because they are of a conservative disposition, and the saying of a new alternative will offend them more than not saying them at all. On the other hand they might be got to

---

[1] *We believe:*
    God is spirit: and they that worship him must worship him in spirit and in truth.
    God is light: and if we walk in the light, as he is in the light, we have fellowship one with another.
    God is love: and every one that loveth is born of God and knoweth God.
    Jesus is the Son of God: and God hath given to us eternal life, and this life is in his Son.
    We are children of God: and he hath given us of his spirit.
    If we confess our sins: he is faithful and just to forgive us our sins.
    The world passeth away and the lust thereof: but he that doeth the will of God abideth for ever. Amen.

appreciate the fact that the omission of the Creeds is real conservatism, besides being a liturgical and psychological improvement—is in fact the removal of one of the mistakes of past innovators. It is on grounds such as these that I believe that the permissive use of alternative creeds would be in principle unsatisfactory; and, while welcoming full liberty for those who would prefer to substitute a new authorized creed, I should point to the entire omission of Creeds from Public Worship as the ideal.

And clearly the old creeds cannot be tampered with. They cannot be amended, nor does it seem practicable even to retranslate them, considering the deep objection that people have to linguistic innovations. They are noble classical expressions of essential Christian values, and magnificent instances of the Church's wisdom in ancient times. They must stand as monuments of which we may well be proud. Their explanation and retranslation belong rather to theology than to liturgics.

Liturgical Use of Creeds To-day

Meanwhile, the rubrics being as they are, some difficulties would be met if the Apostles' Creed were sung by the choir as an anthem, and thus treated like the Nicene Creed as in some measure an act of worship. In this way their "religious reconstruction" for the expression of their permanent values would be helped; though none of the creeds are shaped for worship as the *Gloria in excelsis*, the *Te Deum*, and the *Gloria Patri* are. Musical settings of the Apostles' Creed (and Dr. Martin Shaw has already composed one) would at least help people to take it less as a drill, and more as an act of worship in the frame of that majestic expression of Christian belief.

It is with some hesitation that I refer in passing to the Deposited Book, since there is a real danger of our becoming unprincipled and treating it as if it had authority, which it has not. But the Bishops have some justification in using it as a standard within which they can sanction small practical modifications. The Deposited Book does not touch the use of the Apostles' Creed; but it allows the omission of the Nicene Creed on days other than Sundays and Holy Days (reverting thus to the First Prayer Book), and both the shortening and the omission altogether of the Athanasian Creed. This at least is a move in the right direction.

The Danger of being Static

The strength of science to-day is that it refuses to be fixed by past pronouncements and is free of false cosmogonies. Scientific writers are believed (sometimes unduly) because they make no claim to finality, and do not require a public recitation of their belief in genes or electrons. Theologians are suspect; their most honest investigations carry little weight because of the fixity that is unjustly attributed to them. Although the very reason for their existence is faith, and faith looks forward, yet the formal parade of belief which is imposed upon them produces the continual impression that they cannot extricate themselves from a past that died with Copernicus.

For that is the result of reciting creeds in Church. They become static, and, being set, they lose their vitality and are taken for *mantras*. Their spell is thrown over even strong minds, with the result, as we are seeing to-day, that born leaders of religion who are in other ways wise and reasonable, are willing to see the fellowship of Jesus Christ dwindle into nothingness rather than abate a jot from the Nicene interpretation of his person. If such a temper should spread, then the urgent work of all who put Christ first, and are trying to follow him and not his resolvers, will be to proclaim on the house-tops the Gospel which he gave to the world, and to make very sure that the Kingdom of Heaven shall not be destroyed from within.

The Church was right in her long reluctance to use any creeds in her worship; for the peril of every age is to bury the future in the past. Even regrets are dangerous. It was Jesus who said, "No man, having put his hand to the plough, and looking back, is fit for the Kingdom of God".

IV

THE NEW CATHOLICISM. I

INTERCOMMUNION

by

T. G. ROGERS, B.D., M.C.

Chaplain to H.M. the King
Hon. Canon of Birmingham Cathedral
Rector of Birmingham

SYNOPSIS

The Position in Outline

In the earliest days of Christianity we have no record of intercommunion between orthodox and heretic. This creates a prejudice against intercommunion in the minds of those who look to antiquity for the norm. But it is a prejudice countered by the appeal to the Spirit of Christ as the criterion. The Catholic Church is in fragments and new precedents and a new policy are demanded. The present position cannot be remedied except by an effective promotion of the spirit of fellowship. Of such fellowship sacramental fellowship is an essential part. It is futile to preach international fellowship and to emphasize international interdependence while concurring in the continuance of exclusiveness as between branches of the Christian Church. Catholicity is not dependent on the form of ecclesiastical government.

The Official Anglican View

That the authorities of the Anglican Church are dissatisfied with the present position is clear from the Reports of the Lambeth Conferences of 1920 and 1930. The statement of the Lambeth Committee appointed after 1920, which included the two Archbishops, affirmed the conviction that non-episcopal ministries are real ministries of Christ's Word and Sacraments in the Universal Church. In contrast with the Roman Church and the Orthodox Church, the Anglican Church, as is shewn by its formularies, refuses to condemn the ministries of other Churches. In the seventeenth century intercommunion with foreign Protestants was common, and in modern times the Lambeth Conference of 1930 sanctioned intercommunion with non-episcopalians in certain circumstances. The hesitation to sanction a wider intercommunion is not based on an official affirmation of any such principle as that implied in the Anglo-Catholic theory of the Apostolic Succession. The reasons for hesitation are secondary rather than primary. The Lambeth Report suggests that full intercommunion is inconsistent with the present "will and intention of Christians to perpetuate separately organized churches". But Christian churches may be regarded as self-governing guilds within the Catholic Church. On the analogy of the British Commonwealth of Nations, or the organization of the United States of America, the will and intention to preserve the unity of the spirit does not exclude some forms of independently organized life. Nor is it obvious why Lambeth should advance the psychological objection that intercommunion should be the goal rather than a means to the restoration of unity. Within the Church of England the Sacrament of Holy Communion is regarded and used as a means to the restoration of unity between various parties and schools of thought. The prior practice of intercommunion facilitated Methodist and Presbyterian reunion, and it is unlikely that without it reunion would have been possible. The Churches with which the Anglicans have discussed reunion stress the importance of prior intercommunion. The course of discussion and negotiation has shewn that further progress cannot easily be made without intercommunion. There has been no hesitation in regarding intercommunion as a means to closer reunion with the Orthodox Church and the Old Catholic Church. It seems that the real ground for hesitation in accepting intercommunion with the Free Churches is the existence within the Church of England of a party which draws a sharp distinction between episcopal and non-episcopal ministries.

A Policy for the Future

The outlook is reasonably hopeful. Even Anglo-Catholics are willing to support intercommunion on special occasions within the limitations laid down by the Resolutions of the Upper Houses of Convocation passed in 1931. At present the Christian forbearance shewn by non-Anglicans inspires them to wait for their Anglican brethren to open heart and mind a little wider. In the Birmingham diocese joint enterprises between congregations have led to congregational acts of intercommunion, and in one important instance to reciprocity. This kind of pioneer advance is in line with the method of development of various Anglican movements in the past, and has the right to claim consideration on the part of Church authorities. The problem of reunion in South India is simplified by the fact that in India, apart from the Roman Church, there is only one branch of the Church working in any particular area; a measure of inter-communion has been practised with Synodical authority among those engaged in formulating a scheme for reunion. The spirit of fellowship cannot conceivably use other channels while ignoring the very Sacrament of Fellowship itself. To this history testifies, as in the Communion in Westminster Abbey of the Revisers of the Authorized Version of the Bible in 1870, and the joint Easter Communion which marked the close of the Jerusalem Missionary Conference.

An Appeal

It ought not to be necessary to await an anti-Christian persecution such as that through which the Confessional Christians of Germany are passing to be constrained to intercommunion. To believers, faced as they are by a wholesale apostasy, our disproportionate concern with "order" is incomprehensible. Anglican eagerness for reciprocity with episcopalian foreigners contrasts unfavourably with our hesitation to practise intercommunion with non-episcopalian fellow-countrymen. The impression is given that Communion is at home a divisive symbol. The time has come when the official leaders of the Church might reasonably be expected to inaugurate a forward move and to give some guidance to the pioneers. Much depends on the ultimate official response to the appeal made to the Bishops by the Evangelical Group Movement, which represents some twelve hundred clergy, for the fostering and regulation of intercommunion. The time factor is of importance. Visions which do not lead to action fade away, often with tragic consequences.

IV

THE NEW CATHOLICISM. I

INTERCOMMUNION

The Position in Outline

WHEN I was invited to write this paper I thought it would be interesting to produce some instances of what might be regarded as intercommunion in early Church history. There must surely be, so I argued, some occasions on record when the Christian spirit of fellowship succeeded in bringing orthodox and heretic together at the Lord's Table. I was assured, however, by a competent authority that I might save my pains. No such records existed and the temper of the times would not have permitted it. Even Origen, who might be regarded not only as a liberal but something even of a rebel, "when charitably received into the house of a wealthy lady of Alexandria, who also had a certain Paul, a heretic, living under her roof, refused, in accordance with the rule of the Church, to eat with Paul". And if this were the attitude of Origen, how much more severe would have been the attitude of lesser men. The history of the Church leading up to and throughout the mediaeval period would appear to be a history of increasing rigidity of rule in the interests of uniformity.

It is quite reasonable, therefore, that those who think of Catholic use in terms of the sub-Apostolic or Mediaeval Church should have a serious prejudice against intercommunion to-day. Even if logic compels them to admit that their own Church cannot make any exclusive claim to be the Catholic Church, it is difficult to set up any standard of orthodoxy which is disinterested. Even if the word "heretic" has dropped out of common use, and even if experience has shewn that the fruits of holiness are displayed equally by Conformists and Nonconformists to the Anglican Rule, there remains the mental attitude which expresses itself in such subtle distinctions as the covenanted and the uncovenanted mercies of God. Probably our inheritance from the past—our long-established Church tradition that orthodoxy implies exclusiveness—accounts for much of the religious opposition which intercommunion encounters in an age and in a situation in which it might seem to be both obvious and desirable.

We are not likely to get very far in breaking down the ecclesiastical barriers which still divide the several parts of Christ's Church from sharing in a common Eucharist until we have the courage boldly to appeal to the Spirit of Christ as the final criterion not only of our personal and national relationships but also of our Church relationships with one another. If the Church has rightly interpreted our Lord's mind by its growing rigidity throughout the mediaeval period, and if the inherited policy of subordinating sacramental fellowship amongst Christians to insistence on the acceptance of "right order" is to be the last word, then there is no use discussing intercommunion in the present distress.

Our plea is that, taking all things into consideration, new precedents and a new policy are called for which are more in accordance with the Spirit of Christ. We have to acknowledge that the Catholic Church is in fragments and that it cannot be unified apart from the promotion of the spirit of fellowship of which sacramental fellowship is a constituent part. Exhaustive historical research justifies us in saying that our Lord laid down no one form of government for his Church, and therefore to forbid inter-communion with other Churches because they follow not with us is to lay down a rule that has no Divine authority and is quite unsuited to the present conditions.

We appeal frankly to the Spirit of Christ, even though in so doing we expose ourselves to the accusation of discourtesy and even of arrogance in claiming to interpret the Spirit of Christ more accurately than those who differ with us conscientiously. But they will understand that where so much is at stake, and where the whole question of the relationship of Christianity to the modern world is being tested, it is natural and legitimate for the plaintiff to appeal to the highest court. We do so without disrespect, realizing that there must be others charged with the responsibility of guarding the institutional life of the Church and challenging on its first appearance each new (or old) principle or precedent which is offered for acceptance in the Name of Christ.

Our position may be illustrated in this way.

In the modern world in which we find ourselves the Church is very largely concerned with preaching and teaching international fellowship. It does so in the Name of Christ, confident that it is taking its stand on a great Christian principle. It views with natural concern the tariff walls and economic barriers that so often impede the normal course of trade. It is critical of such economic nationalism as may tend to isolate any State as an independent unit. In the name of Christian fellowship it urges collective policy and collective responsibility. Where disputes arise it urges arbitration, and it does not hesitate to recommend to the nations some surrender of their sovereign rights in order that the foundations of a larger unity may be well and truly laid. All these are commonplaces of the Christian teaching to-day. The air is full of our remonstrances to the nations that refuse to accept the full implications of interdependence and pursue their egotistic or imperialistic way.

It is essential, if we are sincere, that what we preach to others we must preach to ourselves and what we ask others to accept in the Name of Christ we must be prepared to accept ourselves. If modern conditions compel the modification of sovereign rights of nations in obedience to the larger unity which we believe to be God's purpose for the world, modern conditions may also demand modifications in the sovereign rights of Churches in the interests of a larger unity. If we believe that Christian fellowship between nations is being strangled by economic barriers, we must be equally sensitive to the ecclesiastical barriers which strangle the Christian fellowship between Churches. We, too, must accept the full implications of interdependence which may be regarded as a new word from God for our day and generation.

This, very briefly, is the modern case for intercommunion. It assumes the position now almost universally admitted outside the Roman Church that no one system of Church government, however august its history, has been ordained to the exclusion of all other. It assumes that the non-episcopal Churches on the Continent and the great Protestant denominations throughout the world which reconstituted their particular forms of government as the result of the Reformation did not thereby lose their Catholicity. It assumes that they are equally members with the Roman Catholic and Orthodox Churches of the one Body of Christ. It assumes that all these various churches ought to be conscious of their interdependence and to acknowledge it. The new movement of the Spirit of God which from the time of the Edinburgh Conference in 1910 has steadily driven the Churches to try and realize their essential unity is intended, we believe, to bring us into close relationships with non-episcopal as well as episcopal Churches. To attempt to differentiate between them in the matter of sacramental fellowship on the ground of invalid or imperfect order seems to us to be unjustified by the evidence and contrary to the spirit of the Christian religion.

THE OFFICIAL ANGLICAN VIEW OF INTERCOMMUNION

It is evident, I think, that the authorities of the Anglican Church are greatly troubled by this question of intercommunion. They recognize that the large-heartedness of their own official utterances afford at least plausible grounds for a request from Free Churchmen that they should be implemented by some considered measure of intercommunion. It would be impossible to find space for a complete catena of these utterances which have gradually prepared the way for the request for intercommunion. There is, first of all, the famous passage dealing with the vision of a united Church which is to be found in the reports of the Lambeth Conferences both of 1920 and 1930:

> The vision which rises before us is that of a Church, genuinely Catholic, loyal to all Truth, and gathering into its fellowship all "who profess and call themselves Christians" within whose visible unity all the treasures of faith and order, bequeathed as a heritage by the past to the present, shall be possessed in common, and made serviceable to the whole Body of Christ. Within this unity Christian Communions now separated from one another would retain much that has long been distinctive in their methods of worship and service. It is through a rich diversity of life and devotion that the unity of the whole fellowship will be fulfilled.

To this may be added the statement of the Lambeth Committee of Anglicans and Free Churchmen, which was appointed after 1920 and of which the two Archbishops were members:

> It seems to us in accordance with the Lambeth Appeal to say, as we are prepared to say, that the ministries we have in view in this memorandum—ministries which imply a sincere intention to preach Christ's Word and administer the Sacraments as Christ has ordained, and to which authority so to do has been solemnly given by the Churches concerned—are real ministries of Christ's Word and Sacraments in the Universal Church.

Room ought also to be found for the emphasis laid on humility (a new and a very modern note in ecclesiastical pronouncements) in the 1930 Conference Report. The Committee on Unity speaks of the need of

> humility in which each Church is willing for a change of mind in regard to its customary teaching. . . . This humility must lead to a readiness on the part of each Church to admit that in some respects it may have been wrong. If Churches fear for their own repute as they seek reunion, they cannot have enough contrition or humility to obtain it.

It is interesting, therefore, to see how the Anglican Church proceeds to guard itself against the possible inference that—whereas no Church is infallible and no ministry is recognized by all, but all are still real ministries within the Catholic Church—acts of intercommunion might be permitted between their several members We can enquire later whether the Anglican Communion is justified in thus guarding itself against intercommunion with Free Churchmen and whether its reasons for so doing are adequate, but meanwhile let us study the ground which is taken up for refusing the anticipated request.

It will be noted that the ground is characteristically chosen. It is not based upon fundamental principle but rather upon reasons of general convenience. The Church of Rome has a clear answer to give. Intercommunion with other Churches is impossible inasmuch as there is only one Church which is Rome, as witness the Pope's encyclical shortly after the Lausanne Conference!

> There is but one way in which the unity of Christians may be fostered, and that is by furthering the return to the one true Church of Christ of those who are separated from it; for from that one true Church they have in the past fallen away. . . .
>
> Furthermore, in this one Church of Christ no man can be or remain who does not accept, recognize, and obey the authority and supremacy of Peter and his legitimate successors. . . .

The Orthodox Church, speaking through the mouth of its representatives at Lausanne, has an equally clear answer to give: "Unless the common faith and confession of the Ancient Undivided Church of the Seven Ecumenical Councils and of the first eight is held in its entirety the question of intercommunion does not arise." "In the matter of faith and conscience there is room for no compromise . . . where the totality of the faith is lacking there can be no communion *in sacris*."

With the Anglican Church it is far otherwise. The formularies of the Church of England are quite decisive in their refusal to condemn the ministries of other Churches:

> And in these our doings we condemn no other nations, nor prescribe anything but to our own people only; for we think it convenient that every country should use such ceremonies as they shall think best to the setting forth of God's honour and glory, and to the reducing of the people to a most perfect and godly living without error or superstition; and that they should put away other things, which from time to time they perceive to be most abused, as in men's ordinances it often chanceth diversely in divers countries.—BOOK OF COMMON PRAYER.

Intercommunion with foreign Protestants was common in the seventeenth century. The testimony of Dr. Mason in his book *The Church of England and Episcopacy* will suffice:

"Communion was freely practised on both sides."

The exigencies of the modern situation as created in the mission field had compelled the Bishops themselves in the same Lambeth Conference of 1930 to sanction intercommunion when through distance or for other special reasons the ministry of a particular church was not available. No Church holding a "fundamental" principle which would prevent intercommunion with non-episcopal Churches would ever have passed this Resolution with or without a footnote!

> The Bishops of the Anglican Communion will not question the action of any Bishop who may, in his discretion so exercised, sanction an exception to the general rule in special areas, where the ministrations of an Anglican Church are not available for long periods of time or without travelling great distances, or may give permission that baptized communicant members of Churches not in communion with our own should be encouraged to communicate in Anglican churches, when the ministrations of their own Church are not available, or in other special or temporary circumstances.

It is reasonable, therefore, to look for secondary rather than primary reasons in the refusal, or perhaps it would be more correct to say in the formulated hesitation of the Anglican Church to practise the intercommunion which to some might seem implicit in its pronouncements. There is no definite attempt to base it on the doctrine of Apostolic Succession as Father Hebert attempts to do in his book on *Intercommunion*. It would be difficult for an Assembly containing within it a scholar like Dr. Headlam to do so without protest. He would no doubt have argued, not without considerable support, the thesis he asserted in his classic *The Doctrine of the Church and Christian Reunion*: namely that Our Lord did not directly institute or command episcopacy. We cannot claim that it is essential to the Church. Equally it is clear that there is no Apostolic ordinance to be quoted in its support. There is no adequate or sufficient evidence that it was instituted by Apostles. . . . The Church should freely create its own ministry, and might presumably also change at some future time what it has itself created, or adapt it to new conditions. We cannot therefore say that any form is essential to entitle it to be called a church, nor are we entitled to say that any particular Christian society has no claim to be considered a part of the Church because it has not a particular form of ministry.

It is true that much is said about the necessity of a ministry universally acknowledged as a prerequisite for reunion. It would be difficult, however, to take this ground explicitly as a prerequisite for intercommunion in view of the fact that the Anglican Church is ready for intercommunion with the Orthodox Church though neither possess a ministry universally acknowledged.

The Bishops proceed much more carefully. Dismissing the difficult subject of the universal ministry with the final comment that they are "persuaded" that the episcopal ministry provides evidence of the "divine intention" to provide one, they approach the subject of intercommunion in the following passage:

We cannot regard the maintenance of separately organized churches as a matter indifferent or unimportant. The will and intention to preserve the unity of the Spirit in the Body of Christ must of necessity underlie all its organization; and where that unity has been broken the earnest desire to restore union makes possible a recognition by the Church, in some respects, of ministries which, in separation, must stand on a different footing. The will and intention of Christians to perpetuate separately organized churches makes it inconsistent in principle for them to come before our Lord to be united as one body by the sacrament of His own Body and Blood. The general rule of our Church must therefore be held to ex-

clude indiscriminate intercommunion or any such intercommunion as expresses acquiescence in the continuance
of separately organized churches.

Here we reach the heart of the matter so far as the
opinion of the highest consultative authorities in the
Anglican Communion are concerned. As the report
is intended to be submitted to the judgement of each
constituent Church and no claim for infallibility is
made, it is not considered disrespectful in the Church
of England to submit the report to careful scrutiny.
Even the Articles of the Creeds are only binding on
the conscience of the Church of England in so far as
they may be proved from Holy Scripture. So much
may depend for the future on the attitude of the
Anglican Church to Intercommunion—so much that
is vital to our conception of Catholicity may be connected with it, that every word of the paragraph,
both in wording and the sense, is of the highest importance.

The wording, I am afraid, will be found on
examination to be very ambiguous, whatever views
may be taken with regard to the argument or conclusion. Apparently "the will and intention to preserve
the unity of the Spirit" is intended to be set in sharp
contrast with the "will and intention of Christians to
perpetuate separately organized Churches", with a
view to subsequent deductions from these two positions. But neither Churches nor individuals can easily
be divided under these two categories. There are
Churches, for example, like the Lutheran, which
laid great stress at the Lausanne Conference on
maintaining their independent witness for the present for the sake of vindicating and preserving the
truth for which they stood, but that is a very different
matter from willing in perpetuity a separate and independent life. Nor does it follow that the will and
intention to preserve the unity of the Spirit excludes
some forms of independently organized life. There

is the obvious example of the British Commonwealth of Nations and of the combination of federal and state authority in the organization of the United States of America. It would appear as if the Committee on Unity was perhaps subconsciously affected by the Roman view that the only alternative to our present separately organized life was the highly centralized, authoritative, and uniform system which it represents, whereas, of course, there are many other solutions open to the Anglican mind. There is, for example, the suggestion of Mr Kenneth Ingram, editor of the *Green Quarterly*, regarding "self-governing guilds within the embracing Christian Church". He writes as follows in his book "Has the Church Failed":

> It is inconceivable that unity will ever be secured by crushing the existing denominational varieties into one uniform pattern—so long, at least, as human minds and temperaments vary.
>
> Christian unity, however, would not necessarily be that indefinite undenominational spectre which Catholics suspect, whenever they are presented with a scheme which invites the intercommunion of sects. It requires no great imagination to conceive a scheme of reunion which would involve no serious compromise of existing principles. Such a Christian Church would require a common basis of belief, but, beyond that, each denomination could remain free to fulfil its own method of government, to follow its own form of worship, and even to differ in its interpretative creed. The denominations could, indeed, remain distinct as self-governing guilds within the embracing Christian Church.

But to return to the text of the Committee on Unity. It will be obvious that if the distinction between Churches holding the Unity of the Spirit and Churches seeking to "perpetuate" separate organizations cannot safely be made and does not correspond with the facts with which we have to deal, it is not easy to see how it would be inconsistent in *principle* for the Churches concerned "to come before one Lord to be united as one body by the sacrament of his own Body and Blood". We are asked in fact to accept a deduction based on what would appear to be an inaccurate analysis of the situation.

Nor does the disparaging reference to "indiscriminate intercommunion" in the same paragraph help us very much, inasmuch as no attempt is made to define what is meant by "indiscriminate". If the word is taken to mean thoughtless or ill-considered or disorderly, there can be no objection to its use, but if it is meant to rule out the possibility of all baptized persons of devout mind being brought into sacramental fellowship with one another at the Lord's Table, then the word is, unfortunately, highly controversial and out of place.

We must look for further guidance to the next paragraph, which is less involved and which perhaps with a certain sense of relief to its authors shifts the argument against intercommunion on to a psychological basis.

Here a new principle is brought to light—that intercommunion should be the goal of, rather than a means to the restoration of unity. It is not to be wondered at, however, if readers are surprised at the briefness of the reference and if they find it difficult to agree that "from what has been already said it will be evident" why such a principle should be held. Careful examination of the document does not disclose any discussion of intercommunion as a means to the restoration of unity. Much less does it disclose any commanding reasons against it.

On the contrary it would be easy to put together very strong presumptions from the report itself in favour of intercommunion. If "we acknowledge all those who believe in our Lord Jesus Christ and have been baptized into the Name of the Holy Trinity as sharing with us membership in the Universal Church"; *if* "we believe that God wills fellowship"; *if* we think of "the great Non-Episcopal Communions, standing for rich elements of truth, liberty, and life which might otherwise have been obscured or neglected"; *if* we admit that it is "the Holy Spirit of God Whose call led us all to our several ministries and Whose power enables us to perform them"; *if* "the times call us to a new outlook and new measures"; *if* "we believe that God Himself is calling us all to 'an adventure of goodwill'," there might well seem to be a *prima facie* case for intercommunion without further delay.

Anyone might be excused in the light of these statements for saying, after the manner of Peter in dealing with the doubtful question of Cornelius' baptism: "What doth hinder that these churches should receive the Holy Communion together?"

We are left, however, with the bald but important statement that the Holy Communion should be the goal rather than the means to Reunion and, as the official case against intercommunion—so far as documents are concerned—rests very largely upon this view of the Sacrament, it will be necessary to examine it more carefully. If it is intended to bear so great a weight as is upon it, it will not be amiss to test its soundness.

There are three questions which would seem to be pertinent in this connexion:

(1) Do we regard the Sacrament of Holy Communion as the goal of restoration of unity in our own Church or do we regard it as a means?

(2) Does the practice of intercommunion between Churches, so far as the evidence goes, retard the restoration of unity or hasten it?

(3) In the proposals which we have made to other Churches for the restoration of unity have we

presented to them this Sacrament of Holy Communion as the goal or a means?

When we have answered these questions we shall be in a better position to judge the validity of the general principle which, perhaps too hastily, the Bishops asserted that they held, namely "that intercommunion should be the goal of, rather than a means to the restoration of Union".

(1) With regard to our own Anglican Church it it difficult to think of the principle being applied. All the varying parties and schools of thought—Anglo-Catholics and Evangelicals, Fundamentalists and Modernists—are encouraged by authority to meet together at the Lord's Table. It is hoped that by the common reception of the Life of Christ in that Sacrament the spirit of loving-kindness may be shed abroad through its constituent members. We do not hesitate reverently and humbly to make use of the service as an appointed means for the appointed end of unity. Such services are arranged regularly in connexion with Chapter Meetings, Diocesan Conferences, and Synods, and they are valued for their psychological effect in bringing people together in a common act of faith and penitence and dedication. They promote the family spirit, and we are not ashamed to value them for this amongst other reasons.

It is true that the Rev. A. G. Hebert in his book on Intercommunion goes so far as to say in reference to the Holy Communion that "we need to be greatly afraid if there is even a suspicion that we may be using it as a means to an end".[1] But he is thinking not of internal but external intercommunion, and in any case the reason that he gives for his warning is not very convincing. It is because "The Sacrament is God's Sacrament and the Table the Lord's Table".[2] Why God should not use his Sacrament or

---

[1] A. G. Hebert, *Intercommunion*, p. 110.   [2] *Ibid.*

his Table as he uses other means of grace as means to ends is not explained and perhaps is beyond explanation. The official silence of Lambeth is not therefore materially helped by this *obiter dictum*.

It may quite fairly be taken for granted that within the Anglican Church itself, as far as the various parties are concerned, there is no desire to establish the general principle that intercommunion should be the goal of rather than a means to the restoration of Union. It is the failure of Evangelical and Anglo-Catholic to communicate together and the loss which the whole Church sustains through their sacramental isolation from one another which is officially lamented. No one is in the least likely to say, "Be careful lest you should come to the Holy Communion with those in your own Church with whom you differ in doctrine or teaching lest either of you should be guilty of using the Sacrament as a means to the end of cementing the bond of union between you". Far from it. Not long ago, with the approval of the Archbishop of York, a conference of Evangelicals and "Catholics" to discuss Eucharistic Unity was held under the chairmanship of the Rev. H. C. Carpenter, now Dean of Exeter. Its object "was to prove to the world that the Church of England is *not* hopelessly divided within itself; to show that reconciliation is possible, and that our underlying unity is far greater than our differences"; the closing words of the Manifesto which was issued by this Conference are significant for our purpose, and may fairly be quoted as shewing that the Anglican Church has no difficulty in thinking of the Holy Communion as a means of promoting Unity at least within its own borders: "we affirm that the faithful use of the Lord's Supper can alone reveal its inexhaustible meaning, and *that in the unity of experience we shall draw nearer to unity in belief*".

(2) In endeavouring to answer the question

whether intercommunion between Churches retards or hastens reunion, it is important to bear in mind that what is under discussion is not the inter-communion of individual members of Churches with no thought of promoting organic reunion behind it, or even the action of representative groups of people of different Churches working for organic unity, but whether the recognition by friendly Churches of the practice of intercommunion by their members retards or hastens reunion.

There would seem to be overwhelming evidence that the first Churches to awake to the new spirit of Unity which marks this present century were Churches which had managed in their separation from one another to preserve still the habit of communicating with one another at the Lord's Table. All the triumphs which so far have been achieved in the realm of organic unity in Canada, Australia, and Great Britain have been achieved between Churches where this relationship already existed, and the claim is repeatedly made that without it reunion would have been far more difficult if not impossible. Dr. Carnegie Simpson, writing of the reunited Church of Scotland, makes this comment: "Would the great union recently consummated in Scotland have had the glimmer of the ghost of success if the pulpits and Communion Tables in the one Church were barred against the ministers and members of the other?"[1] The same view is held by Methodist leaders with regard to the success of Methodist reunion in this country. It may be regarded as beyond doubt that the non-episcopal Free Churches at any rate regard the practice of intercommunion as helping and not hindering reunion. The general verdict is that they could not have gone on without it.

There is also a mass of evidence to shew that Reunion between the Church of England and non-

[1] *Call for Christian Unity*, p. 133.

episcopal Churches is being held up through the postponement of intercommunion. In generous recognition of the special difficulties of the Church of England some Free Churchmen in this country do not officially advocate intercommunion. This attitude is taken up not on principle but as an accommodation to what is still the dominant view in the Church of England. Until the Church of England is ready for it many do not think it dignified to press for it or to accept the limited "one-sided reciprocity" which is sometimes offered. Some of the Free Church leaders are also naturally very much impressed by their contacts with Lambeth and acquire a certain reserve on the subject in deference to the Anglican atmosphere which they have unconsciously assimilated. But when the Free Churches abandon "the principle of economy" and speak their whole mind on the subject of the steps necessary to reunion, stress is always laid upon the value of considered acts of intercommunion. Sometimes the case is put in the very modest way in which Dr. Carnegie Simpson puts it in his essay in *The Call for Christian Unity*:

> Union movement cannot live on conference and declaration alone, but the words of union must be accompanied by acts of union. The acts of union I mean are, or include, occasional interchange of pulpits and occasional intercommunion—the former not to talk about union, but to preach Christ, who is our common Lord, and the latter not as "hospitality", but because the Lord's Table is not our own, but His.

More often the case is stated in wider and more comprehensive terms, as set forth in the reply of the Federal Council of the Free Churches to the recent Manifesto on Church Unity addressed by many leading Anglicans (including several diocesan Bishops), to the Free Churches of Great Britain and to the Church of Scotland:

The Council values the readiness shewn in the Manifesto for practical steps which would give expression to the spirit of unity. In particular, it has always maintained that admission to the Lord's Table of one another's communicant members would be a great advance in the cause of unity. The Council cannot accept the position that intercommunion should be regarded as the goal, not as a means of union. The Lord's Table is the meeting-place of Christ with His people and of His people with one another in Him, and His people should be welcomed in all branches of His Church in His name.

This request for intercommunion has been reiterated once more in the Resolution of the Council passed after consideration of the Report from the joint conference of Lambeth which submitted to it *A Sketch of a United Church*. After welcoming the *Sketch*, the resolution proceeds as follows:

In so doing, the Council reiterates its repeated assertion that schemes of unity such as this, must, if they are to have effect on the mind of the Church generally, be accompanied by acts of unity . . . and it feels justified, after the lapse of some fourteen years since the inception of the joint conferences, in asking what practical steps in the expression of unity the representatives of the Church of England are prepared now to take?

And when we turn to the negotiations for Reunion with the Church of Scotland we find that the trouble over the lack of intercommunion has become still more acute. Here we are dealing with a Church very conscious of its historic independence and its national importance. Without any discourtesy to the Free Churches in this country, whose oecumenical importance is quite equal to our own, it may be said that here in this country they are very much overshadowed by the prestige of the Church of England and, if the phrase may be permitted, it is not very easy for them psychologically to negotiate with the Church of England on equal terms. It is very different, however, with the Church of Scotland, whose scholarship makes it formidable in debate and whose national consciousness makes it particularly sensitive to its spiritual independence. Here the damaging effects of the failure to accept intercommunion as "a means" to Reunion may be expected to be felt in their full rigour.

The General Assembly of the Church of Scotland has interrupted the peaceful proceedings of its own joint conference with the Anglican Church on the subject of Reunion by instructing its members to inform the Anglican representatives "with a view to prevent any possible misunderstanding that any agreement with regard to the Orders and Sacraments of the conferring Churches can only be based on the recognition of the equal standing of the accepted communicants and ministers in each".

In other words, the Church of Scotland asks for full intercommunion with the Church of England as the first step towards the realization of a closer unity.

Whatever view may be taken of the action of the Assembly, which by a small majority decided to throw this bombshell into the conference chamber, it is clear that further progress cannot easily be made without some reconsideration of the subject of inter-communion, and it can hardly be denied that this lack of intercommunion is a serious hindrance to the restoration of mutual confidence and goodwill which are the essential preliminaries of Reunion.

When we come to the third question, whether we have in fact presented to other Churches the Sacra-ment of Holy Communion as the goal rather than the means of reunion, we are bound to face that other question which, though kept out of sight in official statements, is really present in the minds of most Anglicans: Do we differentiate in this matter between Episcopal and non-Episcopal Churches? If we are really serious in regarding intercommunion as the goal of organic reunion, then we would expect the same reserves in dealing with Old Catholics and the Swedish Church and the Greek Orthodox Church as with the Lutheran, Presbyterian, and the English Free Churches. But in reality it is not so. The bond of episcopacy seems to be closer than any other bond which unites us to these Churches of the Reformation spirit and tradition. To stand "in the succession of the Reformed Churches" does not seem to be accounted quite as noble as to stand in what is called the Apostolical Succession. That is at least the imputation to which we expose ourselves by our handling of the subject of intercommunion.

For many years the Anglican Church has been interested in trying to arrange for intercommunion with the Orthodox Church. "Terms of Intercommunion suggested between the Church of England and the Churches in Communion with her and the Eastern Orthodox Church" were published as far back as 1921 under the auspices of the Archbishop of Canterbury's Eastern Churches Committee. These terms of intercommunion received quasi-official sanction at the Lambeth Conference of 1930, and a good deal of the time of its Committee on Unity was taken up with exploring the possibilities of intercommunion with the Orthodox. There was no hesitation in regarding intercommunion as a "means" of promoting closer unity.

Similarly with regard to the Old Catholics, a small and relatively unimportant body but one possessing episcopal orders and the "Apostolical Succession," the Anglican Church proved itself very ready to arrange for intercommunion. Considerable progress was made in this direction at the Lambeth Conference which received a delegation from the Old Catholic Church, and complete intercommunion was agreed upon at the Conference held at Bonn, July 1931, and ratified the next year by Convocation. Without waiting for organic unity, while indeed actually asserting their "independence", the Church of England and the Old Catholics entered upon full inter-communion with each other.

The terms agreed upon are important, indicating how far the Church of England is in reality prepared to go where the non-episcopal complex does not arise:

(1) Each Communion recognizes the catholicity and independence of the other and maintains its own.

(2) Each Communion agrees to admit members of the other Communion to participate in the Sacraments.

(3) Intercommunion does not require from either Communion the acceptance of all doctrinal opinion, sacramental devotion, or liturgical practice characteristic of the other, but implies that each believes the other to hold all the essentials of the Christian Faith.

In view of these facts it seems hardly worth while to examine further the official attitude of the Church of England to Intercommunion. It is evident that we are dealing with a process of rationalization in which a position arrived at either intuitively or on the grounds of expediency is defended by arguments that do not properly belong to it. Intercommunion *does* foster the spirit of unity within our own Church. Intercommunion *has* as a matter of history made it much easier for Churches which have preserved the practice to reunite. If the problem before us were simply confined to uniting with other Churches enjoying episcopal orders and the "Apostolic Succession", we should probably never have heard of this distinction between "the means" and "the goal". We should everywhere take full advantage of the psychological and spiritual possibilities of sacramental fellowship to prepare the way for organic reunion.

The policy outlined at the Lambeth Conference must be regarded as an interim one. The results of scholarship as well as the new spirit of charity and the hard facts of the situation make it impossible for the experienced leaders of the Church to condemn inter-communion. It is so obviously the corollary to their own policy of conciliation and fellowship. But a large part of the Church still draws distinctions between episcopal and non-episcopal ministries, which were bequeathed to it by the Oxford Movement. It may be that this fact accounts very largely for official hesitation. We are continually embarrassed by the knowledge that we are not a homogeneous Church.

A Policy for the Future

We may now turn to consider questions of future policy, and I think we may be prepared to do so in a reasonably hopeful frame of mind. Not only is there no decisive barrier to be found in our formularies or erected by our Episcopate against Intercommunion, but the whole temper of the modern mind whether in Evangelical or even in Catholic circles is sensitive to intercommunion. Quite a large number of "Catholics" are prepared to support intercommunion of the limited kind which allows non-episcopalians on special occasions to receive the Holy Communion with their Anglican brethren according to the Anglican rite. The conditions under which this arrangement is sanctioned by authority is set out by the Resolutions of the Upper Houses of Convocation passed in 1931. They permit

(*a*) baptized communicant members of other churches "cut off by distance" from their own church to be welcomed to Communion.

(*b*) In Schools or College chapels communicant members of other Churches belonging to the

School or College may communicate together according to the Anglican rite.

(c) On special occasions where Anglicans and non-Anglicans are engaged "in some form of Christian endeavour" and are in sympathy with the project of visible and organic unity the Bishop may approve the holding of a Corporate Communion according to the Anglican rite.

Under the heading (c) many conferences now have the happiness of meeting together round the Lord's Table, and though the present Bishop of Derby recently refused his sanction or permission to the semi-official body "The Friends of Reunion" to hold such a service at Swanwick, compelling them to look out for another site situated in more friendly episcopal country for the next year's conference, there is usually little difficulty in securing the required permission. It may be taken for granted that unless the whole reunion movement receives some quite unexpected check this procedure will become normal. Already we have begun to laugh, Catholics and Evangelicals alike, at the old days when furtive invitations at dead of night would be given by Anglicans at such conferences to their Nonconformist friends "to come next morning to the Holy Communion". So long as "no public invitation" was given it was superstitiously felt that Church order had not been broken! It may well happen that equally amusing stories will one day be told of "the one-sided reciprocity" which characterized the intercommunion services during the years of our Lord 1930–40. But meantime they do go on bringing a real sense of fellowship, thanks to the Christian forbearance of the non-Anglicans who are content to wait for their Anglican brethren to open their hearts and their minds a little wider.

In some places this opening of the heart and mind

a little wider has begun. Some Bishops have begun to recognize that ordinary Christian congregations which have been drawn into close touch with one another in service for the Kingdom of God may be regarded as groups "engaged in some form of Christian endeavour" and "in sympathy with the progress of visible and organic unity" and have sanctioned intercommunion services. This is not only a welcome widening of the boundaries but an important recognition of the psychology of intercommunion. It has too easily been assumed that it ought to be the prerogative of the chosen few and that ordinary congregations were not ripe for it or could not be prepared for it. Whereas if the argument of this essay is sound that sacramental fellowship is the healing balsam that God intends for the recovery of the Church's unity, it shews true insight to begin its application where it is most needed. Church leaders have already reached a position of mutual fellowship and intercourse far in advance of their followers. They cannot hope to implement such schemes as are set before us in *A Sketch of a United Church* unless congregations of different denominations, and more particularly Anglican and Free, are drawn into closer sympathy and understanding with one another.

It is for this reason, therefore, that the carefully planned advances which are associated with the Birmingham diocese and of which the Parish Church of St. Martin has been regarded as the centre, should be studied without prejudice—certainly without malice—and even it may be with sympathy and encouragement. It was recognized from the start, which dates back to 1925, that no hasty intercommunion between congregations was desirable, but that such a spirit of fellowship and intercourse "in some form of common endeavour" should be created as would eventually justify congregations in sealing their unity in sacramental obedience to their common Lord. Through a long series of joint enterprises for the Kingdom of God culminating in the great Inter-denominational Crusade of 1930, typical congregations such as St. Martin's and the Methodist Central Hall learned to work and think together and share in a common life. After years of such campaigning in Christ's work and with the hope of a larger and more satisfying unity ever before the mind, sacramental fellowship has been from time to time congregationally enjoyed according to the Anglican rite. Nor has this in any sense been imposed from above. For in the case of St. Martin's not only had the approval of the Bishop and the Rector been secured but a unanimous vote of the Parochial Church Council endorsed the venture. Similar steps were taken "on the other side" to ensure that the Act of Intercommunion carried with it full corporate significance.

Quite recently the question of "reciprocity" was faced and answered after careful consideration by St. Martin's congregation. Representative members accepted an invitation to the Central Hall to receive, on a special occasion, the Holy Communion at Methodist hands according to the Methodist rite. This action, admittedly of a pioneer character, passed with surprisingly little comment, much to the satisfaction of those who were concerned only with the witness given and spiritual blessing received. No greater testimony to the value of careful preparation through a period of years and to the wisdom of the policy that sacramental fellowship is something to be "earned" could be found than the quiet acceptance of this service by the religious community of Birmingham as something really guided and inspired by the Spirit of God. No one thought of bringing against it that most painful of all accusations to those filled with a deep spiritual concern—that its pro-

moters were engineering a stunt. Even the newspapers, which might have surrounded the service with
a setting which would have spoiled its spiritual significance, said nothing to rob it of its dignity. It was
generally regarded, even if not according to strict
rule, as having earned its right to appear on the
horizon.

The question of how far pioneers may be allowed
to advance in front of the main body is one which in
the Church of England has a quite special and
unique importance. History has shewn them constantly at work innovating within the established
order and creating new precedents which in their
turn have become established customs. "The Rule
of the Church" has adjusted itself in this curious way
to the demands of new movements of the Spirit. The
lack of homogeneity in the Church and the extreme
clumsiness of the machinery for regularizing and
authorizing change largely accounts for the importance of the pioneer in the Church of England. It
cannot be claimed that he has always acted wisely or
that every innovation has made good or finally
established itself within the constitution of the
Church of England, but to an extent quite amazing
to the foreign onlooker he has proved successful and
has eventually imposed his belief or practice on
the Church to which he belongs. To an extent too,
which is hard for others closely governed by the will
of an assembly or by a strictly codified constitution
to realize, the authorities of the Church of England
have acquiesced in this initiative, exercising a kind
of judicial function in assessing the value of the
results. In theory this arrangement is very vulnerable,
but, like many other English institutions based on
the empirical method, it continues to work and provides a way of escape from the purely static. From
this point of view the pioneer, though technically
outside the law or the usage of the moment, is helping

to shape the rule of the Church in accordance with some new movement of the Spirit of God. Provided that he is not merely self-willed but is willing to submit his experiments to the final judgement of the Church to which he belongs, he is fulfilling, and is increasingly recognized to be fulfilling, a useful purpose. He may even be doing more than this. Sometimes he may be saving his Church from the dead hand of the past and staking out for it at the same time a claim to new life in the future.

At any rate his position is fairly recognized in the Church of England, and though the treatment he receives naturally varies with the opinions which authority forms of his sincerity and intelligence, he receives on the whole a sufficient modicum of sympathy. If, moreover, he is a genuine pioneer, he will be content to carry on with no sympathy at all provided the work is not hindered.

It is in this way that those who advocate, and who, on some occasions where they believe themselves to have been so guided, practise reciprocity, would desire to present themselves to their brethren who may be critical of their teaching or their practice.

They would ask for patience and that their sense of vocation in the practice of sacramental fellowship may be tested by results. They are confident that they are blazing the trail for the road-makers of the Reunion highway who follow after. Time will tell, and, if the practice be of God, the Church will do well to have escaped the stigma of thwarting it.

There are some who think that the South India scheme of Reunion may be quoted as an outstanding scheme of Reunion between Anglicans and Free Churchmen which has been brought within measurable distance of success without the aid of intercommunion and are inclined to argue from this example against the usefulness of the policy outlined above. But the general principle of the Comity of

Missions usually brings it about that there is only one branch of the Christian Church (other than the Roman which rejects the principle *in toto*) working in a particular area, and the question of inter-communion does not arise as it does at home through the pressure of immediate contact. Further, where circumstances demand it owing to the communicant being separated from his own Church, intercom-munion with full reciprocity is freely practised in the mission field in accordance with Resolution 42 of the Lambeth Conference. And as regards the South India scheme itself the earnest desire for inter-communion as a stepping-stone did make itself so strongly felt that in 1932 Anglican members engaged in the negotiations were left free by Synodical authority to engage in reciprocal intercommunion, and such services were actually held to deepen the growing spirit of unity. The scheme contemplates a period of thirty years after fusion has taken place during which episcopally ordained and non-episco-pally ordained clergy will be living together in the same communion and will presumably often come to the Lord's Table together. It would certainly be un-wise to quote the South India scheme as a *bona fide* exception to the general principle laid down in 1909 by the present Bishop of Durham in the course of a lecture on Reunion:

> Intercommunion is the necessary expression of full re-cognition, and therefore is the true preliminary to any useful discussion of corporate union. When the Churches have entered into the religious covenant of Christian dis-cipleship, of which the common reception of the Holy Communion is the appointed symbol, then they can dis-cuss without suspicion or humiliation the further ques-tion, whether they should or should not merge their separate organizations.

I do not think that anything in the future can really hold up the practice of intercommunion as "a means to an end". It is impossible to think that the spirit of fellowship will pour itself through every other channel and ignore the sacrament of fellowship itself. History indicates an incurable tendency where hearts and minds are moved towards unity to seek to express it in sacramental form. We see the revisers of the Authorized Version of the Bible, Anglican and non-Anglican, gathering round the Lord's Table in Westminster Abbey in the year 1870 to consecrate the fruit of their labours. Long afterwards in the fulness of time we see a far larger company, this time of missionaries, likewise Anglican and non-Anglican —meeting spontaneously on Easter Day—on the Mount of Olives at the close of the Jerusalem Conference to dedicate their work together at the Table of their common Lord. Some day the whole Church will feel the shame that some of us experience when we recall that all mention of that most memorable of services was omitted if not expunged from the official report. The deep impression that service produced on one of those privileged to be present to take part may be gathered from these words written by the Rev. G. H. Harris, at that time Editorial Secretary of the Church Missionary Society:

Easter morning on the Mount of Olives. The high wind which had been blowing continuously for some days and nights had dropped. The stillness was broken only by the birds whose Easter anthem greeted the sunrise. The city was soon bathed in the soft light of early day: the Temple enclosure and the buildings of the old city were luminous. Jerusalem seemed to float between heaven and earth, bright and mystical. The morning: the view before us: the song of the birds: the quiet: all combined to speak to the soul the triumphant message of victory and peace: "He is risen".

With full hearts we gathered in the Meeting Hall for our Easter Communion. Late last night the business of this momentous conference had ended. This morning the Hall was filled once more that now, discussion, debate, hard thought and careful planning laid aside, we all might renew our fellowship with the Risen Lord and with each other, and express that fellowship in the way which He ordained.

Had ever such a Eucharist been celebrated before? Sons and daughters of forty and more nations, members of many different branches of the Church, all divisions and barriers done away in the unity of Christ. As we kneel in the silence the purpose of all our labour in this place becomes clear and sanctified. We are called to be members of His Body; we are renewing our life for service by Communion with our Lord this Easter morning. We are showing to Him, to each other, and to the world, that all races and tongues are one loaf, one Body.

The Service begins. It is intensely simple in form; utterly real; lacking all aesthetic aids to worship, yet instinct with His Spirit. He is Risen; but He is here. The sacred elements are blessed and are brought to us by those who are assisting the celebrant. Indian and Chinese join with brothers from America and England in administering to us "the ration bread of God's army; the stirrup cup of His saints". We sit in the silence until the great company has received the Gifts. Then the Lord's Prayer; the Gloria in Excelsis; the Benediction, and last of all the ancient Easter Greeting: "The Lord is Risen", and with one voice the response is made: "He is Risen indeed".

We pass out again into the sunshine, conscious of fellowship renewed, spiritualized, and of a new joy in fellowship rising in our hearts. We have been obedient to our Lord's command. We have turned from all the ecclesiastical divisions and concerns which mar that fellowship and deaden our witness, unto Him. For many of us the realization of Communion in its fullest sense has never been so real. Our conference together has been lifted up on to the highest of all levels. God give us strength of purpose, readiness to suffer and to sacrifice, until all His children everywhere can make this corporate dedication of life, and offer to Him this perfect expression of the Fellowship which is the Spirit's highest gift to the Church.

Some day such an experience in the quiet setting

of an English village or in the heart of a great city may inaugurate a new epoch in the history of the Reunion movement of this country. The spirit of expectancy and receptivity has begun to make itself manifest in congregational life. And what has been experienced by scholars and missionaries in great moments of inspiration has become available for simple folk. So we trace the gradual fulfilment of God's purpose and rejoice in the ever-widening use of the Sacrament of Redeeming Love as a means to unite his people in closer bonds of fellowship and service.

An Appeal

It remains to make an appeal to our Fathers in God to be willing to reconsider their own attitude in the light of the arguments now presented to them. Must we wait until the persecution, which is bound eventually here as elsewhere to fall upon the Church if it is faithful in its witness to its Lord, to break down the barriers which divide us from our brethren? We know in our hearts that these "confessional" Christians in Germany who are willing to face the horror of concentration camps for the sake of loyalty to our Common Lord have justified their right to every acknowledgement of their Catholicity that we can give them. Is it conceivable that we should refuse to admit them to Holy Communion if they came to this country or refuse to communicate with them in their own?

Do we realize the astonishment that it causes them when they find the English clergy who go out to confer with them so preoccupied with questions of "order" when the fundamentals of the Christian Faith are in such grievous peril? To them living in the midst of wholesale apostasy it is the possession of a living faith, not the possession of a particular form of Government, which is the pre-requisite for sacramental fellowship. Do not our theologians, who so often give the appearance of treating the Sacraments as a subsection of the question of Order, need to recover their sense of proportion?

Or, again, do we realize how our refusal of reciprocity with non-episcopalians at home combined with our eagerness for reciprocity abroad, wherever Episcopal Orders are forthcoming, affects our influence on the national life. We have set forth no really convincing reason for refusing, and the nation comes to regard religion as essentially a divisive rather than a unifying force. Some of the more impatient of the younger generation are inclined even to ignore the Sacrament of Holy Communion altogether on the ground that it is the symbol of division rather than of unity. The result is a serious weakening in the effective witness which we might give to the nation.

In these circumstances it does not seem wholly unreasonable to ask the leaders of the Church to inaugurate a forward move. We are all conscious of the dangers to which pioneers are exposed. It is easy for them to make mistakes and to be guilty of extravagances if in their enthusiasm they get too far ahead of the opinion which is slowly consolidating behind them. In vindicating a great principle there is always need of wise leadership, and we appeal to the Bishops to indicate the best line of advance towards the realization of reciprocal sacramental fellowship amongst those who have the will to unite. It is perhaps too much to expect of the Bishops to put themselves at the head of such a movement—even one which their own wise statesmanship has helped to create. The role of the Anglican Episcopate in such matters has rather been that of considered restraint or benevolent encouragement. But to leave the movement for intercommunion just as it is at present and its pioneers wholly without guidance would be deplorable.

It is therefore much to be regretted that the recent resolution passed in April 1934 by the Anglican Evangelical Group Movement, representing some twelve hundred clergy and respectfully presented to the Bishops, has as yet received so little consideration. This resolution, which was submitted to the various groups of the Movement throughout the country before submission to the Episcopate, ran as follows:

> That this Conference of the Anglican Evangelical Group Movement records its conviction that the time has come when further steps should be taken in the matter of Intercommunion between the Church of England and those non-Episcopal Churches whose ministries have already been acknowledged to be real ministries of Christ's Word and Sacraments in the universal Church, and respectfully urges the Bishops to foster and regulate such Intercommunion as may seem desirable in the general interests of Reunion.

This resolution sums up with exactitude the position which we have reached to-day whether we view it from inside or outside the Church of England. It represents the natural deduction which seems to be implicit in the episcopal pronouncements on Reunion and to correspond to the whole trend of our new conception of how we are related to one another within the Catholic Church. It is very far from being a "Bolshevik" resolution. It makes its appeal to the proper quarter and recognizes the need for guidance.

What reply will eventually be forthcoming? The writer believes with the utmost conviction that on the ultimate answer depends the further progress, the success or failure of Reunion with the Presbyterian Church and the Free Churches with which we have been so long in conference. He believes, too, that the time factor is of the greatest importance. St. Paul attributes the amazing success of his own spiritual adventure in Christ Jesus to the fact that he "was not *disobedient* to the heavenly vision". Visions fade where there is not the courage or the skill to implement them. History is strewn with the wreck of such visions and with the tragedy of those who were "disobedient" to them.

Those words which when first uttered awakened a thrill in every heart—

> The vision which rises before us is that of a Church, genuinely Catholic, loyal to all Truth, and gathering into its fellowship all "who profess and call themselves Christians" within whose visible unity all the treasures of faith and order, bequeathed as a heritage by the past to the present, shall be possessed in common, and made serviceable to the whole Body of Christ

—become more challenging every day. Presently they may become ominous if they are repeated too often without the fulfilment which should accompany them. It is in the earnest hope of doing something to throw open the road through sacramental fellowship to ordered unity that this paper has been written.

V

THE NEW CATHOLICISM. II

THE INTERCHANGE OF PULPITS

by

CHARLES E. RAVEN, D.D.

Chaplain to H.M. the King
Regius Professor of Divinity in the University of Cambridge
Canon of Ely
Chancellor Emeritus of Liverpool

SYNOPSIS

A New Impetus

THE Great War gave a new impetus to interdenominational relationships. Free Churchmen were not infrequently invited to occupy Anglican pulpits, but ecclesiastical authority was niggardly in imposing conditions, and while granting principles, haggled over details. Nevertheless the practice of inviting members of other denominations to preach in our churches and cathedrals has been sufficiently established to make its continuance certain. It may well be that canonically the practice is justified if the bishop grants a licence to the preacher, but however that may be it is certain that men who were not Anglican clergy have in the past been occasionally admitted to Anglican pulpits, while from the beginning of the present century there has been a revival of this practice.

The Lambeth Conference of 1920

Owing to the effects on religious life and thought of the upheaval of the Great War, the Lambeth Conference of 1920 met under a sense of urgency and need. In recognizing the spiritual reality of non-episcopal ministries it swept aside such secondary questions as the technique of ordination. In countenancing, under certain conditions, invitations to non-Anglicans to preach in Anglican churches it admitted the necessity for mutual understanding and granted opportunities for its development.

The Sequel

The warmth and spontaneity of the Lambeth Conference, the belief that the fact that existing denominational barriers are largely obsolete was about to be accepted in practice, encouraged the hope of further developments. The sequel was disappointing although the Convocations approved of the Conference Report. Bishops who had been enthusiastic began to repent. Organized and influential opposition to any advance made itself strongly felt. Inspiration was dissipated in prolonged debate. However, the Conference's sanction remains, and, though there has been no general comradeship, there has been much individual fraternizing.

THE VALUE OF INTERCHANGE OF PULPITS

I. UNITY EMPHASIZED

The motive of the sanction by the Lambeth Conference of interchange of pulpits was the promotion of reunion. Though missionaries and ex-chaplains had come to realize the essential unity of the reformed Churches the parochial clergy and their congregations had not made any such discovery. But the custom of inviting preachers of other denominations has revealed to congregations how much in common the various churches possess, and has served to dispel ignorance and misunderstanding.

II. ENLARGEMENT OF SYMPATHY AND INCREASE OF VITALITY

In an ancient Church developments have so elaborated the simplicity of the Gospel that the distinction between the primary or universal and the secondary has become confused. A visiting preacher of another Church naturally concentrates on matters of vital import and thus recalls the congregation to the centre of Christian experience. It is an advantage to be able to avail ourselves of the knowledge and inspiration of men whose training is somewhat different from that of the Anglican clergy and who by their traditions attach a special importance to the prophetic aspect of the ministry.

III. REINTERPRETATION OF THE FAITH

In view of the new knowledge and outlook of the last century, its wide diffusion among the multitude and the rapidity of present changes in the world of thought, the task of theological reinterpretation is urgent and difficult. On one side is the danger of a premature synthesis, on the other the danger of stereotyping some dogmatic position of the past under the influence of the panic cry, "the Faith in danger". In these circumstances denominational exclusiveness should not hinder full co-operation and collaboration in a task which is common to all Christians. It is not enough that there should be such co-operation in the Universities. It should touch the mass of church-people. The interchange of pulpits helps greatly to this end.

COMRADESHIP AND THE CHALLENGE TO CHRISTIANITY

Everywhere there is emerging a plain alternative between the religion of Christ and a humanistic idealism. In the last generation the restraints of privilege and tradition, which in the past favoured religion, have disappeared, and agnosticism has become popular. The need for mutual understanding between the denominations is great, while the divisions between the Reformed Communions are mostly concerned with matters of little interest to the laity. The discreditable divisions and the tone of denominational controversies alienate many people from religion. The practice of the interchange of pulpits is a practical demonstration that we are rising above the old exclusiveness. It helps us to transcend ecclesiastical antipathies. The distinction between holding joint meetings in a secular hall and admitting preachers from other churches to preach in our churches is based on no principle. A church should not be regarded as an exclusive club, but as a home in which we welcome the stranger and wish to do him honour.

LAW, LOVE, AND LIBERTY

Many would counter the objection which is made on legalistic grounds to interchange of pulpits by challenging the conception of the Church as analogous to a nation or empire. The Christian relationship is not like a relationship imposed by legal obligation and administered by statutory authority. An illustration of the distinction is provided by the contrast between the tone of the Lambeth Conference of 1920 and the tone of the Lambeth Conference of 1930. The history of the past fifteen years makes it clear that our hope must rest not in concordats between the heads of Churches, but in the growth of mutual trust and friendliness based on co-operation between the members. Anglo-Catholicism, which has won its position by flouting authority, is not consistent in appealing to authority to suppress action which it finds uncongenial. In fact a constitutional attack on interchange of pulpits is now unlikely. Liberal churchmen must see to it, by their own action, that interchange of pulpits does not come to be regarded as a mere amiable extravagance practised at a few centres.

The New Alignment

For those who accept the modern outlook and the results of the new knowledge, the old denominational barriers have lost their meaning. The future promises to bring a fresh alignment of Christian groups. The issues involved lie deeper than the more conspicuous subjects of ecclesiastical controversy. Those who accept the new outlook find themselves drawn into a real unity with those in other Churches who share their convictions, a unity unaffected by Church Order or other superficial divergencies. It is a unity of the Spirit. There are differences of ethos and atmosphere reflecting the characteristic qualities of different denominations; but it is an enrichment to experience these. Approach from another angle corrects and solidifies our own vision.

A Call to Action

The writer's experience of co-operation with other Churches has taught him the spiritual value of such activities and convinced him of the vastness of the opportunities open to the Church of England in promoting closer relationships. A great and important field of activity lies open and Modern Churchmen should enter on it with eagerness. We should be bold to use and extend our liberties. We should not allow the official desire for safety and stability to discourage experiments. The dominant official policy is one of stabilization, theological and otherwise, the regimentation of new developments by the exercise of episcopal control, and the filling of key ecclesiastical positions by "safe" men. The worst dangers threatened by this policy can only be counteracted by the action of those who are conscious of them. An obvious means is the cultivation of Christian friendliness with our fellow-workers in other Churches.

V

THE NEW CATHOLICISM. II

THE INTERCHANGE OF PULPITS

A New Impetus

It was August 4, 1915, and the parish church, huge and usually desolate, was crowded for the United Service which the new incumbent, greatly daring, had arranged. Both in general and in detail the venture had been an anxious one. He had been brought up in circles in which Free Churchmen were styled dissenters and never mentioned except with contempt, and though he was learning to speak of them as "our Nonconforming brethren" he was not yet free from self-consciousness in so doing. Moreover, the little town had three chapels—Congregationalist, Baptist, and Wesleyan—and how to find parts for their several ministers in an Anglican Evensong was a delicate question. There would be two lessons: that would satisfy two-thirds of the problem. There remained prayers and sermon. Was it more irregular to allow the Baptist, the senior and most prominent of them, to preach or to pray? He had decided to take the service himself—partly to avoid difficulties about the Absolution, partly from a well-founded distrust of his prophetic powers. But the dilemma had been very worrying.

Never mind: the town obviously approved: the Church was full: there was a war on: and the atmosphere was charged with appeals for unity. Surely he had acted properly. A glow of satisfaction and the stirring of something less unchristian made his wel-

199

come to the three visitors to his vestry almost cordial: so much so that when the Baptist diffidently suggested that he supposed he ought to preach from the lectern, his caution forsook him. "You really can't preach when you've got the head of a brazen bird between you and the congregation—and you can't be heard except from the pulpit. Of course you must preach from it."

A week later came an interview with the Bishop. "Yes, I see your difficulty about his taking the prayers. Perhaps you were justified in asking him to preach. After all the times are exceptional. But you had no sort of right to allow him to use the pulpit. You really must be more discreet in future." It was kindly said. The Bishop had not disapproved of the service: instead he had fastened upon a detail in which common sense came into conflict with tradition. "Ask him if you like; but be sure to put him in his proper place. Ask him; but make your invitation an insult." That was how the incumbent, who was far more angry than if his whole action had been condemned, interpreted the warning.

That incident is typical. In the past twenty years such ventures have become frequent. The good seed sown by Father Plater and Bishop Gore, Will Reason and Miss Lucy Gardner when they established the precedent of interdenominational co-operation in social and industrial affairs, has borne a great harvest. United services have become frequent, and the interchange of pulpits less than rare. But is it unfair to say that authority has spoiled every advance by its niggardliness in imposing conditions—that it has granted principles and haggled about details—and that in consequence a real and most necessary development has been made to look mean and precarious? In this matter of the interchange of pulpits the Church of England has in fact swallowed the camel: the strain on its digestion makes it the more eager to discover and reject every conceivable gnat.

For that the practice of admitting members of other denominations to preach in our churches and cathedrals has not only been securely established but has received sufficient official support to make its continuance certain can hardly be disputed. Our present purpose, which is to discuss the value of the practice, will not demand any examination of the canons of the Church or of its tradition and customs in the past or of the origins of our present liberty. It may well be, as has lately been argued, that canon law does not exclude anyone who has the Bishop's licence or confine that licence to Anglican clergy; and that therefore a Bishop who chooses to sanction any preacher is acting within the law. It is certain that for long periods and indeed almost throughout its history men who were not Anglican clergy have been occasionally admitted to our pulpits. It is also true that the revival of such hospitality goes back to the beginning of the present century, and was powerfully advocated by some who have since been conspicuous for their conservatism. But this ancient history was made irrelevant by the Lambeth Conference of 1920; and it is from its resolutions and Encyclical Letter that the student of the present situation will make his beginning.

The Lambeth Conference of 1920

It is not unlikely that the historian of the future will reckon the Lambeth Conference of 1920 as the turning-point in the record of the Church of England, the high-water mark reached by the old type of institutional and traditionalist Anglicanism. The war had disclosed the weakness of organized Christianity: the younger generation of clergy had been set free from the conventional routine of parish and congregation: many of the most active had resolved never to return to it, and the majority was impatient and critical of authority: though the passing of the Enabling Act had brought a measure of encouragement, liberty would be of little value if life and leadership were lacking: the Conference met under a strong sense of urgency and of need. Its achievement was in accordance with its penitence and its hope. The three Bishops, of Hereford, Peterborough, and Zanzibar, then representative of liberal, of evangelical, and of catholic opinion, who united to describe it, claimed that they had experienced in it the power of the Holy Spirit; and their claim was borne out by the evidence. The Conference, especially in its findings upon reunion and in the tone and contents of its Appeal, rose to an unexpected height of generosity, of vision, and of unity. In recognizing unreservedly "the spiritual reality of the ministries of those Communions which do not possess the Episcopate", since they "have been manifestly blessed and owned by the Holy Spirit as effective means of grace", it swept aside as secondary all those questions as to the technique of ordination and the mechanism of its succession which loom so large in ecclesiastical debate, and appealed directly to Christ's own standard, the test of fruits. In asserting that "the removal of barriers will only be brought about by a new comradeship" and that "in view of prospects and projects of reunion, a bishop is justified in giving occasional authorization to ministers, not Episcopally ordained, who in his judgement are working towards an ideal of union such as is described in our Appeal, to preach in churches within his diocese," the Conference admitted the necessity for mutual understanding and sanctioned opportunities for its development. The Appeal was universally welcomed as evidence of a new and sincere intention; the resolutions were taken as the outline of a policy for its fulfilment; a thrill of awakened enthusiasm stirred and invigorated the Church. Ten years of the sort of co-operation foreshadowed in the Report, and already familiar to the clergy who had served with the forces in the war or had been members of the Student Christian Movement in their college days, should surely make possible decisive results when next the Conference met.

THE SEQUEL

There was indeed a warmth and spontaneity about the proposals of 1920 such as are not usually associated with gatherings of the hierarchy. It looked as if, for once, the policy of "Safety first" had been forgotten, as if churchmen had begun to realize that Christian character does not depend upon the precise mode in which a Church is governed, as if there was to be a resolute attempt to face the plain fact that the existing denominational barriers are largely obsolete. Those who had made this discovery were at least encouraged to hope for developments; and for some months believed that the new era would be one not of decline but of fulfilment. They had not made allowance for certain factors in the situation—the enormous conservatism of the Established Church; the existence in the Report of safeguarding clauses which could serve as pretexts for evading its plain meaning; and the contrast between the inspiration of a great Conference and the lonely business of carrying out its decisions. The Church was not ready—perhaps will never be ready—for large-scale changes; and the Bishops who had been enthusiastic for the Appeal speedily began to repent and to excuse themselves for their share in it. Although the Report was endorsed by the Convocations of both the English Provinces, and though a few Bishops, notably the then Bishop of Manchester, acted upon it by inviting prominent Nonconformists to preach in their dioceses, it was evident that progress would be slow; and when, within a year of publishing his eulogy upon the Conference, the Bishop of Zanzibar, in a letter to the *Church Times*,[1] repudiated its findings and denounced those who had acted upon them, it ceased to be united. Since then the promise of 1920 has only been fulfilled by the action of Liberal and Liberal Evangelical churchmen, and at the cost of organized and influential opposition.

The vision of the Great Church, which had been the animating influence of the Conference and of which the permission for the interchange of pulpits was the sequel, swiftly faded. It was one of those illuminating ideals which can only be realized if they are put into immediate practice. The Bishops took no decisive action: the opportunity and the inspiration were dissipated in years of debate: and by the time of the Faith and Order Conference at Lausanne in 1926 Anglicanism had revived its interest in legalisms and argumentation. In 1930 the next Lambeth Conference, though compelled by the situation in South India to renew something of its former faith, was in regard to reunion at home cautious and retrogressive, confining its report to a stilted and self-conscious defence of Episcopacy as a trust to which it must at all costs be true. We are not here concerned with the larger question of Christian unity; and need only note that whereas in 1920 the Church of England seemed ready for adventure, it has now reverted to a contented acceptance of its position as a "bridge", ignoring the fact that it is in reality like Britain an island, and unwilling to join up with either bank.

But despite the failure of the reason for interchange, the Conference's sanction remains and has been freely used. If there has been no general "comradeship", there has been much individual fraternizing. If the main bodies of the several de-

---

[1] Issue of October 28, 1921.

nominations still remain entrenched, an increasing number of friendly visits break through the isolation; and though many Bishops are timid and some hostile, any attempt at an official condemnation of the practice of mutual hospitality would hardly be supported, and if successful would certainly be disobeyed. The pity of it is that a practice so valuable in itself, so consistent with the character and history of the Church of England and so full of promise for the future, should now be regarded not as the general policy of the episcopate but as a mark of liberal (or lax) opinions.

THE VALUE OF INTERCHANGE OF PULPITS

Of the value of the interchange of pulpits proof can be found in the three following directions. It testifies to the essential and existing unity of Christians: it enlarges the sympathies and increases the effectiveness of the separated Churches: it promotes the universal and urgent task of reinterpreting the faith.

I. UNITY EMPHASIZED

It was, as we have seen, with the intention of promoting reunion that the interchange of pulpits under episcopal sanction was approved by the Lambeth Conference. It is probably true that the failure of the policy then outlined was in fact due less to the opposition of certain sections of church-people than to the ignorance and consequent suspicion and apathy of the great majority. Prior to 1920, though missionaries and ex-chaplains had discovered that the differences that now separate the reformed Churches were far less significant than their essential unity, the parochial clergy and their congregations had had no occasion to make any such discovery. Interdenominational meetings might occur under the aegis of the

Bible Society or occasionally to consider social problems. But in general church and chapel rarely met, and had no great desire to do so. "We *do* love our little Bethel" was as true of the one as of the other. Where now there are a dozen fields of co-operation actively cultivated there was fifteen years ago hardly more than one. The first benefit derived from the custom of preaching in each other's places of worship has been to reveal to the ordinary churchman how close is the existing agreement.

Anyone who has had experience of visiting and being visited by members of other denominations will realize how deep have hitherto been our misunderstandings. Naturally on such visits the preacher will speak on some fundamental tenet of the faith, and unless specially invited to do so will avoid controversial subjects. But with this condition in mind he will in fact be free to declare himself without reserve and without self-consciousness; will find that his message is not only welcomed but recognized as familiar; and will be told that his hosts had no idea that such-and-such beliefs were held by his Church. To see and hear a minister of one of the great Nonconformist communions declaring the selfsame gospel is to realize that Christianity is not to be estimated in terms of one's own congregation or of Anglicanism; and in these days when there is so plain a need for Christians to act together the recognition of the vast resources that are or should be available is to gain new courage.

For in spite of the increase of co-operation, in spite of C.O.P.E.C. and the World Call, parochialism and an exclusive concern with our own denomination are still characteristic of the average congregation. Social snobbishness, persistently surviving from the days of Test Acts and Anglican privileges, partially accounts for it. The exaggeration of ecclesiastical at the expense of religious teaching, that evil heritage and breeding-ground of sectarianism, must bear a large part of the blame. But most of it is due to sheer ignorance and to the misrepresentation that attaches to the unknown. So while the enlightened churchman is fully aware that the points of division are trivial when compared with those held in common, and realizes that the situation is so full of peril and of opportunity as to demand a closing of the ranks, such knowledge is still beyond the reach of the majority. Until a change takes place, the movement for reunion will remain a theme for academic debate.

II. ENLARGEMENT OF SYMPATHY AND INCREASE OF VITALITY

To widen the sympathies and increase the vitality of the Churches is the second purpose served by acts of interchange. The more fully we realize the world-wide and all-embracing character of Christ's religion, the more it becomes obvious how difficult it is to keep the proportion of the faith. We may talk about "putting first things first", but in an institution as ancient as the Church centuries of development have so vastly elaborated the simplicity of the gospel that it is well-nigh impossible to discriminate between universal and primary truths and the secondary traditions, usages, and dogmas in which they have been enshrined. This difficulty is much increased so long as a congregation is solely dependent for its teaching upon a single individual. However well-balanced and clear his own hold upon essentials, he starts with an incomplete grasp of the fulness of Christ: and as his ministry develops he is apt to pass beyond the simple elements to refinements and idiosyncrasies which may be of absorbing interest to himself, but are neither necessary nor, if emphasized, edifying for his people. Most of us, if we have had a long period of service in the same place, find it difficult to preach the old and central facts with any freshness. We slip into an insistence upon niceties, inflicting our own interests and fads upon our hearers and fostering in them an eccentric and often gravely perverted concept of religion.

In such circumstances the welcoming of visitors to our pulpit can be of use in two directions. A stranger will usually concentrate upon matters of vital import —matters familiar but apt to be on that very account neglected. He will thus recall the congregation to the centre of its Christian experience, and remind it of matters which can never too often be considered. The visitor has always this advantage over the "man on the spot"; and if he belongs to another Church and has his own characteristic method and dress and turn of phrase, the value of his testimony will be all the greater. It will come as news, or at least as something new; and to discover that in reality it is a primary element in any real Christianity is to regain a sense of perspective for surveying our own position.

Again an interchange can be used not to focus attention upon the centre but to bring into view some unfamiliar aspect of the circumference. None of us, however versatile, can be acquainted with the whole range of Christian interests; and in these days of specialization there are many subjects of real import-ance on which few are competent to speak. The Church of England with its rigid system of parish, deanery, and diocese, and with the recent enormous increase of administrative and financial duties laid upon its ministry, is no longer a training-ground of experts. Our University courses and doctrinal studies are still devoted largely to questions of Archaeology and hardly recognize the existence of Church history later than A.D. 451, or of modern science and psycho-logy, or of sociology and Christian Ethics. Nor is ex-pert knowledge fostered by Theological Colleges and the G.O.E., whose effect is to turn out a standardized mediocrity. The supply of experts diminishes almost as fast as the demand for them increases. It should be possible for us to call upon our partners in other denominations to help us in this respect. If, as is clearly the case, any series of volumes attempting an authoritative survey of modern knowledge from the Christian standpoint would necessarily include certain Free Churchmen among its contributors, the same will be still more the case if a course of sermons on similar lines is attempted locally. There are probably more preachers qualified to speak on such matters among the Nonconformists than among Anglicans; for on the whole their training is more closely related to contemporary life; they attach more importance to the prophetic than to the pastoral aspect of the ministry; and the sermon with the study preparatory to it takes a larger place in their work. In any case such co-operation by a "team" of preachers covering a careful syllabus is of great value as testifying both to the unity and the breadth of the Christian message.

III. REINTERPRETATION OF THE FAITH

In this connexion arises the third contribution which the interchange of pulpits can make to the well-being of the Church. We are constantly and justly warned that among the chief tasks of our time is the adjustment of our presentation of the gospel to the new knowledge. It is probably true that the discoveries in every field of human interest during the past century have been more momentous and far-reaching than those which accompanied the Renaissance and gave rise to the Reformation. Moreover, whereas in the Middle Ages familiarity with new ideas was confined to the few, these are now broadcast to the world at large, often before their validity and significance have been tested. The result is not only a vast confusion in half-trained minds, but for us all the greatest difficulty in formulating any wide or coherent outlook. Religion, if it is to survive except as superstition, must possess a philosophy, and if it is to hold the allegiance of mankind must express its philosophy in terms at once valid and intelligible. Yet to assess the influence of the new is only possible for those who combine clear insight with wide interests, and when novelties are of almost annual occurrence is at best like writing on the sand. It is small wonder that at such a period men should either fall back upon a resolute obscurantism or fling themselves into a disproportionate pursuit of the latest craze. It is difficult for any generation, especially for one faced with practical tasks of unusual urgency, to be content to hold its judgement in reserve—to keep its mind alert to grasp fresh truth and its principles clear so that it can be seen in its proper perspective.

Those who are prepared to admit that the changes now taking place in man's whole outlook must have their corresponding effect upon his religion will probably agree that a premature attempt to reach a synthetic reinterpretation might well be disastrous. We must be willing to be patient, to endure a lifetime of experiment and exploration, during which many issues will have to be left open and all formulations be regarded as tentative. This is, of course, not altogether a loss; for religion can never be identified with a static body of beliefs and practices, without sacrificing its characteristic quality. It is always the quest of a horizon: its followers have here no abiding city and must be ever on the march. But there is grave danger that in the supposed interests of efficiency or under the threat of fear the authorities of the Church may be driven into pronouncements that represent an exaggerated and temporary movement and commit us to positions that restrict growth and jeopardize the future. We owe too much to the balance and comprehensiveness of the Creed of Chalcedon to contemplate with satisfaction any attempt to stereotype one of the several dogmatic positions that have been found consistent with it. The decision of the Convocation at York in reference to Dr. Jacks' sermons at Liverpool was an instance both of the influence of the cry "The faith is in danger" and of the distortion to which legislation under such circumstances is always liable. For the Bishops in accepting as the criterion of orthodoxy a particular phrase from the Nicene Creed seemed to enforce an Apollinarian and ultimately mythological interpretation of the Incarnation, such as is at the moment in fashion but will ultimately be found to surrender true belief in the manhood of Jesus.

We would urge then that the work of reinterpretation must be long and thorough, that while it is in progress there should be a wise tolerance of what is avowedly empirical and tentative, and that if it is to be adequate it must involve an examination not only of the new but of the old. The history of the past century has surely proved that neither Scripture nor creeds, neither doctrine nor system of government in the Church can escape being assayed afresh in the crucible of the new learning; that nothing can be regarded as inerrant or irreformable; and that to refuse to reconsider the findings of the past is to gain a temporary shelter at the expense of ultimate discomfiture. There is a certain pathos in the spectacle of disciples of truth clinging first to one and then to another cherished formula in the hope of evading thorough investigation. Even the Englishman's genius for accepting traditional structures and making them serve purposes for which they were never intended has failed again and again to do more than delay the process of reform.

For such a Reformation as is inevitable the maintenance of denominational exclusiveness is a grave handicap. The situation is too serious and the need for effort too urgent for us to refuse any possible co-operation. There should be the fullest collaboration between all professing Christians in a venture common to them all. Adherence to a particular type of theology or system necessarily limits the sympathies and leads to the neglect of factors essential for any final synthesis. Moreover, the points on which schism has taken place are either obviously out-of-date or represent exactly the questions upon which enquiry is most necessary. With some Churches, as for example the Presbyterians, there would seem to be no difference on any matter of primary importance; for in view alike of the history of the ministry and of any proportionate concept of religion it is surely a trivial matter whether the Church is presided over by an annually appointed Moderator or by a permanent Archbishop. With others, where as with Congregationalists or Quakers the value of tests and ordinances or indeed of institutionalized religion is in dispute, we are brought face to face with one of the most important subjects of enquiry; and can hardly be expected to form a sound judgement unless with full knowledge of the opposite view to our own. In any case our own religious life and therefore our power to interpret the gospel cannot but be strengthened by learning to know and love those who display the fruit of the Spirit without conforming to our type of spiritual culture.

If it is urged that in this matter of restatement there is already in our Universities full co-operation between the scholars upon whom must rest the main task, and that the interchange of pulpits will not contribute to it, the answer is plain. It is only as the mass of church-people recognize the need, broaden their sympathies, and begin to understand differences of outlook and tradition, that there will be any prospect of the acceptance of the scholars' work. Everyone who can be helped to realize that his own denomination has not got a monopoly of Christianity, and that the fundamentals of the faith are not identical with the teaching and usage of his own parish church, becomes thereby an asset to the cause of reform. Moreover, he is released from the tendency to "thank God that he is not as these Dissenters," which is perhaps the most frequent and certainly the most grievous of the sins of the religious.

Comradeship and the Challenge to Christianity

It has thus been argued that the interchange of pulpits has the effect of emphasizing the unity of the faith in regard to essential elements, of revealing the many-sidedness of its application to life and thought, and thus of promoting a wide and coherent understanding of its meaning. In the more immediately practical sphere its advantages are certainly as great and probably more obvious. All over the world, and not least in our own country, there is emerging a plain alternative: on the one side the religion of Christ, and on the other a humanistic idealism to which we commonly give the name of secular civilization. In the old days when Christianity and in England Anglicanism held a privileged position and was nominally at least accepted by all responsible authorities, individuals might challenge its claims, but could make little impression against a public opinion which regarded the Establishment as the chief safeguard of national order and private morality. To profess unbelief was to expose oneself to the suspicion of treason to the realm. Christ and Caesar had come to terms with one another, and, provided Christians kept their religion free from enthusiasm and complacent to the respectable vices, the State would guarantee them immunity from attack and use its influence to enforce a minimum of conformity. A century ago when the reign of privilege was coming to an end, there was no clear-cut alternative to the Church. Public opinion still looked askance at the sceptic and maintained the outward signs of a conventional and even puritanical faith. It is only in the last generation that these restraints upon unbelief have finally disappeared, and that agnosticism, once a lonely and wistful conviction, has become popular, flippant, and irresponsible. Men and women find it easy to fill their lives with interests wholly mundane, and to put the social virtues and a general desire to leave the world better than they found it in the place of any definite religion.

We are not concerned to enquire into the causes or to assess the gains and losses of the change. That it is not wholly deplorable is manifest; for complacency and security are deadlier to the soul of a Church than persecution: if Christianity costs us little, it will not be worth more to us or to the world. Nominal authority maintained at the cost of compromise is destructive of sincerity and can hardly avoid the debasement of religion. But if we can no longer rely upon the favour of public opinion, and are not to see the Church transformed into a pietistic sect bent only upon the saving of its members' souls, the need for closer comradeship among Christians is obvious. The nation may not in fact be less Christian than of old: that seems to many of us an open question. But that the Church of England is rapidly ceasing to be in any real sense national is certainly true. If we are to bring effective pressure to bear upon the life of the country, and if, as is unquestionably the case, Christian opinion is already agreed upon many issues and with mutual understanding between the denominations would find still larger agreement, then the case for the interchange of pulpits gains fresh strength. For not only would it most powerfully assist the formation of a united Christian opinion and of co-operative action, but it testifies to the world the fact that Christians share strong convictions which no politician or government can lightly ignore.

Moreover, such evidence of goodwill would remove one of the most widespread and genuine grounds for unbelief. The divisions and conflicts between denominations, which, so far as the Reformed Communions are concerned, are mostly concerned with matters of little interest to the laity, have probably done more than any other single cause to alienate the sympathies and provoke the contempt of the ordinary citizen. He realizes the paramount need for better relationships between races, nations, classes, and individuals: he has heard it said that in Christ there is neither Greek nor Jew, bond nor free, male nor female. He admires and longs for friendliness, courtesy, generosity, and a sense of proportion: he knows the claim that the fruit of the Spirit is love, joy, peace, long-suffering. Yet he sees that despite the distraction of the times Anglicans do not in their dealings with other denominations practise the unity that they preach, but rather indulge in controversies, whose bitterness would be discreditable in secular life, over issues irrelevant to any of the urgent problems of the day. He thinks it merely hypocritical for Christians to advocate international agreement or to expect employers and employed to get together or to deplore the extravagances of the *Daily Express*, when churchmen will not co-operate with other Christians, when the admission of a Nonconformist to an Anglican pulpit is denounced as a scandal, and when the weekly organs of the chief parties in the Church are more violent and quick to impute evil than any secular journal. Unfortunately our excuses and explanations merely intensify his distrust of us: only action, only the definite proof that we are rising above the old exclusiveness, will avail against it.

There can be little doubt that among the multitudes no longer attached to any denomination but keeping in touch with religion through books and broadcasting this failure of the Church to set its own house in order is a primary and legitimate cause of criticism. Some of us know by concrete evidence how vast a mass of lay support is available for those who have had the courage to welcome Christians of other denominations to their pulpits; how eagerly such hospitality is accepted; how happy are its results. If the Fourth Evangelist is right in representing our Lord as praying for unity because only so will the world believe, we must needs long for organic re-union. But meanwhile, and now that the practice of interchange has been admitted, to resist such co-operation is surely to deserve the condemnation of God and men.

That to some strict churchmen such liberty is a scandal is still no doubt the case; and as they are the folks who write at once to the Bishops and send indignant protests to the *Church Times*, their influence seems large and intimidating. Such an attitude, uncharitable and unchristian as it is, cannot be overcome by concessions. To eradicate it—and surely it is a hideous evil—the authorities should press on with the policy which they have already initiated and approved. No man can see and hear any of the representative preachers of other denominations without realizing that his ministry is, in the words of the Lambeth Report of 1920, "manifestly blessed and owned by the Holy Spirit", or that an occasional visit from him is a privilege and an inspiration. If it is a sound principle, when one begins to think contemptuously of a stranger, to make his acquaintance, the same is no less true of our ecclesiastical antipathies. There seem to be folks in whose minds the word Baptist or Methodist (and still more of course Unitarian) produces a mist of rage, and who see its bearer in a distorted caricature. If so, let him sit at the feet of such an one, as he proclaims his faith. He may come to scoff: he will surely go away to pray and to repent.

"But why admit them to our pulpits? By all means let us hold joint meetings in secular buildings: but in our churches our people have the right to hear their own accredited clergy." That is a common argument; and so far as it welcomes co-operation, it is at least an advance upon the past. But it is not easy to see on what principles it is based. Is the consecration of a building a means not of dedicating it to the service of God but of making it taboo? Is the reserving of the pulpit for the ordained anything but a survival of a primitive idea of the untouchability of the sacred? If not, how can a man who is fit to speak of Christ in a public hall be creating a scandal if he is asked to do so in a church? Probably the true reason for such a distinction is that to most of us our church is much more like a club than a home—a club with an exclusive members' list and where we have a right to be free from intruders and to blame the management if the fare is not to our taste: the priest-in-charge is under obligation to give his people the statutory services and to take responsibility for the preaching: innovations of any sort are apt to be resented. There may be grounds for some such arguments. Indeed many of us would deliberately restrict the Open Pulpit to services other than the offices and liturgy, not because we believe that there is any well-founded objection to the preaching of Free Churchmen at Matins or Evensong, but because we would not offend consciences sensitive in the matter. But it must be urged that if the church is indeed not a club but a home, then by all the rules of hospitality our attitude should be wholly different. We ought to welcome the stranger and do him honour; to treat him as a friend of the family and to give him of our best. To say "We will gladly meet you on neutral ground: we cannot let you visit our house" is not friendship's way; nor according to Jesus is it God's way even with his prodigals.

Law, Love, and Liberty

To many, and particularly to the ecclesiastically minded, such an appeal will no doubt seem sentimental. They will argue that the question must be settled not by goodwill, but by canon and statute, in accordance with the usages of diplomacy; that emotion has no place in negotiations between the denominations; that the situation demands the most cautious and delicate handling; and that while conversations are proceeding among the statesmen of the Churches any departure from precedent by the rank and file will only complicate the existing difficulties and may well betray interests which the Anglican Communion holds in trust.

In this paper the legal approach to the question has been deliberately kept in the background, and for reasons which seem worthy of consideration. Many of us would wish to challenge, and challenge vigorously, the modelling of Church life upon the pattern of nation or empire. This transformation of the "blessed community" into the likeness of a civic power is part of the damnable heritage that the Church of the Dark Ages took over from imperial Rome; and whatever its value for the disciplining of barbarian tribesmen or mediaeval barons, it was always a reversion to a sub-Christian status. The relation of person to person, the fellowship and brotherhood of the family, is a totally different thing from that imposed by legal obligation and administered by statutory authority. Probably the whole system of dignitaries and officials, of preferment and lordships, is open to the same criticism: certainly the

real argument against Episcopacy is that the official
rapidly ceases to be human, and is compelled, whatever his resistance, to live not by love but by law. So
long as the negotiations between Churches are conducted in the method and spirit of International
Conferences by delegates whose chief concern is to
maintain their own vested interests and prestige, we
shall not see any such unity as the Spirit of Christ
inspires.

The contrast is sufficiently illustrated by the example already quoted between the Lambeth Conference of 1920, where the Bishops for a moment realized
their own brotherhood and saw Christendom in the
light of that experience, and the dreary proceedings
that have been its sequel. Many of us, encouraged
by the temper of the Appeal, believed for a time that
bishop and prophet might become synonyms, or at
least that having once broken out of the prison of
officialdom the hierarchy might lead us into a new
age of comradeship and spiritual freedom. The last
fifteen years have done little to justify that hope. The
story of Prayer-book Revision with its record of
bargaining and compromise, of bad tactics and worse
strategy, recalled the ugliest features of secular diplomacy. The Lausanne Conference, despite the heroic
faith of its chairman, was dominated by prudence and
caution. Lambeth 1930 spoke with two voices, giving
us the inspired wisdom of its first section, but when it
dealt with reunion relapsing into self-consciousness
and self-assertion. It has become evident that any
real change of method and temper in interdenominational contacts must first come not by concordat between their heads but by the growth of mutual trust
and friendliness based upon understanding and co-
operation between their members. Those of us who
are spared the burden of official responsibilities must
use our freedom, and not be afraid to let our hearts as
well as our heads guide us.

If we want precedent for such action, the example of the party in our own Church which is now most vocal in insisting upon strict observance of law is open to us. There is indeed something mildly amusing in the warnings against anarchy and the fulminations against innovation which now proceed from those whose influence was established by a continuous and deliberate flouting of episcopal authority, by the courage which was ready to go to prison for its beliefs and the perseverance which refused to be silenced either by argument or by violence. It does not seem likely that in the present case, and despite Lord Hugh Cecil, a similar course of legal persecution will have to be faced. Interchanges have already been so numerous, are indeed so much a regular part of the activities of influential parishes and cathedrals, that the danger is not of constitutional attack but lest the practice be regarded merely as the eccentricity of a few recognized libertines. It is here that the importance of persistence by liberal churchmen will be of value. The work of churches like St. Martin's-in-the-Fields or the parish church of Birmingham should be followed up by all who realize the significance of the issue. Otherwise it may be dismissed as a mere amiable or theatrical extravagance.

The New Alignment

For indeed the essential importance of the matter has hardly yet been disclosed. To describe it in detail does not fall within the scope of this paper. But no one who has had experience of close contact with British Nonconformity can fail to realize that for those who accept the modern outlook and the results of the new knowledge the old denominational barriers have lost their meaning. The real cleavage in Christendom to-day is between the new and the old, between those who admit and rejoice in the changes that the scientific movement and its method of study involve, and those who deplore and resist them. Here is a division that runs through almost every denomination, even the seemingly immovable and uniform Church of Rome; a division that already creates vital and deep-seated differences of faith and practice and that promises a fresh alignment of Christian groups in the near future. Ultimately it is a division that depends upon our whole concept of the nature of the universe, of the creative process and of mankind, and therefore of the nature and character of God. The issues involved in it lie deeper than any of the usual subjects of theological and ecclesiastical debates, though inevitably every one of these is affected by them. It is probably because he is dimly aware of these wider problems and feels that the clergy do not face them, and that most clerical questions are really irrelevant so long as they are ignored, that the educated layman is nowadays so impatient with the Churches. To those who accept the new outlook, it brings a richer appreciation of Christ's revelation, a clearer grasp of the unity and scope of the Divine activity, and a fuller belief in the reality and work of the Holy Spirit. Certainly they find themselves not only cut off from many of their brethren by disagreements far more radical than those of denomination or party, but drawn into real unity with the members of other Churches who share their convictions. When we meet there is at once a conscious community of experience and thought which is unaffected by the source from which we drew our commission to the ministry or by divergences in our formularies and acts of public worship. We know that we worship the same God, have a similar understanding of his dealings with mankind, and are at one in all the fundamentals of our teaching. Consequently we can preach in one another's pulpits without the slightest constraint or self-consciousness, or any sense of caution or insincerity. We do not need to make a great occasion of it or to assume an air of aloofness or of geniality. We are in fact at home with them as they are with us. When one has had experience of such comradeship over a long span of years, it is impossible to deny that here is a real unity of the Spirit or to contemplate anything which would cast doubt upon that unity or restrict its consequences.

That there remain many points of difference within this realized fellowship is of course manifest. Church Order and usage have their influence—though it is relatively slight and secondary. Between modern Christians of whatever name there is no such gulf as there is to-day between liberal and fundamentalist or liberal and infallibilist. But there is to those who are sensitive to it a distinct difference of ethos or atmosphere, a diversity of temperament, between Anglican and Methodist or Anglican and Congregationalist. It is not a matter of principle or of theological disagreement, but is rather a habit of mind reflecting the characteristic quality of the denomination. As such it greatly enriches friendship; for it means that we bring to our common quest varying points of view or approach our one objective from unfamiliar angles. It is more like the difference between a painter and a musician than between artists who use the same medium but belong to different schools; and as such if we are sure of our essential purpose in the service of truth it promotes a fruitful and uncontroversial partnership. We have learnt to express our religion in varying forms, and when we come together have the joy of discovering how the fresh angle of approach corrects and solidifies our own vision—which is after all just what friendship always accomplishes. Whatever may be the constitution of the Great Church of the future, we may hope that it will not cultivate so strict a uniformity as would wipe out such varieties of experience and expression.

A Call to Action

It would be improper and impossible for one who has been given so full and perhaps so unique an opportunity of the interchange of pulpits to print his first paper on the subject without a word of acknowledgement and gratitude to those who have made his adventures possible. It was as dean of a Cambridge College with responsibilities towards undergraduates of all denominations that I first came into touch with interdenominational work through the Student Movement and the College Christian Union. This led necessarily to invitations to Free Churchmen to preach and to the acceptance of similar hospitality from them—in days when a sudden telegram from a Bishop inhibiting one's sermon was not unlikely. The war deepened my conviction of the wrongfulness and unreality of our divisions: when men are facing death, Christ matters more than Paul or Cephas or Apollos. C.O.P.E.C. provided its secretaries with the right of entry to all quarters; and the Bishop of Liverpool's courageous leadership gave occasion for the return of invitations to those who had made me welcome. During the past fifteen years there has seldom been a month in which I have not spoken or preached to some other denomination, and once I visited the four largest Free Churches in a single week. I have spoken in a Unitarian Chapel on the divinity of Christ, and been violently denounced in the *Church Times* for doing so; and at the London Meeting House to the Society of Friends on my criticisms of Quakerism. Before the Union I addressed the Assembly of the United Free Church in Edinburgh, and after it the great Congress of the Forward Movement in Glasgow. I have conducted public worship in the chapels and according to the use of Presbyterians, Congregationalists, and Methodists, and have taken hundreds of "free" services in Anglican Churches. Such visits have brought me some of the most valued friendships and the most searching religious experiences of my life; they have never for a moment made me doubt the reality of the existing unity or the value of co-operation; they have continually deepened my sense of the vast possibilities open to the Church of England, of the ease with which she could promote closer relationships, and of the obligation upon her as still the National Church to welcome their promotion; they have given me continual evidence of the limitless resources, the power and many-sidedness of Christ's religion, and a recurring tonic against depression or impatience.

I have ventured to describe these activities partly "as in private duty bound" for gratitude's sake, and partly because the recital may encourage other Modern Churchmen to find a similar scope for their energies. It is still the case that most of us who, like F. D. Maurice, know that we can never be acceptable to any party in the Church find ourselves ineligible for positions of influence in it. So far as this frees us from the temptation to careerism or manœuvring for preferment it is an unmixed blessing: but it often leaves us without much apparent scope. Many of us find an outlet in the direct service of interdenominational movements or in work outside the sphere of parish or diocese. For others I believe that the development of co-operation with the Free Churches might be an invaluable as it will surely be a well-rewarded task. The openings are innumerable, and the effect upon the future will be far-reaching. In any case here is a direction in which Modern Churchmen should be able to act at once and with eagerness.

For unless by individual effort we are bold to use and extend our liberties, we may well find them seriously restricted, not so much by direct official action as by the pressure of the movement for centralization, uniformity, and mechanical efficiency. It is highly improbable that any attempt to repudiate the principle of occasional interchanges will be made, though individual Bishops may follow the Bishop of Peterborough in declaring that at present such action is unwise. But the general process of regimenting the Church, to which the Enabling Act in spite of "Life and Liberty" has so powerfully contributed, is already endangering our independence and threatening to substitute official for human relationships, to give the Diocesan Secretary and the Board of Finance supreme authority, to strengthen the party causes and its proctorial nominees, and to discourage experiments under the pretext of securing safety and stability. To "bring the clergy into line", to standardize orthodoxy on the principles of *Essays Catholic and Critical*, to denounce all co-operation with the Free Churches as damaging to our hopes of reunion with the Holy Orthodox, to fill all the positions of influence with "safe" dignitaries, and to answer every new project by submitting it to episcopal control and quietly smothering it—that is at present a popular policy. Some day the tale of the extent to which it has been carried in the past decade will have to be told. Meanwhile a sufficient number of clergy and laity recognize and resent it to make it certain that, if they are willing to resist, they can avert its worst dangers. It is because the cultivation of Christian friendliness with our fellow-workers in other Churches is an obvious means for counteracting it that the effort to do so should have a chief place in any Modern Churchman's activities.

Q

VI

THE CHURCH AND SECULAR LIFE

by

LT.-COL. SIR A. T. WILSON, M.P., D.S.O.
K.C.I.E., C.S.I., C.M.G.

SYNOPSIS

RELIGION is the most important thing in life because it leads to a final conception of God as the supreme and only reality which, as such, is present within each of us. This conception influences our action at every point and gives significance to the search for truth. History proves the truth, so far as society is concerned, of the revelation and teaching of Jesus Christ, on whose life and death is founded the idea of Progress and of the Church as a *societas perfecta*. The Christian Church accepts the world as its platform. Its primary object is to inculcate a distinctively Christian personal morality and to strengthen the family as the one essential social unit. A general atmosphere of benevolence and tolerance is no substitute for the quest after personal righteousness. The first part of our Lord's summary of the Commandments, love of God, should be emphasized rather than the second, love of neighbour. Love of neighbours may be no more than a vague goodwill towards others.

PREACHING

Preaching is the only means by which a clergyman may influence the large silent part of his flock. Good preaching is an English tradition. Addresses and sermons when published command a wide reading public, but the influence of the printed word cannot compare with that of the spoken message of the sincere preacher who has a real message which he desires to impart. The temptation to deal *ex cathedra* with matters of current controversy should be resisted by the preacher. He usually has not the specialized knowledge which would make what he has to say on such matters of real value, and he gives an unfortunate impression of speaking *ex parte*. If, as is probable, a clergyman deals unsatisfactorily with secular questions, some of which are of extreme difficulty, his spiritual influence is weakened. It is better to keep before men the ideal of a *Civitas Dei* than to urge the acceptance of particular remedies, such as the League of Nations or Birth Control.

TEACHING

The teaching office of the Church is not confined to the pulpit and ought to be shared with the clergy by the laity. It is unfortunate that the influence of the more ultramontane type of Anglo-Catholicism has tended to widen the breach between clergy and laity, a tendency which has been reinforced by the recent demand for a formal delimitation of the functions of Church and State. The clergy should devote more attention to the preaching of "the Word", which was never more earnestly desired or more readily heeded by the laity. The episcopate in particular and the clergy in general should seek rather to arouse the public conscience to deal with disclosed evils than themselves to espouse particular remedies or palliatives. They should leave responsibility for action to competent laymen.

ALMSGIVING AND SOCIAL SERVICE

England is covered by a network of public and voluntary social services which deal with all kinds of misfortunes and disabilities. Working people find the procedure connected with these services complicated and puzzling; and they are often in need of guidance from a friend in whom they have confidence. The clergy should inform themselves about the social services and seek, in co-operation with laymen, to make the general public aware of the existence of voluntary and State agencies established for their benefit. In the distribution of alms, laymen should be associated with the clergy and care should be taken that financial help should be given in cases where it will do permanent good and no claim lies against the public purse, cases far more numerous and distressing than is generally realized.

THE TEACHING OF CHRISTIAN MORALS

The primary object of the Church is the inculcating of a distinctively Christian personal morality; but the full moral implications to the individual of the Christian faith are seldom examined. The Church can best exercise its influence over secular life by teaching the causes and remedies of moral failure. We need to be reminded that "each man must bear his own burden".

Religion and Economics

Before the Reformation economics were a branch of ethics and ethics a branch of theology. Two centuries after the Reformation economics and religion were regarded as parallel and independent provinces. To-day they are regarded as parallel but not independent. The doctrine of absolute separation is only held by Marxians and, at the other extreme, by ultra-pietists. Economics are in the last resort a branch of aesthetics: we can have many things but at the expense of others. To help men to decide at what they should aim in the economic sphere is one of the functions of religion: how they should attain it is a secular rather than a religious question.

Relations between Church and State

The connexion with the State is an antidote to the inclination to confine religion within the limits of individual emotion or belief. The basis of society is the personal character of the citizen, which rests on principles which find their true development in Christian doctrine. To expound these principles is the function of the Church, to apply them the function of the State. Material prosperity has increased during the last two centuries and there is good ground for the belief that we are moving forward to a still higher level. The Church with its message of faith, hope, and love should stand firm against that sour pessimism which is the modern form of *Accidie*. Membership of the nation invests short and humble lives with dignity and meaning. The Church should be national in outlook and teaching and hold fast to the righteousness that exalteth a nation, whilst opposing at all costs a narrow racialism and recognizing as allies the national churches of other Christian confessions. The establishment of National Churches in India, Persia, and China is a forward step.

VI

THE CHURCH AND SECULAR LIFE

By "the Church" I refer to the Church of England in the sense of the nineteenth of the Thirty-Nine Articles:

> a congregation of faithful men, in which the pure Word of God is preached, and the sacraments duly administered according to Christ's ordinance in all those things that of necessity are requisite to the same.

By "Secular Life" I refer to the daily life of the men, women, and children who make up the population of this country, as well as to the communal, corporate, and commercial activities of the nation, its assemblies and its ceremonies, and indirectly to those of the British Empire.

I write as a layman whose scientific studies have led him to regard the universe, in the words of Professor J. S. Haldane, C.H., as one "from which chaotic activity of every sort is progressively disappearing—a view which harmonizes with the conception of biological evolution, or the religious conception of the universe as a progressive manifestation of God's activity".[1] With him, I regard religion as the most important thing in life, because it leads, like scientific interpretations of our experience, to a final conception of God as the supreme and only reality, and of God present as such within each of us as Personality and giving to each of us the only reality which we possess. The recognition in our conscious behaviour of this conception influencing our actions at

---

[1] *Materialism* (Hodder & Stoughton, 1932), pp. 120-37.

every point constitutes religion, and gives significance to the search for truth in every walk and aspect of life.

I believe further that Jesus Christ, in whom the Holy Spirit was manifested, as in no other man before or since, was sent to redeem the world by his preaching and his example and, above all, by his death, and that history, rightly studied, proves the truth, so far as concerns human society, of the Christian revelation and teaching. The Act of Redemption gives hope and meaning to society, for, to me, on it and on it alone is founded the Idea of Progress, of man's perfectibility and of the Church as a *perfecta societas*. Without it, we may gain the whole world, and lose our own soul. Societies can change rapidly when there is no fixed moral code, but for the worse, for men's nature does not change, and without a fixed moral code human society cannot long survive.

Christian ethics are based on something far higher than the experience of mankind and on "common sense". The readiness of men and women, young and old, to risk their lives, and to endure the greatest agony, to save others who are to them strangers, is not instinctive, not inborn. "Common sense" dictates that no man should risk his own life for that of another perhaps less "valuable"—and in non-Christian countries any other attitude is regarded as surprising and in some cases as wrong, for it is held that able-bodied men are of more use to society than women and children and should not lightly imperil their lives or the prospects of their family for the sake of weaklings or strangers. That the opposite view is held and acted on in Christian countries, is a proof of the profound effect of our Lord's example and of the belief not that men are equal in ability or merit but that all are "worth while" and that we all have some measure of responsibility for each other.

The nature of Christianity made necessary a profound change in the secular framework of society. That change was the separation of Church and State and delimitation of their respective spheres of influence. This separation was the fundamental contribution of Christianity to secular progress, because it made it possible to combine the conception of a fixed moral order with the secular evolution of society.[1]

The Christian Church accepts the world as its platform, avoiding on the one hand the Oriental concentration on personal other-worldiness, and on the other the Western concentration on material welfare and inventive ingenuity, as proper goals of human endeavour.

Thus, to me, the primary object of the Church is to inculcate the belief in and practice of a personal morality which is distinctively Christian, in every relation between man and his fellows, and between man and God. The whole Christian conception of life is built up on the reciprocal obligations of the members of the family to each other, and the antecedent rights of the family against the State, which cannot destroy the family without destroying its own foundations.

I hold, therefore, that the primary concern of the Churches with secular life should be, firstly, to inculcate a strong Christian morality in the individual and, secondly, to strengthen the family as the essential basis of human society with a greater claim on our consideration and loyalty than the State, the nation, or the race.

A close study of the Reports of recent Lambeth Conferences and of various bodies set up of late years by the Archbishops, has left on me the impression that there has been, on balance, a tendency during my lifetime to emphasize the second to the detriment of the first part of Christ's summary of the Ten Commandments.

[1] Douglas Jerrold, *Orthodoxy sees it Through*, p. 222.

Goodwill towards men, and a desire to be just towards one's neighbour, are not distinctively Christian tenets. A general atmosphere of benevolence and of tolerance, whether of things we regard as evil, or as merely out of place, or the outcome of misconceptions, is no substitute for the desire and the attempt to ensure personal righteousness. The inculcation of the pacifist principle of non-resistance to evil, for example, is apt to result in a passive acceptance of injustice to others and of the wicked practices— which is not easily distinguished from selfishness.

> (Jesus answered), The first of all the commandments is Hear O Israel: The Lord our God is one Lord. And thou shalt love the Lord thy God with all thy heart, and with all thy soul, and with thy mind and with all thy strength: this is the first commandment (Mark xii. 30).

No recorded saying of our Lord is more explicit and more emphatic. The injunction to love our neighbour as ourself is secondary and, relatively, unemphatic.

My understanding of "the first of all the commandments" is that the primary duty of the Churches is to bring the individual to a realization of his responsibility for his own life and his own soul—to tend and develop the Spirit of God within him. Success in this direction will be the measure of the individual's influence on others. All experience seems, to me, to confirm this view of the primary obligation of the Church Militant here on earth. Rich and poor, old and young, dwell with thankfulness and humility on the influence exercised by individual ministers and Christian workers of all denominations on their individual lives.

Every one of us has personal knowledge of the profound changes wrought in the lives of others by the example and teaching of Christian men, who, by their life and doctrine, shew forth God's true and lively word and rightly and duly administer it. More often than not they are unknown beyond self-imposed and often narrow limits; but the seed thus sown by the Church bears a hundredfold. The best work is more often than not accomplished in privacy. Seldom, if ever, does God speak to man in a crowd.

PREACHING

The Church cannot in the nature of things seek only to influence individuals, though that will always be, in my view, the domain in which the most valuable work will be done. The preaching office of the Church is of importance both as to its influence on individuals and on a community. Preaching, whether in Church or elsewhere, and whether by way of a formal sermon or homily, or informal addresses, is the only means by which the large silent part of an incumbent's flock can be reached. Good preaching is an English tradition. Donne and Knox, Whitfield and Wesley, influenced men profoundly. Addresses "printed by request" in tens of thousands, and Collected Sermons, issue by scores from the presses every year; they are not profitable to their authors, but they are not published at a loss. The output of religious literature was never larger than it is to-day; yet the influence of the printed word is not to be compared with that of the preacher who has something to say, which he desires to impart, which he believes, and desires others to believe. Let no one underrate the great importance of preaching—or the potential effect on men's lives and thoughts. Men and women need it: they feel the absence of good preaching even though they do not understand it all. I once took to the same village church, on successive Sundays, a young Member of Parliament and a farm labourer. Each, in his own tongue, paid a tribute to the preacher as we walked home over the fields.

"That's the sort of thing does one good to hear," said the former, "clear and fresh and alive—he must be a learned man."

"I liked his sermon," said the farm labourer: "I didn't understand it all but I reckon he's a straight man: I'd like him to marry me, I would, and I would go to him if I wanted advice. A good parson makes a lot of difference to a village." Yet that man seldom had a congregation of over thirty, and he had preached twice on Sundays for twenty years.

A good preacher must often be tempted to deal *ex cathedra* with current controversies: his views must sometimes be distorted, or at least tinged, by the medium through which those events are presented to him. The clergy are mostly busy men: their means are narrow and they cannot afford to buy or even borrow many books: least of all have they the time or the specialized knowledge necessary to enable them to analyse and criticize the assumptions and figures relating to the public affairs of which they read. I seldom read or listen to a letter or homily by a Bishop or lesser dignitary of the Church on a particular aspect of some secular question without feeling that he is speaking *ex parte* and that it is inconsistent with his office and profession that he should be doing so. The clergy tend, when dealing with secular affairs, to take the short view rather than the long, to emphasize the desirability of "ideal" solutions and to speak vaguely of ideals, forgetting that ideals that are not practicable may well be delusions the indiscreet pursuit of which may be, and often is, disastrous to the causes advocated.

Monetary Reform, the Minimum Wage, Economics—"the oppositions of science falsely so called" —Disarmament, the League of Nations and Sanctions, International Debt, Unemployment, and the Peace Ballot, to take current topics at random—are secular questions of extreme difficulty. A minister of

Christ should not speak on such topics without even more thorough preparation than a Minister of the Crown, for so far as events prove him to be misguided, or falsify his anticipations, his spiritual influence will be weakened. On such matters the Churches should, in my view, offer every encouragement to men and women to take an active and distinctively Christian part, and to lead public opinion. But they should not as a rule enter the arena in support of a particular thesis. Experience suggests that, wherever this policy has been followed, Christianity has gained rather than lost thereby. It is better to keep before men the ideal of the *Civitas Dei* than to urge upon them, with insufficient knowledge or authority, particular legislative solutions, each bearing within itself the seed of fresh ills, so long as human nature remains unchanged.

The Archbishops and Bishops in particular should, to my mind, "keep the door of their lips" on such matters, except in the House of Lords where they may, as of right, raise any issue at their convenience, not *ex cathedra* but in Debate with their Peers. The unwillingness of the Bishops in recent years to make full use of this opportunity, unique in the constitutional practice of the world, is surprising and, to me, a matter of profound regret.

TEACHING

The teaching office of the Church is by no means confined to preaching in places of worship. At all times in our history the parson, as in Chaucer's *Canterbury Tales*, was an important figure in society, though his status and his influence with particular social strata varied from time to time. The whole question was very fully investigated by an exceedingly strong Commission of Inquiry appointed by the Archbishops in 1917: their Report[1] was compre-

---

[1] *The Teaching Office of the Church* (S.P.C.K., 1918, 1s.).

hensive, critical, and constructive. No franker statement of the difficulties of the clergy, their failure in some directions, and the limitations placed upon them in others, has ever been published. It emphasizes, also, the responsibility of the laity who are "essential organs of the Church, with a clear duty to spread the message for which the whole body of the Church is responsible", bearing in mind that "teaching given by laymen often carries with it special weight and influence". The Report contrasts the enthusiasm of those who advocate certain political and ethical views with the indifference or inability displayed by the majority of the laity in bearing intelligent witness to their faith. It discusses the failure of home influence, of "the great dangers we are in by our unhappy divisions", and urges on churchmen of all schools of thought the duty of teaching positively rather than negatively, constructively rather than controversially and, in the sense that the words have come to bear among us, with due regard to the proportion of faith.

Lord Davidson spoke in the House of Lords in 1920 of "the Church—that is, the Bishops, together with the clergy and laity". These words again emphasize that the teaching office of the Church is as much the concern of the laity as the clergy. The Church Assembly has come into being, but has not fulfilled the high hopes of its promoters. Some activities and some public utterances of Anglo-Catholic clergy of the ultra-Montane type, whilst not in truth representative of the Movement as a whole, have tended to widen the breach between the clergy and the laity and between the Church of England and the State. These manifestations have synchronized with public references, in which violent language is sometimes used, and not only by Bishops, to the necessity of at least a formal delimitation of the functions of Church and State.

Recent developments in Germany and Mexico, Spain and Russia, should make us pause before seeking on logical grounds to make a change.

Holding firmly, as I do, to the ideals of the Church as a *perfecta societas,*

> I can [in the words of Dr. Mandell-Creighton[1]] think of nothing so tending to debase the ideal of the State as to talk about 'freeing the Church from the bondage of the State'. This representation of the State as something inherently unholy, something stifling to spiritual aspiration, something from which the high-minded man longs to be delivered, is very dangerous teaching. . . . Disestablishment—or as I prefer to call it, the repudiation of a Christian basis of the State—would go far to give real vitality to such opinions. I do not see on what grounds it could be deprecated by those who rashly raise so large an issue to gain such a trivial advantage—for it is a large issue which is raised when it is proposed that the English State should divest itself of its religious character.

That is still the view of the vast majority of lay churchmen. They note that the demand for a re-arrangement, or for a disconnexion, of the relations of the Church and State have come, not from nonconformists, nor from secularists, but from within. It is often accompanied by what is widely regarded as a self-satisfied sacerdotalism which, as remarked by H. B. Wilson in *Essays and Reviews* (1860), can succeed in keeping peace only within the walls of emptied churches, and which entails the belief in certain individuals, ordained in a certain way, as the exclusive channel, in the Divine Covenant, of Sacramental graces. It is distinguished by what is regarded by the majority of laymen as undue emphasis on ritual observances and ceremonies, which our forefathers had, wisely or unwisely, abolished or at least omitted to retain. No discussion of this question is possible here, but it is, in my judgement, one

---

[1] *Primary Charge to the Diocese of Peterborough in* 1894.

of the principal causes of an apparently increasing estrangement between clergy and laity.

The clergy are appointed to be Ministers of the Word and Sacraments, and one of the main differences between the Churches in England and the Roman Catholic Church is the emphasis, in our ordinal, on "the Word". The influence of the Church, as defined by Lord Davidson, on secular life will be great in proportion to its ability to teach "the Word". "Vast numbers of the clergy", wrote the Bishop of Oxford in 1918, "are frightened by Biblical criticism, and lose all power of teaching the Bible." They cannot, even now, proclaim from the pulpit that the contents of the opening chapters of Genesis, and much else, are in the words of St. Gregory "doctrines in the form of a story".

The laity earnestly desire instruction on the Bible: they regard it, by tradition and instinct, as by far the most important function of the clergy. A preacher, be he priest or layman, who can explain passages, particularly well-known portions of Scripture, and who can tell them of the history and significance of our liturgy, is, in my experience, assured in every gathering of an attentive audience and a wide influence. Laymen often regret, and sometimes resent, the application of isolated texts to particular problems of secular life. The personal influence of clergy with their parishioners is, I must here repeat, often weakened by persistent or emphatic insistence on the adoption of specific secular policies as being in accord with the teachings of Jesus Christ and, conversely, the claim that alternative policies are inconsistent with "God's will" and the teachings of the apostles. Laymen who are at all familiar with Holy Writ, with the circumstances of the world in which our Lord lived, and with the legal bonds and social conventions of his hearers, have no difficulty in quoting texts and advancing arguments in the contrary direction. They do not accept the Bench of Bishops as keepers of the national conscience, nor the clergy as arbiters on current social questions: they question their qualifications to be judges of such matters as the Contagious Diseases Acts, the raising of the School Age and the Age of Consent, the administration of Public Assistance, Housing, White Slave Traffic, Women Police, Birth Control, the Reform of the Licensing and Betting Laws, and Indian Constitutional Reform, and British Colonial Policy. Upon all these and many other secular subjects, laymen are accustomed to hear episcopal and other pronouncements delivered not indeed *ex cathedra* but uttered upon occasions[1], and in circumstances, which are clearly intended to invest the speaker with greater authority than attaches to a private individual. Laymen note that on such matters the clergy in their private and individual capacity are often not in agreement with the Bishops, and that the Bishops habitually differ from each other. They find it hard to believe that men with such heavy duties can devote the time necessary to a right appreciation of all sides of these problems, which are being dealt with by the Government of the country—and by Parliament, as well as by special organizations. They do not question the right of the Bishops and clergy to speak on such matters: they often question their competence and that of their usually anonymous advisers.

I am led, not without hesitation, to the conclusion that on grounds of expediency, and in view of the immensity of the task before the Bishops and clergy in their own peculiar sphere—the interests of the Church are best served by those clergy who deliberately abstain, as a general rule, from active partici-

---

[1] *E.g.* at the Lambeth Conference, which demanded among other things more women police, commended Prohibition in America, and passed judgement upon half a score of other controversial topics.

pation in secular matters to which informed laymen are capable of devoting themselves, and from taking sides upon current secular questions. This is not to say that there are not occasions when they may not usefully do so, and that they should not take the lead, when the spirit moves them from time to time, in matters to which they have given thought and adequate study. The result of close and detailed investigation of any specific social or other problem has usually led me to views very different from and often diametrically opposed to those which I held before I commenced to study the question with care. To arouse the public conscience by disclosing the existence of evils is a proper function of all His Majesty's lieges, and not least of the clergy of an established Church, whose position, if financially narrow, is normally secure and independent of local opinion. But the public conscience having been aroused, and competent laymen having assumed the responsibility for action, the clergy will usually do well to stand apart.

Almsgiving and Social Service

The Church needs religious orders for priests who, as mission preachers and preachers at large, shall specially consecrate themselves to influence secular life by study, meditation, and preaching. It needs the academic scholar who, as theologian, critic, or philosopher, can occupy himself with great matters which are too high for the ordinary man. It needs, in great numbers, clergy who will keep in touch with their parishioners and who, in the exercise of the pastoral office, may give them help and advice in matters affecting their daily life. This brings us to a further aspect of the relation of clergy to secular affairs. England is covered to-day by an elaborate and complicated network of public and voluntary social services which deal, however inadequately, with almost every form of disability and misfortune which may befall the working classes. These social services are, almost without exception, admirably administered by expert officials, often with the assistance of local committees. The regulations under which they work are of necessity complicated: investigation is necessary before public money is expended on outdoor relief, on old-age pensions, on additional benefits; several authorities must often be consulted. Working men and women, particularly in old age, are little better able now than were their grandparents to put their case and lucidly explain their title to such services. They are confused by the various forms, hurt by questions, often ignorant of their rights and duties. There is great need for a skilled *amicus curiae* in every parish—someone who knows the regulations and those who administer them, and can help the helpless whilst at the same time facilitating the work of harassed officials.

It is not without significance that in almost all official forms provision is made for attestation or confirmation of statements by Justices of the Peace or ministers of religion, in preference to and often to the exclusion of any other persons.

This work, if well done, adds greatly to the parson's knowledge of the world in which he works, and is a link of real value between the Church and the street. It is not always a mere formality. Not long ago a youth desiring to join the armed forces of the Crown applied to a Justice of the Peace, with the usual printed form, for a character. He had fallen once by the way. The honest Justice refused to give a testimonial. The boy applied to the vicar of the parish, equally honest, who made full enquiries as to the nature of the offence in question, and wrote a detailed letter to the Recruiting Officer on the subject. The boy was admitted to the Service, where he has done himself and his parents great credit. But they have not forgiven the J.P.

Let those who have read these lines ask themselves whether in the parish in which they live there is anyone who can answer, or ascertain quickly the answer to the following random questions:

To whom should application be made for the services of a nurse or midwife?

What hospital or institution in the neighbourhood will take lying-in cases, and at what cost?

Where should a birth be registered?

How can birth certificates be obtained and at what cost?

Is any action necessary by a parent who wishes to keep a child at school after 14?

Where are the officers of the local Juvenile Employment Association?

Is there a local Hospital Savings Association?

Where is the local Isolation Hospital? the County Sanatorium for cases of pulmonary T.B.? Where can treatment be given, in conditions of privacy, for certain maladies and disabilities?

Where should a boy apply who wishes to join the Services, or to enter a training-ship for the mercantile marine?

How is application made for an old-age pension, and where does an appeal lie?

Such questions arise daily in every parish, and much depends on the replies.

The clergy could do more in such matters, but it is primarily the responsibility of well-disposed laymen and women, organized by the clergy. Whether viewed as a body corporate or a society, the Church should seek to harmonize its activities with secular agencies and, in its own interests, to avoid duplication of effort. Vast sums collected by means of voluntary subscriptions are devoted annually to an immense variety of social needs. The Churches are active agencies for the collection of several million pounds a year—through offerings during Divine Service and otherwise: over the expenditure of a large proportion of money thus subscribed they have no control, and some of it is devoted to purposes which however socially desirable have no direct relation to the work and teaching of the Churches.

The decision as to what objects money collected in churches should be devoted is often left in large measure to Parochial Church Councils, but it is reasonable to suggest that the clergy in the exercise of their duties should impress upon these Councils the importance of strengthening the Church to which they belong in preference to dispensing charity through many channels. The clergy in every parish should have funds at their disposal for the assistance of parishioners: they should be in a position to give financial help in cases where it will do permanent good, when no claim lies against the public purse. Such cases are often numerous and always distressing. In their own interests clergy will be well advised to associate a few laymen with them in the work of almonry. Church men and women as a body desire to provide for the sick and needy: and specially to them that are of the household of faith. They dislike to be told, as a matter of form, "to let their light shine before men"—they would prefer to hear any of the other sentences whilst Alms for the Poor are being received by the churchwardens. But they wish to be assured that the money is being wisely spent, for the sums now collected by the State for the relief of the poor, the sick, and the needy have vastly increased in the last ten years.[1]

---

[1] The sum devoted to outdoor relief in 1914 was £2¼ million: in 1934 £16¾ million.

THE TEACHING OF CHRISTIAN MORALS

When beginning this essay I set down as the primary object of the Church the inculcating of belief in and practice of a distinctively Christian personal morality. "The neglect of this subject", observes Professor H. L. Goudge,[1] "is probably the worst evil of the present system, and the evil is now widely recognized." Christian morals have their basis in Christian doctrine, and the attack upon Christianity to-day is directed against Christian morals rather than Christian doctrine. It is easy to retain Christian theology and reject Christian morals. The full moral implications to the individual of the Christian faith are seldom examined: there is indeed a notable willingness in many quarters to assume that they may be equated with a general willingness of the community at large to delegate responsibility for the relief, rather than the prevention, of invalidity, sickness, poverty and distress in general, with little regard for ultimate consequences. Failure to consider whither we may be led by the various short-term remedial measures which a superficial examination of social conditions may suggest reacts unfavourably upon the acceptance by laymen of the moral teaching of the Church as a whole, and this in turn reacts upon its doctrinal teaching. Laymen feel that the Church can best exercise the influence which it can and should have over secular life by teaching the causes and remedies of moral failure and how they may be overcome. "The whole armoury of God" must surely include great emphasis upon personal conduct and upon personal responsibility. We are often told that we must bear one another's burdens. But as St. Paul added, "each man must bear his own burden". Of this great truth we are less often reminded.

[1] P. 119, App. IV, "The Teaching Office of the Church", *op. cit.*

The reactions between religion and politics are as old as humanity—older by far than our present civilization. The one must react on the other—a man's religion must affect his outlook on life—and his outlook on life *plus* his temperament to a large extent determines his politics. There is only one attitude of mind which is really untenable—and it is born of ignorance—that is the "secularist" attitude which says in effect "Render all unto Caesar . . . for there is no God. . . ." The glorification of "the State" —the will of the majority—tends in this direction. Majority rule is necessary, but it is workable only on condition that minorities are not made to feel that, whatever their size or personal merits, they have no voice or status. The best rough test of a civilized state is the treatment of minorities within its borders.

This is the real problem presented to Christians by the growth of Authoritarian States during the last fifteen years.

Our belief in the Fatherhood of God carries with it the implication that we are all children of one father. This general statement is perhaps sufficient in itself, but it should be considered in the light of the following passages from Scripture:

> Whosoever will be great among you, let him be your minister, and whosoever will be chief among you, let him be your servant.
> This is my commandment, that you love one another, as I have loved you. Greater love hath no man than this, that a man lay down his life for his friends. Ye are my friends if ye do whatsoever I command you. Henceforth I call you not servants: for the servant knoweth not what his lord doeth.
> Inasmuch as ye have done it unto one of the least of these my brethren, ye have done it unto me.

Behind these passages is a common spirit—which we must as Christians seek to apply. The change of outlook which placed economics above all other aims

—the contraction of the territory within which the writ of religion was conceived to run—is of recent growth.

RELIGION AND ECONOMICS

When the age of the Reformation begins [writes Mr Tawney], economics is still a branch of ethics, and ethics a branch of theology: all human activities are treated as falling within a single scheme, whose character is determined by the spiritual destiny of mankind: the appeal of the theorists is to natural law, not to utility: the legitimacy of economic transactions is tried by reference less to the movements of the market than to moral standards derived from Christian teaching.

The Church itself was a society with practical as well as theoretical authority over a nation.

Two centuries later the divorce between economics and religion was complete. They were regarded as parallel and independent provinces, governed by different laws, judged by different standards, amenable to different authorities. That is the case to-day—but with a difference—for though they are regarded as parallel they are no longer looked upon as *independent* provinces. The doctrine of absolute separation is confined to Marxians on the one side and to the following of Karl Barth, the extreme pietists on the other. It has never counted for much in this country, where politics have never been officially cut loose from morality, but on the contrary are allied at every point with Christianity. It is clear that, in the words of the 69th Psalm, "the things that should have been for our wealth" (in the classical sense of the word) "have become unto us an occasion of falling": it has happened before and it will happen again. All forms of national prosperity which arise from the levying of tribute from foreign possessions (which we have long ceased to practise) or from the possession of slaves (which we have long ceased to own) are full of peril to the national character and eventually to the stability of civilization. But perhaps we still practise these things indirectly, by having invested too largely abroad and by depending too much on exports.

Plato is emphatic on the subject (*Laws*, iv. 704):

> Had you been on the sea, and well provided with harbours, some mighty saviour would have been needed, and lawgiver more than mortal, if you were ever to have a chance of preserving your state from degeneracy and discordance of manners. . . . The sea is pleasant enough as a daily companion, but has indeed also a bitter and brackish quality, filling the streets with merchants and shopkeepers, and begetting in the souls of men uncertain and unfaithful ways. . . . There is a consolation, therefore, in the country producing all things at home; and yet, owing to the ruggedness of the soil, not providing anything in great abundance. Had it been abundance there might have been a great export trade, and a greater return of silver and gold, which as we may safely affirm, has the most fatal results in a state whose aim is the attainment of just and noble sentiments.

This is the philosophical and indeed the religious justification for developing home industries, even if it means a lower standard of life for some of us; and for bringing back agriculture, the most vital of industries, to its proper place in the national economy. We shall, I believe, do so, and emerge better, wiser, stronger, and nobler from our trials.

Relations Between Church and State

> We must erase from the mind of the country [said Disraeli in October 1862] the idea that the Church of England is a clerical corporation. The Church of England is a national corporation of which the clerical element, however important, is only a small element.

Our sovereign is crowned by the heads of the Church, by a Christian ceremony: the proceedings of

Parliament are opened daily by prayer—and no one who is accustomed to attend those prayers can fail to realize that they are a reality, and that they have an influence on its proceedings. In all our legislation the appeal to Christian standards is implicit: in our discussions in Parliament the appeal is often explicit. To quote Disraeli once more:

> Those who advocate the abolition of the union between Church and State have not carefully considered the consequences of such a course. The Church is a powerful corporation of many millions of Her Majesty's subjects. . . . Restricted and controlled by the State so powerful a corporation may be only fruitful of public advantage, but it becomes a great question what might be the consequence of the severance of the controlling tie between these two bodies. The State may be enfeebled, but the Church would probably be strengthened. . . . I doubt whether it would be favourable to the cause of civil and religious history.

The connexion with the State is a powerful antidote to the inclination to confine religion within the limits of individual emotion or belief, and keeps up a sense of the intimate relations between Christian faith and character on the one hand, and human interests and social justice on the other. Let us modify and modernize the connexion, but keep it. Politics without religion would be poorer: religion divorced from the State would be less fruitful of good. Let us in a word bring religion into politics, but keep politics out of the Churches.

The basis of any form of society must always be the personal character of the citizen: this in its turn rests upon certain principles which, in my belief, find their true expression and surest development in Christian doctrine. To expound these principles is the function of the Church: to apply them the function of the State, aided by men of goodwill who by long training and experience are qualified to advise the leaders of the nation. No greater disservice can be rendered to the State than to lend the authority of religion to ancient catchwords and discredited nostrums which aim at the diffusion of general prosperity by systems which, however ingeniously expounded, are derided by economists and rejected by thinking men.

Many factors combine to retard the rate of growth of material prosperity: that it has risen steadily for the past two hundred years is not in doubt. That a rapid growth in the population of the world has synchronized with an amelioration over the greater part of the world of the conditions under which human beings live is not seriously questioned. That want, misery, and sickness are less common than heretofore is demonstrated by all accessible documentary and statistical evidence. There is every ground for hope, and for confidence, in the record of human progress in the last century. There is every reason to believe that we are, at the moment, emerging from a period of depression, the direct result of war, to a higher level of material prosperity; but unless the spirit of man is raised to a higher level our efforts will be in vain. *Nisi Dominus frustra*, Unless the Lord build the house their labour is but vain that build it.

Let the Church then, with George Meredith, "look at the good future of man with some faith in it, and capacity to regard current phases of opinion without letting our sensations blind and bewilder us". "We see events forced on us", to-day, as Emerson saw them a century ago, "which seem to retard or retrograde the civility of ages. But the world spirit is a good swimmer, and storms and waves cannot drown him. Through the years and the centuries a great and beneficent tendency irresistibly streams."

Our ancestors held *Accidie* (ἀκηδία) or sloth to be the fourth cardinal sin. It shews itself to-day in the deadly form of a sour or hopeless pessimism which proclaims its faith in humanity in general whilst exciting in men the deepest distrust of each other, and asks each successive generation at school and college to believe that an unfriendly world has in store for them nought but misery and prostration. Against these prophets of doom the Church should stand four-square with its message of hope, faith, and love. Love of, and the desire to live with and to serve, each other, and to transmit to those who come after a legacy worthy of the great company of men who, having served their generation, died strong in the hope which we inherit from them. Faith in the future, though it is hidden from us as it was hidden from our forefathers. Remembering how dark to their eyes was the road which they trod, we shall face it more boldly in our secular life if the Church will proclaim from every pulpit the great lesson of her long history —that faith conquers. Hope, based not on self-deception but on the faithful record of God's guidance of his creatures through the ages, to which the Psalms, too little expounded, and the great hymns of the Church bear witness, of which mankind longs to hear from the pulpit—and it is by hope for their children that men and women are moved to endure hardness and to run with patience the race that is set before them.

The individual dies, but the nation, of which he was during his lifetime a living part, endures. This is an immortality which all can understand, and a conception which invests short and humble lives with dignity and meaning. For this reason, if the Church is to carry weight and to extend its bounds to cover the world it must in every country be national in its outlook and teaching—no narrow nationalism indeed, but an explicit recognition of the duty that every human being owes to the secular society in which he lives.

A century ago the Church bid the Christian have regard rather to the future than to his present life. Eastern allegory and metaphor was given the most literal interpretation. To-day we are too often bidden to regard only our own lives and to think little, of what we can know so little, of immortality and eternal life. With a better understanding of the nature of time will come greater insight into the truth underlying the promise to Christians of eternal life—the life immortal. Meanwhile may the Church, standing above secular causes however great, with a message greater than the greatest of secular heralds can proclaim, hold fast, like Job, to righteousness—the righteousness that exalteth a nation—and to that good thing which has been committed to it, by the Holy Spirit which dwells within us all, and by the words of our Lord Jesus Christ.

The oldest charge to clergy is that of St. Paul (I Timothy vi.):

> But thou, O man of God . . . follow after righteousness, godliness, faith, love, patience, meekness. Fight the good fight of faith, lay hold on eternal life, whereunto thou wast called. . . .
>
> Charge them that are rich in this present world, that they be not high-minded, nor have their hope set on the uncertainty of riches, but on God, who giveth us richly all things to enjoy; that they do good, that they be rich in good works, that they be ready to distribute, willing to communicate; laying up in store for themselves a good foundation against the time to come, that they may lay hold on the life which is life indeed.
>
> O Timothy, guard that which is committed unto thee, turning away from the profane babblings and oppositions of the knowledge which is falsely so called: which some professing have erred concerning the faith.
>
> Grace be with you.

This to me is the true function of the Church in relation to secular life, and to those clergy who pursue it is vouchsafed, in my experience, the confidence and trust of their flocks in the fullest measure; to them is given an influence upon the minds of men which transcends that of experts and philosophers. To such men the secular world will listen to-day as readily as ever in the past. With such men in my mind, in all humility and gratitude, I have written.

VII

RELIGION AND SEX

by

DOUGLAS WHITE, M.A., M.D.

Author of "Forgiveness and Suffering" (C.U. Press)
and of "Modern Light on Sex and Marriage" (Skeffington)

SYNOPSIS

THE RELATIONSHIP BETWEEN RELIGION AND SEX
IN HISTORY

RELIGION is necessarily related to morality, and sex morals form the basis of all morality. Human inheritance involves both body and spirit. All human capacities are interrelated; sex is not an adjunct, but pervades the whole of life. There are three primary instincts—the self-regarding instinct, the altruistic instinct, and the sex instinct, the sex instinct forming a bridge between the other two. In early historic times sex symbolism was bound up with sympathetic magic. Oriental religions were full of sex symbolism and practice as exemplified in temple prostitution. Hebrew religion was contaminated by such practices and the religious rites of the Greeks and Romans were of a licentious character. In the early centuries of Christianity there was a rebound to a violent asceticism based on a philosophy, still prevalent, of a final hostility between flesh and spirit. To-day a harmonization between the two elements is called for.

Religion and sex are never really segregated. The sexual *motif* is still apparent in expressions of religious emotion—in hymnology and in the phenomena of mysticism. There is a parallelism between sex and religion. Each requires emotion tempered by intelligence. The finest sexual love is a beautifully spiritual thing.

SEXUAL MORALS NOT STATIC BUT PROGRESSIVE

The principles of morality have been progressively perceived as man has grown in intellectual, moral, and social insight. Conscience—the apprehension of the good—has grown in sensitiveness since primitive days. There has been a gradual progress from negative commandments to positive principles. Increasing knowledge has played an important role in the development of moral conceptions, especially within the sphere of sexual morality. Sexual morals have developed concurrently with biological knowledge. The growth of biological knowledge accounted for the change from the matrilineal to the patrilineal concept of descent. The discovery in the seventeenth century of the ovum, and the discovery in 1850 that the male sperm makes organic contact and actual fusion with the ovum, in principle counteracted the mediaeval exaltation of the male as the real life-giver so far as this was based on Aristotelean biology. Conscience has been enlightened as knowledge has increased. Advance has recently been real, but public conscience still lags behind knowledge.

The Economy of Sex in Nature: Its Use and Abuse

Man and woman are just so different as to fit each other in every way, and yet so similar as each to have some understanding of the other. In each there is a reaction between sense and soul. The sensuous may be refined but not eliminated. There is a serious need for some knowledge before marriage of the physiology and psychology of sex function. The ecclesiastical attitude on sex relations has led to a dichotomy of the sexual life. Prostitution, though not primitive, has flourished since the early days of civilization. It has been regarded as a necessary rampart for the defence of marriage. The feeling that occasional promiscuity is beneath human dignity is causing prostitution to fall into disuse among the better classes in Britain. The regulation of prostitution has increased the evils against which it was aimed. Affectionate liaisons of a more or less lasting character, far though they are from the ideal, constitute an advance on the system of prostitution. The independent value of the sex factor in marriage must be recognized if marriage is to become the norm of sex relationship. In sex, as in religion, the sensuous is a factor.

The Proper Ground and Condition of Monogamy

In the white races, and apparently in all human races, more males are born than females. This excess is more than counteracted by a greater infant mortality among males, so that in adult life there is a preponderance of women. This preponderance is being steadily reduced for the rising generation *as a result* of the reduction of infant mortality, so that by the year 1950, it is calculated, the number of marriageable men and women will be approximately equal. The decline in the birth-rate will in about ten years bring about a stabilization of the population. This need not necessarily cause anxiety; but the fact that the birth-rate is differential between the classes may have a dysgenic effect. Parity of numbers between the sexes demands monogamy, the only alternative being sexual anarchy. It also demands a single standard of sex conduct.

The Church: Marriage and Divorce

Monogamy does not necessarily imply indissolubility. Western Christianity has moved toward the doctrine of indissolubility. The Eastern Church has regarded marriage as being dissoluble for adultery and other causes. The Western view is avowedly based on the words of Christ, but there is the alternative explanation that originally the doctrine of indissolubility was based on a desire to leave room for repentance on the part of the erring husband or wife. The words of Christ should be understood in the light of the Hillel-Shammai controversy, and there is the further question as to whether he was in fact acting as a legislator. The Church and the State are to-day in agreement as to the ideal of marriage even if they disagree as to the methods of attaining it. The English law of divorce is to-day in an evil state. Modern thought desires that when a marriage has actually come to an end the State should give relief. Divorce is the friend, not the enemy of marriage, while indissolubility has proved in experience to be unfavourable to good morals. The sanctity of marriage comes from within and is the creation of neither Church nor State. Marriage cannot rightly be described as a sacrament unless there be spiritual communion. Though it is argued that the indissolubility of marriage is to the benefit of the children, children are not benefited by being brought up in an atmosphere of bickering and bitterness between the parents. The ultimate court of appeal for the Christian State is the Christian conscience. The doctrine of "the other cheek" does not restrain the State from using a police force. Divorce is a remedy for failure, though unfortunately there is in England no other means of escape from the ruin of a marriage except by committing adultery.

Birth-Control and Abortion

The ideal is that the newly married woman should experience the complete gamut of a woman's sex life; but for very many there may be good reasons to the contrary. Children should come by design, not by accident. There is general agreement as to the duty of limitation of families; but there are differences as to method. Abstinence involves a drastic limitation of the sexual relationship. The so-called "safe period" is not safe, and it is the period during which women least desire connexion. Our knowledge is incomplete. Sexual intimacy has an independent value of its own as the sacrament of love. It is not merely for the procreation of children. The present methods of contraception are not ideal, but the spacing of children is essential both for mothers and children. No woman ought to be subjected to an annual pregnancy. To forbid marital relations invites extra-marital intercourse. The alternative to the use of contraceptives is, in too many cases, the practice of abortion. In many European countries there is a growing demand for the legalization of abortion, but this would decrease if the knowledge of efficient contraception were more widely spread. An allied question is that of eugenic sterilization. Such questions should be studied without prejudice in order to find a solution for them in accord with basic moral and religious thought.

The Sublimation of Sex

Sublimation means refinement and enhancement. The sublimation of the sex instinct is its refinement and partial diversion into other channels than that of its primary flow. Without such diversion civilization stagnates. The potential energy of sex may be compared to a river flowing through land which needs irrigation. The river flows on to the sea and cannot all be used up for the derivative purpose of irrigation, but it can be partially dammed up and the overflow so used. The secretion of the sex glands can be partially reabsorbed and serve creative purposes other than physical. Abundance of sex energy creates difficulty, but if the possessor exercises self-control he will be compensated to a very special degree by the enrichment of his personality. At the same time, the overflow should have some outlet, as in marriage. There is great variation in sexual strength. Its transmutation demands no little effort and that over long periods. An adequate motive for the effort can be provided, especially in times of stress, by religion alone.

The Readjustment of Sex to Religion

Religion and sex are not opposed forces but are ultimately different aspects of the same energy—the energy of Love. The early Christian contempt of sex is unjustifiable though, in view of the degradation of sex in the later Roman Empire, understandable. Sex ought to be judged by its highest level. To the best thought of to-day Sense and Spirit are no longer regarded as in final opposition, but as capable of beautiful harmonization. The finest love means giving and receiving, losing one's self and thus finding it. Marriage has difficulties which are intensified by the progress of culture, difficulties traditional, biological, and social. A sense of subjection or serfdom of the woman (patriarchy) is fatal to marriage. Biological changes, especially in the woman, cause difficulties. Culture produces a high individualization which makes it difficult to secure a congenial mate. But the prize is great. Life is unsatisfying without a personally centralized affection. A new orientation of thought about sex is required, not dissociated from but reintegrated with religion.

VII

RELIGION AND SEX

The Relationship between Religion and Sex in History

Does the title of this paper sound incongruous for a book concerned with the religious outlook? Are not sex and religion incompatibles, like oil and water, which, shake them up together as you may, will never coalesce but only form a muddy emulsion? Such a view is as common as it is mistaken. Religion, morals, and sex form a basic unity in the human constitution, whether individual or communal. If you separate religion from general morals (that is, from standards of social conduct) you are killing religion; a live religion must express itself in social righteousness. But what is the relation between morals and sex? If I mistake not greatly, sex lies at the very root of all social ethic. When you call a man or woman immoral (without further definition) you mean sexually immoral. And that is not merely a habit of language; it represents a fundamental of life.

Human society is built upon a sexual basis; that is inescapable. This basis implies inheritance, not only of the bodily structures and functions, but of the instincts, the mind, and that whole intangible make-up which we call "spirit". All our human capacities are interrelated. The sex organs are not mere specialized appendages, isolated from our general life: they influence, and are influenced by, our whole spiritual activity. All ideas of right social conduct, all altruism, and alternatively all selfishness, seem to be rooted in the concept of sex as it takes shape in the

264

minds of races and peoples. Sex also has laid civilization under tribute for all the finer arts of life; hear Dr. Maudsley:[1] "Were man robbed of the instinct of procreation and of all that spiritually springs therefrom, that moment would all poetry, and perhaps also his whole moral sense, be obliterated from his life".

Consider now the three great instincts or urges of human life.

First, the instinct of self-protection and self-advancement. Good and necessary up to a point; but man cannot live to himself alone; if only for his own benefit, he must keep in active touch with his social group on which his life and hopes depend. That is the second, the herd instinct. But something more is needed than protective association; there must be a sentiment of loyalty, springing out of some sort of affection. Here comes in the third great instinct, the urge of sex, whereby the individual is drawn affectionally towards one of the opposite sex; this forms the bridge between self-interest and altruism; the sexual affection becomes for him the centre whence radiates his emotional feeling, first for the family, then for the group, tribe, or clan. So it becomes clear that, if religion and ethics are inseparable, sex and religion cannot be very distant cousins. Indeed, they always have been closely related, though, after the manner of cousins, their behaviour to each other is not always predictable.

In simple fact, the historical bond between religion and sex is beyond question. When primitive animistic ideas began to acquire some sort of intellectual focus, the first conception of God would be that of creator. It might well then be thought that man's creative powers bring him into close relation with God. Such an argument may, or may not, explain

---

[1] Maudsley, *Physiology of Mind*; quoted by Havelock Ellis, *Psychology of Sex*, vol. vi. p. 140.

the outspoken—not to say blatant—sexual symbolism, and sexual practices suited to it, which constantly obtrude themselves in practically all early Oriental religions. That aspect still survives in India and elsewhere. It had a footing among the Hebrews: the story of the fall in Genesis is cram-full of sexual symbolism—the serpent, the apple, the tree of knowledge (they knew—that they were naked)—all emblems of sexual passion and desire.

The early history of Israel shews how largely sexual practices figured in the worship of the tribal god; the whoredoms of the country (groves, high places, and the rest) were constantly attacked by the indignant prophets. In those early days, clearly religion and sex were closely combined. The gross practices, indeed, fell into disuse as the concept of God's character enlarged and improved; yet the symbolism remained even into Christian times, though its interpretation was entirely changed. The cross itself, and the fish ($\dot{\iota}\chi\theta\grave{\upsilon}\varsigma$), originally phallic emblems, were translated into Christian symbols, which, now for long, have quite lost their original meaning.

The story of the interrelation of sex and religion exhibits many phases, with strange alternations of alliance and hostility. In early historic times the alliance was striking: it took the form of sympathetic magic.

When multiplication of flocks or the fructifying of crops was desired, men sought to propitiate the proper god or goddess by special festivals of fertility, exhibiting their needs symbolically by indulgence in promiscuous sex relations. At other times, by contrast, sexual abstinence was enjoined, in order to avert the malice of unfriendly spirits. Later on, temple prostitution, for both sexes, was used (and is still used) to symbolize, and in some sense to effect, union of the worshipper with god or goddess. We read of such practices in Palestine, to which the Israelites, if not already habituated, became easily acclimatized. The religious rites of the Greeks and Romans were also of a licentious character; and after the Christian era, some, at least, of the mystery religions were not free from the taint. Thus the close relation of sexual practices with religion in the past is quite plain. The effect of such widespread habits (perhaps specially at Rome in the latter half of the first century) was found to be debasing both to religion and morals. Disgust at the excesses of sexual laxity produced, by way of rebound, various styles of asceticism. These were by no means confined to the Christian religion; they had existed before it, quite independently. But after the first century many prominent figures in the Christian Church exhibited extreme forms of asceticism, with the object of subduing and expelling carnal lusts. John the Baptist had been an ascetic; Christ was not; untainted himself, he did not disdain to be called the friend of publicans and harlots; his attitude towards the adulterous woman shews, not only his generous attitude towards such, but also throws light on the sexual laxity of the men of his generation, not one of the accusers being able to throw a stone at her. But, even before the close of the first century, asceticism had begun to grip the Christian Church. St. Paul, indeed, does not condemn marriage, though he commends virginity. Virginity is praised in the Apocalypse, though the Epistle to the Hebrews declares the marriage bed to be undefiled. The influence of St. Paul, however, became paramount; his views on marriage ("better to marry than to burn") do not suggest an exalted conception;[1] his grudging permissiveness of marriage set the standard of thought

---

[1] Except for the description of the Church as Christ's bride, in the doubtfully authentic Epistle to the Ephesians (Eph. v. 22 ff.; but cf. also 2 Cor. xi. 2).

for succeeding centuries, till, gradually, complete sexual abstinence became the hall-mark of high Christianity; woman, as woman, came to be regarded as a sewer of iniquity, so that in some monasteries the name of woman might not even be mentioned. The penitentials (dating from about A.D. 950–1300) concern themselves almost exclusively with sexual sins, penance being ordered even for lustful thoughts with no external expression. All this was the result of a philosophy of dualism—the spirit against the flesh and the flesh against the spirit; it was to be a fight between them to a finish. But you can't use a pitchfork to Nature. Not yet could humanity discern the "gracious equilibrium of Nature". The balance of sex had been forcefully tilted right over from licence to anathema.

Neither limitless carnalism nor exclusive spiritualism (pardon the expressions) will fit any comprehensive philosophy of life. History makes plain two things: first, that reckless sensuality wrecks nations; second, that you cannot eliminate from life its sexual foundation. The only remedy lies in the harmonization of the two elements, each of which is part and parcel of the human make-up. Religion must claim them both. The present generation has now, perhaps for the first time, the chance of building up such a harmony: a new philosophy of science, a new philosophy of religion, a new philosophy of sex; and these three must be one.

In history, then, it is clear that sex is closely tied up with religion; like a see-saw, swinging first one way, then the other, with religion as the fulcrum. What about the position to-day? On the one hand, we must admit that in families with a religious outlook all sexual manifestations are still regarded with suspicion: boys and girls are warned against any form of sex activity; the attitude is one of negation; positive teaching is rarely given. The need of positive knowledge is beginning to be recognized, even by the Churches; but, as yet, with little effect. On the other hand, the close nexus between sex and religion is tacitly acknowledged in many ways. Let me explain my meaning; how the current ideas of our relations with God are by no means independent of a sexual *motif*. Let us take the primary concept of union with God. Except in some pictorial form, personal union with the Great Spirit of the Universe is difficult to conceive at all; between human personalities, a merging of will and feeling is possible, and pre-eminently through sexual love; it is, I think, by that analogy that the idea of mystical union with God is reached.

This thought, indeed, ought not to sound shocking, or even strange, to Christian ears; for the Song of Solomon, an idyllic and plainly erotic composition, having found its place in the Canon of the Old Testament, has been interpreted (in the headings of each of its chapters in our Authorized Version) as expressing in fitting terms the mutual relations of Christ and his Church. Many of its passages are familiar to evangelical ears.

Moreover, the experiences of saints, specially of women mystics, have often been, quite patently, closely allied to the sexual rapture.[1] But, apart from the rapturous mystical experience, there is, and always has been, a very close bond between religious and sexual emotion; where religious enthusiasm is high-pitched, sexual ardour is not far to seek. It was found so in the very early days[2] of Christianity, and so it is to-day. Uncontrolled religious fervour often leads to sexual decontrol.

Again, look into our hymn-books, and consider the more intensely devotional hymns, specially those addressed to Jesus: you cannot fail to see the sexual type of thought; such verses appeal to the feminine

---

[1] Cp. H. Ellis, *Psychology of Sex*, vol. i. App. C, p. 310 ff.
[2] Cf. Didache, § 11.

mind, though alien to masculine thought. It is just as well that we should be conscious of the erotic element in religious emotion.

Do not think I am poking fun at religious emotion. The sexual impulse is potentially noble, though, like every noble thing, capable of debasement. So also is the religious impulse. Degradation of sex activity also degrades religious feeling; exalted thoughts of sexual love bring with them a heightened religious sensibility.

It seems, indeed, that sex and religion run along parallel lines. To attain any worthy result, each must implicate the whole personality. The indulgence of a temporary sexual emotion between two persons is harmful to both; in the highest love, the physical attraction and emotion are both right and necessary: but these should be under control of the spiritual— the intelligence and higher social sentiments; for in the case of sexual love, the physical supplies its intensity, and the spiritual its permanence. The same is true of religion. A religion based upon a violent passing emotion is not enough to satisfy for long; the emotion must have behind it the intelligence, the mind, in full vigour; love of God must embrace the whole personality.

Conversely, in religion the intellect is not, by itself, sufficient; pure intellect is cold; it needs the drive of hot feeling. So also with sexual love; mere intellectual sympathy or similarity of tastes is inadequate; there must be an emotional drive; the one supplies the power, the other the guidance and, where necessary, the brake.

One last thought on the intermingling of sex with religion. Love between man and woman—love in its full and all-embracing sense—is the most beautifully spiritual thing the world has ever seen. When such a love dawns on the soul of man or woman, the world becomes to them a new world; that is the high moment when one sees right through to the truth of things—when one comes into close and almost immediate contact with that Love which lives at the centre of the Universe and which we call God. In such an experience we are able to believe, despite contrary appearances, that God loves his creation: and at last we feel sure that we can be children of God, sex and all. Can you wonder, then, that men and women in love tend to desire some religious sanction for marriage—even if they dislike the institutional form—just because they feel that sex and religion are somehow twin emotions? Surely men and women must needs love the highest when they see it: they only want a guide to lead them up the mountain and shew them the view.

Sexual Morals not Static but Progressive

The fact of evolution is beyond doubt, though the factors in its production are still in debate. Alongside of the structural and physiological progress there has also occurred development in the mental and psychological sphere. These changes have not ceased but are still going on ceaselessly. The moral outlook cannot be, and has not been, immune from corresponding change and development. Such changes need not always mean, and have not always meant, progress; but on the whole, through history, progress is plain, if slow. This is not only true of general morals, but is particularly true in the sexual region. Are there then, you may ask, no fixed principles of morality? Yes, there are; but these principles have only been gradually perceived by man as he has grown in intellectual, moral, and social insight. Is not conscience, then, the infallible guide that we have supposed? For the individual, indeed, it is the best guide he has, and, as such, is bound to follow. But conscience too—the apprehension of the good—is progressive, and has progressed from the most primitive days to the present. All along the long line, men have arisen with consciences sensitive to condemn current practices commonly accepted as right, and their moral judgement has, through time, won general approval.

Abraham was perhaps the first to perceive that God did not require propitiation by the slaughter of his son. Later on the prophets taught the Hebrews that God required justice and not sacrifice. Moral concepts advanced with advance in concepts of the Divine. The ten commandments were a great improvement on the previous code; yet even they were (with one exception) of a negative character, "Thou shalt not". They expressed condemnation of existing practices; and that is the method by which gradual moral progress has happened. But negatives are not enough; we need some positive principle by which to judge current practice; and that was given by Jesus, when he pronounced the golden rule, compounding it of two passages of the Old Testament (Deut. vi. 5 and Lev. xix. 18). In the light of that principle moral progress has been made ever since. Just as, in the physical world, the facts of astronomy, electromagnetism, wave radiation, have existed all along, but were only recently discovered and made available for man's thought and use. The same sort of thing is true of morality, sexual or otherwise. Call it revelation, if you like; I can see no clear distinction between discovery and revelation; all comes through man, and all from God. The law of love is the great principle which awaited, and still mostly awaits, its application as between individuals and nations. Its application is difficult; but once discovered there can be no reversal of a true principle, whether in physics, physiology, psychology, or religion.

I wish now to emphasize the role which increasing knowledge has played in our conception of morals, specially in sexual morals. Apart from intelligence, the higher degrees (perhaps any degree) of active morality are impossible. Knowledge is not morality; but morality seems to be nothing else than the application of intelligence to the well-being of our fellows and of the world at large.

Apply this to the development of sexual morals. At the first dawning of man's intelligence, he can have had no understanding of the process of fertilization and pregnancy. The dependence of pregnancy on sex intercourse was not known. Tribes at this stage of knowledge still exist to-day, and must have existed generally in the earliest days of humanity. Sex intimacy was, at first, as with beasts, just the gratification of a natural instinct; the thought of paternity did not arise. At such a stage sex relations would be very free among young adults, guided by mutual predilection; but no responsibility was attached on either side. Thus society was at first matrilineal, *i.e.* pedigree was traced on the mother's side: pregnancy was credited to spirit agency. At this stage of knowledge, marriage gave the pair the social position of man and wife, the sexual relation being taken for granted.

This sounds very primitive; but it contains a serious lesson for ourselves; for primitive marriage was instituted for the happiness of the individuals and the contentment of the community. It was based on mutual predilection, sexual and temperamental, which carried with it, as it still does, the prospect of a lasting union. But for us, at the moment, the point is that the sexual code of morals flowed naturally from the knowledge of the day.

This sort of stage must have lasted for, perhaps, thousands of years. By the time we reach the historic period, the earlier concept had faded away.

Agriculture had now been established; the analogy from the seed planted in the ground probably helped towards a new conception of the significance of sex intercourse. The man was the sower of the seed, the woman the soil in which it was planted. This idea formed the basis of patriliny and patriarchy, which prevailed all through historic antiquity, among Hebrews, Greeks, and Romans. The pedigree of Jesus himself, both in Matthew and Luke, is traced exclusively through the male line. You will remember that, in the Epistle to the Hebrews, "Levi was still in the loins of Abraham" when Abraham met Melchizedek. And this notion—the patrilineal notion—has been at the bottom of our concept of marriage up till quite recent times: the code of morals which grew out of it has prevailed for a second series of millennia. Woman thus became man's property: the mother of *his* children, the instrument of *his* pleasure.[1]

The excess of females (as there always has been up to the present) would form the rationale either of a limited polygamy or of prostitution, or both. And this was what actually happened. Not that the seed-and-soil notion went unchallenged. Hippocrates, the father of medicine, held that the woman had an active function in the begetting of children; Aristotle, too, in a narrower sense, believed the woman to be possessed of a material which had to be vitalized by the male seed. Aristotle's view favoured the father as the real life-giver; and, through the influence of Aquinas, the Church followed Aristotle. This conception was bound to exalt the estimate of men, and to lower the position of women.

In the seventeenth century, history repeated itself in the scientific controversy as to whether father or mother played the chief role. The ovum was first discovered, and it became the predominating factor,

---

[1] Here we may note that, from Greco-Roman days until the present century, these two purposes have been separated—children and pleasure. The legal wife was taken mainly for the begetting of children, while extra-marital connexions were formed for sexual pleasure. Can anyone say this idea is obsolete to-day?

though Harvey insisted that the father's influence was necessary for its development. Some twenty-five years later, Leeuwenhoek discovered "animalcules" (now known as spermatozoa) in the male semen: then came a battle-royal between "ovists" and "animal-culists". Not actually till 1850 (less than a century ago) was it proved that the male sperm makes organic contact and actual fusion with the female's ovum; that the result of this fusion was the fertilized cell, the first element of a new creature.

Still further has knowledge advanced in this century; now we grasp something of the deeper mystery of the chromosomes—those living elemental threads in the nucleus of the male and female cells, which at fertilization form a quadrille with their opposite numbers, so that every new life is heralded by a bridal dance in very miniature; so that the infant-to-be is symmetrized, perfect in every detail—an unimaginably complete fusion of the minutest subdivisions of the nuclei of two minute cells, far outstripping the vision of the naked eye. Yes: and the more we study these micro-reactions of sperm and ovum, the more they seem to reflect the mutual activities of full-grown men and women. Marvellous as it all is, is it not plain that knowledge gained is bound momentously to affect, as it has affected, the current concepts of sexual morals? Of course it is. To say that moral notions may, must, and do develop, certainly means that they must change. But it does not mean that there is no ideal towards which they move. Such an ideal we must keep steadily in view, following the growing light of knowledge, doing violence neither to our physical nor to our spiritual instincts, so that our code of sexual ethic shall be in accord with the highest truth as well as the deepest need of our nature.

Think of it: as we look back on the millennia, is it not strange that our own Women's Property Act is but half a century old; women's rights as citizens but a thing of yesterday, following—albeit perhaps unconsciously—in the wake of our knowledge of life? Slowly and with back-slips does mankind rise toward the higher values of sex life, as indeed toward all ethical values, among which sex has pride of place. In this very century, change in ethical concepts is marching at a pace such as never before. Think of the brutal cruelties of the Middle Ages and even of the great seventeenth century, approved then by masses and leaders alike, and you will see how in days of comparative ignorance the progress of real morals has lagged. What about to-day? are the relations of men and women approaching any ideal? Enlightened consciences to-day are clamouring for much needed reform, not only of laws and customs, but of men's minds and hearts. To-day it is for us to incorporate into our system of the future the finest and truest elements in the thought of the past, but placing them in a new framework, in the tapestry of which the warp shall be the happiness of the individual and the woof the stability of society.

The Economy of Sex in Nature: Its Use and Abuse

In every person, the dawning of sex consciousness brings with it the possibility of new and fine ideals. But if ideals are to be realized, even in part, the actual facts of life must be envisaged. If you want to see the stars, your feet and your telescope must be fixed on solid earth.

What is sex to mankind? wherein does it consist? Man and woman are so fashioned, both in body and spirit, as to be complementary, that is, so to fit into each other that each can fulfil the other's needs. Legend has it that when the first woman was brought to the first man, they both laughed. Each was just what the other wanted. Different indeed they were, but with points of contact; not a separate race. In every man and woman are common features that make for mutual sympathy. Each man has in his make-up something of the woman, and each woman something of the man. They are not totally differentiated, either in body or in spirit. The man has the rudiments of the breast, essentially a feminine character: the woman, too, has a small but important structure, which corresponds to the male sexual organ. Both man and woman are just so different as to fit each other every way, and just so similar as each to have some, though imperfect, understanding of the other. Some men have more of the woman in them than others, and some women more of the man. And it is a fact of observation that the most virile men are attracted by the most feminine women, while the men with a higher degree of femininity tend to mate with the rather more masculine type of woman. That is a gracious provision of Nature; it keeps the balance fairly steady. Sex pervades the whole organism both of man and woman, not only in the bodily sphere, but in the spiritual too. It is not merely a specialized adjunct to the body, but a pervasive dynamic.

Man is the more active and aggressive; woman the more passive and receptive. Normal men, after puberty (the age of about 16 to 18) experience desire for bodily contact with a woman, the desire being concentrated on the sexual organs. With a woman, at puberty (some two years earlier) desire is more diffused, not consciously sexual till aroused by male contiguity. With woman, it has been said, love usually proceeds from the soul to the senses and sometimes does not reach so far: with the man it usually proceeds from the senses to the soul, and may never complete the journey. The ideal of marriage can only be reached if both journeys are completed; for then

only can there be full mutual adjustment of personalities at all levels of consciousness from the humblest to the highest.

Evolution has proceeded from the simpler to the
more complex; from the humbler to the higher; from
the sensorial to the spiritual. But the sensuous is
fundamental; it cannot be eliminated, but rather refined, as we rise to the spiritual. The facts of sex
ought to be understood by anyone contemplating
marriage. Instinct in man is not enough; sufficient
in animals, it is blurred and unfocused in man, and
needs to be guided by intelligence.

Even to-day it is unbelievable how crassly ignorant many young men and women, of all classes, can
be of the very elements of sexual structure and
function, and even more so of sexual psychology, the
appreciation of which is a pre-requisite to satisfactory
marital relations. Every man and (I think) every
woman ought, before marriage, to obtain some elementary grasp of these things. It is as necessary
from the Christian standpoint as from any other. If
consummation is an integral and vital part of marriage (as all tradition insists), then it ought to be
accomplished in an intelligent manner, befitting a
relation so refinedly sacramental.[1]

The beauty and satisfaction of sexual intimacy lies
in the mutual awakening of, and response to, desire.
The lover's art, like every art, requires care and deli-
cacy. For the lack of it, many a marriage has come
to failure. A marriage may be wrecked, even on the
first night, by the clumsiness or stupidity of the
bridegroom, or by the ignorance or false modesty of
the bride. In the communion of bodies, there should
be no force, nor fear, nor shame. It is the high place
of love.

---

[1] Such information is now happily available in many books. A
simple exposition has been attempted in a pamphlet, *Right Marriage*,
published by the Christian Student Movement Press.

Not only at the beginning, but all through marital life, the utmost consideration and forbearance must be forthcoming. The needs, positive or negative, of each should, so far as possible, be the guiding motive of the other. High love demands high chastity: but, be it remembered, chastity is a thing of the spirit, and is not the equivalent of mere abstinence. The highest chastity may, at times, demand the fulness of love. It is a true paradox.

Although physical consummation has always been held necessary to the completion of marriage, yet the specifically sexual side of marriage has been frowned upon or neglected by the Catholic Church (Roman or Anglican), the main purpose of the union being regarded as the begetting of children (an idea carried over into Christianity from the Greco-Roman concept), excluding, so far as possible, the element of sexual pleasure (obviously intended by Nature). This outlook has determined the separation of sex activity into two streams: the one, marriage, for the ulterior purpose of children; the other, fornication, or extra-marital liaison, for the immediate purpose of sexual gratification. This separation has been unfortunate, but it has a long and powerful tradition behind it. It is bad, because it leads to a damaging dichotomy of a man's personality—a double life, the one domestic, the other sensual.

So we are led to the subject of prostitution. Prostitution is not primitive, seeing that in primitive humanity sex relations were, except for certain incest tabus, untrammelled by inhibitions, and followed mutual predilection; commercialization had not arisen. But it did flourish in Palestine, Greece, and Rome; and it has flourished till our day. We cannot shut our eyes to the close interrelation between marriage and prostitution. Indeed, up till the present century, the accepted idea, by both Church and State, has been that prostitution is a necessary defence of marriage. Augustine lays it down quite definitely. "Take away prostitutes", he says, "and you will wreck society through lust." Aquinas, in the thirteenth century, follows his lead, telling us that prostitutes are as necessary to marriage as sewers are to a palace. Similarly our own Lecky, in a famous passage: "She [the prostitute] remains, while creeds and civilizations rise and fall, the eternal priestess of humanity, blasted for the sins of the people". So too Balzac: "They make of their bodies a rampart for the protection of respectable families"; and Schopenhauer speaks of them as "a human sacrifice on the altar of monogamy".[1] That was, in fact, the dominant view of Christendom for 1600 years, and prostitutes were alternately licensed as an unfortunate necessity or brutally persecuted. Havelock Ellis refuses this hypothesis, denying the "rampart" idea, but propounding that marriage and prostitution are but part and parcel of one system. That ought to set us a-thinking. But a third view of the relationship of the two is possible; namely, that they represent two competing sexual systems—competing not only as between social groups, or even between individuals, but even competing within the mind of the same individual, in different moods; the one taking cognizance of spiritual ideals, the other exploiting the merely sensual.

But that is to philosophize. Look at the facts today. Among the better classes in Britain, prostitution is largely passing into disuse, since both men and women feel that occasional promiscuity is beneath human dignity, divorced as it is from affectional relationship. It has therefore given place to affectional liaisons of a more or less lasting character. This is far from ideal; yet, for anyone who knows, or can imagine, the horrible evils of prostitution, and specially of regulated prostitution, it must be re-

[1] Havelock Ellis, *Psychology of Sex*, vol. vi. p. 281.

garded as an advance.[1] The prostitute is commonly regarded as the fountain-head of disease; but the demand for her is created by the very men who use her, despise her, and inflict on her the diseases which she spreads.

The best elements in civilization desire that marriage should be the norm of sex expression in a nation. That can never be the case until religion has fully and freely acknowledged and welcomed sex gratification, as well as the procreation of children (to which indeed it is a powerful adjuvant), as essential to a high-spirited and full-blooded marriage. This much-needed change of attitude is gradually infiltrating the better classes of society, and is even coming within the vision of religious bodies, slow as they are to break free from traditional authority.

The attempt, in sexual matters, to dissociate the sensuous from the spiritual is as unreasonable as it would be in religious worship. In religion we recognize architectural, liturgical, musical beauties, all as potent adjuvants to the spirit of worship. They are all sensuous, through eye, ear, and even smell, and are used as means of creating and heightening the spiritual atmosphere. All these things can be abused, yet we do not despise them. In despising sex, we have despised (so says Maudsley) that which is the only final elevating principle of life.

---

[1] The fight against State-regulated and licensed prostitution, started by the heroic Josephine Butler in the latter half of last century, has made slow but steady progress in Europe: State regulation has been abolished in Scandinavia, Switzerland, and elsewhere; while France stands at the head of the Latin countries, refusing hitherto to abolish the anachronism of licensed women and licensed brothels. That system, during the last 150 years, has aimed chiefly at the reduction of venereal diseases; but now it has been made clear that disease is more rampant in regulated countries than in unregulated. It has also been proved that regulation is the mainstay of the White Slave international traffic.

The Proper Ground and Condition of Monogamy

A recent writer advocates polygamy as a cure for present evils, seeing that in Great Britain there is a considerable excess of women. There is indeed such an excess: in England and Wales the excess was, in 1911, 1,220,000; in 1921, 1,804,000; in 1931, 1,684,000; and now it stands at about a million and a half. To-day for each 1000 men there are 1084 women. But the figures need interpretation; we shall be misled if we build on the sand of shifting figures. Rapid changes are in process. Let us begin at the beginning.

For some reason not yet fully understood, by the grace of Nature, in the white races, and apparently in all human races, more males are born than females, in the ratio, here, of about 104 to 100. That is, at birth; but at conception the male excess is certainly greater, probably between 20 and 30 per cent. But at all ages now the mortality of males (up to old age) is greater than of females, specially so during embryonic life, so that a large proportion of the excess males conceived are choked off before birth.[1] Of the infants born, too, many more males die in the first year of life than females (up to 1900 about 25 per cent), so that the male excess was then practically wiped out in the first year or two of life. But the excess male mortality still went on, so that before adult life there was a considerable excess of females. Until 1900 there was a high infant mortality (about 150 per thousand); after that, more care was taken of children, and the mortality figures have fallen from 150 to 60—a vast change, so that the excess of males born tends to continue into adult life.[2] To-day,

---

[1] It has been stated that in some backward races the whole male excess is eliminated before birth.

[2] Girl children are still more easily saved than boys; and although the excess *per cent* of male infant deaths is now even greater than it

indeed, males are in excess up to the age of nearly 20, and by 1950 this figure will rise to somewhere near 30, the result being that, by that time (apart from wars, or excessive male emigration), the numbers of marriageable men and women will be about equal.

The importance of this fact, a new fact in the nation's history, has not been grasped; in it lies a real national importance of the reduction in infant mortality. Moreover, the infant mortality is capable of a further drop, perhaps to about 35 per thousand; if that happens, there might, in a generation, be even a slight excess of marriageable males, which some authorities think desirable, since there are thought to be more men than women who do not desire to marry.

Thus we see that the natural religious impulse to save infant life, in itself of doubtful national utility, is justified by its indirect result in securing equal opportunity of marriage for all in later years.

Another point: During the last fifty years the birth-rate has fallen from 35 to 15 per thousand. But the true state of affairs is better seen from the actual number of births. Though the birth-rate was slightly falling from 1876 to 1900, the peak of actual numbers born was reached in 1903, when just under 950,000 babies were born in England and Wales. Since then the numbers have fallen steadily (save for a sharp oscillation during the War) to below 600,000[1]—a matter of profound significance. The population as a whole, indeed, is still increasing, because people are living longer; but in about ten years the population will become steady, the number of births and deaths becoming equal. This need not cause anxiety unless the excessive fall in births continues, which is not likely. What we want is quality, more than quantity.

was (about 33 per cent), yet the excess of males born is maintained till adult life.

[1] In 1933 and 1934.

And here is the ground for anxiety. The capacity for the procreation of children (fecundity) does not vary greatly in the different grades of society, yet the actual production (fertility) is widely divergent. The so-called upper classes produce least; while the unskilled workers produce most. It has been truly said that civilization is a lamp which burns at the top and is replenished from below; the finest blossoms of ability will probably come, as they have in the past, from the vigorous humbler gentry, artisans, and farmers; but we cannot hope for great things from the progeny of the mentally backward. Like tends to mate with like; dull and backward parents tend to produce children duller and more backward than themselves, having a double dose of deficiency. What is the positive moral? Surely that, in the interest of the country we love, young couples of good antecedents and average vigour ought to aim at producing a family of at least three or four children, so long as there is a reasonable prospect of bringing them up under reasonable (not luxurious) conditions of comfort and nutrition.

What bearing, you may ask, has all that on religion and morals? Just this: In a country of advanced civilization, such as ours is gradually becoming, infant mortality ought so to be reduced that, when the children attain adult years, the numbers of men and women shall be approximately equal. For such a society, monogamy is the natural form of sex relation: the alternative is some form of sexual anarchy. That, however, does not mean that such monogamy need be indissoluble. Incidentally also, equality of numbers postulates a single standard of sexual conduct for men and women; but neither does this determine what that single standard shall be. Shall the men rise to the standard they have expected from their women, or shall the women accommodate themselves to what they have expected of their men?

That is a critical question, which the upgrowing generation must answer according to its sense of responsibility.

The Church: Marriage and Divorce

Monogamy, I have said, need not imply indissolubility. The marriage might last just as long as the partners desire; or until the children reach, say, the age of 16; or it might be dissoluble for various causes of offence, matrimonial, civil, or criminal; not as a punishment of the offender, but as a relief for the injured party.

The Roman Church first pronounced marriage to be indissoluble (as a fixed doctrine) at the Council of Trent (1545–63). Several provincial councils had judged otherwise, but the general stream of Western thought flowed in the direction of rigidity. The Eastern Church has always taken the opposite view, marriage being dissoluble both for adultery and other causes.

The Roman view, and, generally speaking, the Anglo-Catholic view, is that marriage is indissoluble because Jesus so ordained. The Papacy draws its authority from Mark and an isolated text in Luke; while the Greek Church follows Matthew's exception for "fornication".[1] But it is not clear that the Marcan text is the real origin of the doctrine of indissolubility. An alternative explanation is at least probable; namely, that the early Christians considered that an erring husband or wife should be given a chance of

---

[1] *Fornication.* Throughout the N.T. there is a clear distinction between adultery and fornication, save for two doubtful cases in the Pauline writings. But Dr. Charles thinks that the word refers to any sexual lapse, and that Matthew was right in introducing the exception, since, among Jews, a man was bound to divorce his wife for adultery. My own view has, for long, been that Matthew inserted the exception in order to cover the case of Joseph, who was minded to put away Mary because of fornication. Matthew did not like any reflection on the relatives or apostles of Christ.

repentance, and therefore the other party should not marry again. This was at first a dictate of Christian charity, but it hardened into an enforcement. Enforced charity is a contradiction in terms.

But as to the words of Christ, assuming that they are accurately handed down, they must be understood in their context of time and place. The controversy of the day was between the schools of Hillel and Shammai; Hillel held that the law (Deut. xxiv. 3) permitted a man to put away his wife for any trivial cause, while Shammai limited its meaning to unchastity. If this was the question put to Christ (as in Matt. xix. 3), he clearly took the stricter view. But the short report does not justify the view that Christ outbid Shammai so as to forbid divorce altogether. Even St. Paul did not go so far as that (1 Cor. vii. 15). The real question, however, is whether Christ was giving voice to an ideal or whether he was legislating. If he were legislating on marriage, it was the only subject on which he did so. He taught ideals consistently; and if he praised permanent monogamy, he stood therein for an ideal which has gained general approval. That is a principle which, to-day, both Church and State desire to promote. But they seek to reach the goal by different routes: the Church, by enforcement of indissolubility, regardless of human needs; the State by providing relief for cases where marriage is a disgrace to the name. We may well wonder which method is in accord with the gracious mind of Christ.

The law of England to-day is a hopeless bungle between the two. It is difficult to see how any decent or clear-thinking man (clerical or lay) can approve of the present English law, which declares that if a man or woman needs divorce he or she *must* commit adultery in order to obtain it; nevertheless, if both are found to have committed adultery, divorce is not possible, except by the Judge's discretion. The law not only demands immorality, but it leads to illicit unions; the Divorce Court is a sink of perjury, as is no other court in England; fraud, in this case, is not disapproved by public opinion, even of the better class, since the law is considered bad; but ecclesiastical opinion stands in the way of reform.

What is marriage? It is, in its finest experience, a union of love; it is doubly creative, both in the physical and the spiritual sense. If the attraction be merely physical, it must lack permanence; it is only lasting in proportion to its spiritual content. But men and women are apt to be carried away by their acute but transitory emotions, so that many unions are bound to fail of success. Modern thought desires that when a marriage has actually come to an end, as in the case of long desertion, a long term of imprisonment for crime, or where conditions are intolerable from one cause or another, the State should give relief. Why should any religious body oppose such healthy reform? Members of any Church, who dislike divorce, need not avail themselves of the facilities offered; but they have no right to enforce their views on citizens who believe (as multitudes do) that increased divorce facilities would make for better public morals. The fixation of marriage, as indissoluble, has never proved to nurture high sex ideals; where it has prevailed, as in Latin countries, marriage has often become a cloak for illicit concubinage; and, though divorce is not allowed (with power to remarry), causes of annulment have been multiplied, shewing how great is the real need for divorce. In this country, permanent separation orders are a crying evil. Thousands of them take place every year, which effectively put an end to the marriage; but neither party can obtain divorce thereafter, except on proof of adultery after the separation, which can rarely be tracked. Result: the separated parties form new affectional, and often good, liaisons, which, however, are technically illicit; and the children of such a union are, by the present law of England, irredeemably illegitimate if *born*[1] while the marriage still subsists; the law of legitimation by subsequent marriage is thus cruelly limited.

Divorce, such as reformers want, is the friend of marriage, not its enemy; reformers want a lasting reality rather than an interminable sham. The persistence of an external bond which has no spiritual counterpart is evil; the continuance of the name, when the reality is dead, brings marriage into contempt. Says George Tyrrell,[2] that straight-speaking Modernist, and sometime Jesuit, "Physical divorce is less evil than rational and spiritual. Are two cats, tied together by the tails, an image of Christ and his Church?"

Do I hear whispers of "sanctity" and "sacrament"? As to sanctity, neither Church nor State can make a marriage other than it is; if there be sanctity at all, it comes from within, not from external ceremony. And if the sacramental aspect be urged, wherein does the sacrament of marriage consist? The traditional doctrine is that of Augustin (of Hippo), who taught that the marriage of baptized Christian couples (and of them alone) involved a metaphysical fusion of personalities—a doctrine which to-day cannot be defended on either psychological or practical grounds. Others have held that the ring is the sacrament: but the ring was adopted after the Christian era from pagan sources. Is there then no sacrament of marriage? God forbid. Marriage is the greatest of all Nature's sacraments. The union of bodies is the

---

[1] They can be legitimized by subsequent marriage if the original marriage has been legally terminated (by divorce or by the death of the partner) before the actual birth of the child. *Complete Statutes of England*, Halsbury, vol. ii. pp. 25-26. Legitimacy Act, 1926: "Nothing in this Act shall operate to legitimate a person whose father or mother was married to a third person when the illegitimate person was born."

[2] *George Tyrrell's Letters*, by M. D. Petre, p. 300.

sacrament which both signifies and intensifies the union of spirits. It is the divinely appointed means to the realization of a spiritual communion which may outlast its carnal expression. The *merely* physical attraction—and who has not felt it?—is ephemeral, having no spiritual reality behind it. Without the spiritual communion, the carnal act is no sacrament—it signifies nothing.

In the New Testament, the references to marriage are mainly concerned with the relation of the sexes as such. To-day the main attention is focused, and rightly focused, on the children. The case for indissolubility is now mainly based by its advocates on the children's well-being; but the argument is faulty. It is almost a commonplace, with men of experience, that the interest of the children is not advanced by being brought up in an atmosphere of bickering and bitterness between parents, but rather by allowing separation, custody being given to the spouse best fitted for it. The atmosphere of a home is, for good or evil, the most potent force which impinges on the plastic mind of a child. But here, too, we must realize that the presence of children is the most powerful influence in keeping the parents together. Rarely does it happen that neither parent desires to hold their children's love; so it is usual that, in case of defended divorce proceedings, the defence is undertaken, not to prevent the divorce, but to secure custody of the children.

But, returning to the reported words of Christ, the matter goes deeper than is commonly supposed. First, it is difficult to see how Christ can have been completely human (as orthodoxy maintains) if he were immune from the poignancy of the sexual urge, to which normal men are exposed; nor can he have been tempted in all points like as we are. That he was subject to such trial is made probable, at least, from the fact that he was attractive to women and was attracted by them; his forceful personality raised the eyes of the humblest of them to the higher values of life. Besides, if he were himself impervious to such emotions, his sayings on such a subject could only have reference to what he saw of the conditions of sexual life of his own time and place, so that he could hardly speak with any degree of universal authority. This is a point which seems to call for a straightforward answer. In the second place, if we admit, for argument's sake, that Christ did forbid divorce to his followers, does it follow that a Christian State ought equally to forbid it? At the Royal Commission on Divorce, Dean Rashdall was asked by the present Archbishop of Canterbury (then of York) whether the Christian conscience might still approve of divorce under certain conditions. His answer was that the ultimate appeal was to the moral conscience of mankind.[1] Surely he was right. It is the only possible court of appeal. It is the actual court of appeal in general practice. The doctrine of "the other cheek" and the "cloke also", does not forbid police action, nor the protection of citizens against assault or theft. We must interpret Christ's words in relation to human needs. In the one case he stood for the principle of unselfishness, in the other of permanent monogamy.

That principle needs to be taught; it is cardinal to civic education. At present there is little or no effort by Church[2] or State to instruct young adults on the implications of marriage, physical, spiritual, and social. To-day (as Havelock Ellis says) marriage is like a rat-trap, easy of entry but mighty difficult of exit. In England there is one means of exit—adultery. The object of reformers is not to break up marriage, but to mend broken lives by permitting those who

---

[1] *Royal Commission on Divorce and Matrimonial Causes:* Evidence, vol. iii. pp. 306 ff. and 310 ff.

[2] The Archbishops' Board has lately instituted excellent lectures, which are given at some Universities and Training Colleges.

have made shipwreck to find salvation in a truer and better alliance, which shall have the sanction of the society in which they live, if not of the Church of which they are members.

Birth-Control and Abortion

It were cowardly for any writer on sex to shirk a subject which is of deep concern to all married persons. That the control of conception brings with it risks of abuse is plain enough, but so also does every invention or discovery. Risk or no risk, the thing has come to stay; it remains to teach its values, and to resist its misuse. There can be little doubt that, shortly after the marriage of any normal couple, it is desirable that the woman should experience the complete gamut of the music of her being—intercourse, fertilization, pregnancy, parturition, lactation. That is the ideal. But here, as often, the best may be the enemy of the good. To-day, for a large proportion there may be a variety of arguments against immediate pregnancy —economic, housing, health, and what not: apart from the fact that the bridal year should be one of freedom to enjoy the new conditions. If pregnancy happens almost immediately, the bride may desire no further sex relations, and her desire should be the husband's law, even if distressful. The Lambeth Conference of 1930 gave a half-hearted approval of contraceptive methods, so long as they were based on Christian principles.

The first general principle, which seems to emerge, is that the begetting of children should be by design and not by accident. Children should not be born unless the parents are able to support them in decency, and to give them their birthright of love and care. Unwanted children are born to unhappiness— a misery to themselves and their parents. Until quite recent times the advent of children was popularly regarded as matter of luck or chance; God would provide. To-day nobody thinks that way. All ecclesiastics (Roman included) admit the duty of prevision, and, in many cases, of limitation of families. They differ in the permissible means of limitation. Abstinence is the obvious way. But abstinence, except where children are desired, means refusal of connubial "rites" except on the very rarest occasions. So jejune a concept has brought in casuistry: the "safe" period is allowed; this means the week or so before menstruation, when conception is least likely, in general theory, though not "safe" in actual practice. This is also the time when the woman least desires connexion; and, even so, our theoretical knowledge is full of gaps. Let us get down to principles.

Is the purpose of sex relation merely the procreation of children, or has sexual intimacy an independent value of its own? Quite clearly it has such a separate value. It is the sacrament of love. It stands unique. By its means the spiritual communion sweeps into its embrace the whole personalities of the pair, mental, emotional, sensorial, reaching down to the very roots of humanity, and equally up to the most delicate flower of love which is thus coaxed into bloom. Not the sensuous apart from the spiritual nor the spiritual without the sensuous, but both together for the mutual adaptation of two complete personalities.

This is not the place to describe the various methods used for such a separation of purposes. None of them is fool-proof; but if carefully used, they do, even now, provide for reasonable safety combined with satisfaction. Most of the present methods are disliked by many women as inaesthetic, and from the scientific standpoint they are crude. But, as yet, no satisfactory physiological method of contraception is discovered, apart from sterilization; and that must be considered permanent.

No one desires that any marriage of normal people

should be sterile. No marriage can be completely satisfying without children, however happy the mutual relation may be. But the proper spacing of children is essential. No woman ought to be subjected to pregnancy each year. An interval of about two years between births is best; children are then near enough in age to play together, and not so near as that the advent of the second shall cause neglect of the first.

To forbid intercourse in the interval is both stupid and ineffectual; morally and spiritually also, worse than doubtful. Moreover, in the average case, before the wife's child-bearing period has passed, the family may already have reached the largest desirable; is intercourse to cease? The call for it may be as urgent as ever. This, in fact, constitutes one of the major troubles of mature married life. To preclude reasonable sex activity within marriage not only endangers the marriage, but invites illicit relations outside. That contraceptives can be, and are, used outside of marriage is, of course, true; but that is no reason to deny their proper and reasonable use in marriage. We must grant that the alternative to their use is, in too many cases, abortion. Now abortion (which means the ending of pregnancy before the child is viable), though condemned by law, except where induced to save the mother's life or health, is, in fact, practised very widely; though, of course, no figures are available, except where it results in accident or death. If induced unskilfully, abortion is most dangerous to the mother; septic conditions, set up by unskilled abortion, probably do a good deal to keep up the figures of maternal mortality. Yet about abortion, in theory at any rate, a few words may be said. From the academic point of view, it would seem that an early embryo, so long as it is incapable of independent life, is part of the mother's body, and the mother might be held to have a natural right to decide its fate. There are, in fact, many women of all classes who, ignorant of the law and innocent of any immoral intention, go to their doctor asking him to terminate an early and unwanted pregnancy. But, we must add, when the child is born, it very often becomes the dearest thing in the world.

In spite of all that can be said against abortion (and it is much) there is to-day, in more than one European country, a growing demand for legal facilities of abortion; the moral ground for this demand will be that legalized abortion, allowed only by skilled operators, will kill off the demand for quack abortion with its direful results. But abortion, at best, is recognized as a dangerous thing: in Russia, where it is allowed, and skilled facilities provided, so that the danger to the woman is minimal, it is now being severely discouraged; and that is a healthy sign, for it is most undesirable, save in exceptional cases. Here, in Great Britain, it is only allowed where there is danger to the woman's life or health. I personally think it ought to be allowed in cases of rape of a girl, where it seems cruel and immoral to enforce motherhood. But the general demand for abortion would decrease with the spread of knowledge of efficient contraception. Whatever be our *prima facie* views on these, and allied questions, such as that of eugenic sterilization, it is well that we should study the problems as they actually exist, without prejudice, in order to find their solution in accord with basic moral and religious thought. Such questions are more urgent for the future of our people than even the important political questions of housing or the distribution of wealth; for this concerns the very stuff of human life itself. Dr. Inge has said that eugenics is an infant science; that is true; but the infant has now begun to talk; it cannot be many years before it will talk to some purpose unless killed by prejudice that masquerades in the dress of principle.

The Sublimation of Sex

The word "Sublimation" is used in chemistry to denote the converting of a solid substance, by means of heat, into vapour, which resolidifies on cooling; metaphorically it means elevation or transmutation to a higher and more refined state of existence. By sublimation of the sex instinct, we mean its refinement and partial diversion into other channels than that of its primary flow. To some extent, at least, civilization demands from all this sublimation. It is probably true that, biologically, sex supplies the main energy of the will-to-live, whether such life be civilized or not. Where its primary and crude impulse is exercised without control, there civilization progresses slowly or not at all. Where it is restrained by submission to the promptings of higher control, there it can be, and is, stored in such a way that its energy can be used for other than sexual purposes. Among such purposes we may mention poetry, art, music; discovery, invention, handicraft.

By way of parable, we may compare the potential energy of sex to a river, such as the Nile, passing through a dry country: the land has sun and warmth, but it needs irrigation. By means of skill and labour, much of the land may be rendered fertile, deriving its supply from the main stream. Yet the river itself must flow on to the sea, and cannot all be used up for the derivative purpose. It seems that this is like the river of sex energy. It can be utilized for the culture, even the intensive culture, of the various potentialities of the personality; yet it cannot be wholly dammed up, but must, in part at least, continue to run in its own natural bed. Thus it happens, at any rate with the man, and perhaps with the woman too, that by means of deliberate suppression of the sex impulse— the energy of which largely (often very largely) exceeds its specific biological needs—the hitherto unfruitful soil of his mind and spirit is so vitalized as to bring forth its proper harvest according to the nature of the soil. That such a result actually takes place is clear enough. The products of sexual energy, through the activity of the sex glands, are always being secreted, with varying intensity; they can either be passed out of the body through the natural channel (in sex intercourse or otherwise) or they can, in considerable part, be reabsorbed into the system and put to other service. There must, indeed, always be some overflow until the later years of life; and this necessary superfluity can be satisfied with the normal sex activity of marriage. But civilization demands that the main stream shall not be recklessly wasted, but employed for other creative purposes than the merely physical.

That seems a fair picture of the part played by sex in civilization. The careless abuse of sex in the years of its effervescence, specially in the years of adolescence and early manhood, dries up the source by which the whole personality might be enriched. The abundance of men's sex energy varies within wide limits, and allowance must be made for cases where it is over-abundant; for such the difficulties of suppression of the natural outlet are unusually great. But there is the compensating advantage, that the man of high sexual energy has also, thereby, the power, through exertion of self-control, of enriching, to a very special degree, his own personality and strengthening his influence over others. For it is true that a man or woman of powerful sex capacity can develop his personal force and influence to a degree that persons of modest or weaker sexuality cannot attain.

But it must also be admitted that the denial, to any normal man or woman, of any natural outlet to their sexual energy, involves a loss to the personality; and that, more serious, in my judgement, to the woman than to the man; though, to the man also, total absence or deprivation of marital communion entails considerable diminution of the richness of life. How often do we see women, and men too, who might have contributed fine offspring to the nation, but who for various reasons have failed to marry, and whose own lives have thereby suffered desiccation and impoverishment. That is why it is highly desirable that opportunity of marriage should be, as near as possible, universal. There will always be some men and women who can so effectually divert their sexual energy into the enrichment of some one particular aspect of their personality that they feel little or even no need of normal sex experience: these are men and women with some overmastering special vocation; but they are exceptional. Men and women vary indefinitely, both in their relative powers of sublimation, and in the natural abundance of their sex energy. Through such wide diversity of gifts has Providence arranged for the progress and enrichment of humanity.

Some degree, then, of this activity—and it is a definite activity—of sublimation of sex is essential to every normal civilized man and woman. But, just as in the world of chemistry (from which the analogy is borrowed) the process of sublimation requires the expenditure of heat-energy, so here, any degree of transmutation demands no little effort, and that over long periods. Such effort cannot be made without a motive: such an adequate motive can be supplied by religion alone.

A high sense of duty towards our neighbour may be adequate while the stream of sex energy flows smoothly; but when it swells into a spate, where are we without a sense of duty to a higher Power? There are few indeed who have not, at one time or another, experienced its torrential force. So, if there be truth —as assuredly there is—in this concept of sublimation, here again we may perceive the inter-dependence between sex and religion, whereby the potency of sex is directed toward the enrichment of culture and the spiritualization of the whole of life.[1]

THE READJUSTMENT OF SEX TO RELIGION

To some readers this paper on Sex and Religion will seem a mixed grill of platitudes and controversy. But sex and religion are so intimately allied that every aspect of each lends colour to the other. If the family is the basic unit of civilization, then nothing of family or marital life can fall outside the ambit of religion.

It would appear, then, that religion and sex, so far from being opposed forces, fighting to the death, are really and ultimately different aspects of the same energy—the energy of Love; the one working downwards from above, the other striving upwards from beneath, both destined to merge at the last. In religious thought, it is said, dependence is primary, love secondary; in sex, love is primary, dependence secondary. For close on 2000 years, in Western Christendom, all sexual manifestations, even within marriage, have been suspect of evil. That was natural where, as in the later Roman Empire, sex was deeply degraded in public practice. This attitude is reflected in the story of the Virgin birth—no part, so far as can be seen, of the earliest gospel tradition—which suggests that the Divine could not mingle with the human through the ordinary channel of human paternity. We cannot accept that. The concept is not only imperfect; it is positively misleading. High-minded Christian ladies have told me that they consider the story of the Virgin birth as no less than a slur on the natural and proper functions of women.

[1] On this subject see Havelock Ellis, *Psychology of Sex* (Heinemann, single volume, 1933), p. 307 ff.

That sex may be bestially degraded is only too true. But human capacities must be measured, not by their meanest expressions, but by their highest achievements; nor indeed by their primitive origins, but by their finest developments. In primeval days, as to-day with the humbler creation, sexual attraction was purely sensorial, without spiritual component or understanding of its purpose. But to-day, for the better walks of life, the spiritual becomes paramount, refining the carnal element into its instrument and sacrament. To the early Christian mind sex was incapable of spiritualization. Human nature was at enmity with itself, spirit and flesh lusting against each other. So, for Augustin, sin had its special seat and symbol in the sexual organs. Human nature was enmeshed in inescapable dualism. How different this from the best thought of to-day. One quotation may suffice: "Under the influence of sexual love, the whole being is exalted, its capacities enlarged, and its sensibilities, mental, moral, and physical, brought to a pitch of fineness otherwise unknown. . . . Courage, truth, honour, enterprise, admiration of moral worth, are all inspired by love as by nothing else in human existence."[1] It is a revolution of thought. The devil is no longer in possession.

Yet, for the human individual, the working-out of this salvation is not all plain sailing. It must be an achievement. The sensual is mighty hard to control. By sensual, I mean the physical urge where it has no spiritual accompaniment. But in the finest love there must always be the sensuous element; the task is to harmonise sense with spirit.

What then is the line of hope for monogamous marriage, to make it lovely, joyous, and permanent? First of all, a high-souled love is manifested in a desire, even a need, to give; to give, not things, but one's whole self. "Love is fed, not by what it takes,

---

[1] J. A. Godfrey, *Science of Sex*, pp. 73 and 138.

but by what it gives." But that is not all: the giving must be mutual. This needs intelligence. A man should be not only the subject of generous emotion, but should consider what the proposed partner has to give. Can there be a reciprocal life at all levels, not only the specifically sexual, but in things of mind and spirit too? Thus a wide divergence of station, upbringing, nationality or race, makes mutual alignment specially difficult, owing to deep-seated difference of outlook. For though the sexual contributes the intensity of love, the spiritual is the only guarantee of its permanence. Marriage ought to bring new values within the grasp of each; only so can it be fruitful in a spiritual sense. It should enrich the lovers themselves, and through them the society in which they live. So that, while love begins in losing oneself in another, it advances to finding oneself—a new and finer self.

But it is no use blinking the difficulties, which are intensified by the progress of culture. The difficulties are traditional, biological, and social. On the traditional side, a long-established patriarchy has engendered a certain feeling of male superiority and female subjection. A sense of possession of the female by the male is poisonous to marriage. In the high places of love, indeed, there is possession: but it is mutual and joyous. The functions of the two, both in mutual and social life, are complementary: any thought of subjection or serfdom is ruinous to a real marriage. Biologically the sweetness of marriage is endangered by the fact that character is liable to change with the years. This is a biological fact, mainly due to the readjustment of the products of what are called the endocrine glands of the body; such variation is more apt to happen in women than in men, owing to the crises of pregnancy, lactation, or the change of life. The man must be forearmed against such developments, and must remember too that he himself is liable to similar changes, though of a more gradual and less dramatic kind. Socially, again: a high state of culture brings its own difficulties. Culture and freedom of discursive thought produce a highly differentiated individuality. It becomes harder and harder for highly educated people to find congenial mates; culture creates a sense of loneliness which is hard to complement; as Westermarck says, "Diffusion of culture makes partnership less easy and more exacting. Ideals are higher and less easily satisfied."[1]

The difficulties truly are great; but so is the prize. The pursuit of other achievements, wealth, power, position, influence—these all have their values; but without a personally centralized affection, life, for most men and women, becomes, at best, unsatisfying. Yet, to attain satisfaction, we need a new orientation in our thought of sex and marriage, not dissociated from religion, but freed from its traditional blunders and exaggerations. Such change is not brought about in a moment; thought takes time to percolate; yet its filtration is more rapid to-day than ever before. The trouble is that while knowledge of things grows rapidly, adaptation of personality to new conditions is painfully slow.

So, we may gather, religion and sex travel, in the history of human thought, along parallel lines. We are taught to-day that parallel lines meet at infinity; but these lines of thought, parallel in each individual, will only find their perfect coalescence at that day when we shall know even as we are known.

---

[1] Westermarck, *History of Marriage*, 5th ed. 1921, vol. i. p. 393.

VIII

ANGLO-CATHOLICISM AND THE TWENTIETH CENTURY

by

FRANK LESLIE CROSS, M.A., B.Sc., D.Phil.

Priest-Librarian of the Pusey House
Examining Chaplain to the Bishop of Bradford
Wilde Lecturer in Natural and Comparative Religion
in the University of Oxford
and
Oxford University Lecturer in the Philosophy of Religion

SYNOPSIS

Permanence and Progress in Religion

Since what is Absolute is not susceptible of progress, a religion which claims to be in possession of principles of absolute validity must so far be unchangeable. But Christianity contains within itself contingent as well as absolute elements. In the Christian Faith there is an element of the "unfinished". The Church is an organism capable of growth, a body able to incorporate within itself a constant succession of new elements. In this way permanence and progress can both find a place in Christianity.

Christianity and Platonism

Every religion seeks to express itself in philosophic terms. The Christian Church was fortunate in that it found ready to hand in the first centuries a view of the relation of the Universe to God exactly fitted to her needs. The Platonic metaphysic was soon discovered to be the *praeparatio evangelica*. In essence, this philosophy was rooted in a doctrine of degrees. Its basis was the belief that God alone is absolutely good,—the *Summum Bonum*,—and that created things were good in so far as they derived their being from that Source. The *malum*, strictly speaking, had no existence; in St. Thomas' phraseology, it was an *ens privativum*. St. Augustine, who had himself come directly under Neo-Platonist influence, summed this metaphysic up in the formula *In quantum est quidquid est, bonum est.*

This doctrine has its counterpart in the belief that all theological formulae are at best approximations. Mediaeval philosophy developed the same idea in its teaching concerning "analogy". Such a view precludes from the sphere of theology the possibility of logical precision and systematic completeness. As long as we are *in via* we must abandon the quest for "infallibilities".

X

CATHOLICISM AS INCARNATIONAL

As a definition of Catholicism we may accept a formula of popular theology which discovers the essence of Catholicism in its supreme emphasis upon the Incarnation. Incarnationalism sees the whole natural order related to the Absolute. It is the function of Christianity to raise all that is good in the natural order to a still higher plane. The Christian Moral Law, for instance, is (as Abelard termed it) the *re-formatio* of the principles of natural ethics. The principle behind Catholicism is *Gratia non tollit naturam, sed perficit.*

ANGLICANISM

A survey of post-Reformation Anglicanism reveals that English religious thought has had a firm and continuous hold on Incarnationalism. Nearly all the outstanding theologians of the classic epoch of Anglicanism,—*e.g.* Andrewes, Laud, Chillingworth, William Forbes, Bramhall, Pearson, Bull,—were Incarnationalists (or, as they were frequently termed by their Seventeenth Century adversaries, "Arminians"). In 1688 the unity of the Incarnational ideal was bifurcated, to produce unfortunate effects which were to be felt over some two centuries. The Tractarian and the Broad Church Schools each emphasized only one side of religion. In the latter part of the Nineteenth Century, largely through the influence of R. W. Church, a synthesis was re-effected. This found unequivocal expression in the pages of *Lux Mundi.*

CREEDS AND FORMULARIES

The Christian conviction that human reason is one of the *bona* made it inevitable that the Church should seek to give, so far as it could, a thought-out explanation of her faith. This found expression in such vehicles as the Books of the Bible, the writings of the Fathers, the Definitions of Councils and Synods, the Encyclicals of Bishops, and the Formulae known as the "Creeds". These different attempts to formulate the Truth possess varying degrees of validity. Obviously to some of them more importance will attach than to others.

In the Church of England the Three Creeds (the

Apostles', the Nicene, and the Athanasian) have come to occupy a position apparently unparalleled in any other Christian communion. There are no intrinsic reasons for supposing them to be absolutely irreformable. But in their positive teaching they have stood the test of time and have behind them the authority of long experience.

(In an Appended Note, three of the clauses of the Apostles' Creed to which objections have been raised in recent years are examined. It is argued that except on the basis of a somewhat stringent literalism, the grounds against them are not serious.)

On the other hand, objections of a weighty character may be urged against the Thirty-Nine Articles. Their spirit is contentious, they are in many respects antiquated, their teaching is at some points opposed to the main current of Anglicanism, and they contain certain positive misstatements of fact. For these and other reasons the Church of England would do well to take steps at the earliest opportunity to secure their abolition.

THE SOCIOLOGICAL IMPLICATIONS OF CATHOLICISM

The Incarnational nature of the Christian Faith imposes upon the Church the task of redeeming human society. Christianity cannot rest content therefore with the conversion of individual souls. At the present juncture there are peculiar opportunities for the Church in this matter. Modern civilization suffers from an intense individualism —nationalism, class-barriers, over-specialization. Even judged by purely human standards, the unitary view of the Universe possessed by the Church must be reckoned a force in the right direction.

In so far as the Church seeks to fulfil her mission in the field of Sociology she must (i) avail herself of the best "secular" evidence at her disposal, and (ii) use modern methods of making her influence felt. An urgent need exists for a Christian press in Great Britain.

CHRISTIAN ASCETICISM

The principle of Christian Asceticism rests in the renunciation of the "material" not on the ground that it is evil (indeed, the "material" is, in its degree, good), but because it is a lesser good which can give way to a greater good. In the Liturgical Year, provision is made for such renunciation, particularly by the weekly abstinence of Friday and by the Forty Days of Lent. The "Religious Life", which is capable of a far fuller development in the Church of England than it has hitherto attained, exists for those who receive the call to more complete renunciation. Two new Orders which may be envisaged are: (*a*) one to be concerned with relating the Christian Faith to the modern world outlook, and (*b*) one devoted to the propagation of Christian Pacifism.

CATHOLIC SACRAMENTALISM

A necessary corollary of Incarnationalism is Sacramentalism. The right use of seemingly unimportant instruments as vehicles of Divine communication was illustrated in the *modus* of the Incarnation. Insistence upon the principle of Sacramentalism is far more important than the methods of its expression. For instance, the problem as to the Number of the Sacraments is relatively secondary. Whereas the Tridentine Canons reaffirmed that there were seven, most Anglican formularies imply that there are only two. The "representative" function of the Sacraments should also not be overlooked. In a Universe wherein the *bonum* finds expression at every turn, the Sacraments are representative of the *bonitas* of created things. The Eucharistic Bread and Wine are representative of the "goodness" of all meats.

LITURGICAL WORSHIP

This is closely connected with Sacramentalism. On Sacramental principles, outward forms can never be merely indifferent. Every Contemplative Religious Order recognizes the importance of its Breviary. In the Church of England the subject of Liturgical worship is closely bound up with that of Prayer Book Revision. Though the Deposited Book of 1927 indicated some desirable reforms, in matters of detail it proved distasteful to many Anglo-Catholics. The less acceptable parts of the Book were the outcome of the method by which it was produced, its compilers tending to conceive it rather as a means for the restoration of discipline than as a manual of worship. Its treatment of the Minor Offices was among the more successful elements in the Book.

In the Eucharistic rite, a more extended "Proper" is a *desideratum*. Reservation should be explicitly legitimized. As forms of regular Sunday Service, Matins and Evensong are no longer those best adapted to modern needs.

ANGLO-CATHOLICISM AND THE TWENTIETH CENTURY

Permanence and Progress in Religion

Religion surpasses every other form of human activity in that it claims to be concerned with the ultimate facts of life. Its advocates maintain that there is no other pathway towards Reality which brings the enquirer so near his goal. They hold that in so far as it is possible for man to apprehend the nature and content of the Real, it is through religion that such apprehension most readily takes place. In religion, they contend, mankind is confronted with a set of principles and ideals by which, if he is in earnest, he must needs seek to guide his life and to interpret its mysteries. Here he will find principles and ideals which, in the last resort, are beyond the possibility of criticism; for to criticize implies the possession of a criterion which transcends the facts to be criticized and *ex hypothesi* no criterion of measurement can transcend the Absolute. Progress, restatement, reform in religion, therefore, can never be revision in the matter of its first principles. Where revision is demanded or desired, it will be conditioned by the perception that what has hitherto been held to belong to the content of religion has been misconceived as such.

In common with other forms of religion, Christianity also claims to be rooted in a set of absolute principles. These principles, she believes, were revealed in the Person and Work and Teaching of her Divine Lord. All those who should accept the supreme revelation in Christ Incarnate had to take into account new principles, the validity of which was absolute. She claims that the Christ brought with him new categories of interpretation, new ideals of action, new demands for discipleship; and that these new principles were to be the guiding ideals of every philosophy of life which should claim the name of Christian.

But while what may be described, in varying metaphors, as the substance, the essence, the kernel, or the leaven, of the Christian Faith was committed to the Church at the outset, the form which that Faith was to assume in its richness and its universality was to be the work of succeeding generations. Those to whom the Revelation was entrusted were themselves to take a part in interpreting it. By their reception of it, they were to be, in some mysterious way, organically incorporated into it. They became more than purely witnesses to the Christ; they became, in the language of the Apostle of the Gentiles, "members of the Christ". In the Mystical Body of Christ there was thus to be continued and developed the content of the revelation. Hence it was to be the function of the Church, guided by the Spirit, to apprehend and set forth the Truth ever more fully. Disciples from far and near were to bring their gold and frankincense and myrrh to the feet of their Incarnate Lord to be transmuted and consecrated and synthesized into the fulness of the Christian Life. To use a daring metaphor of St. Paul, they were to "supply the deficiencies" ($\dot{a}\nu\tau$-$a\nu a\pi\lambda\eta\rho o\hat{v}\nu$ $\tau\dot{a}$ $\dot{v}\sigma\tau\epsilon\rho\dot{\eta}\mu a\tau a$; cp. *Col.* i. 24) of Christ —those "deficiencies" inherent in the categorical structure of historical events and persons which entail that a man cannot be, *e.g.*, a St. Augustine and a Shakespeare and a Newton simultaneously,— so that ultimately in Christ God may be "all in all" (cp. 1 *Cor.* xv. 29).

CHRISTIANITY AND PLATONISM

Since the Christian Revelation claimed to be vastly more than a merely speculative account of the Real, the elucidation and development of that Revelation could never be wholly, or even primarily, the work of theologians. Nevertheless, as far as the *intellectual* content of the Revelation was concerned, it was upon her theologians and philosophers that the task of interpretation necessarily devolved. It was to be their mission to expound its theoretical principles, and to relate them to the categories of thought outside the Revelation. Certain facts were soon perceived to belong to the very "deposit" of Revelation. There was the fact that in Christ was to be discovered the inmost nature both of God and man. There was the fact that God judged men's actions not by their conformity to external or ceremonial laws, but by their inward springs. There was the fact, implied by Christ's whole attitude to nature and presupposed by the Old Testament background of his thought, that the relation of our Universe to God is a relation of Creation. Facts such as these were to be the necessary point of departure of every philosophy which sought to give a *rationale* of the Christian Faith. But beyond such basic facts, there was room for a wide range of freedom.

Reflection on the facts soon made it clear to the Church that one of the most characteristic notes of a Christian Philosophy was that it must needs be a "Mediating" one. A Christian philosophy must involve what the late Friedrich von Hügel used to term an element of "tension". The doctrine of Creation, for instance, was perceived to be intermediate between a Pantheism which would equate the whole of Reality with God and a Dualism which, with other forms of Pluralism, would defend the existence of beings other than and totally independent of God. Similarly, the doctrine of the Incarnation insisted that Christ can be understood neither as God alone nor as man alone, but that he is to be conceived somehow as both God and man at once. Christian ethics, again, was neither purely world-accepting nor purely world-renouncing, but in some mysterious way both world-accepting and world-renouncing at the same time. The Christian path was thus to be a *via media*.

It so happened that when Christian speculation set out on its course it found ready to hand a philosophy which exactly suited its needs. The metaphysics underlying the Platonist doctrines was just such a "mediating" philosophy. This philosophy proved to be, in fact, the *praeparatio evangelica* in the realm of metaphysics. Patristic theology, as history shewed, was the outcome of a long series of attempts to understand the Christian Faith through the eyes of Platonism. The more philosophically minded of the Fathers—St. Clement of Alexandria, Origen, the Cappadocians, St. Dionysius the Areopagite, and St. Augustine—were all Platonists. The result was that the root-principles of Platonist metaphysics were destined to play for two thousand years (and perhaps for all time) an organic and all but inseparable part in every Incarnational interpretation of the Christian Faith.

The essence of this philosophy was its emphasis upon the doctrine of degrees. The Universe was conceived of as a graded structure wherein God alone possessed Absolute Reality while other entities possessed a relative degree of reality depending upon their nearness to the Absolute. The only unconditioned Real was the *Summum Bonum*. Created things were *bona*; and such reality as they possessed, they owed to their participation in this Supreme Good. St. Augustine well summed up the essence of this metaphysic in the formula *In quantum est quidquid est, bonum est.*[1] The only things which were altogether devoid of being were, accordingly, the *mala*. They alone possessed the metaphysical status of "nothing".

This Platonist metaphysic was to be further worked out and refined in the Scholastic era. The important contribution made to the development of it by Mediaeval Thought was the introduction of the concept of Analogy. The Scholastics argued that since God's goodness exceeded all human goodness, human language could never be "adequate" to the expression of it. Our use of language in relation to God must therefore be "analogical". For instance, they pointed out that we can never apprehend Divine Justice in its fulness. But though this is so, Divine Justice and human justice cannot be thought of as totally different; recognition of the limitations of language must not lead us to agnosticism. Hence philosophers must strive after a *via media*. They must conceive of Divine and human justice as related *per modum analogiae*.

The doctrine was developed as follows. It was commonly held, for example, that God's justice was indistinguishable from his very essence; but in a just man, his "justice" and his "humanity" were two different things. Here was one distinction between Divine and human justice. Moreover, when Divine and human justice are compared, they are seen to differ vastly in degree. Such justice as man at his highest can claim is but a shadow of the full and unsurpassable justice of God. Corresponding relations naturally hold true of the other attributes of God, such as his wisdom, his purity, and his love. Perhaps the clearest view of this doctrine is obtained from the image of the ladder, constantly employed by the exponents of it. The top of the ladder represents God, who is absolute Being, absolute Justice, absolute Love, and so on. The bottom of the ladder represents

---

[1] *De Vera Religione*, c. 21.

"nothing" (*non-ens*), which, as has been indicated, was the metaphysical status commonly assigned by theologians to evil. Human existence, human justice, human love, in so far as they derive the being they have from God, who has created them out of nothing (*ex nihilo*), are represented correspondingly by stages up the ladder. "God", wrote St. Thomas, "is not a measure proportionate to any single thing; yet he is said to be the measure of all things on the ground that each individual thing has the more being, according as it the more resembles him."[1]

Nevertheless, however fundamental to Christianity this Platonic (or "Mediating", or "Analogical") element has been, it has continuously been in danger of supersession. Theologians and controversialists have been tempted at every turn to abandon it in favour of a method which allowed of greater logical precision. They have tried to substitute for the *per modum analogiae* the *Entweder-Oder*. Words, they have argued, must be capable of exact and univocal usage. Theology must provide formulae which answer with just precision the questions propounded to it. The Christian Faith cannot be content to describe Reality by means of shadows and pointers. It must be possessed of infallibilities and systematic completeness. And this appeal for Absolutes has been a constant threat to Platonism, for it is only in so far as theology abandons the Principle of Analogy that it can reach exactness.

Perhaps the Church of England has fared better than most of her neighbours in this matter. As a number of recent students of Anglicanism have pointed out,[2] Platonism has proved deeply congenial to the English religious mind. Indeed, Anglicanism

---

[1] *Deus autem non est mensura proportionata alicui. Dicitur tamen mensura omnium, ex eo quod unumquodque tantum habet de esse quantum ei appropinquat* (*S. Theol.* i. q. 3, *art.* 5, *ad* 2).

[2] *E.g.* C. C. J. Webb, *A Century of Anglican Theology*, pp. 7-11; W. R. Inge, *The Platonic Tradition in English Religious Thought, passim.*

can fairly claim that in modern times the Platonist approach to the Christian Faith has been more marked within her limits than anywhere else in Western Christendom. As to how this has come about, opinions may differ. Some may ascribe it mainly to the historic circumstances of the Reformation in this country, others to the peculiarities of the English character, others to an exceptional degree of theological penetration. But of the Platonic temper of Anglican theology there is room for no serious division of opinion. Whether we examine the religious philosophy of Colet or of Hooker, of the Cambridge "Latitudinarians" or of Joseph Butler, of Law or of Wordsworth, of Newman or of F. D. Maurice, the same fact is impressed upon us. It is reflected no less strikingly in the singularly small part which confessional formularies play in the life of Anglicanism. The Church of England has no set of modern dogmatic formulae which occupy a place in her life corresponding to the Decrees of the Tridentine and Vatican Councils on the one hand, nor to the Confessional Formularies of Continental Protestantism on the other.

Catholicism as Incarnational

In our analysis of the nature of Catholic principles, we may take as our point of departure the summary formula of popular theology that "Catholicism is rooted in the doctrine of the Incarnation, Protestantism in the doctrine of the Atonement". Such is at any rate a rough approximation to the current sense in which the words "Catholicism" and "Protestantism" are used. The Theology of the Protestant Reformation tended to concentrate its attention upon a single element in the plan of Redemption. It believed that the whole faith was contained in the death of Christ on the Cross and its implications for mankind. Here was the one and only fact in the realm of created being which was possessed of merit and goodness in the eyes of God, and of this goodness even the most faithful Christian disciple could never partake. At most, this goodness could be imputed to him through his acceptance of the Redeemer. For, as the Formula of Concord of 1576 expressed it, "original sin . . . is so profound a corruption of human nature as to leave nothing sound, nothing incorrupt in the body or soul of man, or in his mental or bodily powers".[1]

This view of human nature stood in sharp contrast with that characteristic of traditional Catholic theology. The Fathers, as we have seen, had a philosophy which regarded the work of Christ as the culmination of an order in which everything in its degree had its value. Moses, Plato, Seneca had received illumination, each according to his deserts, from the Logos who was fully revealed in Christ. The Incarnation was thus the culmination of a long process. Wherever in the Universe goodness was to be discovered, it was necessarily related to that of the Incarnate Son. Mediaeval theologians came to regard the Christian Moral Law as, in Abelard's phrase, a *re-formatio* of the law of Natural Morality. It was a view which implied that the virtuous deeds of the heathen were to be regarded not—as some theologians (forgetting their Incarnationalist principles) even in Patristic times occasionally expressed it—as "vices", but rather deeds which through their participation in "the light which lighteneth every man" were good as far as they went. Christianity did not condemn all that had gone before. It raised the best of the past to a new level. *Gratia non tollit naturam, sed perficit.*

Accordingly, every account of the Christian Faith

---

[1] Articulus I, Affirmative, § iii.; Schaff, *Creeds of Christendom*, iii. p. 100.

which claims the name of "Catholic" and sets out from Incarnationalist principles must conceive of the Christian Revelation as related to the whole range of human experience. It must consider it to be the end of religion to consecrate every form of experience by raising it from the "natural" to the "supernatural" level. As R. C. Moberly well put it in a famous volume of essays devoted to the subject of Incarnationalism, the Christian Religion "professes to have for its subject-matter, and (in a measure incomplete, but relatively adequate) to include, to account for, and to direct the whole range of all man's history, all man's capacities, explored or unexplored, all man's destiny now and for ever. . . . To the religious man . . . the fulness of Christian evidence is as many-sided as human life. There is historical evidence—itself of at least a dozen different kinds—literary evidence, metaphysical evidence, moral evidence, evidence of sorrow and joy, of goodness and of evil, of sin and of pardon, of despair and of hope, of life and of death; evidence which defies enumerating. Into this the whole gradual life of the Christian grows; and there is no part nor element of life which does not to him perpetually elucidate and confirm the knowledge which has been given him. Everything that is or has been, every consciousness, every possibility, even every doubt or wavering, becomes to the Christian a part of the certainty, an element in the absorbing reality, of his creed."[1] There can be no fragment of the Real which stands out of relationship to the Christian Faith.

ANGLICANISM

If we are right in using the word "Catholic" to describe every view of Christianity which holds it to

---

[1] R. C. Moberly, "The Incarnation as the Basis of Dogma" in *Lux Mundi* (ed. 1890), pp. 230, 232.

be all-inclusive (καθολικός) and Incarnational, then the Church of England, judged by the standard of history, can claim to be a Church whose spirit has been outstandingly Catholic. The Protestant theories of Justification, though zealously advocated in some quarters during the unsettled times of the sixteenth century, soon ceased to exercise any effective influence upon the main stream of Anglican thought. Caroline theology in its characteristic representatives was through and through Incarnational. James I's suspicions of "Arminianism", imbibed from his Calvinist antecedents, were never a serious rival to the Incarnational theology of such men as Andrewes, Laud, Chillingworth, Forbes, Bramhall, Pearson, and Bull. No less Incarnational was the thought of the small but influential group of "Latitudinarian" scholars, already referred to, who have since their day become known as the Cambridge Platonists. However much they may have differed in some important respects from the divines whose names we have just cited, they agreed with them (as against the Calvinists) in the way in which they conceived the Universe related to God, while in their emphasis upon the essentially reasonable character of the Christian Religion they were unceasing. The seventeenth century thus saw Incarnationalism permanently established in the National Church.

In 1688 came the Revolution. It brought to its term an era of Anglican theology no less than an epoch of English political history. The theological result of it was that the Anglican ideal was bifurcated. The Caroline divines had recognized that an Incarnational interpretation of religion found its full expression only in a unity which includes thought and life, prayer and cultus, contemplation and action. It understood that Incarnationalism requires that the *Summum Bonum* should be reflected in all these different *bona* in varying degrees; and to a great extent the Anglican Ideal, as it had been realized in the seventeenth century, was a comprehensive whole of this nature. But at the Revolution the division of the Church into two parts brought with it the dissolution of this unity. Henceforward the "intellectual" aspects of religion were to be cultivated all but exclusively by the "Jurors", while the "mystical" and the "sacramental" elements of the Faith were to be the peculiar possession of the "Non-Jurors"; and thus at one blow the magnificent unity of Caroline theology was shattered, to remain disunited for nearly two hundred years.

The effects of this bifurcation are brought out clearly in the history of the earlier stages of both the Tractarian and the Broad Church Movements. On the one hand, the leaders of the Oxford Movement are seen to have been concerned almost solely with the traditional, the mystical, and the Sacramental side of religion, to the neglect of its broader philosophical aspects; while on the other hand, the first phase of the Liberal Movement, though it courageously faced the intellectual problems which discoveries in natural science, in Biblical criticism, in archaeology, and in other fields created for religion, only too frequently betrayed little understanding of the Sacramental aspects of the Faith and sometimes even deeply suspected them. Happily much has happened since the days of the *Tracts for the Times* and of *Essays and Reviews*. The last half-century has seen the growth of an Anglican theology which can find room for the manifold elements of religious experience and life, and yet be in immediate contact with the best "secular" thought of the age. The work of theologians such as those whose names are to be found among the contributors to the collections of essays known as *Lux Mundi, Foundations*, and *Essays Catholic and Critical*, shews how far we have moved from the standpoints both of the eighteenth and of the early nineteenth centuries. It may justly be said that "anyone who comes fresh from reading the Caroline Divines to Gore and the other essayists of *Lux Mundi* will feel that here . . . he has picked up again the straight continuity of direction".[1]

CREEDS AND FORMULARIES

The Christian who believes that human reason is related *per modum analogiae* with the Reason of God will recognize at once the importance of a rational account of his faith. And if he goes on to hold—as surely he certainly must—that in Christ Incarnate was revealed in the most complete form possible under human conditions the nature and being of God, he will turn to this Source for the solution of his deepest speculative questionings. This is, of course, what happened in the early history of the Church. As soon as Christians began to meditate upon the implications of the Revelation which had been committed to them, they found themselves face to face with the issues of metaphysics. The Primitive Church could not have understood what was meant by Incarnation, by Divine Sonship, by the conceptions of "Messiah" and of "Son of Man", by the facts of forgiveness, of salvation, of perfection, without bringing them into mutual relatedness in a Christian Philosophy. Believing that to her care had been entrusted the Truth, she was convinced that the study of the Revelation made in the Incarnate Christ would reveal to her members progressively more about the world, and that what was dim and obscure would be made clearer by the promised guidance of him who was the Spirit of Truth. As time went on she found that, partly under the stress of controversy, partly through more

---

[1] P. E. More, "The Spirit of Anglicanism", in P. E. More and F. L. Cross, *Anglicanism*, p. xxxi.

directly constructive influences, the details of the Faith came to receive fuller elucidation and clearer definition. What had hitherto been fluid and undeveloped became crystallized in such forms as the literature of the Bible, the writings of the Fathers, the authoritative pronouncements of Bishops, the formulae of the Creeds, the definitions of Councils, and so on.

The vehicles just named are among those through which the Faith of the Church has come to expression. The use of such created instruments for the embodiment of eternal truth will be seen to be in complete harmony with the Incarnational principle. Man stands at the point of juncture of the temporal and eternal, and hence necessarily perceives the eternal under the language and forms of time. To have recognized the importance of the part played by the empirical factor in human knowing was one of the profoundly Christian elements in St. Thomas' system. As Dr. Kirk remarks with much justice, Aquinas is "perhaps the first Christian philosopher to take the corporeal character of human existence calmly".[1] In modern philosophy, one is reminded of the similar insistence made by Kant upon the relatedness of the temporal and the eternal factors in cognition. We thus see here another instance of a principle in the natural order which is no less applicable—but *per modum analogiae*—to the conditions of the communication of supernatural verity.

A necessary corollary of this consideration would seem to be that no revelation of truth can reach us altogether divorced from an element of contingency. "Infallibilities", that is, are never to be met with in religion. The authority which attaches to any particular element of revealed truth will be partly dependent upon the nature of the organ through which it receives expression. There must be, therefore,

---

[1] *The Vision of God*, p. 384.

degrees of dogmatic authority. Some authorities clearly have more inherent claims to be trusted as witnesses to the truth than others. More weight—always *ceteris paribus*, of course—will attach to the solemn decisions of a General Council than to the utterances of the individual Bishops who compose it; to the pronouncements of the Bishop of an important see than to those of an obscure divine; to the utterances of Christians of outstanding saintliness than to those of the worldly or the contentious; to the judgements of the learned than to those of the superficial or ignorant. We have, however, no indication in the teaching of the Gospels that to any of these particular vehicles was to be entrusted the capacity of producing infallible statements; on the contrary, such a presumption would be difficult to reconcile with the conditions under which on the principles of the Incarnation the communication of Divine Truth alone seems possible.

As a concrete illustration of the foregoing, the Creeds may be examined in somewhat more detail. To these summaries of dogmatic truth greater importance has probably been attached in the Church of England than in any other Communion in Christendom. Anglicanism, indeed, seems to be unique in considering the "Three Creeds"—the Apostles' Creed, the Nicene Creed, and the Athanasian Creed—as a set of dogmatic formularies *sui generis*. In the Primitive Church there existed a large number of Creeds, but their content and language was fluid, and they differed considerably from place to place. As regards our own familiar Creeds, the origin of all three of them is obscure. The view generally current in the Middle Ages that the Apostles' Creed was compiled by the Twelve Apostles has universally been abandoned by modern scholars. This Creed is now known to be the result of a long growth and believed not to have reached its present form before the eighth century. The origin of what we know as the Nicene Creed is also veiled in darkness. The Creed certainly received Conciliar authority at the Council of Chalcedon in A.D. 451, but it seems probable that the divines of that Council were under a misapprehension when they asserted that it had been promulgated at the Council of Constantinople in A.D. 381. At all events it belongs to a much later date than the Council of Nicaea in A.D. 325. Wrapped in still more obscurity are the origins of the so-called Athanasian Creed. It was certainly not written by St. Athanasius, for it is a Latin composition. Such authority then as attaches to the Creeds must belong to them in virtue of other circumstances than the traditional views of their genesis.

Nevertheless, the authority which these Creeds possess is immense. From time immemorial, they have proved invaluable as summaries of the Christian Faith. Through a period of some fifteen centuries they have found a continuous place in the life and worship of the Church and they give expression to the Christian Faith as, in its main outlines, it is still all but universally held. Even in the case of the Athanasian Creed, the objections sometimes raised to it are directed not so much against the positive content of its teaching—which is for the most part admirable—as against the anathemas which are attached to it and the suitability of its form to public worship. Occasionally objection is taken to a very few (hardly more than three) clauses in the Apostles' Creed—namely, "born of the Virgin Mary", "the third day", and "the Resurrection of the Body" (*resurrectio carnis*). But even here, except on a rather rigid literalism, the grounds upon which these clauses are questioned have (so, at least, it may be argued) not sufficient cogency to require the rejection of this

Creed from the position which it has come to acquire in historic Christianity (see Note, p. 344).

The Creeds may be taken, then, as instances of dogmatic formularies which, if viewed from the standpoint of broad principle, have stood the test of a long history. The fortunes of the vast majority of such formularies, however, have been less favoured. As an instance of a set of formulae which history has discredited may be taken our Thirty-Nine Articles. Unlike the Creeds, these consist of a number of *theologoumena*, drawn up *ad hoc* by theologians in an epoch singularly ill-fitted to legislate for the thought of succeeding generations. They cannot claim the prestige of an extended history, and if they ever possessed any usefulness, they have long since outgrown it. To turn from the Creeds to the Articles is to turn from historic fact and clear principle to narrow partizanship and contentious bickering. Some of the teaching set forth in the Articles implies a view of human nature that is doubtfully Christian, and many of their assertions are quite irreconcilable with an Incarnational view of the Christian Faith. There can be few theologians to-day, for instance, who could concur with the teaching of the Thirteenth Article that the good deeds of the heathen, so far from being "pleasant to God", "rather, for that they are not done as God hath willed and commanded them to be done, we doubt not but they have the nature of sin". Perhaps there are still fewer who would wish to impose *as an article of religion* the assertion in the Thirty-Seventh Article that "it is lawful for Christian men, at the commandment of the magistrate, to wear weapons and serve in the wars". Moreover, some of the assertions in the Articles are definite misstatements of fact. The tiro in Church history knows that it is untrue to refer to the Canonical Books of the Old and New Testament as those "of whose authority there was never any doubt in the Church". There was, of course, considerable difference of opinion about the Canonicity of certain of the New Testament books until well into the fourth century.

It may, no doubt, be argued that the specific teachings of the Articles no longer exercise much influence in the Church of England. The present writer has recently had occasion to read the examination papers of some 500 Ordinands on the subject of Christian Morals, and though there has been the fullest occasion for the expression of such views, not a single candidate has indicated that he held the view about Works done before Justification set forth in Article XIII. Perhaps the acquaintance of some Ordinands with the Articles is not vastly greater than that of the seventeenth-century candidate who, when his Bishop confronted him with the searching question, "how many there were of the Articles", boldly replied, "Two and twenty".[1] But it is highly undesirable that a totally antiquated and seemingly useless set of formulae should receive the assent on oath of every candidate for Holy Orders, and that the disproportionately large congregation which comes to church to welcome the newly appointed Incumbent should hear these obsolete theological pronouncements read out as though they epitomized and heralded the teaching which it was his duty to impart. By the retention and use of such formulae, the Church suggests to the uninstructed that she has lost contact with the intellectual, moral, and spiritual needs of the age. In our own view it is much to be wished that at the first opportunity the necessary legislative steps may be taken to abolish the Thirty-Nine Articles to that limbo whither many

---

[1] Referred to by N. Sykes, *Church and State in England in the Eighteenth Century*, p. 109. The Bishop was Kidder, who held the see of Bath and Wells from 1691 to 1703.

of the other contemporary formularies have now been consigned.

The Sociological Implications of Catholicism

From the Incarnational character of the Christian Faith, it follows that the Gospel has immediate implications for human society and its ideals. No province of human life can lie without the frontiers of a faith which claims to be all-inclusive (καθολικός). The Church, therefore, must seek to understand, as far as she can, the individual and corporate strivings of mankind, and endeavour to unify and guide them. It is her sociological vocation to redeem the natural elements in the social order, and to transmute them into a "new creation". The principle again is *Gratia non tollit naturam, sed perficit.*

There are, indeed, some Christians who urge (misguidedly, so the Incarnationalist must believe) that the Church ought to take no part in such matters. They contend that her concern is purely with "personal" religion, and that her one mission is to bring men into the right religious relationship with God—to teach them how to say their prayers, how to repent of their sins, how in a word to "find salvation"; and they argue that beyond this point the Church's function ends. In justification of this view they sometimes maintain that when men have "got right with God", all political, social, and economic issues will look after themselves. But such an attitude is radically at variance with an Incarnational philosophy. *In quantum est quidquid est, bonum est.* Political, economic, and social ideals—the sum-total, that is, of those ends which may be described in a wide sense as "Sociological"—are, for the Catholic, ideals which stand in immediate relationship to God, the *Summum Bonum.* Of several contending sociological doctrines an Incarnational religion must needs hold that only one of them is the "best"; and hence it must seek to discover which one this is and then endeavour to actualize it. The Church, if she is to be true to her vocation, is bound to give guidance to those seeking it on the great issues of contemporary human life.

The demand for the Church to exercise her consecrating and directive influence upon human culture is peculiarly pressing at the present time. Her aim is unity, whereas contemporary civilization is impeded and threatened on all sides by forces which make for disruption. At every turn we find disunity—a strongly developed class-consciousness, high tariff-barriers, and intense nationalism—facts which are the sociological counterparts of over-specialization in thought, in learning, and in science. Even more disconcerting is the absence of unity in personal morality. Clear canons of choice have been abandoned and men are unable to decide between conflicting claims. Probably never before in history have the resources which make for technical efficiency been greater than they are to-day. Manufactures are pouring out of our industries at so lavish a rate and with so little physical exertion that the labour market is flooded with the unemployed. And yet everywhere the world is crying *Quo tendimus?* It is to this question that the Church believes that she alone can provide the answer. She claims—almost without rivals, be it noted—to be possessed of a principle of unity which can permit of these *bona* being understood in a comprehensive and unified setting.

In relation to the carrying of this task into effect, two points need emphasis. The first is that the Church should recognize that if her decision is to be of any value, it ought to take the fullest account of the best available "secular" evidence. The pronouncements of some clergy upon sociological questions, it must be feared, suffer only too often from a deplorable "amateurism". Beyond and above all "secular" evidence, the Church has indeed to reckon with evidence belonging to a new Order, facts which have reached her through the Gospel. The possession of such data will enable the Church to arrive at principles and to outline a policy based upon them vastly superior to those which are open to those whose vision is limited by purely "secular" considerations. But when all this is perceived, the Church must not forget that the natural order also has its place in the Divine economy, and that the Christian Sociologist must understand it to the best of his ability.

The other point which needs emphasis concerns the method by which the Church should seek to make her voice heard in a world which has lost the desire for unity. There is no doubt that the Church has not as yet sufficiently adapted to the present age her somewhat stereotyped and now partially antiquated methods of commending her faith. The pulpit is a vehicle which to-day reaches only a small proportion of our population, and these not always the most critical. We imperatively need a daily newspaper which is definitely and uncompromisingly Christian in outlook. To illustrate what is required, reference may perhaps be made to the treatment week by week of foreign affairs in the opening "Summary paragraphs" of the *Church Times*. The reader finds here Christian principles brought to bear upon matters of international importance by what is widely recognized to be a singularly well-informed and judicious criticism. But presumably the *Church Times* circulates almost exclusively among those who already claim the name of Christian; and like other religious journals is looked upon by its readers as a Friday religious appanage to the secular press which is studied exclusively on the other six days of the week. The Church undoubtedly requires a daily newspaper which shall circulate on its own merits, whose outlook from the first page to the last is Christian, and wherein at every turn Christian principles are brought to bear upon the course of events, whether in literature or in politics or in art, or in whatever else may be the subject of the hour.

CHRISTIAN ASCETICISM

In virtue of the "tension" to which reference was made at the outset of this essay, Christianity is both world-accepting and world-rejecting. It therefore not only allows a place to "asceticism", but sets a high value upon it. An account of the Universe which was unreservedly Pantheistic could find no scope for renunciation. On purely Immanental premisses every action, no matter what its motives or what its consequences, would be an expression of the Divine Nature, and therefore necessarily absolutely good. At the other end of the scale, Dualistic thought, by refusing to allow the possibility of any goodness attaching to things *hic et nunc*, requires the complete renunciation of all that is held in estimation by human standards, and asserts that pleasures as such are evil. Christianity pursues a path between these two philosophies. It holds that whatever is truly human *ipso facto* shares in its degree in the goodness of God. But it also maintains that not all human actions are *equally* good. The fact that goodness has its grades demands that growth towards perfection should go hand in hand with the renunciation of the lower in favour of the higher. "If any one will come after me, let him deny himself, and take up his cross and follow me" (Mark viii. 34). Certain pleasures, therefore, are to be renounced by the Christian, not because they are intrinsically evil nor, on the other hand, because renunciation is an end in itself, but because indulgence in them is a hindrance towards the fullest Christian life.

Such is the theological justification for the great emphasis which in the history of the Church has been set upon a measure of asceticism. According to a careful definition, asceticism is "the practice of evangelical renunciation which is either demanded by the Christian law or is simply counselled as a means of more certainly tending towards Christian perfection and of more effectively contributing to the common good of the Christian Society".[1] There is thus no call to renunciation of pleasures for their own sake. When the call to the sacrifice of pleasure is heard, it comes simply because indulgence in it is an impediment to other and more important claims. Indeed, so far is pleasure from being in itself undesirable that, *ceteris paribus*, a world in which there is more pleasure is "better", and therefore from an Incarnational standpoint more "Christian", than one in which there is less.[2] Yet from the earliest times the Church has sought to encourage *ascesis* among her members, and for this she has made provision in two ways. By the one she has sought to prescribe a minimum amount of mortification upon all her faithful; by the other, she has given opportunity for a much enhanced degree of it to such Christians as receive the call to it.

The former means of discipline is fostered by the place which Days of Fasting and Abstinence occupy in the Liturgical Year. Friday by Friday, the Church bids abstinence in remembrance of the Friday on which the Lord effected the supreme sacrifice for the salvation of the world. In Lent and Passiontide, she recalls the Temptation of the Son of Man and impresses upon her members that only through suffer-

---

[1] *La pratique du renoncement évangélique exigé par la loi chrétienne ou simplement conseillé comme moyen de tendre plus sûrement à la perfection chrétienne ou de contribuer plus efficacement au bien commun de la société chrétienne* (Du-Blanchy in the *Dict. de Théol. Cath.* i. 2055).

[2] As H. Rashdall constantly, and rightly, insisted.

ing can they hope to reach the joy of the Resurrection. By her Ember Seasons, with their emphasis upon the close association between prayer and fasting, she reminds her children that the Christian ideal of prayer is not uncontrolled mystical rapture, but a life of disciplined communion. In ways such as these, the Church sets the ideal of *ascesis* before all her members.

But for those to whom the vocation comes to a life of fuller renunciation the Church has sought to make further provision. From the rich young man of the Gospel, there have been those who have heard the call to "perfection"; and it has been the especial function of the Religious Orders and Congregations to train in saintliness and renunciation those who have heard this call. With the varying needs of individuals and the changing circumstances of times, the Religious Life has assumed, as all students of Church history are aware, very different forms; but the record of many of its triumphs and its fruits, both in the spiritual and the temporal orders, belongs to the history of Western civilization. It would be difficult, indeed, to overestimate the extent to which the course of European culture has been modified by the work of such religious as St. Anthony and St. Basil, St. Benedict and St. Bernard, St. Francis and St. Dominic, St. Ignatius Loyola and St. Theresa. If Monasticism has here and there had its dark patches, it has been on the whole an enormous influence for good. Moreover, it is of deep significance that the achievements of the Religious Orders, so impressive even when judged by purely "secular" standards, have been brought about by men and women whose ideals were essentially "otherworldly". Whatever be the explanation, it seems to be a fact that a life modelled on the world-denying counsels is found often to lead to more permanent and fruitful results in the temporal order than those which issue from ideals more immediately and consciously philanthropic.

In the Church of England, the last hundred years have seen a remarkable revival of the Religious Life. Such names as Cowley, Mirfield, and Wantage, to mention no others, have become household words throughout the length and breadth of *Ecclesia Anglicana*. But there is still scope for a much fuller growth of the Monastic life amongst us; and as it is possible that the next developments of it will proceed along somewhat less traditional methods than those followed by the existing Orders, we will conclude this section by venturing to suggest lines upon which two possible future Orders might be conceived. Each of these Orders would, we believe, meet an outstanding need of the present time.

The first of these would be an Order whose function it should be to study afresh the bearing of the Christian Faith upon the intellectual background of the age. It would set out to do for to-day what St. Dominic's Order did for the thirteenth century. From the nature of the case, such an Order could not be "enclosed". It would have to keep in immediate contact with the development and progress of contemporary thought; and hence it would be desirable that it should be centred either in a University town or in some other focus of intellectual life. It might be a matter of some difficulty to prescribe what freedom should be allowed to its members; probably this would have to differ more from individual to individual than is the case in most of the now existing Orders. In such an Order, no rule could reasonably require a man to spend so many hours a day at his desk, or to produce so many words for the printer each week. It could not profitably require even that he should devote all his activities to one particular piece of work—to the elucidation, say, of one particular problem or to the writing of one particular book; for doubtless the all but universal experience of scholars is that they derive stimulus from change of work. The freshness which comes from relaxation and diversion of activities would thus have to be fully allowed for. But somehow the community in question would have to insist that each of its members should be willing to subordinate all his other activities to the one particular piece of work which the community assigned to him.

From such a co-operative effort, carried out with determination and purpose by men of tried ability, results of enormous value might be expected. Few theologians living "in the world" to-day are able to give unfettered attention to their vocation. Their energies are constantly diversified into a vast number of channels—preaching, organizing, tutoring, lecturing, examining, reviewing, controverting, conferring, and so on (to say nothing of such claims as matrimony and their implications). On the other hand, those who are least hindered from study by the interference of such obstacles are apt to suffer seriously from isolation. In a community in which the activities of its members were properly directed such hindrances would be obviated. Great freedom would have to be allowed, of course, for differences of theological opinion. No study can be unfettered if the results at which the student is to arrive are prescribed to him from the outset; and a ludicrous situation would arise if a member of the community were to find that when his studies had reached a certain stage he was liable to suspension or expulsion by reason of his conclusions. Further, it would be imperative that the life of the community should be kept in touch with contemporary culture to the greatest possible extent. The lections at meals might sometimes be the Lives of the Saints—the traditional stand-by of the refectory pulpit—but they might more often be the writings of the Huxleys or Mr. Lloyd George's latest programme for economic reconstruction or the newest set of Gifford Lectures.

The other Order that it is possible to visualize is one which would concern itself with the propagation of International Peace. The masses of the world in revolt against Militarism have as yet no leader, and perhaps under no other leadership except under that of him who is the "Prince of Peace" will they ever make their convictions effective. An Order whose purpose it was to preach in season and out of season the futility and, what is far more important, the immorality of War, and which aimed at uniting men and women throughout the world in groups determined to resist it in all circumstances, might reasonably hope to achieve what other methods have hitherto failed to effect. Indeed, it may be doubted whether anything short of religious motives will ever prove a successful weapon against the potent forces of all kinds and descriptions which make for war.

The members of such an Order would presumably be itinerants. They would be constantly on the move from place to place, preaching in the market-place and conducting missions in such parish churches as were placed at their disposal. They would attest their sincerity by their selflessness—by accepting no more from the world than was necessary to satisfy their modest needs. They would proclaim incessantly that, however estimable in themselves were the sentiments of "loyalty", such sentiments must be resisted with might and main if exploited by a Government in favour of a war. They would unite those who accepted their principles into an Association pledged religiously to active anti-Militarism.

A comparatively small Order of thoroughly devoted and disciplined men, fired with this sense of vocation, might exercise a determining influence upon the destiny of Western Europe. Through their agency there would come into existence a united body of Christian people, definitely bound to do all in their power to hinder a Government when it contemplated entry upon a war. On the occasion of a threatened or an initiated war they would have no hesitation in being "disloyal", knowing that "loyalty" to a Government in such circumstances would be no more justified than "loyalty" to a Government which sought to re-introduce slavery or to stamp out Christianity. The vast majority in every nation are opposed to war and (as circumstances in this country in the last war proved) can be induced to take part in it only by "conscription"[1]; but hitherto they have been effectively silenced on the outbreak of every war, as they have possessed no concerted plan of action. No Government in Europe, however, would venture to embark on a war if it knew that such a course would be resisted within its borders by a large mass of convinced and "Militant Pacifism".[2] At the present time there are multitudes who are awaiting an uncompromising lead from the Church in this direction.

Catholic Sacramentalism

A further principle which is intimately connected with the Incarnation is that of Sacramentalism. The

[1] Statutes enacted by those whom Mr. A. A. Milne terms "Elder Statesmen" to impel the young to acts of "heroism".

[2] A phrase from the *Church Times* of March 15, 1935. Anyone in doubt of the extent of "militant pacifism" among Christian people in this country should read and weigh the correspondence which this letter occasioned. What other religious ideal except Pacifism could at the present time bring 7000 men to a meeting at the Albert Hall, as happened on July 14, 1935? As Canon H. R. L. Sheppard insisted on that occasion, few things shew more clearly the gulf between much contemporary ecclesiasticism (a vice by no means confined to "ritualists") and the best ideals of the modern generation than the indifference of the former to the cause of Peace.

Christian Faith is built upon the conviction that the key to human life is to be found in the life and death and resurrection of One born of humble stock and nurtured in comparative obscurity. In this circumstance is discovered the guarantee that the least pretending elements in creation may serve as vehicles for Divine revelation. Popular theology has become accustomed to summarize this conviction in its formula that the Sacraments are "the extension of the Incarnation". Through seemingly unimportant outward instruments, the Godhead makes contact with the human world-order.

The emphasis laid by those Christians who value the name of "Catholic" upon the Sacramental elements in religion is too familiar to require elaboration. The particular forms which Sacramentalism assumes in current practice are the outcome of a long development. In this principle in Christianity the outward elements in religion necessarily receive especial prominence—for a Sacrament is, as the Catechism phrases it, "an outward and visible sign of an inward and spiritual grace"—and hence it is natural that Sacramental forms, as external ordinances, should be exceptionally susceptible to the external changes which mark the world of history. Recent Anglo-Catholicism has borrowed much in this field from Rome. For instance, the Tridentine doctrine of the Sacraments, with its insistence upon their sevenfold number, has found increasing favour. But as long as the principle of Sacramentalism is conserved, there is no reason to suppose that any particular form of Sacramentalism will be permanent nor that the differences between the several forms of it are of major importance. Unlike the Tridentine theologians, the Tractarians for the most part followed their Caroline ancestors in restricting the term "Sacrament" to the two "Sacraments of the Gospel"— Baptism and the Eucharist. On the other hand,

z

before the thirteenth century the term was frequently applied to a much larger number of the rites than the seven of Trent. Hugo of St. Victor enumerated no less than thirty *sacramenta*.[1] Perhaps Lancelot Andrewes was not far wrong in suggesting that often discussions about the number of the Sacraments was not more than a λογομαχία.[2]

In connexion with Sacramental theology, it should also be noticed that the Sacraments are not only channels of Divine communication but are possessed, in addition, of a representative function. Here again their relatedness to the Incarnation becomes evident. Just as Christ was representative of the human race, so correspondingly the Eucharistic Bread and Wine are representative of all bread and wine and, ultimately, of the whole of created nature. The reverence due to the sacred species is thus representative of the reverence due to God's presence throughout the external world. A similar representative function attaches to other religious objects whose character is in essence Sacramental. The Bible is representative of every form of great literature, the Cathedral or the Parish Church of all that is great in the realm of art; and hence the respect paid by the Christian to such things is expressive of his proper attitude to every fraction of created being. For, on the principle of analogy, the world is through and through Sacramental. Every fragment of creation shares to some degree in the goodness of God and, in so far, can claim our reverence.[3]

Liturgical Worship

Closely connected with Sacramentalism is the subject of Liturgical Worship. The Forms of Liturgy

---

[1] Cf. *De Sacramentis Fidei Christianae, M.P.L.* clxxvi. 471-2.
[2] Cp. Extract No. 174 in P. E. More and F. L. Cross, *Anglicanism,* p. 414.
[3] Leaving litter on Hampstead Heath or on the Bournemouth sands is thus an un-Christian act.

are the outward dress with which Christian devotion is normally clothed, and as such are another expression of the Incarnational principle at the heart of the Christian Faith. For the Incarnationalist the ordering of worship can thus never be a subject of indifference. Indeed, those who have penetrated most deeply into the meaning of interior prayer have usually been among those who have emphasized most the importance of its external forms. What Order of Contemplatives, for instance, would dare to dispense with its Breviary?

In the matter of Liturgy, Incarnationalism makes the same demands as elsewhere for "mediation"; and not without justice many Anglicans hold that the ceremonial ideal of the Church of England is a *via media*. When Simon Patrick approved of "that virtuous mediocrity which our Church observes between the meretricious gaudiness of the Church of Rome and the squalid sluttery of fanatic conventicles",[1] he was uttering no vain boast. The same eulogy of "the mean" is to be discovered in George Herbert's poem, "The British Church",[2] and the divines of the Savoy Conference summed up over a hundred years of our liturgical history with the assertion that "it hath been the wisdom of the Church of England, ever since the first compiling of her Public Liturgy, to keep the mean between the two extremes of too much stiffness in refusing and of too much easiness in admitting, any variation from it".[3] The *via media* both in the extent to which ceremonies have been prescribed and in the amount of freedom permitted in respect to what has been ordered has marked Anglicanism throughout its history.

But if it is possible for the Church of England to

---

[1] Quoted in P. E. More and F. L. Cross, *Anglicanism*, p. 12.

[2] *Ibid.* pp. 11 f.

[3] Preface to the Book of Common Prayer. Cp. also P. E. More and F. L. Cross, *op. cit.* pp. 167-9.

justify the liturgical ideal she has set before herself, she can hardly claim that her present Liturgical forms are altogether satisfactory. Indeed, it is all but universally recognized that the existing Book of Common Prayer is no longer fully suited to modern needs. The intellectual, political, social, and economic changes of the three centuries which have now nearly elapsed since 1662 have been so vast that unless we are to believe that Christian worship stands unrelated to these aspects of life, it could scarcely be expected that the devotional forms of the existing Book should be those most adequate to the requirements of the present day. The very fact that our Liturgy uses a "language understanded of the people" makes those who use it the more conscious of the need for change. Consequently the desirability of a revision which should take account of these altered conditions is widely admitted. Certainly few Anglo-Catholics would have any objections to revision in itself, and most Anglo-Catholics would warmly welcome a measure of it.

The reason why the Deposited Book of 1927 was distasteful to so many Anglo-Catholics is to be accounted for by the circumstances of its origin. Briefly summarized, they appear to be these. From about the middle of the last century onwards, a certain latitude in interpreting the rubrics of the 1662 Book became widespread, and as time went on some of them came to be universally broken. Dissatisfaction with the letter of the Book was thus felt on almost all sides; and individuals, believing that there was little immediate hope of securing through the legislative channels a revision such as they desired, introduced changes on their own initiative. In one church, for instance, the Athanasian Creed would be omitted from Morning Prayer on the days on which its use was prescribed; in another, Eucharistic prayers and ceremonial would be introduced which the rubrics did not countenance or even forbade; in a third, services for which there was no authority in the Book of Common Prayer—Mission Services, Harvest Thanksgivings, the Three Hours' Service, Compline, Devotions before the Blessed Sacrament —would be used.

It was with this situation that the Royal Commission on Ecclesiastical Discipline sought to deal when in June 1904 it held its first meeting. The natural outcome was that the projected new Prayer Book came to be envisaged by its compilers rather as an instrument to enable the re-creation of uniformity than as a manual of worship. As the attempted revision proceeded through its various stages, the disciplinary aspects of the Book were increasingly emphasized while devotional and liturgical considerations receded more and more into the background. When at length those charged with the revision were faced with the practical issue as to how the Book would be received by the legislative courts—the Church Assembly, Convocation, and Parliament—the one motive which seems to have been dominant among its supporters was the determination to secure at any price that the Book should be accepted. Successive changes in the Book thus were made, not because they were demanded by any devotional or liturgical or theological principles, but almost solely (so at least it seemed to many Anglo-Catholics) because they were more likely to make the Book commendable to the legislative bodies concerned. A comparison between the 1927 and the 1928 Book makes it abundantly clear that this was so in the final stages of the revision. It is not surprising that a Book produced in this way should have proved from the liturgical point of view a failure. The severe judgement on the 1927 Book of Mr. F. E. Brightman, probably the most outstanding English liturgiologist then living, is well known. "As to the Book as a whole I would say . . . that on almost every page of it I find something irritating, something inexact or untidy or superfluous or ill-considered or unreal."[1]

Nevertheless a revision in the near future of certain parts, at least, of the Book of Common Prayer is esteemed by many Anglo-Catholics a great *desideratum*. The Occasional Offices are particularly in need of modification and reconstruction. In the Office of Baptism, the Book of 1927 indicated the direction in which alteration is desirable by its excision of the phrase "conceived and born in sin" and its substitution in their place of the words that "we are taught in Holy Scripture that God willeth all men to be saved, for God is love". The references to the Ark and to the Red Sea could also very profitably be removed. In the Marriage Service, the existing introductory exhortation with its assertion about the institution of matrimony urgently demands considerable modification. The services for both the Visitation of the Sick and the Burial of the Dead are likewise in need of reform. In all these cases the Deposited Book supplies many suggestions as to possibilities; for it was in its least controversial parts that that Book naturally achieved most success.

In the matter of Eucharistic worship, most of those who call themselves Anglo-Catholics would like to see not only Reservation of the Sacrament definitely legitimized, but also provision made that the reserved species should be kept in a tabernacle and not in an aumbry or locked chapel. The methods of Reservation countenanced by the promulgators of the Deposited Book were ostentatiously inconvenient. They aimed at erecting obstacles to devotion, and by removing the Sacrament from the altar tended to dissociate it from the idea of Communion. Many Catholics would also wish to see at any rate Devotions to the Blessed Sacrament, if not Benediction, pro-

[1] *Church Quarterly Review*, July 1927, p. 222.

vided for. Some measure of reform in the Eucharistic Rite would also be welcome. In the light of our extended liturgical knowledge and modern needs, our present Canon is evidently susceptible of considerable improvement. The range of Proper Collects, Epistles, and Gospels should be greatly increased to make provision for the now widespread practice of Daily Celebrations and the observance of many Saints and Commemorations. Proper Introits, Graduals, Offertories, and Post-Communions should also be given official recognition. The Ten Commandments could profitably be removed. Not only are their moral precepts not specifically Christian, but their cosmology rings uncouth in modern ears; it is undesirable to convey the impression that the Church holds that "in six days the Lord made heaven and earth".

Perhaps the greatest anomaly in Anglican worship, however, is the place which Matins and Evensong have come to occupy in it. Based upon Offices intended primarily for Monastic Orders, these services have in the majority of Anglican churches come to be the normal form of Sunday worship. The long tradition which lies behind this use of them demands respect, for liturgical forms and customs, somehow, acquire sanctity through usage. But, this consideration apart, it would be hard to conceive of two services more ill-fitted for their purpose. By a curious anomaly their contents are predominatingly pre-Christian. On an average Sunday, the worshippers at Matins will hear from five to seven passages from the Old Testament, and not more than two (*i.e.* the "Second Lesson" and perhaps the "Benedictus") from the New. Such a form of worship might be well suited to those who, nurtured in the Christian tradition and familiar with its principles from childhood, as it were grew into it and interpreted it with Christian associations; but it may be seriously doubted whether it is likely to meet the needs of a generation which needs to be instructed almost *ab initio* as to what the Christian Faith is.

In the preceding sections the attempt has been made to expound from a particular standpoint some of the principles of the Christian Faith in their relationship to contemporary conditions. By such readers as have had sufficient patience to proceed thus far, several judgements may have been passed. The considerations urged may have been deemed rash or commonplace, individualistic or partisan, antiquated or modernistic, rationalistic or credulous. The writer is fully conscious that they may well have suffered to some extent from all these limitations in different places.

An Incarnationalist interpretation of the Faith, however, cannot be final. It will seek not merely to tolerate but to encourage criticism. It is based upon the conviction that every human exposition of the truth is made by those who are themselves within the time-process. Every historic individual views Reality not *sub specie aeternitatis*, but from a concrete situation *hic et nunc*, and hence every human account of the Faith must reflect the historically conditioned background and prejudices (*praejudicia*) of its author. As long as we are pilgrims, we necessarily approach Reality δι' ἐσόπτρου ἐν αἰνίγματι. The shadows will depart only later. *Ex umbris et imaginibus in veritatem.*

NOTE

It is perhaps worth examining a little more closely each of the three clauses of the Apostles' Creed referred to in the text on page 325.

(1) *"Born of the Virgin Mary."*—The current objection to this clause rests on the two assumptions that to profess it implies belief in the Virgin Birth of Christ and that this belief has been rendered untenable or improbable by recent investigations. As regards the latter of these assumptions, the question under consideration is far from proven. Admittedly there is no clear evidence that either St. Mark (the earliest Evangelist) or St. Paul was acquainted with the tradition. But, granting the possibility that Christ was born in a miraculous way, it would be a subject the knowledge of which the Blessed Virgin might very well have imparted to only a small circle, and thus not have found its way until a late date into the Evangelical Tradition. As far as the Gospels go, there is no historical evidence "against" it. The main ground upon which the belief is questioned is probably connected with the objections felt by some modern theologians to miracle as such. It would take us too far afield if we were to enter upon a discussion of this subject here. But it may perhaps be noted that philosophically the objections to miracle to-day would seem to be far less serious than they were a generation or so ago when Absolute Idealism was the regnant philosophy.

But, to return to the Creed, it may be seriously doubted whether the clause in question really commits those who profess it to the belief in Our Lord's miraculous birth. As a matter of Church history, it seems pretty clear that the clause found its way into the Creed in order to emphasize not the "supernatural" character of Our Lord, but his Humanity. There is little doubt that its original purpose was anti-Docetic, and that it was thus meant to assert that Christ was born of a truly human Mother. The fact that this woman was the *"Virgin* Mary" would thus be no part of the original emphasis of the phrase; and if so, it is arguable, as Dr. Goudge has suggested, that we are no more committed by the Creed to the belief that Christ's Mother was a virgin than to the belief that Pilate's first name was "Pontius".[1]

(2) *"The third day he rose again."*—The objections to this

---

[1] Cf. *The Church Times*, Oct. 5, 1928, and the continuation of the correspondence in subsequent issues.

clause also rest largely on the "prejudice" (*praejudi-cium*) against Miracle. But even those who find difficulties in the traditional view that the physical body of Christ was resuscitated from the Tomb can hardly deny, unless they deny the Christian Faith altogether, that the Resurrection of Christ was a definite "event" of some kind, and presumably must have taken place at a definite moment. It may be difficult, if not impossible, to reconcile the Gospel accounts in their details. But practically all the evidence concurs towards the hypothesis that it was "on the third day" that something (whatever it was) took place.

(3) "*The Resurrection of the Body*."—To this clause the objections are perhaps more serious than those to the other two. It points forward to a "final resurrection" when the material particles of our bodies will be brought together again. But in the Christian Church a wide divergence of opinion in matters of eschatology has always been permitted and the clause may still be patient of an acceptable meaning. Investigations in physics in the last few decades, though they may not have refuted Materialism (as is sometimes, and not altogether without basis, asserted), have at any rate shewn how uncertain is the view of matter traditional in pre-twentieth-century physics, namely, that it is *res extensa* or something like it. Even when the clause is interpreted just as it stands, there are no conclusive scientific difficulties against it. But surely the clause stands as an approximate (may we say, an "analogical"?) way of expressing two things which go beyond the mere letter—first, the belief in a final Divine Judgement on every human soul; and secondly, the fact that the Christian belief about the future life implies more than a doctrine of "mere immortality".

IX

EVANGELICALISM AND THE TWENTIETH CENTURY

by

LEONARD ELLIOTT-BINNS, D.D.

Late Hulsean Lecturer in the University of Cambridge
Examining Chaplain to the Bishop of Hereford
Fellow of the Royal Historical Society

Author of *The Evangelical Movement in the English Church* (Faiths Series); *Erasmus the Reformer*; *Innocent III*; *The Decline and Fall of The Medieval Papacy*; *Jeremiah* (Westminster Commentaries); *Numbers* (Westminster Commentaries); *From Moses to Elisha* (Clarendon Bible); *The Jewish People and Their Faith, Religion in the Victorian Era*, etc.

SYNOPSIS

INTRODUCTION

NEITHER Evangelicalism nor Liberalism in isolation fulfils the spiritual needs of men. The future needs to be studied in the light of the past. Especially is this so in the case of Evangelicalism, which to-day is standing at the cross-road, and faces a future of promise and opportunity but also of much hazard.

THE PRESENT SITUATION

Our age is one of restlessness and rebellion, and in this reminds us of the state of Germany in the sixteenth century. Many have been led astray by a misunderstanding of the New Psychology and have drawn false deductions from it. Old sanctions have disappeared and the widespread abandonment of belief in immortality has caused an increased value to be attached to the satisfaction of carnal appetites. The results of the disintegration of morals and manners are masked for the present by the continuance of the tradition of Christian civilization; but already the modern form of Humanism is breeding disillusionment and weariness. There is hope that a new presentation of the gospel will win a response from the younger generation.

THE OLD EVANGELICALS

The Evangelical Movement grew out of Methodism and had the same characteristics, but the early Evangelicals were strong churchmen. It was in reaction against the Oxford Movement that the Evangelicals became Low Churchmen. They held strong dogmatic beliefs. Their theory of a sacrificial Atonement led many in the direction of Tritheism. The older Evangelicals believed in Biblical verbal inspiration, but avoided many of the dangers involved in their belief by a method of interpretation which was largely allegorical. They laid more stress on the emotions than on the intellect. A prominent feature in their system was the emphasis on the direct influence of the Holy

Spirit on the heart of the individual believer. In the early years of the nineteenth century the power of Evangelicals in the Church was not commensurate with their spiritual predominance. At a later period, when their ecclesiastical prestige was high, their spiritual power had begun to decay, and in the middle of the reign of Queen Victoria Evangelicalism was in a bad way. Its weakness was bred of an undue reliance on the past and an unwillingness to adjust itself to meet new conditions. Especially were the Evangelicals unable to deal effectively with Biblical Criticism. Recovery was made through Revival Movements and the establishment of Theological Colleges for the training of Evangelical ordinands.

THE LIBERAL EVANGELICALS

The fruit of the foundation of the Theological Colleges ripened a generation later in the formation of the Anglican Evangelical Group Movement, a Movement which for eighteen years remained private and almost secret. Its object is to discriminate between what is essential in the Evangelical position and what is traditional and fleeting. During the first stage of the Movement it included very few men of social or clerical influence or of reputation as preachers or scholars, but it did include many men of determined character who knew what they wanted. Gaining influence in their party, they ultimately gained influence in the Church at large. They brought into the Church the methods of the business world from which most of them had sprung. They introduced a new type of Bishop. The advantage of efficiency, however, is dearly gained if it should prove to be at the expense of spiritual power.

THE OLD AND THE NEW EVANGELICALS

The new Evangelicalism is fundamentally at one with the old in its insistence on the need for redemption and sanctification, the stress it lays on unrestricted access to God, and the high place it gives to the Bible. It is, however, less rigid in doctrine, especially as regards the doctrine of the Atonement. It appreciates more adequately the meaning of the Incarnation, and has thus gained a more balanced outlook. It has abandoned the theory of verbal inspiration and regards the authority of the Bible not as arbitrary and external but as based on its religious and spiritual appeal. The only final standard is the Mind of Christ. In spite of differences, the new Evangelicalism stands in the same succession as the old.

The Future

The greatness of the past of Evangelicalism does not necessarily assure its future importance. The line to be followed is that laid down by the Liberal wing, and Evangelicals must continue to throw themselves into the life of Church and Nation. The A.E.G.M. is active in promoting schemes of study among its members, but there is still need for more scholarship among Evangelicals. An excessive activity is not conducive to study.

The Danger of Liberalism

Addiction to an extreme Liberalism may lead Evangelicals into rationalism. Scholarship ought not to be divorced from life. The predominant school of Biblical criticism has an inadequate conception of revelation, which it equates with discovery. Christianity is a religion of the supernatural. Much modern theological thinking about the subject of miracles reflects the mechanistic determinism of the nineteenth century.

The New Knowledge

That we are on the verge of great spiritual discoveries seems the natural and faithful conclusion from the fact that we belong to an age of vast scientific discovery and achievement. Mentally and philosophically mankind is living in temporary lodgings which must be changed frequently. The new philosophy, when it comes, will be one of conciliation rather than comprehension. In the meantime the theologian must claim the scientist's right to propound new hypotheses for the purpose of discussion and testing. But for most people religion is primarily an emotion or experience. Evangelicals must, however, not acquiesce in the conception of two truths, one scientific, the other religious.

The Need for Catholicism

Evangelicals should learn from Catholicism a more adequate valuation of history, and a clearer realization of the importance of the religious community or Church. Otherwise they are in danger of an excessive subjectivism.

ETHICS

The present widespread confusion in ethics and the shifting of moral standards cannot continue indefinitely. Settled standards are necessary. Christian ethics are related to doctrines which give morality its sanctions. The sense of sin follows on the possession of a vital sense of a living God. Ethical principles based on evolutionary philosophies, being bound up with the temporal and imperfect, fail to be absolute. Religion involves consecration of life and activity to the service of God, and such dedication leads on to a clearer and higher ethical judgement. The growth of a new Puritanism is desirable, though this will not lay so much stress as the old Puritanism on suppressions. It will combine sternness to self with tolerance towards others, and will attach a religious value to beauty. A greater simplicity of life will enable people to support larger families and will check the dysgenic effects of the practice of conception-control.

WORSHIP

Evangelicals will demand the right to make further experiments in worship while learning a wider tolerance of forms which are not congenial to themselves. They must also beware of neglect of private prayer and devotion in too exclusive a reliance on hard work and efficiency. The A.E.G.M. has attempted to help those who, for various causes, are in danger of weakness in the devotional life by the institution of the Cromer Convention, but it has not yet really "caught on".

THE JUSTIFICATION OF EVANGELICALISM

The future of Evangelicalism is dependent on its effectiveness in the parish. The new Evangelicalism must preach a full gospel, social as well as individual. New methods will be used as new wisdom comes, but Evangelicals will continue to draw from the treasury inherited from the older Evangelicalism.

IX

EVANGELICALISM AND THE TWENTIETH CENTURY

INTRODUCTION

EIGHT years ago, in a volume entitled *The Evangelical Movement in the English Church*, I tried to foretell the future of Evangelicalism. What I now write has behind it the further experience which those years, spent mainly in literary activities, have brought with them. In reading through my old essay I am not conscious of the need for anything but slight modification in the opinions there expressed; I am still profoundly convinced that neither Evangelicalism, with its emotional susceptibilities, nor Liberalism, with its tendency to follow scholarship divorced from life, is adequate to meet the problems of the day, and to bring to man, on any large scale, that inner unity and peace without which he can 'serve neither God nor his fellows as he ought, and as, in his highest moments, he sincerely desires to do.

In view of the incalculable vicissitudes of human affairs, as the race proceeds on its long march beneath the changing aspects of the years, forecasts are always precarious. They may easily be also irresponsible and harmful. If it is hard to interpret the past, harder still is it to make prophecies of times and seasons which, we have been warned, the Father himself holds in his own keeping. The solemnity of this thought has, I hope, never been absent from me, and what I have attempted has been little more than to suggest possible developments and possible perils which may arise from the continuance of

353

2 A

existing tendencies in the light of their past history. Contemporaries, knowing only the past and the present, judge events by their causes alone; the historian, as he looks back, has the advantage of being aware, in part at least, of their effects. Thus the study of the past, whilst it does not rob the historian of the power to recognize the daring of those who prophesy, helps to quicken whatever ability he may possess in tracing the sequence of events.

The careful study of history shews that the Church, though constantly being called upon to face new situations, never, or but rarely, finds them entirely novel. Somewhere in its long history similar difficulties have been met and overcome, similar assaults have been parried and repulsed. To recollect this gives courage in an age when Christian beliefs, and the definite view of life based on them, are being, in many quarters, persistently rejected. None the less we must once again examine our principles and our ideals, bringing them before what Sir Thomas Browne has called "the areopagy and dark tribunal of our hearts". By so doing we shall be able to see how far modification of them is necessary; how far they still commend themselves to our judgement in the light of fresh knowledge, and the clearer insight into the Will and Purpose of God which such knowledge has brought.

Such an examination is especially necessary for Evangelicals, since the task which lies ahead of them is most urgent. Evangelicalism more than any other party in the Church is standing at the cross-roads; it must either shew itself capable of adaptation to the new conditions, or it will lapse almost into nothingness. The future which lies ahead of it is one of much promise and of much hazard; it has amazing difficulties and glorious hopes. Perhaps the most striking feature of hope is the robust and indefatigable spirit in which it is facing that future. Liberal Evangelicalism, as Archdeacon Storr, its greatest living leader, has said, "is not enamoured of trenches; it prefers the open field".[1] One may not anticipate triumphs which time alone can achieve; but it seems to me that Evangelicalism, by God's grace, has a future greater than anything that lies in its past. At the same time its leaders must not forget that sometimes the highest courage, as well as the highest wisdom, lies in the ability to recognize the necessity for withdrawal; they must be willing to face the sneers and to accept the suspicion which inevitably follow every strategic retreat. "Moral courage", as Disraeli once wrote, "is the rarest of qualities, and is often maligned." It is certainly hard at times to distinguish it from defect of temper, or even from its very opposite, lack of scruple.

The Present Situation

Our age is one of unrest and even of rebellion. Many are proud, it would seem, to turn their backs defiantly on the moral and spiritual heritage of the race. Like the age of the Reformation in Germany, it is suffering from the abolition of old sanctions and the repudiation of ancient authorities. For just as the North German of the sixteenth century found himself "at sea" when the guidance and control of an infallible Church was withdrawn, so men and women to-day are floundering in cross-currents. Parents and teachers no longer have the restraining influence which once was theirs; whilst the authority of Church and Bible are often unknown or gladly forgotten. Through newspapers and sensational novels loose and perverse opinions obtain wide circulation; and young and inexperienced readers, possessing as they do but a slender stock of sound principles or elevated standards by which to test them, are easy victims. Many have been led astray (by a mistaken following

---

[1] *Spiritual Liberty*, p. 127.

of what they regard as the teaching of the New Psychology) into the belief, so acceptable to the self-indulgent, that to curb the natural desires is dangerous and that such "repressions" are liable to lead to "complexes" and a neurotic condition. Such aberrations are worthy only of censure and their falsity has been exposed by Professor McDougall. He states plainly enough that

> much vague acquaintance with the doctrines of Professor Freud is widely spread, and grossly false deductions from them are widely current and countenanced in not a few books. Of all such misrepresentations that of the dangers and evil consequences of "repression" is most widely accepted, just because it seems to give licence to unrestrained indulgence, to excuse us from all efforts at self-control. And so we hear much nonsense about living out our nature, and about free self-expression and about our rights, and especially women's rights, to happiness and experience, and what not; and much scornful comment on old-fashioned conventions and restraints. I would assure the reader that neither Professor Freud nor any other judicious psychologist countenances the popular deductions to which I refer.[1]

The real truth seems to be, as Professor James Simpson proclaimed in *Man and the Attainment of Immortality*, that the course of evolution seems to depend upon man's ability to deny his lower instincts the unreasonable gratification for which they crave, and by so doing to co-operate in the purpose of God which underlies the whole process. Evolution is not only a moving forward, but a moving upward as well.

In times past the belief in a material heaven and a material hell served to keep weaker souls in the path of virtue; nowadays such beliefs have hardly any operative force. This is not all loss, for an obedience which rested on such a basis had but little moral value, and can hardly have been well-pleasing to a

---

[1] *Character and the Conduct of Life*, p. 39.

God of Love. Not only has belief in a material heaven and hell been abandoned; but immortality itself, the idea that man survives death, is widely repudiated. The result is natural and inevitable. To the man who believes that his mind and soul will perish with the body which is their instrument, the things of the senses, the satisfaction of carnal appetites, are bound to loom large. In many a rude and overbearing manner, a tendency to be inconsiderate and self-assertive, is apt to manifest itself; their "natural graciousness of mind" having given way "to overpressure from the times and their disastrous issues".[1]

What the ultimate outcome of a continued neglect of Christian moral laws will be cannot yet be foreseen, for

> the present generation is still living on the tradition of Christian civilization. The modern agnostic is benefiting by the ideals which have soaked into the minds of men, and now that they are beginning to evaporate we are face to face with moral disturbances from which earlier generations were saved.[2]

Alongside this neglect of Christian morals, and probably in part a consequence, in part a cause, of it, there has arisen in some a confidence in man and his ability to meet all the requirements of life without the aid of any power outside him. Such people are, as Henry James in quite another context once put it, "wedded to the immediate and the finite"; and when once reality is limited to the time-process it is but a short step to the belief that there is no God but man. Humanism, as it is called, attracts many. But of these a great part are soon convinced that such a gospel brings nothing but disillusionment; man, when isolated in the cosmos, seems so meaningless and humanity itself a lost cause. A feeling of dis-

---

[1] Wordsworth, *Prelude*, xii. 50 ff.
[2] Father M. D'Arcy, *Mirage and Truth*, pp. 71 f.

illusionment was excusable, as it was common, in the generations which experienced and followed the War; they saw so many great movements come to nothing, so many promises unfulfilled, so much apparently vain sacrifice. For them, in their weariness, life and existence seemed but a desolate autumn burying their ideals beneath

> Leaves pallid and sombre and ruddy,
> Dead fruit of the fugitive years.

The younger generation, although it has gone through lean years and difficulties, has really no such excuse; and perhaps it is growing up to face things with a readier spirit. The situation has never been quite so bad as to some it seemed. Shadows were dark, but, as Ruskin has observed, shadows are "commonly more conspicuous than the things which cast them". This new generation, avoiding much of the foolishness of its immediate predecessor, will be more capable, one hopes, of being touched to noble issues. From it the response will come when once again the message of the gospel is proclaimed in such a way as clearly to shew its ability to be, as so often in the past, the saviour of a wearied and decaying civilization.

But the new presentation of the gospel, when it comes, will grow out of the old. New systems are not planted in virgin soil, nor as they develop do they escape the challenging growth and influence of rival creeds. It will be well, therefore, before looking to the future of Evangelicalism, briefly to survey its past, and to trace the gradual emergence of the more Liberal spirit with which alone that future lies.

THE OLD EVANGELICALS

The Evangelical Movement grew out of the earlier Methodist Revival. Those who remained loyal to the teaching and directions of John Wesley, when his autocratic control was removed, formed the Evangelical party in the Church of England; the rest, in defiance of his specific orders and in face of his warnings, seceded. Their action was not without excuse, however, for Wesley, in spite of continued expressions of loyalty to the Church, had acted in such a manner that the eventual separation of his followers was made almost inevitable.

A movement attracts adherents in part by the loftiness of its declared aims, in part by the motives which it puts forward as inspiring them, but above all by the character and personality of its leaders. Leaders must exhibit the ideals for which the movement stands already in process of realization; otherwise their principles, however pure and noble, have the weakness of being merely academic ideas. The Evangelical Movement was fortunate in its early leaders. It is true that no outstanding genius such as Newman emerged; but they had saints in plenty, men who were notable, not for originality or depth of thought, but for strength and variety of character; men who promoted the objects of the Movement more by the nobility of their example than by the novelty of their teaching. Among them there were wide differences in character and temperament, in training and habits of thought; but one and all were marked by a high spirit of purity and devotion, by vigour and zeal—a zeal, perhaps, not always checked and controlled by discretion—and by an intense desire for the salvation of their fellow-men.

The characteristics and special doctrines of the Evangelicals were substantially those of the Methodists from whom they took their origin; but with one important difference—the Evangelicals were loyal churchmen. This we should naturally expect, otherwise they would have followed the stream and drifted into Dissent. Charles Simeon was even accused of being more of a churchman than a gospel-man, whilst Henry Martyn, rejected, as a matter of course, the invitation to preach in a Methodist chapel.[1] It was one of the fruits of the Oxford Movement that the Evangelicals were driven into the "Low Church" group; they came to feel that undue emphasis was being placed on the "Church" and, in order to avoid misunderstanding, they gradually refrained from teaching doctrines so capable of what they regarded as perversion.

The Evangelicals, in spite of the high place which they gave to the emotions, had certain very strongly held dogmatic beliefs; the scheme of salvation was carefully worked out. Wilberforce, in his famous *Practical View of Christianity*, went so far as to attribute the decay of religion to the failure of nominal Christians to obtain "a firm intellectual grasp of the fundamental truths of their religion". These truths were simple and vivid. The belief that man was by nature alienated from God; the necessity of arousing in him a sense of sin; the certainty of everlasting punishment for those who neglected their opportunity; and the need for accepting, through faith, the atoning sacrifice of the death of Christ. By many the form in which this last doctrine was preached led straight to Tritheism—the belief in three gods, with an angry Father who was placated by the death of his Son. In any case the over-emphasis of the Atonement, to the neglect of other aspects of the Christian Faith, made it almost seem, according to the old, crude Evangelical teaching, that if Jesus had simply come to this earth and died, that would have been enough to enable the gospel to be preached in all its fulness. Judged by this standard, he himself did not "preach the gospel". This had been stated quite definitely by Martin

---

[1] On the Evangelicals as churchmen see further my volume *The Evangelical Movement, etc.*, pp. 38, 48 f., 112 ff.

Luther, who in the Preface to 1 Peter recommended his followers to read St. Paul's Epistles, as they were "more a Gospel than Matthew, Mark, and Luke. For these do not set down much more than the story of the works and miracles of Christ; but the grace which we receive through Christ, no one so boldly extols as St. Paul".

The older Evangelical had a firm belief in the inspiration of the Bible, even to its very words; and he made no distinction between the level of inspiration in the Old and New Testaments; in both the scheme of salvation was revealed to those who had insight to see it. Fortunately the Old Testament was so used that the harm which might have come to ignorant men and women from treating its moral standards, and the habits of some of its great men (Abraham, David, and so forth), as worthy of imitation was avoided; for only lip-service was paid to its writers. With strange perversity those who professed to think that everything written in the Bible was inspired by God, shutting their eyes to the plain facts and teachings of many of its narratives, twisted them so as to fit into a preconceived scheme. The method by which this process was carried through was largely that system of interpretation which is called allegorical.

The older Evangelicals, in spite of the intellectual gifts of some of the leaders, were not greatly interested in intellectual things. They made their appeal to the emotions. This was, and is, the most certain line of approach, for as Archdeacon Storr has recently written: "Men are not saved by logic or the intellect; they are saved when they surrender their entire being to the God who loves them".[1] To this surrender they were helped by the work of the Holy Spirit in their hearts; without him no words could move the sinner or allow access to his soul. Emphasis on the work of

[1] *Spiritual Liberty*, p. 17.

the Third Person of the Trinity was ever a notable feature of the Evangelical faith; its strength and effectiveness varied indeed as this feature was forgotten or made prominent. By the work of the Spirit in the heart of each individual soul, and the possibility of each individual soul being inspired by him, the immediate access of the believer to his God was assured. This, too, was a great feature of the Evangelical message, which left no room for intermediaries of one kind or another. What place had they when God's ear was always open and his Spirit ever at work?

Inspired by the consciousness of a great mission, the Evangelicals, in the early years of the past century, swept through the religious life of the English Church, and their power and influence have been admitted even by those who did not share their views. It is true that for some time they were not allowed to play any prominent part in the higher counsels of the Church; but apart from that they were predominant; especially in philanthropic schemes and missions overseas. Then, largely through the influence of Lord Shaftesbury, they began to receive higher preferment, and Evangelicals were not altogether loath to undertake stations of prominence, even though they involved them in odious publicities. But by this time the old fervour of the Movement was passing, success had brought into it many who were unworthy, and the novelties that had their rise at Oxford and were graced by the names of Newman, Pusey, and Keble began to draw away the finer spirits in the Church. There can be no shadow of doubt that in the middle years of Victoria Evangelicalism was "in a bad way". Already in 1863 Mark Pattison, not a sympathetic witness, could speak of its ruins cumbering the ground; whilst Lord Shaftesbury confessed that it was no longer a party, but only a theological term of doubtful meaning. Even in the

Mission Field its force seemed to be exhausted and the supply of both men and money began to shew signs of failing. Bishop Moule quotes a Roman Catholic periodical as prophesying triumphantly—though a little mistakenly—that "Ere long the sectarian societies will be looking in vain for missionaries, as heresy dies out".

The weakness of Evangelicalism in this epoch must not be passed over, especially by those who wish to try to assess its future. There are fanatical adherents of the Movement who see in any attempt to face the real facts of the situation only treason and disloyalty. They remind one of the Oxford professor of a bygone day who, not wishing to speak evil of a king who had freed the Church and Nation from the iniquitous domination of Rome, dismissed Henry VIII with the words: "The later years of this great monarch were clouded by domestic troubles". Such a course is cowardly and foolish, for the causes which led to the weakness of the Movement in the sixties and seventies of last century may well operate again. To state and expose them is the best way of making for their avoidance in the future. What then were the causes which led to this weakness?

Two stand out prominently: an excessive reliance on the past and, following on it, unwillingness to adjust itself to meet new conditions. Evangelicalism had grown accustomed to living on the gathered harvests of previous generations and its own vast reputation. The lustre of departed days clung around it, and its leaders were unable, for a time, to recognize that such a lustre was no guarantee for the future. Mental immobility had fallen upon them and they were quite incapable of meeting new conditions. Their minds, like shuttered casements, refused to open to the light. Especially the matter of Biblical Criticism troubled them; to it they could make no effective reply, and were content to repeat the old shibboleths without doing anything constructive. But before such formidable omens as the days revealed action was necessary if the Movement was not to lapse into insignificance. Relief and new strength came from two sources: spiritually from the Revival Movements which arose about this time,[1] intellectually from the foundation of Theological Colleges for the training of Evangelical candidates for the ministry.[2]

The Liberal Evangelicals

It was from the Theological Colleges thus founded, especially from Wycliffe and Ridley, that a new Liberal type of Evangelicalism at length emerged. But it was not until the lapse of more than a generation that it took real form and substance, finally to come out into the open as a definite Movement under the title of the Anglican Evangelical Group Movement, or A.E.G.M. as it is usually called. This development was so important that something must be said of its origins and the policy which directed it.[3]

The early years of the new century found the Evangelicals much as they had been before. There was little apparent awareness of the changes that were taking place all around them; the same old cries were being repeated; the same old leaders held their power, and held it with a tight grip; suspicion of anything new was as easily roused as ever; and, in fact, the party seemed safely fixed in its rather narrow groove. Among the younger men, however, there was much dissatisfaction; some left the party, others remained on, hoping and working for better things. Amongst the latter was a small group of

[1] The efforts of Moody and Sankey first obtained real prominence owing to their mission in London in March 1875. In that same year the Keswick Convention was begun.

[2] St. John's Hall, Highbury, was founded in 1863; Wycliffe Hall, Oxford, in 1877; and Ridley Hall, Cambridge, in 1881.

[3] The following account is abstracted from *The Evangelical Movement in the English Church*, pp. 69 ff., where full details will be found by any who are interested.

men in Liverpool, and from them the Movement had its beginning.

There are many versions of the influences which first led the members of this little group to band themselves together; talks at Ridley Hall in graduate days and the possible suggestion of Douglas Thornton are among them. Some time in 1905 three of them had lunch together: A. J. Tait, Principal of St. Aidan's College, Birkenhead (now Canon of Peterborough), C. Lisle Carr, Vicar of Blundellsands (now Bishop of Hereford), and Guy Warman, Vicar of Birkenhead (now Bishop of Manchester). These three felt that something must be done to arouse Evangelicals to a sense of the dangers they were in through their internal divisions and through their failure to understand the needs of the times. They began by inviting the co-operation of a few like-minded friends in their own area; later, similar groups of sympathetic friends were formed up and down the country, hence the first name of the Movement, "Groups". To preserve some kind of common policy an annual Conference was also instituted where the members of the different groups could meet and share their conclusions. In consequence of the unwillingness of the members to add yet another to the numerous Church societies, the organisation remained for more than eighteen fruitful years a private, almost a secret, organization. The small groups continued to meet together in prayer and study, for the Movement was careful both for the devotional and the intellectual life of its members. Study from the first was one of its great objects; for the need to think out afresh the doctrinal position of Evangelicals, and to state in new terms the contribution which they had to make to the life and thought of the Church, was felt to be most urgent. So it continued until events in the Church at large, the creation of the National Assembly, the rapid spread of the Anglo-Catholic Movement, and above all misunderstandings and disputes amongst Evangelicals themselves, together with the realization that secrecy meant suspicion and distrust on the part of those outside, caused the movement, at a Conference at Coleshill in June 1923, publicly to declare its principles and to invite application for membership.

On coming out into the open, the Movement took a title which was cumbrous and lacking in elegance, but had the merit of representing the various elements combined in it. It is Anglican because the members wish to express their loyalty to the Church of England, and their "claim to share in its rich heritage"; it is Evangelical because its members feel that much as they may differ from their spiritual fathers in many things, yet by their emphasis on spiritual religion, on freedom, on reliance on the Gospel rather than on tradition, they stand in a true succession to them. The whole Group Movement was an attempt to discriminate between what was essential in the Evangelical position and what was merely traditional and fleeting. It was an attempt to abandon mere party cries, narrow and limiting as these cannot fail to be, and to adopt a more courageous policy.

The significance of the rise of the Group Movement, which was social as well as religious, has never hitherto been fully realized, nor the greatness of the achievement of its first members. Socially it was a symptom of the rise of the middle classes to power in the Church as well as in the State. Among its protagonists there were no Gores, or Lytteltons, or Talbots, not even the Ashleys and Waldegraves of the older Evangelicalism. They were for the most part sons of the counting-house and the factory rather than of the parsonage, and their outlook on life was swayed by no clerical antecedents. Educationally they were the product of the big day-schools of the country; only Linton Smith (now Bishop of Rochester) and E. N. Sharpe (now Archdeacon of London) came from the older public schools. Thus their social and clerical influence was small. So was it intellectually, for there was among them not a single fellow of a college, indeed the only first-class men were A. J. Tait and Dawson-Walker. In the second generation men who had had distinguished academic careers were to join them; such were E. A. Burroughs, the late Bishop of Ripon, and J. W. Hunkin, now Bishop of Truro. But at first this was not so. There were not among them, as might have been expected, any preachers with more than a local reputation. Yet in spite of these drawbacks a surprisingly large proportion of them attained to positions of power and prominence in the Church. The question may be asked: How did they do it?

The answer is, I think, as follows. They were for the most part men of determined character, who knew what they wanted and let nothing come between them and their goal. They stood together, and the comparative insignificance of the individual was forgotten in the importance of the group. Beginning by obtaining influence in their own party, they went on to obtain it in the Church at large. By adequately occupying the less prominent positions in the ecclesiastical system they demonstrated their fitness for higher posts; though their gifts did not as a rule include any great imagination or vision. In this they were a little like the "safe" Bishops of the eighteenth century, though if they fell short of them in learning they surpassed them in energy. Energy indeed was the leading trait of this group of men, that and efficiency and adroit finance. In fact they brought into the Church the methods, and even the ideals, of the business world from which most of them had sprung. They really introduced a new type of Bishop. Whether this new type is really for the Church's good is a question that needs pondering over. The older Evangelical Bishops, like the Anglo-Catholics, were fathers-in-God; some of the modern Bishops, I hope the comparison is not too unkind, might almost seem to have taken as their model the general manager of Marks & Spencers or the International Stores.[1] Both types may be necessary, and some of the more spiritual Bishops have not been noted for

[1] The contrast between the different types of Bishops was brought home to the present writer by the following incident, for whose truth he can vouch. A certain priest was offered livings in two different dioceses over which an Evangelical and an Anglo-Catholic Bishop respectively ruled. He went to see the former, who received him with great cordiality,

their business-like habits. But the original question comes back in a different form: Was the Church intended to be "run" on business-like lines? Neville Figgis, at any rate, had come to his own conclusion on the matter and, in his paradoxical way, had declared that "if the Church should become really efficient its days as a spiritual power would be at an end".[1]

THE OLD AND THE NEW EVANGELICALS

At this stage one naturally seeks to enquire how far the new Evangelicals were a geniune development from the old, and what modifications they introduced into Evangelicalism. Their point of view was certainly different, in many respects, from that of their fathers; for not only did they make use of new methods, but also, by their wider sweep of the religious horizon, brought in new materials for consideration. But fundamentally they were at one; for both alike insisted on the need for redemption and sanctification, both alike regarded the unrestricted access to God as essential, and both, although in

shewed a minute knowledge of the conditions of the parish, but gave no word of spiritual counsel or advice. (The interview was largely taken up by a detailed account from the Bishop of the manner in which he had, not exactly on Pauline lines, proved the worth of his office to the leading laymen of the diocese by his dexterity in some obscure financial transaction.) The interview ended with a hearty handshake, but without any prayer; and in the atmosphere in which it had been conducted prayer would have seemed both an affectation and an intrusion. In the other interview all was different and at its close the Bishop took the priest into his private chapel and prayed long and earnestly with him, finally dismissing him with his blessing.

[1] *The Gospel and Human Needs*, p. 66. I had completed the above paragraph when I read the report of the speech of the Archbishop of Canterbury at the Mansion House on June 19, 1935. The following passage, referring to the energy of the modern Bishop, seems to me to be so appropriate that I quote it without comment: "I sometimes conceive of a new order of Bishops, who would spend their time instructing their clergy in sacred learning and conducting retreats for the clergy and their people. Their task should be, 'first be still, then you will be strong'."

different ways, gave a high place to the Bible as authority and guide.

One point at which the difference in outlook revealed itself was in relation to dogma. The Liberal Evangelicals were much less rigid in their schemes of salvation, and more diffident in their attempts to explain and define the things of God. They saw that on many points it was necessary to suspend judgement and to leave undefined much that an earlier generation had professed to know. In this they followed, if unconsciously, the method of Erasmus in the days of the Reformation.[1] The older Evangelicals had inherited the schemes and systems of doctrine of Melanchthon and Calvin, and had continued to use their methods. In regard to the doctrine of the Atonement the difference of outlook was specially marked. Though the Liberal Evangelicals retained a full realization of the supreme importance of our Lord's work of redemption, they deliberately discouraged attempts to enquire too closely into the manner in which it was accomplished. The theory of the older Evangelicals was certainly a crude one, for they held that Christ died, not merely on behalf of sinful man, but in his stead. Charles Simeon went so far as to declare that Christ

in his death "became a curse for us, that he might deliver us from the curse" to which we were doomed. Thus did

---

[1] I feel that this is such an important point that I hope I may be pardoned for quoting a passage from my Hulsean Lectures, *Erasmus the Reformer*, p. 62, in which his principles are described: "In regard to doctrine as a whole he desired more freedom than was usual amongst Catholics of his day, realizing that suspense of judgement is often the only safe attitude in face of the many obscurities of existence; he dreaded the cramping effect of multiplying articles of faith, and the consequent limitation of the number of subjects upon which it was still permissible to have mere opinions; hence the refinements and subtle distinctions of the Schoolmen were an abomination to him. In the preface to the *Enchiridion*, written at Basle in July 1518, he pleads for simplicity in dealing with the statement of the faith, and a single sentence gives the key to his position: Quae pertinent ad fidem, quam paucissimis articulis absoluantur."

he not merely die in our stead, "the just for the unjust", as a common victim in the place of the offender, but he fully discharged our debt in every particular; so that neither law nor justice can demand anything further at our hands.[1]

This doctrine was central in all Evangelical teaching and preaching. What Sir James Stephen said of Whitefield could be said, with but slight modification, of all the early leaders:

His thirty or forty thousand sermons were but so many variations on two key-notes. Man is guilty, and may obtain forgiveness; he is immortal, and must ripen here for endless weal or woe.[2]

For the older Evangelical the Atonement was all in all. This undue emphasis was corrected amongst the Liberals by a more adequate appreciation of the meaning of the Incarnation; a truth which, no doubt, they owed to the influence of Westcott, and even to Gore and the *Lux Mundi* school. By reason of this more balanced outlook they were enabled to welcome the possibility of hallowing all human activities, and to bring within the scope of religious influence matters, such as the drama, which their fathers had condemned as utterly "worldly".

Then as to the Bible. The theory of verbal inspiration was of course rejected by the Liberal Evangelicals in view of the new light which had come to them from the researches of scholars and archaeologists. This light they regarded as adding to rather than diminishing the spiritual value of the Scriptures, though at the same time it revealed the large human element in their composition. This is all to the good for the coming generation. For those who have been brought up to believe in an infallible Bible, even though by God's grace they may gain their freedom

---

[1] *Horae Homileticae*, xi. p. 591.
[2] *Essays in Eccles. Biog.* vol. ii. p. 98.

from it, are never or but rarely the same as other men. The mark of their struggle is upon them, and in times of difficulty there is often a wistful looking back. The coming strength of the Evangelical party lies in the fact that, whereas the past generation had to find for itself a firmer basis for its faith than the belief in an inerrant Bible, a whole generation has now grown to manhood which has no need for any such emancipation, because from the first it has been accustomed to regard the Bible in the light of modern knowledge.

But though the spiritual value of the Bible is fully recognized by the Liberal Evangelicals, it is not accepted as "an external authority imposing itself arbitrarily upon the human mind"; it is to be accepted because it makes a "religious and spiritual appeal to mind, will, and conscience".[1] Nor is the possibility of revelation exhausted by the account, preserved in the Bible, of God's dealings with Israel. Value is given to the spiritual experiences of other races; although they may not have been so highly favoured, yet they were not "left without witnesses" from on high. So with all truth and knowledge; it is to be welcomed, after due scrutiny, as adding to our knowledge of God and his ways, as a fresh gift from him who is Truth absolute.

Thus the Bible is not accepted as an infallible authority. In fact no "external" authority of any kind is given this position. The Church is valued as expressing "the common mind of Christian people", but, in words quoted from Dean Inge, it "has no accredited organ, and claims no finality for its utterance".[2] There is only one supreme authority and one final standard by which to test "religious developments whether theological or ecclesiastical", that is, the Mind of Christ.[3] This is a noble standard; but

---

[1] See Storr, *Spiritual Liberty*, pp. 54 f.
[2] *Ibid.* p. 61.   [3] *Ibid.* p. 65.

perhaps, in view of the very diverse conceptions of the Mind of Christ, the question may be allowed: Who is to say what that Mind is on any particular point?

It must not be forgotten that the New Testament knows nothing of the Mind of Christ apart from the Community of his followers. As Canon Quick says:

> If the New Testament records be at all substantially correct, what we see in them is the progressive actualization and interpretation of a teacher's ideas through the continued operation of his living spirit in the society of his followers.[1]

This can be well seen by noticing the attitude of St. Paul. In his epistles there are no appeals to the actual teaching of our Lord while here on earth, but a confidence of his presence in the heart of Christians to guide, inspire, and direct them.

Thus it may, I think, be fairly held that the Liberal Evangelicals, although they may differ from their fathers of past generations, yet stand in the same succession. It is with them, as any historically minded observer is bound to conclude, that the future of Evangelicalism belongs. Otherwise there will have to be a complete reversion to the past, to what is called Fundamentalism. Such a conclusion is unthinkable.

The Future

The greatness of the Evangelical party in the past cannot be denied. Splendid as are the names which adorn the records of other parties, none shine more brightly than those which God saw fit to call into his service through this school of thought. It had its pioneers from Henry Martyn and Bishop French to Bishop Hannington and Douglas Thornton; its godly laymen from the Clapham Sect to Lord

---

[1] *Liberalism, Modernism, and Tradition*, p. 92.

Shaftesbury and Eugene Stock; its devout women from Hannah More to Catherine Marsh; its devoted parish priests and Bishops from Charles Simeon and the Sumners to Bishop Ryle and Handley Moule. The names of these men and women will live as long as the Church in which they found the opportunity of serving their Master. But history shews quite clearly that eminence in the past is no guarantee of eminence, or even survival, in the future. What of the future of the Evangelicals?

If that future is to be secured, the Movement must develop along lines already laid down by the Liberal wing; though it must avoid certain dangers which seem to threaten such development. It must above all be willing to continue to throw itself fully into the stream of life of both Church and nation. To abstain was one great mistake of the older Evangelicals; it followed, indeed, from a too narrow idea of revelation, and a too narrow idea of the scope of redemption. They failed to see that religion was no specialized function of one part of man's nature, but the consecration of his every activity in the service of an Incarnate Lord. To many of them the Bible, as the divinely inspired Word of God, contained all that was necessary for man to know for the salvation of his soul. To go outside its covers might be, so thought some of the more timid, to exercise an undue curiosity, and even to partake of the nature of sin. The truth was contained in Holy Scripture, why seek to know more? The weakness of this position has been sufficiently exposed by Principal Tulloch.

> The Evangelical school [he wrote], with all its merits, had conceived of Christianity rather as something super-added to the highest life of humanity, than as the perfect development of that life; as a scheme for human salvation authenticated by miracles, and, so to speak, interpolated into human history, rather than as a divine philosophy. Philosophy, literature, art, and science were conceived

apart from religion. The world and the Church were severed portions of life divided by outward signs and badges; those who joined the one or the other were supposed to be clearly marked off.[1]

Furthermore, these same activities were under-valued by the Evangelicals as, in their opinion, having no direct bearing on the state of the soul. The world of culture was not so much avoided as for-gotten, and the mind left, as Thomas Arnold once put it, "a fallow field for all unsightly weeds to flourish in". As a result Evangelicalism never made any deep impression on the higher intellects of the nation. In the vehemence of their passion for indi-viduals all else was forgotten and much that gives grace and dignity to life cut off. Carried away by the urgency of their task, they had not sufficient poise to see life steadily and see it whole. But let those blame them whose love for their Master and whose concern for the spiritual welfare of their neighbours can com-pare with the all-consuming zeal by which they were distinguished. None the less the Evangelicals, by their neglect of culture, and above all of scholarship, have failed, hitherto, to make their proper contribu-tion to the Church's intellectual life. Here and there isolated members of the party have struggled to serve God in this manner; but in the old days suspicion, and even denunciation, was their lot, and even in more recent times all they could anticipate was the dubious guerdon of neglect. The A.E.G.M., by promoting schemes of study among its members, has tried to do its part, but the results of its efforts have yet to be seen. The neglect of real study among the clergy—reading small manuals is not study—is reflected in the uninstructed condition of the laity. At present it would probably be true to say that the Evangelical (old as well as new) is the least carefully

[1] *Movements of Religious Thought in Britain during the Nineteenth Century*, p. 15.

instructed of all churchmen, and this in spite of Dr. Griffith Thomas' warning that "There can be no full Christian life without definite, careful, clear, and continuous instruction".[1]

Many reasons may be given for this weakness in the party. Some, especially of the older type, think that learning and knowledge lead to coldness and indifference; some rely so entirely on the emotions that the powers of the mind are despised; some believe that the individual, with no outside help, can obtain all that he needs from reading the Bible; many—this applies especially to the members of the clergy—are unable to find time for study because all their energies are taken up by the calls of an active life. Over-activity is the bane of Evangelicals, and not only does it involve them in a dangerous neglect of scholarship, but in the still more dangerous neglect of the care of their own souls. To this last point we shall return later.

The Danger of Liberalism

The fears of the Conservatives that learning leads to indifference have a measure of justification, for some of the younger men, dazzled by a superficial and second-hand knowledge, are apt to be led too far in a Liberal direction. Reacting strongly from the obscurantist position of their fathers and of contemporary Fundamentalists, they become too rationalistic, and, as such, ashamed of the somewhat naïve and simple faith of the older generation. For the Evangelical who gives himself up too freely to the Liberal tide may easily find himself in strange seas of thought. Liberalism is a strong solvent and the cleansing process may be too drastic. The "task of pure ablution" has been dignified by one of our own poets as "priest-like"; but so vigorous is the Liberal

[1] *The Catholic Faith*, p. 17.

nurse that her charge, after being scrubbed clean, is sometimes so attenuated as to be in danger of sharing the fate of the baby in the German proverb, and being poured away with the bath-water. Liberalism is an ally much more dangerous to Evangelicalism than to Catholicism; for the latter, having greater stability and balance, as well as greater knowledge, is less likely to be fascinated by novel views. For it is the supposed novelty of Liberal views which proves so attractive, and Liberal teachers always like to be able to say:

> We were the first that ever burst
> Into that silent sea.

Catholics, however, who sometimes know more of the history of the Church than their brethren, have a knack of treating such novel ideas as a mere "hashing-up" of ancient heresies.

Between Evangelicalism and the ultra-Liberal scholarship which thrives in the rarefied atmosphere of certain lecture-rooms at the Universities and can find in the gospel narratives, not a portrait of Jesus, but merely "a whisper of his Voice . . . and the outskirts of his ways", there can, of course, be no alliance. Scholarship divorced from life offers no reliable guidance. But it may be that there will again flourish a school which, following the great Westcott, Hort, and Lightfoot tradition—now so strangely and so sadly ignored—is not out of touch with the real world.

The school at present predominant in criticism is defective, not only because it is out of touch with life, but also because it has an entirely inadequate conception of the meaning of revelation. This it equates with discovery. There is, of course, a danger in making the antithesis between discovery and revelation too sharp, for God is not only the object of our seeking but is himself present in us who seek: he is the Way by which we travel as well as the

Truth which crowns the journey. None the less revelation has a meaning, and in Christianity there is an element of "givenness" which is additional to what man has discovered for himself. Evangelicals must preserve the "initiative of the eternal", to adopt A. E. Taylor's striking phrase, and not allow their religion to be reduced to merely human proportions. "Christianity is nothing if not a religion of the supernatural", writes Archdeacon Storr.[1]

This brings us to the question of miracles. Much theological thinking of the present day and many theological utterances on this subject seem to reflect the point of view of the nineteenth century. As Storr says (after pointing out the utter impossibility of eliminating miracles from the gospels without reducing them to chaos), "our whole modern attitude to the miraculous is much more sympathetic than it was when a mechanistic science was in the ascendant".[2] The presuppositions of those who criticize orthodox Christianity need to be scrutinized as well as those who defend it; and in particular the strange prejudice which seems to take it for granted that the orthodox are always in the wrong, unless they can prove the contrary.

THE NEW KNOWLEDGE

The tremendous scientific discoveries of the present age should remind us that revelation is not at an end (for man's "discovery", although it may not exhaust "revelation", is a great part of it), and we are compelled to ask if their coming at this epoch has any special significance. They are, of course, evidence of man's vast progress as the master and

---

[1] *Spiritual Liberty*, p. 139. In this connexion it is interesting to notice the conclusions of Professor Irving Babbitt, who is not a Christian. In his recent volume *Humanism and America*, p. 39, he declares himself to be "unhesitatingly on the side of the supernaturalists".   [2] *Op cit.* p. 51.

maker of instruments, of his ability to collect and co-ordinate data; but are they anything more? To those who believe in the guidance of a Divine providence surely they are. To them such achievements are also evidence that the race has reached a stage when it is capable of using such knowledge, not merely in the material, but also in the spiritual sphere. Bergson has complained that the effect of scientific progress has been to give man a bigger body for which his soul is inadequate. May we not believe that man's soul will also grow; that we are, in other words, on the verge of spiritual discoveries which will rival and complete those in the material world? Such seems the natural and faithful conclusion. Natural, because man hitherto has proved equal to the task of rising to his needs; faithful, because trust in God will not allow us to think that such needs, especially as they are spiritual, will be allowed to go unsatisfied. (It may be that the longed-for outpouring is delayed until these newer acquisitions have been fused with the spiritual truth and essential beauty which are already ours.) That man is faced by certain definite problems in the spiritual sphere is an assurance of the proximity of their solution; as Hort has finely said, "human search precedes Divine revelation".[1]

For the present the Church must adopt an attitude of suspense. New discoveries come in like a flood, and before one series of facts, and the new ideas which they suggest, has been assimilated, another series is upon us. Mentally and philosophically mankind is living in lodgings; and, like a touring theatrical company, has to shift them almost weekly. The new philosophy when it comes, and the hour of its birth is not yet, will be one of conciliation rather than of comprehension. The craving after such a philosophy has always been observable in the Church

[1] *The Way, the Truth, the Life*, p. 3.

whenever mental energy has been quickened. It is the philosophy in which Clement of Alexandria and Origen, as well as St. Augustine, made many earnest essays; and to seek it is no unworthy aim.[1] But the relating of new knowledge to religious truth is a long and gradual process in the course of which experiments will have to be made by individual thinkers, many of which may well be wrong or misleading. But the theologian, if real progress is to be made, must claim the scientist's right to put forward, for the purpose of discussion and testing, hypotheses which may in the end prove to be unsound or defective.

In working out new systems of thought, however, it must ever be remembered that, interesting as may be the processes of the savant, there are deeper needs. Men do not want systems, they want a living God. They are not greatly concerned about the logic of their faith, but they care intensely for the things that give them strength to meet life's trials and difficulties. For most people religion is primarily an emotion, or perhaps better an experience, and though it may be necessary to formulate the experience the formula may become a mere skeleton and the religion "anatomical" in consequence. This is also true of the beliefs handed down from the past. Orthodoxy, if made an end in itself, can hardly avoid that self-complacency which inevitably accompanies any realized correctness, and may become barren and dead. The dogmas which constitute it are simply the crystallized experience of the Church. To make them real they must again be liquefied and the original experience recaptured. In conclusion one thing needs to be said. Evangelicals must never acquiesce, even by default, in any kind of doctrine of "Two Truths"; such as certain philosophers were willing to accept in the Middle Ages.[2] If a thing is true in science, it

---

[1] See Dean Church, *Occasional Papers*, vol. ii. pp. 310 ff.
[2] See Elliott-Binns, *Decline and Fall of the Medieval Papacy*, p. 82.

must be true also for religion; God's world is one, and cannot be divided into mutually exclusive spheres.

The Need for Catholicism

If the Evangelical is to be on his guard against a too-ready submission to Liberalism, he ought, on the other hand, to endeavour to overcome some of his shyness in the face of Catholicism. It has lessons to teach him of which he stands in sore need. One of them is the need for a more adequate appreciation of the value of history. Liberal Christianity has always been deficient in this respect because it takes no account of the growth and development of the Church. It looks to origins only, the rest may be dismissed, or even treated as degeneration. More than two thousand years ago both Plato and Aristotle, here in agreement, taught that the highest life for the individual can only be realized in a community. The truth of this is coming more and more to be recognized in the sphere of religion. "The tide of desire for a truly Catholic Church is rising", says Dean Bate.[1] We are bodies as well as souls, and we have to live in a material universe; some form of institutional religion is therefore necessary, though it may be remarked in passing that the cult of Professor Royce's "Universal and Beloved Community" is, apart from its manifestation in history, a vague and meaningless devotion. Evangelicalism is a necessary foundation for the individual, by itself it is incomplete.

The need for a Catholic Church was discovered in the later years of the nineteenth century by many leading Nonconformist teachers (personally I think that this discovery saved Nonconformity, its politi-

---

[1] In a volume entitled *The Future of the Church of England*, p. 176. In the same volume there is a good exposition by the late Bishop of Winchester of the meaning of Catholicism (*op. cit.* pp. 224 ff.).

cal importance having waned, from lapsing into a number of self-centred societies with ever-diminishing spiritual power), though their idea of Catholicism was not entirely that of the historical Church. Episcopacy, for example, was not one of its characteristic notes. To make the structural form of the Church primary and essential may be what Dr. Carnegie Simpson dubs "ecclesiastical materialism";[1] but it has to be remembered that history knows of no Catholic Church which was not based on some form of episcopacy, and that Christian bodies which do not possess the historic episcopate have witnessed to its value by adopting similar types of office. The logic of circumstance thus seems to disprove the old quip that episcopacy might belong to the *esse* of the Church, but that it certainly did not belong to its *bene esse*. The Liberal Evangelical, to judge by Archdeacon Storr, would agree with the Nonconformist and refuse to "come to terms with any view of the Church which would make some particular form of organisation essential to its being".[2]

The Church is necessary as a source of strength for the congregation and as a bulwark of doctrinal truth. It is also necessary as a source of strength for its members. Less and less must we place reliance on the religious feelings and experiences of the individual. Such subjective matters, if they stand in isolation, are at the mercy of psychology; and in any case, need modifying by the experiences of others, and of the Church as a whole. Private interpretation may well lead astray. God, be it remembered, is transcendent as well as immanent. So the individual must be taught to see that religious experience has a much wider content than, as a Protestant, he had been accustomed to imagine. So, too, in the Church he must receive the training which, in spite of all his

---

[1] *The Evangelical Church Catholic*, p. 26.   [2] *Op. cit.* pp. 90 f.

"religious experiences", he so badly needs. In the volume from which I have just quoted, Dr. Carnegie Simpson makes the interesting admission that it has been one of the mistakes of Protestantism to "assume that everyone is mature and able to guide himself . . . and in consequence to fail to provide sufficient helps, especially for the young and simple".[1]

ETHICS

So far we have been thinking of the future of Evangelicalism in regard to its mental needs, as a system of thought and belief. From doctrine we must now pass to conduct. What has it to say on all those questions which concern man's moral being? what message has it in the sphere of ethics?

The confused state of ethical thinking and the repudiation of the standards which guided the moral life of previous generations are a commonplace, and reference has already been made to them. In part they are the fruit of taking too much for granted—moral rules of conduct are often based on ungranted assumptions—in part from the cardinal error of identifying amiability and character. This state of confusion and unsettlement cannot continue indefinitely; no people can remain content to blunder and deviate in its ethical life, or acquiesce permanently in continually shifting moral standards. It will demand that freedom and ease which come from an assured basis upon which to conduct the manifold business of living.

Ethics are the product of the collective memory of society and enshrine the best of the world's experience; they cannot therefore be defied with impunity. Sooner or later it will be found that disaster and disillusionment await those who attempt it. Expediency may seem to triumph over principle; but

---

[1] *Op. cit.* p. 63, n. 1.

principles have a knack of asserting themselves, and theories, which seemed forgotten, of springing up to a lease of new and more powerful life as they prove capable of allying themselves with the needs of the times. We used to be taught that "moral ideals are the work of Reason",[1] but nowadays a much more prominent place is given to instinct. Perhaps this has some justification. There is certainly no infallible method by which, for example, the man who places pleasure above virtue can be refuted. Moral truth must be grasped immediately, it cannot be proved.

In framing our schemes of morals we must gaze with discriminating eyes on the whole drama of humanity, taking account of the grovelling commonplaces of life as well as of the romantic harmonies of devotion. So will they be less liable to suffer shipwreck when faced with the vivid facts of besetting experience. Provision must also be made for expansion and contraction, for the alternating passions which possess the hearts of men. The recognition of this will enable us to avoid drawing our circle too close for the Divine geometry. In any case no ethical system can ever be final, for

> To mortals 'tis but given
> To work rough border law of Heaven.

The widespread sense of failure and disillusionment, to which reference has already been made, is a hopeful factor, since it may herald a fresh consideration of the Christian scheme of things. In spite of the belief of some Humanists that man is self-sufficient and even self-redemptive, experience plainly reveals his need for some power outside himself. He envies those who hold that supernatural resources are available in the struggle. For the uniqueness of Christian ethics lies in the fact that they do not stand alone; they are related to doctrines which give

[1] Hastings Rashdall, *Religion and Philosophy*, p. 62.

morality its sanctions and are, moreover, part of a greater whole in which "means of grace" are provided as well as guidance.

Certainly "there is no use talking about life", as Dr. Carnegie Simpson says, "unless we will recognize that, somehow, there has got into it a moral poison", and because of this "human life is not its own saviour and often is its own destroyer".[1] The realization that man is incapable of raising himself by his own efforts, that he has "made a mess of things", may be widespread; but it falls far below what theologians call a sense of sin. That is, as Canon Barry has said, "rather an advanced stage in our moral and spiritual experience", and follows on our having a vital sense of a living God. This, rather than a sense of sin, is the essential need of our age.[2]

The natural man is satisfied, or thinks he is, to live in a world which is largely of his own making; his chief endeavour is to make that world more comfortable, more "liveable in". His ethical schemes, therefore, are limited to what will further this aim or retard it. Sin for him is crime, something which disturbs society and makes itself a nuisance; or on a slightly higher plane, something which interrupts the process of evolving a better world. Evolution, and the philosophies built upon it, ignore eternity and the possibility of any world beyond that in which we now have our being. Their outlook is limited by the present, they have no vision of that far-off future—

> When time into Eternity
> Falls over ruined worlds.

Any ethical principles based on them must of necessity fail to be absolute, since they are bound up with the temporal and the imperfect. The older Evangelicals certainly had their limitations, but, as Bishop Woods has said, "they saw life in the vista of

---

[1] *The Evangelical Church Catholic*, pp. 43 f.
[2] See *The Relevancy of Christianity*, p. 190.

eternity, and that is a point of view which we dare not let go".[1]

For the Christian morality means ultimately but one thing—doing the will of God; and finding therein, as Dante well knew, our own peace: "*In la sua voluntade è nostra pace*".[2] To do the will of God involves the consecration of every activity of mind, body, and soul to his service. Life itself is to be regarded as the raw material from which the Christian shapes his offering, the opportunity for fulfilling the law of his being. This is the ideal; and it is an ideal which expands as we learn more of God. Absolute moral truth may be unattainable in this life; but we shall not approach nearer to it except by following the promptings of the voice within us, and cherishing the idea of God revealed in Jesus. It is to those who have thus dedicated themselves that fresh light will be vouchsafed in moral as in spiritual matters; for they alone possess that fine power of penetration which comes when the faculties have been reduced, by the hammerings of fate, into a kind of sacred hardness.

Here the older Evangelicals have still a lesson to teach their latest descendants. Their lives shew us that, in religion as in other things, power comes from selection and concentration. Modern religion is so apt to be dissipated and uncontrolled and to miss that highest of all healthy joys, the joy that comes from self-conquest. Life, and religion with it, has been robbed of much of its hardness, and so, what Professor Toynbee calls the Stimulus of Pressures has been removed.[3] Virtue itself is sapped by comfort and the absence of difficulties to be overcome. "The child is destroyed by unalloyed pleasure, the State by ease."[4] So I would plead for a revived

---

[1] In *The Future of the Church of England*, p. 222.
[2] *Paradiso*, iii. 85.
[3] See *A Study of History*, vol. ii. pp. 112 ff.
[4] Father D'Arcy, *Mirage and Truth*, p. 190.

Puritanism. This Puritanism, however, must differ in many ways from that known to history; for it must recognize that no complete life can be built up on omissions and suppressions. Its great merit will be to demonstrate that there can be fulness of life without some of its perilous excitements, and that it is possible to combine sternness towards oneself with a tolerant attitude towards the weaknesses of other people. This last is important, for lenience to the ordinary is a virtue which Puritanism has always found it hard to come by; and there was no little truth in the old gibe that the Puritans objected to bear-baiting, not because it gave pain to the bear, but because it gave pleasure to other people. So, too, the new Puritanism must have an appreciation of beauty and of beautiful things such as found no place in the older type; and those to whose temperaments such an appreciation is foreign must grant at least that there are others who, like Walter Pater's Marius, can only be made perfect in the love of visible beauty. The conception of all true beauty as something in which God himself delights, or even as something in which he is revealed, is an important one for Evangelicals to grasp, since with them the idea of "separation" is so vital. If beauty is not of God, then it is a danger and to be avoided as "worldly" in the bad sense. If it is of God, then it is to be invoked and cherished.

One result of a greater simplicity of life would be that larger families would again be common among religious people. At present there is no doubt that we are breeding largely from our inferior stocks; the middle and upper classes are failing in their duty in this matter. So we have multitudes of small houses with space for a garage, but no room for a nursery. This selfish refusal to face responsibilities is at bottom irreligious, and it is questionable whether those who marry with the deliberate intention of avoiding the procreation of children ought to seek the Church's blessing on their union. Such a union is mainly an opportunity for self-indulgence. The object of Christian marriage, as the Prayer Book plainly states, is to bring into the world a future generation to be educated in the knowledge and fear of God. Both parts of this object are frequently ignored by those who imagine that they are good churchpeople. The older generation handed on their own faith to their numerous children, not only by example, but by definite teaching. The present over-occupied and over-indulged generation is too often content to leave this duty to the schoolmaster and the clergyman. It is interesting to notice that the Roman Catholics, by their obedience to these two commands, are steadily regaining possession of territories which once they lost. Humanly speaking, in the course of a few generations they will be pre-dominant once again in Scotland and in the New England States of North America, into which the French-Canadian farm labourer is pouring in large numbers. It is quite possible that the verdict of history, which seemed to declare that these lands should be English-speaking and Protestant rather than French and Catholic, will be reversed.[1]

Worship

As this subject is treated elsewhere there is no need for me to say much about the attitude of Evangelicals towards it, save to affirm that they will demand the right to make further experiments and will desire to avoid anything that is "fussy" and pretentious. They will also, I hope, learn to be more tolerant of forms of worship which their fathers dreaded as savouring too much of Rome and "false doctrine".

[1] This has been worked out in an exceedingly interesting manner by A. J. Toynbee, *A Study of History*, vol. ii. pp. 71 ff.

Here some brave words of Dr. Carnegie Simpson may well be quoted:

> Evangelical Protestantism would do well to learn from, on the one hand, a Roman Mass, in which not the voice of man, but the supernatural presence of God, is so distinctly—even if in ways we think are not free from error—made primary, and, on the other hand, a Quaker meeting, where the worshipper silently waits upon God.[1]

But it is not only in public worship that Liberal Evangelicals need to learn from other types of Christians. There is an alarming tendency among some of them to neglect private prayer and devotion. In the fight with the world and the powers of evil they look too much to hard work and efficiency and are apt to forget the spiritual weapons which are available. This is true especially of those who rise to positions of eminence in the Church. The harassing responsibilities and temptations to over-activity which such positions bring are bound, unless special care is taken, to sap the spiritual life. Not a few Liberal Evangelicals as they advance in ecclesiastical status noticeably decline in spiritual power and influence. They become incapable of spiritual leadership because their own lives are overstrained; times of quiet and meditation are crowded out, or rendered impossible by the excited state of their minds. Even the public services of the Church bring them no relief for they are not attuned to them. With them to work is to pray; and work is the only kind of prayer of which they seem capable. In some few cases this excessive absorption in the practical duties is virtually a recognition of their unsuitability for their calling; they grasp every excuse for avoiding the true work of the ministry, the pastoral care of their people. It has, they hardly know why, become distasteful to them. In others, and again one hopes that their

[1] *The Evangelical Church Catholic*, p. 77.

numbers are few, the ministry is looked upon not as a vocation but as a career. Their one desire is for promotion. This is gained, so they observe, not by careful and devoted work in the parish or even the diocese, but by attendance at Committees and Conferences, by keeping their names before those in authority. But the vast majority of Liberal Evangelicals have a genuine vocation and a real desire to fulfil it with no ulterior object; but even these often find themselves growing cold and dead. Perhaps they are troubled by questions of criticism and doubts of one kind or another; and in any case they suffer from that ceaseless over-activity to which reference has, more than once and with deliberate emphasis, already been made. The A.E.G.M. has attempted to meet their need by the Cromer Convention, intended to be a kind of Liberal Keswick. So far, although attended by not inconsiderable numbers, Cromer has not really "caught on". Rumour has it that some of the speakers are too "high-brow"; certainly its potentialities as a source of spiritual power, not only for the clergy but for the laity as well, have not yet been exhausted.

The Justification of Evangelicalism

I come now to my final observation on the future of Evangelicalism within the Church. Its ability to survive and flourish is not a matter which can be decided in advance by discussion and argument, by canvassing hopes or assessing probabilities based on contemporary tendencies. It is in the practical life of the parish that the answer will be found and the question decided. The double task of the Church is to spiritualize Christians and to win non-Christians to the allegiance of the Lord. In the ultimate event this is carried out, not by the thinkers and leaders, but by multitudes of faithful workers. It is there, in the common round, the daily task, that the only hope for the healing of the race from sin and evil is to be discerned. And here it is necessary to recognize that all our problems, of whatever nature, are ultimately spiritual problems, and can only be solved on the spiritual plane. The economist and the politician, valuable though their work may be, deal only with symptoms; the disease that lies behind them is a disease of the soul.

The new Evangelicalism must therefore preach a full "gospel", a message based not merely on the needs of the individual but of society as a whole, a message above all which is derived from the gospel which Jesus himself preached. This gospel alone is adequate to meet the needs of a broken and divided world, and by the proclamation of the revelation of God as Love, to bind up its wounds and stop their bleeding. The true Evangelical is he who desires to preach this gospel, not he who is content to stand exactly where the fathers stood a century and more ago. The Spirit of Christ is moving over the chaos of this present age and revealing to his servants new methods and the wisdom which comes from a wider experience; to reject his guiding is to shut oneself off from the light. The past must not be allowed, like a chrysalis, to cramp the growing organism. New forms must be found and new ways of expressing the new life. But the great and glorious heritage handed down from the older Evangelicals is neither to be despised nor ignored. From its rich treasuries, fearlessly and boundlessly, the younger men must draw their stores; not falling to the temptation of being led aside by the desire for mere novelty. The gospel must be fitted to the age, but the age must also be made to conform to the gospel.[1]

[1] The above paragraph is borrowed, with slight modifications, from *The Evangelical Faith, etc.*, pp. xii. f. and 139.

X

NOVA ET VETERA

by

G. L. H. HARVEY, M.A.

Rector of Sutton Coldfield

SYNOPSIS

Retrospect

EVER since the Reformation there has been within the Church of England a conflict, and, at the same time, an interpenetration of ideals. These ideals have come to a clearly formulated expression at certain focal points, one of which was constituted by the publication of *Essays and Reviews* in 1860. The principles which inspired the contributors to this book were: (1) loyalty to truth in all its forms, (2) loyalty to the guidance of reason, (3) loyalty to the moral judgement. It met with a hostile reception from Tractarians and Evangelicals alike. The reversal by the Judicial Committee of the Privy Council of the condemnation pronounced by the Court of Arches on two of the contributors, Wilson and Williams, was followed by a panic agitation and the formal condemnation of *Essays and Reviews* by Convocation. Prominent ecclesiastics who were regarded by the public as spokesmen of the Church led the agitation, and, though men of wiser and cooler judgement deplored the prevalent ecclesiastical obscurantism, the Church still suffers from the consequent damage to its reputation.

"Lux Mundi"

In the Universities a succession of great scholars pursued the search for truth in an atmosphere free from the fever of ecclesiastical controversy. Their influence was reflected in *Lux Mundi*, which, published in 1889, accepted as legitimate the methods of Higher Criticism. As Liddon saw clearly, *Lux Mundi* marked a break with the older Tractarianism.

The Parting of the Ways

Lux Mundi abandoned the traditional Catholic conception of an inerrant Scripture as the ground of faith, maintained throughout the ages and reaffirmed by Pope Leo XIII. Liddon knew that it had broken with historic Catholicism on a matter of fundamental importance.

CREED AND CRITICISM

The literary criticism of the Gospels has produced assured results. Whether the two-document or the four-document theory be accepted, the student can discover something of the tendencies of the Evangelists. He has been rescued from the false assumption that a twofold or threefold attestation of a saying or event is any guarantee of its authenticity. Biblical criticism had its repercussions in the theological sphere. It led Gore to the formulation of his Kenotic Christology. A subconsciousness that his position as a Liberal Catholic was equivocal may have prevented him from travelling far along the road of Liberalism. *Lux Mundi* prepared the way for a further advance, a definite stage in which was marked by the publication of *Foundations* in 1912. The Bishop of Zanzibar challenged *Foundations* as heretical, and three years later excommunicated the Bishop of Hereford because he had preferred one of the contributors to a canonry. It aroused a keen controversy in the course of which several distinguished theologians defended the validity of the views impugned. Gore and the Bishop of Zanzibar publicly objected to the consecration of Dr. Henson to the see of Hereford on the ground of heterodoxy. An aftermath of the *Foundations* controversy was the abortive attempt of Rev. C. E. Douglas in 1921 to secure the trial of Dr. Major on a charge of heretical teaching on the subject of Resurrection. Since 1912 Liberalism or Modernism has spread rapidly and has deeply influenced Anglo-Catholicism and Evangelicalism. Leading Anglo-Catholics have abandoned Gore's insistence on the acceptance of the Creeds literally interpreted, and recognize a mythical element in the Biblical accounts of the birth and resurrection of Jesus.

RASHNESS AND RETICENCE

The reticence of ecclesiastical leaders is largely responsible for the fact that the laity are in large part ignorant of the changes which have taken place in the theological world, and the effects of this reticence have been reinforced by the rash utterances of ecclesiastics, frequently more conspicuous for piety than learning, who do not hesitate publicly to propound traditionalist views as if they were authoritative. The result is the alienation from the Church of many of the more intelligent lay-people. Courage and frankness, even at the cost of some risk, are demanded by the present situation.

The Jesus of History

The Liberalism of which Harnack was a leading representative held that the study of the Gospels reveals a historic Jesus whose words speak to us across the centuries with the freshness of the present. Under the influence of an intensive study of the writings of the Jewish Apocalyptists the Eschatalogical school of criticism presented a picture of Jesus as one who belonged to the bizarre world of Apocalypse. The Roman Catholic Modernists held that this interpretation of the Person of Jesus afforded a justification for the later developments of Catholic theology. This view met with some acceptance in Anglo-Catholic circles. Though the depreciation of the moral element in Christ's teaching as a mere *Interimsethik* was unacceptable to Anglican Liberals and in other respects they had little sympathy with Continental Modernism, by a curious twist the appellation of Modernist came, in common usage, to be attached to Anglicans who stood in the line of succession of *Essays and Reviews*. Barthianism was profoundly affected by the eschatological interpretation of Christ and Christianity. In principle it attaches no importance to history and is prepared to accept the most negative results of radical Biblical criticism. Its influence in England has been in a diluted form. Form Criticism seeks to penetrate to the stage which preceded the written documents which are incorporated in our Gospels, the stage of oral tradition. The assumptions made by the Form Critics are questionable and their conclusions are widely divergent.

The Christ of the Creeds

The critical movement in the Church of England was, up to 1919, predominantly of the Liberal type. It was overlapped by another movement which, under the influence of Loisy and Schweitzer, attached only subsidiary importance to the historical. This has influenced the Liberal Catholic to lay a more exclusive stress on cultus and traditional dogma, a tendency which has been reinforced by the vogue of Otto's theory that the basis of religion is a sense of the numinous. If the believer is content with this basis of belief, he can not complain if he finds that scientific materialism claims the world of actuality, and leaves him to indulge in "an attitude towards the universe". The more recent phase of radical criticism may be held to account for a certain reinforcement of emphasis on the metaphysical abstractions of classic Christian theology. The danger involved in the mental manipulation of abstractions is illustrated by the bastard Aristotelianism of the doctrine of Transubstantiation and St. Augustine's theory of evil. Dr. Tennant in his *Philosophical Theology* seeks to provide an apologetic which is free from these dangers. He criticizes immanental and incarnational Christology, and suggests as an alternative the acceptance of Christ as "a manifestation of God in the flesh and as the unique revealer of God". He faces the problem of the "break-down of theology" acknowledged by the present Archbishop of York a generation ago. The problem of to-day is to express the Christian Faith in terms of the modern *Weltanschauung*.

EVOLUTION AND ORGANIZATION

Loisy, as a Roman Catholic, appealed from an unknown Jesus to a known Church which has evolved from him as a tree evolves from its seed. The Eastern conception of the Church lays less stress on organization than does the Roman conception. Berdyaev's conception of catholicity is more spiritual. The Anglican conception of catholicity is intermediate. The holy Catholic Church is "the whole congregation of Christian people dispersed throughout the world". The more sectarian Anglican uses the word "Catholic" as the antonym of "Protestant", though he himself would not be recognized as a Catholic by continental Catholics. Loisy justified later doctrinal developments by an appeal to evolution. The corresponding Anglican method is the appeal to the guidance of the Holy Spirit. It is thus that a Divine sanction for episcopal organization is alleged. The result is a hardening of attitude towards the Nonconformist section of "the whole congregation of Christian people". This is reflected in the insistence that no one can be included in the parochial Electoral Roll unless he affirms that he does not belong to any religious body which is not in communion with the Church of England.

The demand for this negative statement is an innovation which is contrary to the general practice of the Anglican Communion elsewhere.

AUTHORITY

The question of authority, Biblical, credal, ecclesiastical, runs like a red thread through the ecclesiastical history of the past seventy-five years. Prior to the question of authority, however, is that of the criterion of authority. Since the time of Hooker Anglicans have appealed to Reason as the Divine criterion. This appeal includes the appeal to the rational moral judgement. As the doctrine of Everlasting Punishment had been rejected at the bar of moral judgement, so, Dean Rashdall contended, unethical doctrines of a substitutionary propitiatory sacrifice of Christ on the Cross must be rejected. This affects the Catholic doctrine of the Mass and the Evangelical Plan of Salvation. If the cultus of the Mass be retained after the doctrine which it expresses has been abandoned, there is grave danger of superstition. Though the liberalizing of Evangelicalism has not been without pain, the right of private judgement implicit in Protestantism has made for a greater freedom in respect to tradition.

It may well be that in the future it will be necessary for the Liberal elements in all parties to unite in the work of stemming the tide of a movement of anti-rationalism.

X

NOVA ET VETERA

RETROSPECT

WITHIN the Church of England there is, beyond question, a conflict of ideals. Yet it would be misleading to leave it at that, for a concurrent mutual interpenetration of ideals is constantly taking place. That is why it is not easy to give a clear-cut picture of the·present position, nor, from an analysis of the factors which enter into it, to predict the future. Unless full regard be paid to the history of the tendencies which have been active in the Church since the Reformation, any enquiry as to the future of Anglicanism can only result in a guess at the solution of a very ambiguous riddle. An admirable survey of the development and interplay of the different tendencies which co-exist within the Church has been made by Rev. R. D. Richardson.[1]

As the student of Anglicanism surveys the vista of the past he sees standing out boldly certain peaks which help him to take his bearings. Such a peak event was the publication of *Tracts for the Times*; another was the publication of *Lux Mundi*. To change the metaphor, there are well-defined focal points which give their full significance to tendencies which hitherto had not come to clearly formulated expression. One of the outstanding landmarks of Church history in the nineteenth century was the publication, three-quarters of a century ago, of *Essays and Reviews*. The contributors to this book

---

[1] R. D. Richardson, *Causes of the Present Conflict of Ideals in the Church of England*.

398

were no more without a theological ancestry than were the writers of *Tracts for the Times*. The Tractarians were the descendants of the Laudian High Churchmen; the essayists were the nineteenth-century representatives of a liberalism or humanism which from the time of the Reformation has found a home in the Church of England and may be held to be of the very ethos of Anglicanism. *Essays and Reviews* appeared in 1860, the year in which Bishop Wilberforce, a typical ecclesiastic of the period, a representative of the pink shade of Tractarianism which was then becoming the accepted colour of "good churchmanship", during his famous debate with Huxley at the Oxford meeting of the British Association, after speaking for half an hour "with inimitable spirit, emptiness, and unfairness",[1] had the insolence to ask his opponent whether he was related on his grandfather's or grandmother's side to an ape, and elicited in reply one of the most crushing and merited rebukes in the history of controversy. Wilberforce was one of those ecclesiastics who attract the limelight to themselves, and he was popularly regarded as one of the leading spokesmen for the Church of England. The layman, not unreasonably, in view of the attitude adopted by such leading ecclesiastics as Wilberforce, believed that the Church was no less antagonistic to the new biology than, in the previous generation, it had been to the new geology.

Essays and Reviews brought to the notice of the general public another factor which might seem to threaten the interests of religion. In Germany Biblical criticism had already made itself felt, but it had not as yet claimed much interest in England. *Essays and Reviews* brought its challenge to English readers and the challenge was repeated two years later by the publication of the first part of Bishop Colenso's

---

[1] *Life and Letters of Charles Darwin*, vol. ii. p. 322.

The Pentateuch and Book of Joshua Critically Examined. Colenso's *Commentary on the Epistle to the Romans* had already given much offence.

A new epoch had opened in the history of the Church of England, an epoch of which the end is not yet. The immediate reaction was one of panic. Those who counted themselves the defenders of orthodoxy girded themselves for battle. Tractarian and Evangelical forgot their quarrels in a common determination to crush the new enemy.

> The candid incline to surmise of late
> That the Christian faith proves false, I find;
> For our Essays-and-Reviews' debate
> Begins to tell on the public mind,
> And Colenso's words have weight.[1]

It is not remarkable that the challenge of the new knowledge met with an unfavourable reception. Its very novelty sufficed to damn it. The religious world was not prepared to give it calm consideration. Of the Evangelicals of that period Archdeacon Storr has said, "Truth for truth's sake, the independent pursuit of truth was no passion with them. . . . Art, science, literature, philosophy, with all the contribution to the fullness of human life which these can make, were viewed by them with indifference or hostility."[2] Ruefully surveying, many years later, the effects of the Tractarian Movement on the College and University which gave it birth, Mark Pattison wrote, "It was soon after 1830 that the 'Tracts' desolated Oxford life, and suspended, for an indefinite period, all science, humane letters and the first strivings for intellectual freedom which had moved in the bosom of Oriel".[3]

But, little though the critics of *Essays and Reviews*

---

[1] Robert Browning, "Gold Hair".
[2] V. F. Storr, *The Development of English Theology in the Nineteenth Century*, p. 70.
[3] Mark Pattison, *Memoirs*, pp. 100 and 101.

suspected it, an essential condition of the conserva-
tion of the religious values embodied in Tractarianism and Evangelicalism was that they should assimilate the principles for which the essayists stood.
These principles find clear expression in the first
essay in the book, written by Frederick Temple, the
future Archbishop of Canterbury. It is true that other
essayists displayed idiosyncrasies of which Temple
could not approve, but he voiced the central principles which inspired them all, principles which were
not of temporary significance only, for they are the
determinative principles of that type of Anglicanism
which has persisted and developed under the successive designations of Broad, Liberal, and Modernist
Churchmanship. They are three in number:

> First comes loyalty to truth in all its forms:
> "He is guilty of high treason against the
> faith who fears the result of any investiga-
> tion, whether philosophical, or scientific, or
> historical."

> Then comes loyalty to the guidance of reason:
> "Not only in the understanding of religious
> truth, but in all exercise of the intellectual
> powers, we have no right to stop short of any
> limit but that which nature . . . has imposed on
> us."

> Thirdly comes loyalty to the moral judgement:
> Conscience is "the supreme interpreter, whom
> it may be a duty to enlighten, but whom it can
> never be a duty to disobey".

If either of these three loyalties or principles may
be described as central, it is the third; for it is conscience which inspires loyalty to all truth and faith-
fulness to the guidance of the light of reason.

Essays and Reviews was the starting-point of the
Odyssey, later stages of which were marked by the

publication of *Lux Mundi, Contentio Veritatis, Foundations, Essays Catholic and Critical*.[1] It is difficult to recapture in imagination the alarm and resentment which it elicited. "Past heterodoxy has become present orthodoxy." Two of the essayists, H. B. Wilson and Rowland Williams, were cited before the Ecclesiastical Court of Arches and adjudged guilty of heresy. They were both held to be guilty of impugning the inspiration of Holy Scripture. Their other alleged errors resulted from the application of the criterion of the moral judgement to Christian doctrines. Williams had criticized as unethical the conception of justification by faith as "merit by transfer". Wilson had ventured to hope not only that after death there may be an intermediate state, but that all men might finally be saved from damnation. It is interesting to note that Colenso earned his reputation as arch-heretic by expressing the same kind of opinions on the same grounds. "The Bible is not God's Word", he wrote, "but assuredly 'God's Word' will be heard in the Bible by all who will humbly and devoutly listen for it." He also was guilty of suggesting that "there is hope in the counsels of Infinite Wisdom and Love for all". He again, on ethical grounds, challenged the dogma that "our Lord died for our sins in the sense of dying instead of us . . . and dying so as to bear the punishment or penalty of our sins".

The Court of Arches sentenced Wilson and Williams to one year's suspension from office, a sentence which was reversed on appeal to the Judicial Committee of the Privy Council, a tribunal which is guided by the traditions of English justice and is free from the disturbing influence of the *odium theologicum*. The Judicial Committee "dismissed Hell with costs, and thus took from orthodox clergy of the Church of England their last hope of eternal

---

[1] A. L. Lilley, *Religion and Revelation*, p. 7.

damnation". The success of the appeal was regarded by Tractarians and Evangelicals alike as an outrage on the Church. An impressive protest followed. Pusey and his followers joined with the Evangelicals to issue a manifesto which, within a few weeks, was signed by eleven thousand clergymen. In 1864 *Essays and Reviews* was condemned by Convocation, Archdeacon Denison marshalling the conservative forces with a skill which even an experienced caucus politician could hardly surpass.

It may, in these bustling times, be suggested that ecclesiastical controversies of seventy-five years ago are of no more than antiquarian interest. They were positively Victorian. Even among our middle-aged theologians there are some who, somewhat unsuitably posing as the bright young things of the theological world, emulate Mr. Lytton Strachey and adopt a patronizing attitude towards those who have the honour of maintaining the great tradition of Victorian Liberalism. But the controversies of the last century were not mere "scuffles in the dark"; they were concerned with principles. Moreover, seventy-five years is not a long period in the history of a Church. The fact that Convocation took the obscurantist line, that respected leaders such as Pusey, that able men like Wilberforce and Denison, who had the ear of the public, led the opposition to the new knowledge and thought of the day, has had disastrous consequences from which we still suffer. Our fathers ate and relished the sour grapes of obscurantism. It is we who are still suffering from the resultant toothache. The Church in the nineteenth century lost the reputation of putting truth in the first place. Its first interest appeared to be the defence of tradition. It takes very much longer to regain a character than to lose it, and the hard fact is that in spite of the splendid devotion to truth of a succession of great churchmen, seventy-five years have not sufficed to enable the Church to win the reputation with the outside world of being the home of truth. The battle for the supremacy of the moral judgement within the sphere of doctrine, for loyalty, on religious and conscientious grounds, to all factual truth, whether scientific or historical, in short the battle of nineteenth-century Liberalism, has not yet been finally won. Its principles, it is true, nowadays receive universal lip-service, but few who followed the history of the recent attempt at Prayer Book Revision will imagine that they have become determinative and formative in the ecclesiastical world.

Happily, even when theological passion was at its highest and ugliest there were men in the Church who refused to be swept off their feet. The wise and learned Bishop Thirlwall regarded the mass panic with contempt. He was quite unimpressed by the large number of the signatories to the manifesto promoted by Pusey and his allies. "I consider them", he said, "in the light of a row of figures preceded by a decimal point, so that however far the series may be prolonged, it can never rise to the value of a single unit." F. J. A. Hort was disgusted by the way in which Convocation dealt with *Essays and Reviews*. "Surely this wretched paltering with great questions must soon come to an end," he exclaimed, "or else the Church itself." [1] Writing to Westcott, he urged that the Essayists had a right to sympathy and support because "they happen at this moment to represent the cause of freedom of thought and criticism". He deplored the attempt "to crush out all belief not founded solely on tradition, and, if possible, to drive from the Church all who, whether orthodox or not, value truth above orthodoxy". Frederick Temple knew what he was about when he joined the Essayists. "I for one", he wrote to the Bishop of London,

[1] *Life and Letters of F. J. A. Hort*, vol. i. p. 443.

"joined in writing this book in the hope of breaking through that mischievous reticence which, go where I would, I perpetually found destroying the truth of religion. I wished to encourage men to speak out."[1] That same mischievous reticence still persists. Its practice is even urged by timid ecclesiastics as a duty imposed by charity. On the respectable ground of consideration for the weaker brethren, it is sometimes advocated by those who ought to know, but apparently forget, that its effect is to alienate the stronger brethren.[2] Even though it be the fashion to speak disparagingly of Victorian virtues, we can hardly as yet congratulate ourselves that we are free from Victorian vices.

"Lux Mundi"

The traditionalists, in their endeavour to stem the flowing tide of knowledge, were the Mrs. Partingtons of the Church. But that lady's ineffectual mop was incapable of doing any positive harm. Unfortunately, the attempt of ecclesiastics to dam the stream of thought and criticism, their readiness to plunge into scientific controversies with which they had no real acquaintance, inflicted an injury on the higher interests of the Church of England from which it has not yet recovered. Their stubborn traditionalism gave the Church a bad name and compromised its reputation not only with men of science but also eventually with the man in the street. Some scientists, it is true, were only too ready, in their turn, to enter temerariously into spheres with which their own acquaintance was inadequate. But this did not better matters. Hort shewed his sense of the gravity of the situation during the latter half of the nineteenth

---

[1] *Life of Archbishop Tait*, vol. i. p. 292.
[2] See "Bishop Barnes on Science and Superstition", by Professor L. de C. Richardson, *Hibbert Journal*, April 1933.

century when, in the course of a letter to E. W. Benson on the occasion of his acceptance of the primacy, he said, "The convulsions of our English Church itself, grievous as they are, seem to be as nothing beside the danger of its calm and unobtrusive alienation in thought and spirit from the great silent multitude of Englishmen and again of alienation from fact and love of fact: mutual alienations both".[1]

Hort, who was appointed Hulsean Professor of Divinity at Cambridge in 1878, belonged to the succession of great scholars whose work in our Universities was far removed in spirit from the feverishness of ecclesiastical strife. Their allegiance to truth was undivided. B. F. Westcott, appointed Regius Professor of Divinity in the same University in 1870, was another. Westcott gave noble expression to the spirit of genuine scholarship when he said, "He who believes that every judgement on the highest matters different from his own is simply a heresy must have a mean idea of the faith; and while the qualifications, the reserve, the lingering sympathies of the real student may make him in many cases a poor controversialist, it may be said that a mere controversialist cannot be a real theologian".[2] At Oxford, S. R. Driver became Professor of Hebrew in 1882, and T. K. Cheyne Oriel Professor in 1885. These men, and others like them, were specialists, and, as such, no doubt had their individual limitations; but each, in his own department, sought after truth and truth only, and regarded the quest as a progressive one.

The Church of England has been advantaged by its close connexion with the older Universities in that its leading theologians have been able to carry on their work free from ecclesiastical control and with-

---

[1] *Life and Letters of F. J. A. Hort*, vol. ii. p. 290.
[2] *Lessons from Work*, p. 85.

out regard to ecclesiastical expediencies. In the long run their work has told. The appearance in 1889 of *Lux Mundi* was an outward and visible sign of the influence exerted by sound scholarship on the younger representatives of the Tractarian tradition. They frankly accepted the right of the Higher Criticism to determine questions of authorship, historicity, and date in dealing with the Scriptures.

They did not, however, realize how far in principle they had departed not only from the older Tractarianism, but from historic Catholicism itself. Tractarianism had enriched the Church by deepening the sense of the value and importance of the corporate aspect of spiritual life, by directing the attention of churchmen to their heritage from the past, and, in accordance with its sacramental emphasis, by stressing the value of beauty and dignity in public worship. It had, above all, nourished a deep and cultured piety. But it had been, on the whole, a backward-looking movement. It had brought precious things out of its treasury, but they had been things old rather than new. Its learning had the same antiquarian flavour as that of the Laudian school; and, as the High Churchmanship of its seventeenth-century predecessor was impotent in face of the eighteenth-century rationalism which questioned not only the authority of the Fathers but that of the Scriptures themselves, so the older Tractarianism was impotent in the face of an advancing Liberalism. No doubt Charles Gore, the editor of *Lux Mundi*, thought that he was doing no more than adapting the older Tractarianism to the needs of the day. Liddon saw more clearly what was happening. He saw that the school which he held to be guardian of true Anglicanism was at the crossroads, and he believed that Gore and his friends were taking the wrong turning.

The Parting of the Ways

Canon Liddon, the revered representative of Tractarianism, had been responsible for the appointment of Gore as principal of Pusey House, and was therefore the more dismayed at the emergence from Pusey House of a portent so threatening to that which Pusey held dear.

> I have been more disturbed than I can say [he wrote] by the concluding pages of Gore's Essay, which have come upon me as a thunderbolt out of a clear sky. It is practically a capitulation at the feet of the young Rationalist Professors, by which the main positions which the old Apologists of Holy Scriptures have maintained are conceded to the enemy, in deference to the "literary" judgement of our time.[1]

Lux Mundi on a matter of fundamental importance broke with historic Catholicism, and Liddon knew it. It is a very superficial judgement which is content to attribute Liddon's repudiation of *Lux Mundi* to the inability of an old man to keep abreast of the times. As Canon Lilley has pointed out in his Paddock Lectures, Catholicism regarded Scripture as the primary and infallible authority. The authority of the Church was theoretically interpretative only, and therefore secondary to that of Scripture. It was merely instrumental. The Catholic conception of Revelation

> meant that the will of God for man's redemption and the manner of its accomplishment had been expressly revealed beforehand to man by God, that without that Revelation man could never have known anything of God's gracious purpose, that that Revelation was contained in the Scriptures of the Old and New Testaments and in certain oral traditions communicated by our Lord

---

[1] *Life and Letters of Henry Parry Liddon*, p. 367.

to His apostles, that this Revelation of Scripture and tradition was infallible in all its parts, that to its original content nothing could ever be added nor from it anything be taken away, and, finally, that its revealed character was guaranteed by the prophetic form in which it was given and by the miracles which God wrought for that express purpose. That was the immemorial foundation of the whole pyramid of Christian truth, that infallible, inerrant, integral, insupersessible Divine Revelation.[1]

No conception of historic Catholicism could be more perversely mistaken than that expressed in the phrase "The Church to teach; the Bible to prove". The Catholic position has ever been, "The Bible to teach; the Church to interpret". The doctrine of the infallibility of the Church has arisen because it has seemed that an infallible Book demands an infallible interpreter. The scholarship of the nineteenth century had undermined "the immemorial foundation" of Catholicism. Rome knew this. Leo XIII was in line with Catholic tradition when, in his encyclical *Providentissimus Dei*, he declared that the total inerrancy of the Bible was the necessary consequence of its inspiration. He but echoed Augustine's "Quam [Scripturam] esse veracem nemo dubitat nisi infidelis aut impius". *Lux Mundi* broke with historic Catholicism on a matter of fundamental importance. That its writers designated themselves "Catholics", albeit hyphenated "Catholics", did not alter the fact one whit. What Pusey would have regarded as the virus of *Essays and Reviews* had infected *Lux Mundi*. The book was not Catholic as Pusey understood Catholicism. Hence Liddon's distress. Liddon's judgement was that of a theologian of weight. The Anglo-Catholic who attaches importance to the fashion of an albe or the cut of a stole as a mark of Catholicity is, by comparison with Liddon, a shallow trifler.

[1] A. L. Lilley, *Religion and Revelation*, pp. 9, 10.

CREED AND CRITICISM

Liddon's accusation that Gore had capitulated at the feet of the young Rationalist Professors was harsh and unfair. The only capitulation was an honourable surrender to the guidance of reason. Gore might well have replied in the words of Frederick Temple, "He is guilty of high treason against the faith who fears the result of any investigation, whether philosophical, or scientific, or historical".

The literary criticism of the Gospels has produced assured results. It is agreed that *Matthew* and *Luke* make use of *Mark* in the form in which we have it or in substantially the same form. It is also agreed that *Matthew* and *Luke* make use of another written document, commonly referred to as Q. Dr. Streeter's development of this theory has received wide though not universal acceptance among scholars. He distinguishes two other written sources which he calls M and L. *Matthew* uses M and *Luke* uses L. He thinks that there were two editions of *Luke*. In the first Q and L were used; in the second, which is our *Luke*, *Mark* was incorporated and the first two chapters added. In *Matthew*, on the other hand, *Mark* was the primary source, and with *Mark* was combined matter from M and Q. It is clear that St. Matthew was not the author of *Matthew*. No disciple of Jesus possessing first-hand knowledge of his life and teaching would find it necessary to use *Mark* and Q in the manner in which they are used in *Matthew*. The Fourth Gospel is essentially a theological work, though it may contain matter of directly historical value.

The results of New Testament criticism have placed in the hands of the student a new instrument. He has been enabled by comparison of the use made in *Matthew* and *Luke* of their common material to discover something of the tendencies which they represent, and thus to attempt to gauge the kind of development which had taken place in the Gospel tradition. His conclusions may be tentative, but he is now able to survey his material from a new and surer standpoint. On the negative side he has been rescued from the fallacious conclusion that a two-fold or threefold attestation of a saying or event is any guarantee of its authenticity, for he now knows that the Evangelists are not independent witnesses.

Biblical criticism was not destined to leave the Creeds inviolate, for, as the Eighth Article puts it, the ground for the acceptance of the three Creeds is that "they may be proved by most certain warrant of holy Scripture". When *Lux Mundi* was published, Liddon saw that the methods accepted therein were likely to affect the traditional view of Christ:

> Is it not remarkable that our Divine Lord, as if in anticipation of the sceptical spirit of our day, sanctioned those portions of the Old Testament which were most strongly objected to by the modern Rationalists? The Flood, Lot's wife, Jonah in the whale, are all used by Him in His recorded teaching. Was He referring to fables which He knew, or—worse still—did not know to be such? [1]

The theological response to this criticism was a form of the Kenotic theory, according to which God incarnate in Christ laid aside some of the attributes of Deity. Gore adopted this theory; but his form of it shared the weakness of all Kenotic theories. They "sought to solve the problem on too narrow a basis" and "were somewhat crudely external in their treatment of the divine attributes". [2] Deity shorn of its attributes is an abstract and mechanical conception, and savours of an inverted Docetism.

Gore's position was equivocal. He claimed to be a Liberal Catholic, but his Liberalism was incon-

---

[1] *Life and Letters of Henry Parry Liddon*, p. 361.
[2] L. S. Thornton, *The Incarnate Lord*, p. 262.

sistent with historic Catholicism. It may have been a subconsciousness that Liddon represented the actual Catholic tradition which inhibited him from travelling far along the path on which he had set out. Within twenty-five years of the publication of *Lux Mundi* it was possible for a Cambridge divine to describe him as "one of the noblest and most persuasive exponents of some convictions that all Christians share, and the most competent apologist of lost theological causes that I know".[1] Whether or not Gore was conscious of the ambiguity of his position there were others who perceived it clearly enough. Shortly before C. W. Townsend, the Superior of the Oxford Mission to Calcutta, went over to the Roman Church, Gore wrote, "He has been reading me, and appears to be definitely of opinion that to admit private judgement and enquiry, as much as I (and all of us lot) do, is Protestantism. Also apparently that the *present* Church authority is meant to be decisive and beyond appeal and the simple question is, 'Which or where is the Church?'"[2] Townsend was right. In Gore, as in the Liberal Catholicism which traces back to Gore, there was a strong, though unavowed, element of Protestantism. He was also right in questioning the value of the appeal to the Church, when the term "Church" is ambiguous.

Lux Mundi made Biblical criticism respectable. It recognized the validity and necessity of critical methods, and by so doing prepared the way for the advance which was in preparation during the first decade of the twentieth century. A definite stage in that advance was marked by the publication in 1912 of a volume of theological essays by various writers under the title *Foundations*. Alarm had already been caused by the publication in the previous year of a

---

[1] J. F. Bethune-Baker, *The Way of Modernism*, p. 131.
[2] G. L. Prestige, *The Life of Charles Gore*, p. 108.

book by Rev. J. M. Thompson, Dean of Divinity at Magdalen College, Oxford. The head of his offence was a denial of the adequacy of the evidence for the virginity of Mary and for the resuscitation of the dead body of Jesus.

> As we may believe with St. Mark that Jesus was born of human parents, and yet call Him divine; so we may believe with St. Paul that His human body remained in the grave, and yet worship Him as risen and alive.[1]

It has been said of the contributors to *Foundations* that they were "for the most part neither very experienced nor very learned".[2] This hardly does them justice. They had all had brilliant academic careers, and ample time had elapsed since their undergraduate days for them to acquire learning sufficient to give their views weight. Among them were B. H. Streeter, now Provost of Queen's College, Oxford; W. Temple, the present Archbishop of York; and A. E. J. Rawlinson, now Bishop of Derby. Streeter had taken his degree sixteen years, Temple nine years, and Rawlinson six years before the publication of the book. They were all men who were in a position to put the pursuit of truth above considerations of expediency. Frank Weston, Bishop of Zanzibar, the most popular leader of the Anglo-Catholic party, and the most influential voice with the rank and file of that party, regarded *Foundations* as heretical, taking special exception to Rawlinson's views on Authority and to Streeter's view that the resurrection of Jesus was not necessarily physical. He attacked them in a lively *Open Letter*. Three years later he formally excommunicated Dr. Percival, the Bishop of Hereford, for appointing Streeter to a canonry. *Foundations* aroused a vigorous controversy in the course of

---

[1] J. M. Thompson, *Miracles in the New Testament*, p. 211.
[2] G. L. Prestige, *The Life of Charles Gore*, p. 344.

which W. Sanday, Lady Margaret's Professor at Oxford, J. F. Bethune-Baker, Lady Margaret's Professor at Cambridge, and H. M. Gwatkin, Dixie Professor of Ecclesiastical History at Cambridge, were among the distinguished theologians who maintained the permissibility of the views impugned. The controversy flared up again in 1917 when Gore, on the ground of his alleged unsoundness on the Creed, protested against the appointment of Dr. Henson, now Bishop of Durham, to the see of Hereford. He withdrew his protest when Dr. Henson gave Archbishop Davidson an assurance that he could accept the Creeds *ex animo*, though in a letter to the Archbishop he admitted that "the letter of H. H. to you caused me bewilderment of mind".[1]

The Bishop of Zanzibar was also involved in the controversy which raged around the appointment of Dr. Henson, and in 1919 he published an Open Pastoral Letter under the title of *The Christ and His Critics* in which he drew the moral of recent events:

> Dr. Henson teaches that our Lord's virgin-birth and bodily resurrection are open questions, that the nature-miracles ascribed to Him are not facts, that His utterances as a teacher need not be received as final, and that He was mistaken in thinking that men were possessed by demons. These doctrines of his were examined by the Archbishop of Canterbury, chiefly on the motion of the then Bishop of Oxford. His Grace decided that they lie within the limits of what the Church of England permits her bishops to believe and teach, and allowed Dr. Henson's books to be taken as showing his *ex animo* acceptance of the Creeds.[2]

From the Bishop of Zanzibar's point of view this was a fair presentation of the situation as it was clarified after a controversy extending over some five years.

---

[1] G. L. Prestige, *The Life of Charles Gore*, p. 401.
[2] F. Weston, *The Christ and His Critics*, p. vii.

When *Lux Mundi* appeared, Liddon saw that its doctrine destroyed the ancient ground of Church authority, belief in an authoritative infallible Bible. Gore himself was no less horrified when he saw criticism laying its hands on the Creeds. He called himself a Liberal Catholic. His Liberalism had expressed itself in *Lux Mundi*. His Catholicism forbade him to come to terms with the claims of criticism to touch the "historical" clauses of the Creeds. They must be accepted, interpreted, and recited in their most literal sense. The Virgin Birth, the resurrection of the body of Jesus are hard facts and must be accepted as such, though it is necessary to give a symbolic interpretation to the clauses which refer to the descent into hell and the session on God's right hand, seeing that here the Creeds deal with matters outside the sphere of present possible experience. In the clause referring to the Ascension, factual and symbolic are blended. "When I say Christ ascended into heaven, I am first of all referring to a certain symbolical, but actual and historical, demonstration which our Lord gave to his disciples forty days after his resurrection."[1] Fearing that he would not obtain adequate support from his brother Bishops in his stand for the inviolability of the Creeds literally interpreted, Gore threatened to resign his see, but "a formula was found which met with general agreement and in which Gore could acquiesce".[2] He finally resigned in 1919, exhausted by a struggle on a double front. Calling himself a Liberal Catholic he found himself during the latter part of his career driven to fight Liberalism on the one side and the Catholicism of the more advanced Anglo-Catholics on the other. An aftermath of the controversy which had its origin in the publication of *Foundations* was the formal charge of heresy brought by Rev. C. E.

[1] C. Gore, *The Basis of Anglican Fellowship*, p. 20.
[2] G. L. Prestige, *The Life of Charles Gore*, p. 363.

Douglas in 1921 against Dr. H. D. A. Major, the Principal of Ripon Hall and Editor of *The Modern Churchman*, on the ground that he openly taught a doctrine concerning Resurrection inconsistent with the Creeds and Scriptures. Nothing came of it. Dr. Burge, the Bishop of Oxford, before whom the charge was laid, submitted the matter to four Oxford theological Professors. They reported that no *prima facie* case had been made out.

The years following the publication of *Foundations* in 1912 constituted a turning-point in the development of Anglicanism. Liberalism, or Modernism, as it had come to be called, spread rapidly and has since profoundly affected both Anglo-Catholicism and Evangelicalism. The controversy which then agitated the theological world has had a formative influence on twentieth-century Anglicanism. Its effects have not yet been felt by the laity of the various parties in the Church, but when they have percolated deeply enough, they will go far to determine the future of the Church. Possibly the younger generation, whose sense of continuity has been impaired by the existence of the gulf of the World War, does not realize the significance for the present of the events of nearly quarter of a century ago. If so, it is to be deplored. Educationalists have seen the importance of instructing schoolboys in the history of modern times. No longer do school histories end at the middle of the nineteenth century. It would be well if those responsible for the training of theological students would take a leaf from the book of lay educationalists and see that those who are in their charge should have at least as sound a knowledge of modern Church history as schoolboys have of modern political history.

Many of the most scholarly Anglo-Catholics have abandoned Gore's position on the Creeds as untenable. Among them is Professor A. E. Taylor, one of the contributors to the Anglo-Catholic volume of essays, *Essays Catholic and Critical*, published in 1926. In his book *The Faith of a Moralist* he rejects the validity of Gore's distinction between the factual and the symbolical:

> Dr. Gore notoriously would include the article *natus ex Maria virgine* among those which must be understood "literally". But how much does he mean by this? We know the interpretation put on this *credendum* by St. Thomas and in the *Catechism* of Trent. Does Dr. Gore mean to insist on the whole of it, or only on some part, and if not on the whole, how does he justify himself from the Tridentine point of view, of not really accepting the article without diminution? Does he regard it as *de fide* to hold that Christ, as a physical fact, *ex mulieris alvo, sine ullo maternae virginitatis detrimento editus est*? If not, is he not permitting a latitude he professedly rejects in the interpretation of the word *natus*? [1]

Approaching the Gospel narratives from the standpoint demanded by the results of critical analysis, it is clear that the Resurrection narratives embody traditions which are confused and inconsistent among themselves and that the opening chapters of *Matthew* and *Luke*, wherein alone is to be found any evidence of the Virgin Birth of Jesus, contain legendary matter. No one could recognize this more clearly than Dr. P. E. More, the learned American theologian, again a distinguished member of that section of the Anglican Communion which makes a special claim to the appellation of Catholic, and co-editor with Dr. F. L. Cross of Pusey House of the volume entitled *Anglicanism*. Of the Virgin Birth he says,

> It is so demonstrably a late intrusion into the life of Jesus, so manifestly legendary in construction, and withal so inessential to the Christian faith, that it has been abandoned by the majority of unprejudiced scholars.[2]

[1] A. E. Taylor, *The Faith of a Moralist*, vol. ii. p. 142.
[2] P. E. More, *The Christ of the New Testament*, p. 269.

While holding that the visions of the risen Christ, though they may be regarded as subjective, were "genuine manifestations of spirit to spirit", he still says that

> The four accounts present so many inconsistencies, not to say contradictions, that one hardly sees how they can go back to a single primitive tradition of actual events. Commentators have made desperate efforts to harmonize the Gospels here, but again, as in the case of the virgin birth, have failed lamentably. And apart from these inconsistencies, the narrative bears the unmistakable stamp of legendary invention.[1]

RASHNESS AND RETICENCE

It is doubtful whether such frank pronouncements as these would to-day shock any Biblical scholar, Anglo-Catholic or otherwise. But it is indubitable that they would profoundly shock nine out of ten of the worshippers in our churches. Dr. A. E. J. Rawlinson, another of the contributors to *Essays Catholic and Critical*, believes that the battle of intellectual liberty within the Church of England has been won, and that not only the intellectual leaders, but "the rank and file also, in so far as they choose, or care", may be intellectually free.[2] This is all to the good, so far as it goes; but, unfortunately, the effect of the attitude of the Church to new knowledge during the past three-quarters of a century has been a steady draining away of the laymen who choose or care to take any interest in the things of the intellect. The average worshipper in the parish church simply does not know what it means to worship God with his mind. He appreciates emotional stimulus and responds to the aesthetic appeal, especially if it suggests the numinous; but the

[1] P. E. More, *The Christ of the New Testament*, pp. 270, 271.
[2] A. E. J. Rawlinson, *The Church of England and the Church of Christ*, p. 70.

enquiring layman for the most part pursues his enquiries outside the walls of our churches.

It is futile to blame our lay-folk for this apathy. On the whole a church gets the laity it deserves. We obviously cannot blame our great scholars. We have had a succession of scholars who, as Frederick Temple put it, in their endeavour to understand religious truth, have not stopped short of any limit but that which Nature has imposed. Their courage has been justified by their success within the sphere of constructive apologetics. But, unhappily, between the scholar's study and the pew of the parish church a great gulf is set. In the nineteenth century it was ecclesiastics like Wilberforce and Denison rather than such scholars as Jowett, Hort, and Driver who had the ear of churchmen. So, to-day, it is not so much great scholars as well-known ecclesiastics, especially Bishops, who have the ear of the laity. And the Bishops, with few exceptions, have continued to find reasons satisfactory to themselves for the practice of that reticence which Temple characterized as "mischievous".

The effect of the reticence of the better informed ecclesiastic is reinforced by the rash utterances of those ecclesiastics who are less well informed. Every now and then we hear astonishing dogmatic utterances from such men affirming that an obligation lies on the clergy to believe in the Virgin Birth of Jesus or his physical resurrection or some other alleged fact which the scholar well knows to be at least highly questionable. Traditionalist ecclesiastics are apt to display all too little reticence. They compensate in unction for their deficiencies in scholarship, and, especially if they happen to be Bishops, occupying important sees, they command a wide audience. They have for their pronouncements the publicity of such occasions as Diocesan Conferences. Their speeches are reported in official diocesan magazines, and not infrequently they appear in condensed form in the public press. The laity, regarding such pronouncements as made *ex cathedra*, attach to them an importance disproportionate to their intrinsic value. We still have our Wilberforces and Denisons, and they are no less harmful to-day than were their precursors in the nineteenth century.

The position is worsened by the fact that if a man goes to church he finds in use a form of worship which was compiled in an age which was ignorant of much which to-day is commonplace to every person of average education. He is, in fact, compelled to say things which he knows to be untrue or to imply untruth. This is not remarkable in view of the period which has elapsed since the last revision of the Prayer Book and of the enormous advance of knowledge during that period. It may even be tolerated for a time as a transitional state of things, the more so because of the religious genius of the Prayer Book. What is remarkable, and no less deplorable than remarkable, is that when an abortive attempt at Prayer Book revision was made a few years ago, hardly any attention was paid to considerations of this nature.

The result of timid ecclesiastical reticence in respect to new knowledge, combined with the rashness of ecclesiastical traditionalists, has been unfortunate. Though the position is not as bad as it was when Hort could speak of "a favourable specimen of the conventional English ecclesiastical scholar, who does not willingly violate truth, but has never discovered that there is such a thing as truth",[1] it is to be feared that even now the Church is not universally regarded as pre-eminently the home of truthfulness. The more intelligent layman suspects his clergyman of practising a good deal of mental reservation. The less intelligent layman believes that

[1] *Life and Letters of F. J. A. Hort*, vol. ii. p. 102.

his clergyman holds pre-critical and even pre-Darwinian views which quite probably he does not hold at all. The position is a false one, and it will only be remedied by a new frankness and courage. A process of evaporation has long been going on and is still going on, and in that process we have lost and are still losing many of the more thoughtful and better informed of the laity. Only the parochial clergyman knows the extent to which the process has been accompanied by the precipitation of a sediment of fundamentalism, a sediment which, in view of his responsibilities within his own sphere, he hesitates to disturb. He has a right to look to the ecclesiastical leaders whose voices carry weight with the average layman to speak out clearly and unambiguously. The academic scholar can do little to help him, for even the names of our great scholars are unknown to the greater part of the laity. Their voices do not reach so far.

It is not only the uneducated who imagine that the Church is hopelessly out of touch with the new thought and knowledge which have transformed man's outlook on the world during the past century. The Bishop of Birmingham has recorded a conversation he had with a girl university student. She was very troubled by the bearing of evolution on religion and her loss of belief in the early Genesis narratives.

> I explained to her that I did not accept these remains of primitive thought, and that they were in no way vital to, or even of importance in, Christian belief. She asked me "But why do you not say so publicly?" I replied that I had done so repeatedly. She looked at me quietly and asked, "May I say what is in my mind?" "Please do. We are talking frankly." "Cannot you say it a little more loudly? It would help so many of us." [1]

The ignorance on the part of the laity of the extent to which educated clergymen accept the results of

[1] E. W. Barnes, *Should Such a Faith Offend?* p. 13.

New Testament criticism is more striking still. It is safe to say that most worshippers in our churches are under the impression that the clergy believe that every saying attributed to Christ in the Gospels is authentic, and that every incident recorded in them is historical. This might not matter much, from the point of view of the ecclesiastical administrator, if it were not that there are at any rate some among the laity who have an inkling of what scholars are saying and thinking. It is they who are being steadily alienated from the Church. The consequent loss is not only quantitative, but, what is more serious, qualitative also. Pending a revision of our forms of worship which will have primary regard to the new knowledge, and, it may be added, to the judgement of the moral consciousness, nothing is more urgent than that ecclesiastics, who have the public ear, and realize the gravity of the present unwholesome position, should lay aside their reticence, even if frankness involves risk. In speaking out they must have in mind in the first place not the question "Is this wise?" but rather the questions "Is this right?" and "Is this true?" The responsibility for frankness lies on the individual. There is no reason to think that the Spirit of Truth is less with the individual who is loyal to the guidance of reason and the dictates of conscience than with any synod or council of ecclesiastics who, while individually perfectly sincere, are in the end commonly driven to exercise their ingenuity in finding a formula to which, by reason of its ambiguity, they all may find it possible, in some sense, to subscribe.

THE JESUS OF HISTORY

The critical examination of the Gospels resulted in the emergence of a picture of the human Jesus, more appealing and comprehensible to the plain man than the metaphysical Christ of the Creeds and the Confessions. This is the practical religious justification of Biblical criticism, though no honest single-minded search after truth is in need of any practical justification. The present writer knows from his parochial experience the high value of such a book as T. R. Glover's *The Jesus of History* in bringing home the appeal of Christ to those who are in danger of losing their way in the misty realm of theological abstractions and archaic rituals.

Adolf von Harnack, the greatest of the New Testament critics and ecclesiastical historians of the latter part of the nineteenth century, was insistent on the importance of history. "History, it is true, never has the last word; but in the science of religion, and especially in that of the Christian religion, it assuredly has the first word." In 1900 he published a series of lectures under the title *Das Wesen des Christentums*, translated into English as *What is Christianity?* in the following year. Though in a popular work of this type such niceties of qualified and balanced statement as are proper in Harnack's more academic writings would be out of place, it possesses value as a broad statement of the position reached by Liberal theology. Harnack, taking a general view of the teaching of Jesus, grouped it under three heads, the Kingdom of God and its coming, God the Father and the infinite value of the human soul, and the higher righteousness and the commandment of love. These three heads were so closely related that the whole of the teaching could be exhibited under any one of them.

> That Jesus' message is so great and so powerful lies in the fact that it is so simple and on the other hand so rich; so simple as to be exhausted in each of the leading thoughts which he uttered; so rich that every one of these thoughts seems to be inexhaustible and the full meaning of the sayings and parables beyond our reach.

But more than that—he himself stands behind everything that he said. His words speak to us across the centuries with the freshness of the present. It is here that that profound saying is truly verified: "Speak, that I may see thee".[1]

But another reading of the Gospels, very different from Harnack's, was rapidly gaining ground. The curious Jewish literature which is known as Apocalyptic was engaging the attention of scholars. It is a literature which came into being during the three centuries between 200 B.C. and A.D. 100, and was bred of disillusionment. Its fundamental presupposition was that this present world was only fit for destruction, and it looked for a miraculous intervention of God, which should bring the present age to a catastrophic end and inaugurate a new age. Some of the later Apocalyptists assigned to a Messiah or supernatural Son of Man a central role in the consummation. *The Book of Daniel* and *The Revelation* are specimens of the apocalyptic writings; but, for the most part, the apocalypses are very second-rate productions. There is no reason to think that they were familiar to the common people whose religious life centred round the synagogue. "The apocalypses with their dreary artificial constructions and difficult symbolism can never have been popular."[2] It was under the influence of an intensive study of these writings that the new school examined afresh the Gospel picture of Jesus. No longer was he regarded as one who speaks to us across the ages with the freshness of the present. He belonged to the bizarre world conjured up by the Oriental imagination of the Apocalyptists.

Alfred Loisy, the great French Biblical scholar, thought that in this new interpretation of the person of Jesus he could find a justification for the later

---

[1] Adolf von Harnack, *What is Christianity?* p. 53.
[2] E. F. Scott, *The Kingdom of God in the New Testament*, p. 31.

developments of Catholicism. His book *L'Évangile et l'Église* was a reply along this line to Harnack's *Das Wesen des Christentums*. It met with some welcome in Anglo-Catholic circles. In a pamphlet, *Harnack and Loisy*, to which Lord Halifax contributed a preface, Rev. T. A. Lacey urged that "The Christ of our altars . . . is surely the historic Christ; not a thin figure drawn from inadequate materials in the Synoptics".[1] But the Roman Church would have nothing to do with this type of apologetic, and in 1908 the major excommunication was pronounced against Loisy.

Loisy was the best known representative of the Roman Catholic movement which the Encyclical *Pascendi* of 1907 stigmatized as Modernism. By a curious twist it has happened that in England the name of Modernist has, in common usage, been transferred to Anglican theologians, many of whom find their affinity with the Liberal movement, the very movement, that is, which the original Modernists regarded as the theological enemy. George Tyrrell, the Jesuit scholar, was the leading representative in England of the original Roman Catholic Modernism. How remote he was from the Anglican tradition which runs through *Essays and Reviews* to the so-called Anglican Modernism of to-day is shewn by his attitude to the ethical teaching of Jesus. English theologians have usually regarded this as of primary importance. To Tyrrell it was secondary and accidental. What mattered was the eschatology, the belief of Jesus that the catastrophic end was near. "Jesus did not come to reveal a new ethics of this life, but the speedy advent of a new world in which ethics would be superseded."[2] So far was the Kingdom of Heaven from what Harnack had imagined it to be that "Righteousness was not of

---

[1] Quoted by W. R. Inge, *Faith and Knowledge*, p. 287.
[2] George Tyrrell, *Christianity at the Cross Roads*, p. 50.

the substance of the Kingdom".[1] The ethics of Jesus were no more than what Schweitzer called *Interimsethik*, an *ad hoc* code of conduct for the interim period before the final catastrophe. "In such a crisis it was not worth while to assert a thousand just claims that, in normal circumstances, could not be inculpably neglected."[2]

Albert Schweitzer's book *Von Reimarus zu Wrede*, published in 1906, and translated in 1910 under the title *The Quest of the Historical Jesus*, gave a great impetus to the eschatological interpretation of Jesus in England. The quest, according to Schweitzer, had had little or no positive result. "Those who are fond of talking about negative theology can find their account here. There is nothing more negative than the result of the critical study of the life of Jesus."[3]

C. W. Emmet's *The Eschatological Question in the Gospels* gives an admirable account of the position of Loisy, Schweitzer, and Tyrrell, along with a judicious criticism of their methods and presuppositions. Schweitzer is arbitrary in his selection of material. He almost entirely neglects the evidence contained in *Luke*. If he had taken into account such parables as the Good Samaritan and The Prodigal Son, it is difficult to see how he could have dismissed the ethical teaching of Jesus as mere *Interimsethik*. He fails to make allowance for the influence of the eschatological hopes of the primitive Church in colouring the Gospel narratives. He illegitimately interprets all Christ's eschatological language in the baldest, crudest sense. Above all, he and his followers fail to account for the fact that the life and teaching of one who, according to them, was the dupe of mistaken apocalyptic fancies, have given birth to a world religion, and that the saints of all ages have

---

[1] George Tyrrell, *Christianity at the Cross Roads*, p. 49.
[2] *Ibid.* p. 51.
[3] Albert Schweitzer, *The Quest of the Historical Jesus*, p. 7.

found in the ideals and teaching of their Master,
guidance on their path through this present life.

The eschatological interpretation of Jesus had a
profound influence on the theology associated with
the name of Karl Barth. Barthianism is a theology
of disillusionment. Hence its vogue during the period
which followed the World War. It was bred of a disillusionment and despair no less profound than that
of the Jewish apocalyptic writers. Neither ethical
aspiration nor human reason can lead men towards
God. Revelation comes exclusively from without. It
is a "vertical miracle". The argument from the
events and processes of this world to the' character
and activity of God, an argument implicit in every
one of the Gospel parables, is to Barthianism
anathema. Schweitzer holds that Jesus' conception
of the Kingdom of God was rigidly predestinarian.
Barthianism teaches predestination. To Barthianism
the historical belongs to the derelict human plane.
Barth replaces *Geschichte* by a highly abstract and
metaphysical *Urgeschichte* which, whatever it may
be, is not historical in any comprehensible sense of
the word. As a consequence of this depreciation of
history Barthianism is prepared in principle to
assent to the most negative conclusions of radical
Biblical criticism. So far as it has had any influence
in England, it has been in a very diluted form. It
has an attraction for some Anglo-Catholics because
it seems to assign to revealed dogma a relative
independence sufficient to place it beyond the reach
of historical criticism.

One of the recent books in which Barthian influence is obvious is *The Riddle of the New Testament*,
by Sir Edwyn Hoskyns, again one of the contributors
to *Essays Catholic and Critical*, and Noel Davey.
The authors do not adopt the negative attitude towards history which Barth professes, but they argue
that throughout the Gospels a Christological dogma

is so closely interwoven with the record that dogmatic interpretation and fact are quite inseparable. "The difficult Christology is lying in the various strata of material which they [the Evangelists] handled, and not only lies there, but controls it."[1] Any such conclusion confronts us with a grave difficulty; for, unless the life and teaching of our Lord are so far separable from the theological interpretation placed on them by contemporaries and the succeeding generation as to enable us in our turn to place our interpretation on them, it would seem that our faith must needs be that second-hand faith which, because it is second-hand and traditional, is hardly worthy of the name of faith.

In the nineteenth century the critics investigated the literary relationship between the Gospels, and sought to throw light on their literary development before they reached their final form. Of late years scholars have undertaken a more ambitious adventure. They are now pushing their enquiries into an earlier period when there was as yet nothing of the nature of a written Gospel. Their *Formgeschichte*, or Form Criticism, as the new criticism is called, makes the assumption that, at a period even prior to Q, M, and L as postulated by the literary critics, stories of the acts and sayings of Jesus were current orally in the various infant churches, which valued them for their applicability to contemporary problems, and used them for liturgical and catechetical purposes. The Form Critics believe that oral units, thus coming into existence, were characterized by definite and recognizable forms, and that they can detect their presence within our written Gospels. The Gospels in fact consist of disconnected units strung together and given a factitious unity by the Evangelists. As to the type and classification of the alleged units there

---

[1] Sir Edwyn Hoskyns and Noel Davey, *The Riddle of the New Testament*, p. 159.

is as yet considerable divergence of opinion among Form Critics.

The underlying assumption of Form Criticism, that, before they were collected and reduced to writing, there was a wide oral circulation of tales about Jesus, has been questioned by scholars of weight. Dr. Burkitt doubts it.

> Luke's patron, "The Rt. Hon. Theophilus", had been instructed in the Christian Religion, but there is nothing to suggest that this included any more of the Gospel history than is included in something like the Apostle's Creed. What Theophilus had been taught was not (as I venture to think) tales about Jesus; it was more likely to have been those first principles of which the Epistle to the Hebrews speaks—repentance, faith, baptism, consecration, resurrection and the judgement to come.[1]

The Epistles in the New Testament certainly do not suggest that their writers or their readers were much interested in the deeds and sayings of Jesus or had much knowledge of them. It may well be, as Burkitt suggests, that St. Mark was in fact a pioneer who turned the Evangel into a Biography.[2]

If, however, the assumptions of Form Criticism be accepted, two questions immediately arise. How far were the stories about Jesus, which circulated in the churches, for one or two generations, the product of the mythopoeic faculty of the earliest communities? To what extent were the sayings determined and even created by the needs of the time? The matter must have been shaped more or less. The only question is whether it was less or more. To these questions different critics give different answers. Dr. Vincent Taylor, for instance, gives a conservative answer,[3] as does Dr. Easton.[4] Professor R. H.

---

[1] F. C. Burkitt, *Church and Gnosis*, p. 142.
[2] *Ibid.* p. 143.
[3] Vincent Taylor, *The Formation of the Gospel Tradition.*
[4] B. L. Easton, *The Gospel before the Gospels.*

Lightfoot, in his Bampton Lectures, is much more radical:

> It seems, then, that the form of the earthly no less than that of the heavenly Christ is for the most part hidden from us. For all the inestimable value of the gospels, they yield us little more than a whisper of his voice; we trace in them but the outskirts of his ways.[1]

The Christ of the Creeds

It is unlikely that any scholar to-day would accept, without substantial reserves, Schweitzer's reading of the Gospels. Yet, though, *pace* Schweitzer, we may still, with Harnack, hear the words of Jesus speaking to us across the centuries, the labours of the eschatological school have not been in vain. They have checked the tendency to make of Jesus a figure of either the nineteenth or the twentieth century. So we may hope, and even anticipate, that in the long run, when the work of the *Formgeschichte* school has been finally sifted and appraised, results of value will remain, and that the whisper of the voice will not be judged to be so faint as to dim the freshness of the words.

During the early years of the present century there was an overlap between two clearly distinguishable critical movements within the Church of England. Up to 1919, the date of Bishop Gore's resignation, the criticism which demanded toleration was predominantly of the Liberal type. It was because the critics attached importance to the historical element in Christianity that they were insistent that no event should be accepted as historical except on adequate historical grounds. Such questions as the historicity of the resuscitation of the crucified body of Jesus were discussed as problems of history. But from the time of the publication of

[1] R. H. Lightfoot, *History and Interpretation in the Gospels*, p. 225.

Loisy's *L'Évangile et l'Église* and the spread of the ideas expressed in Schweitzer's *The Quest of the Historical Jesus*, a tendency to regard the historical as of subsidiary importance gathered strength. To Loisy it did not much matter what Jesus actually said or thought or did. As Harnack remarked, Liberal Protestantism did not seem to Loisy to be sufficiently sceptical. Loisy counted on filling up the void created by his more radical scepticism by an appeal to the Church which has been, which is, and which is to be.[1] His position is summed up in the phrase, "The Christ in the Church and God in the Christ". The Roman Church repudiated this line of apologetic, refused to abandon the immemorial foundation of Catholicism, the "infallible, inerrant, integral, insupersessible Divine Revelation" contained in the Bible, and cast Loisy out. Schweitzer made of Jesus a dim figure shrouded in eschatological mist, a stranger and an enigma to our time, a figure which, we must be prepared to find, "will not be a help, but perhaps even an offence to religion". Form Criticism has continued the work of dissolution, while Barthianism denies significance to the wraith of the historical Jesus which remains when radical Form Criticism has done its work.

The outcome of the controversy which died down some fifteen years ago was a victory for Liberalism. It only remains that the spiritual fruits of that victory should be made more widely available, that those who know what has been gained should "say it a little more loudly".

The second critical movement has not given rise to any clear-cut controversy within the Church, and it is difficult to assess its influence, though it is

---

[1] An article by Harnack in *Theologische Literaturzeitung*, January 23, 1904, quoted by A. Houtin, *La Question biblique au xxᵉ siecle*, pp. 269-71.

clear that it has been and still is considerable. Few Anglican scholars would go to such extreme lengths as Schweitzer and Loisy; but it is not too much to say that, especially under the influence of Form Criticism, a vague but wide uncertainty regarding the extent and even the possibility of knowledge of the historical Jesus has spread. This has stimulated Liberal Catholics to lay a more exclusive stress on cultus and the traditional dogma which lies behind cultus. As "the thin figure drawn from inadequate material in the Synoptics" becomes more tenuous, the emphasis on the Sacrifice of the Mass becomes more insistent. It is forgotten that "it was an essential condition of the old scheme that the events with which it was concerned had happened just as they were believed".[1]

Christianity, like Judaism and Islam, and unlike the great religious systems of the Far East, is a historic religion, and at its very heart stands the historic figure of Jesus. If the historic Jesus is destroyed by the acid of criticism or judged to be unknowable, Christianity will doubtless persist, but it will be so changed as to be a different religion. The doubts which have been thrown on the possibility of knowledge of the Jesus of history account, at any rate in part, for the vogue of Otto's theory that religion is based on a kind of apprehension which he calls the apprehension of the "numinous". Under this one term he includes such widely different experiences as the dread of the eerie or uncanny which a savage feels while wandering in dark forests or amidst dismal swamps, and the religious sense of the Holy, felt by Isaiah in his vision in the Temple. According to him the specifically religious veneration of the Holy is a rationalisation or moralisation of the dread felt by the savage when faced by what he does

---

[1] J. S. Boys Smith, *Christian Doctrine and the Idea of Evolution*, p. 24.

not understand. The origin of religion lies in "the dark daemonic murk of primaeval shudderings".[1]

Otto regards the numinous as another Kantian *a priori* category; but, in truth, the sense of the numinous is nothing more than a feeling, and an irrational feeling at that. To base religion on feeling is a suicidal way of evading the challenge of radical historical criticism. Religious feeling is secondary to religious faith. It is not and can not be its ground. If we are prepared, with Otto, to identify religion with the sense of the numinous or holy, we need not complain if we are taken at our word, and the conclusion is drawn that a religion without God is possible and legitimate.

> I said just now that the moral theology of Communism lacked apparently a doctrine of God. If this should be so, it does not seriously affect the existence of the sense of the holy.[2]

The idea of a theology, Communist or otherwise, which lacks a doctrine of God seems to involve a contradiction of terms. To *base* religion on the sense of the numinous is to assent not only to the possibility of a Christianity without Christ but to the legitimacy of a religion without God or, at best, with an unreal God who is the projection of an irrational emotion and has no connexion with actuality. Scientific materialism will rule in the realm of actuality, while religion will be granted permission to indulge in an "attitude towards the universe".[3]

The negative tendency of the present phase of radical criticism has led to a reinforcement of emphasis on the metaphysical abstractions in which Christian doctrine was early formulated. The theologian is always subject to the temptation to cut loose from the contingencies of history, and never more so

---

[1] B. H. Streeter, *The Buddha and the Christ*, p. 325.
[2] Joseph Needham in *Christianity and the Social Revolution*, p. 435.
[3] *Ibid.* p. 436.

than to-day. Though the Jesus of history may vanish into mist, at any rate the Nicene Creed remains. A Christian teacher of repute may not be tolerated in an Anglican pulpit, even at an extra-liturgical service, unless he is prepared to give his assent to the metaphysical doctrine of God and Christ's relation to God, elaborated in the fourth and fifth centuries. Formulated, as it was, under the influence of "the old loving nurse" of Christian theology, Platonism, it was a highly abstract doctrine. The conceptions with which it worked, such as Person, Substance, and Nature, were abstractions distilled from actuality in the crucibles of philosophic speculation.

Indeed it may be said that from Tertullian to Aquinas the expounders of the doctrine of the Trinity were seeking to find a notion of a kind of entity, denoted by the technical term "Person", which is neither an individual nor the attribute of an individual, but is intermediate between the substantival and the adjectival; or which is the ground or basis of a special function rather than a special function, and yet stops short of being an individual subject.[1]

To move securely in the world of such abstractions without tumbling into patent absurdities demands a special mental discipline. Unfortunately, metaphysical abstractions exercise a strange fascination over minds which are quite untrained. The popularity of Christian Science bears witness to this. Mrs Eddy's "Scientific Statement of Being" is a very farrago of disordered abstractions, floating buoyantly in mid-air without any attachment to the world of hard fact.[2] But it is not necessary to turn to Reason's Underworld for cautionary examples of the dangers which beset the method of abstraction. The bastard Aristotelianism, which determined the

---

[1] F. R. Tennant, *Philosophical Theology*, vol. ii. p. 268.
[2] See the chapter entitled "Bunkumismus or Reason's Underworld" in *Return to Philosophy*, by C. E. M. Joad.

mediaeval doctrine of Transubstantiation, provides a sufficiently striking example. First of all the attributes or accidents of a thing were *mentally* abstracted from its substance, and then the accidents were regarded as *actually* separable from substance. This was indeed "Aristotle turned topsy-turvy and metaphysics gone mad".[1] Yet another example is provided by St. Augustine's ingenious argument whereby he sought to demonstrate the unreality of evil. As Dr. Tennant points out, if we start from the world as we know it, the world of actual experience, the fact that evil exists is knowable with much more immediacy and certainty than is the being of God. It might, with equal force, be pointed out to the Christian Scientist, who argues that pain is an illusion, that the fact that I have toothache is more directly known to me than the fact that I am made in the image of God.

> Evil in the abstract is indeed nothing existent, and cannot be said to resist the good; but evil wills none the less resist good wills. St. Augustine, in teaching that the evil will or act has no efficient cause, stated that it is due to *not* setting the will upon God; but he overlooked the fact that evil volition also consists in actually setting the will upon something other than God. Thus the positive element in moral evil was suppressed by *substituting an abstraction for a concrete fact*, and by adopting a negative form of words where a positive form is equally called for. Even the will is an abstraction: the only actuality is an agent willing; and he is the efficient cause which the deficiency-theory failed to find because, by a mere verbal device, it had left him out.[2]

In 1857 Frederick Temple wrote to a friend, "Our theology has been cast in a scholastic mould, *i.e.* all based on Logic. We are in need of and are being gradually forced into a theology based on psychology." "The transition, I fear," he added, "will

<hr>

[1] P. E. More, *The Catholic Faith*, p. 142.
[2] F. R. Tennant, *op. cit.* p. 182.

not be without pain; but nothing can prevent it." Though the transition did not develop as rapidly as, perhaps, Temple anticipated, Anglican theology has now definitely entered on the transitional stage. In this connexion Dr. Tennant's book *Philosophical Theology*, published five years ago, is of significance. It may well prove to have a great and even formative influence. It certainly provides a corrective to the tendency of theology to hypostasize abstractions, and to bestow "a substantival name on an abstracted adjectival characteristic". Starting from the world of actuality and fact, inclusive of man, Dr. Tennant builds up a powerful argument leading to a reasonable faith in God. In that argument considerations of psychology play an important part. His thought is certainly cast in no scholastic mould. The difference of method inevitably affects the form and, in a measure, the substance of the final conclusions.

It may be urged that in any reformulation of Christology the traditional term Incarnation should be retained on the ground that it emphasizes the importance of the fact that Jesus was in the full sense a man as against the Docetism which is constantly cropping up in one form or another. Yet, if the old formula is retained, it must carry with it much which is of a new significance. "The whole world is incarnation in process; in man it becomes increasingly personal: and in the course of the process, 'in the fulness of the times', in Jesus Christ the manifestation of God in Humanity reached its highest stage." [1] This conception of Incarnation relates it closely with Divine Immanence. Dr. Tennant draws a sharp distinction between Immanence and Incarnation. He also urges that "if 'incarnation' is to have any meaning *sui generis* it must signify that God was either one of two subjects, or else the sole subject involved in Christ's experience. . . ." An alternative to an immanental

---

[1] J. F. Bethune-Baker, *The Way of Modernism*, pp. 124, 125.

or strictly incarnational Christology is an acceptance of Christ as "a manifestation of God in the flesh, and as the unique revealer of God". Dr. Tennant faces a position the gravity of which the present Archbishop of York frankly admitted twenty-three years ago.

> The formula of Chalcedon is, in fact, a confession of the bankruptcy of Greek Patristic Theology. The Fathers had done the best that could be done with the intellectual apparatus at their disposal. Their formula had the right devotional value; but it explained nothing. . . . The formula merely stated the fact which constituted the problem; it did not attempt solution. It was therefore unscientific; and as theology is the science of religion, it represented the breakdown of theology.[1]

The undoubted need of reformulation of doctrine is not simply a matter of intellectual apparatus. Our categories of thought, our whole *Weltanschauung*, differ from those of earlier ages. In a valuable pamphlet, *Christian Doctrine and the Idea of Evolution*, Rev. J. S. Boys Smith has examined the repercussions on theology of modern thought and knowledge. He points out that it is not enough to cling to the old theological terminology, interpreting it in some sense which will be congenial or at any rate tolerable to modern thought. "To accept, in its *verbal* sense, a doctrine which belongs in another context and to another age, is not to accept the old doctrine, but a different and almost invariably a worse one." [2] To answer the modern seeker after truth by pointing him to the Nicene Creed is a confession of weakness amounting to impotence, and it is no less futile than weak.

It is of primary importance that the Liberal tradition which goes back from so-called Anglican Modernism to *Essays and Reviews* should be maintained. The Church of England, ever since the Reformation, has been its natural home. Dr. Sanday,

---

[1] W. Temple in *Foundations*, pp. 230, 231.   [2] *Op. cit.* p. 4.

one of its great exemplars, in his last published writing expressed what it stands for: "It stands fundamentally for what I have called elsewhere 'the unification of thought'. The liberal feels that he cannot at any point stop short of this. It is the same mind that has to think of things secular and of things sacred, and the processes of thinking for both are the same." [1] Failure to attain unification of thought is liable to reduce the thinker to the plight of being a philosopher on Mondays, Wednesdays, and Fridays, and a theologian on Tuesdays, Thursdays, and Saturdays.

It may well be that, as Frederick Temple prophesied, the process of winning a theology for our own age will be not without much pain. No advance in the realm of religious truth has been won without pain. If that be the price, it must be paid. The truth should be spoken in love, but it must be spoken. The practice of reserve, even on the honourable ground of a distaste for religious controversy, submission of honest and informed opinion to the censorship of current conceptions of orthodoxy, constitute no Truce of God. The law of God's Kingdom is a law of growth, and acceptance of the *status quo* is no qualification for membership.

EVOLUTION AND ORGANIZATION

Loisy appealed from an unknown Jesus, a Jesus of whose ways we can trace but the outskirts, to a known Church. Jesus was the seed, the Church the growing tree which had sprung from that seed. Along such evolutionary lines he identified the Church with the Christ, though it may be objected that it is morally and religiously intolerable that Jesus of Nazareth should be identified with the historic Catholic Church, that figure "splendid, but

[1] William Sanday, *The Position of Liberal Theology*, p. 31.

terrible, with the light of contemplation and the fire of devoted enthusiasm in her eye, but splashed with innocent blood, like the rider of the Apocalypse, even to the horse-bridle, the cruel oppressor of liberty, the bigoted enemy of truth".[1]

Loisy knew what he meant by the Church. It was a definite institution, the organized world-wide body of which the Pope is the head. The Easterns regard the Church from a different standpoint. The Russian word *sorbonost* denotes a Catholicism which is not primarily institutional. To such a theologian as Nicolas Berdyaev the Church is primarily mystical. Its significance is cosmic. "The Church is all; it constitutes the whole plenitude of being, of the life of humanity, and of the world in a state of Christianization."[2] It is "the order of love and freedom", and may properly be defined as "the true beauty of existence". The visible Church is secondary, "the partial actualization of the invisible Church". Unity of organization is a horizontal unity, belonging to the plane of ecclesiastical statecraft; schemes of external reunion are therefore to be distrusted. It is necessary to "go deeper and higher rather than attempt to move on the surface of things". The universal Church is so wide as to embrace even the activities of a Goethe and a Nietzsche.

> The limits of the universal Church do not coincide with those of the visible historic churches; the soul of the Church is one, and to it there belong, not only the members of the different churches, but even those who are outside the visible Church altogether. There is a great spiritual brotherhood composed of Christians to which not only the Churches of the East and West belong, but also all those whose wills are directed towards God and the divine, all in fact who aspire to some form of spiritual elevation.[3]

[1] W. R. Inge, *Faith and Knowledge*, p. 287.
[2] Nicolas Berdyaev, *Freedom and the Spirit*, p. 331.
[3] Nicolas Berdyaev, *ibid.* pp. 356, 357.

The Church of England is not an Eastern Church, and is more concerned than is Berdyaev with the horizontal plane; but it is nearer to him than to Rome when in its Bidding Prayer it speaks of "Christ's holy Catholic Church—that is, the whole congregation of Christian people dispersed throughout the world". The more sectarian Anglican, however, uses the word "Catholic" as the antonym of "Protestant", while, at the same time, claiming that he himself is a Catholic. The non-Protestant European world pays no attention to his claim. To the cultured European the Catholic Church is the Roman Catholic Church as distinguished not only from the Protestant Churches, but from the Orthodox Church, and, most certainly, from the Church of England. If he has so much as heard of Anglo-Catholicism, he regards it as an insular vagary with no more than an insular significance. The attitude of the Roman Catholic Church is not in doubt. The Pope no more regards the Archbishop of Canterbury as a Bishop of the Catholic Church than the War Office regards Miss Evangeline Booth as a commissioned officer in H.M. Forces.

Loisy justified later doctrinal developments on evolutionary grounds. Some Anglicans, in seeking a justification for certain ecclesiastical developments, take a similar line; though for Evolution they substitute the Holy Spirit. The episcopal organization which had become general by the middle of the second century had, they hold, the authorization of the Holy Spirit and was therefore sacrosanct. It is not enough, apparently, to point out that something like an episcopal system was demanded by the position in which the Church found itself; that, under the circumstances of the time, episcopacy patently had great value; and that we can make reasonable conjectures as to the way in which presbyterial or poly-episcopal local organization developed into non-episcopacy, the episcopate representing the unity of the Church. This might well seem to constitute a sufficient justification for episcopal government in the early Church. But under different conditions a different form of organization might be demanded. Along similar lines the Roman Catholic would justify the later developments of the Papacy, while the Protestant would affirm that, under the conditions which existed at the time of the Reformation, a non-episcopal organization of the Reformed Churches was desirable. To meet this difficulty the special guidance of the Holy Spirit must be postulated for the earlier but not for the later developments. So episcopacy is endowed with a divine right, and the acceptance not only of episcopacy, but of an episcopacy which lays claim to an "apostolic succession", is made a pre-condition of Reunion. This facile evocation of the Holy Spirit to justify a method of ecclesiastical organization is as much open to objection as Loisy's justification, on evolutionary grounds, of questionable doctrines. It is as undesirable as it is convenient thus to produce the *deus ex machina* to strengthen the weaker links of an argument.

The ambiguity of the word "Church", and, no less, the ambiguity of the word "Catholic", are responsible for much unconscious sophistry and questionable argument. If, for example, by Catholicism is intended Roman Catholicism or pre-Reformation Catholicism, it is undoubtedly true that the retention of episcopacy constitutes a link between Anglicanism and Catholicism. If, on the other hand, by Catholicism is meant the Catholicism of the Bidding Prayer, or the *sorbonost* of the Russian Church, it is no less clear that insistence on the necessity of episcopacy creates a deep fissure between Anglicans and the majority of those Catholics who are of their own race and language.

The same reasons which drove Loisy from the Jesus of history to the Christ existent or incarnate in the developing Church have driven some Anglicans to seek in the Catholic Church, as they happen to envisage it, a final court of appeal. When "the Church teaches" this or that, discussion is finished. Rome repudiated Loisy. Anglicans who take a line similar to his are in a plight almost, if not quite, as embarrassing, for they are appealing to a Catholicism from whose authoritative belief they have, as Canon Lilley points out, during the last fifty years drifted away so gradually and imperceptibly "that there is hardly left among them to-day even one who would maintain it in the full measure of its ancient rigour".[1] They seek escape from their embarrassment by an insistence, as a matter of Catholic principle, on the importance of episcopal organization. The result has been a hardening of Anglicanism as against the Free Churches.

This was reflected in the exclusive character of the declaration which is now imposed on applicants for inclusion in parochial Electoral Rolls.

> I declare that I . . . am a member of the Church of England *and do not belong to any religious body which is not in communion with the Church of England.*

This explicit exclusion from the Electoral Roll of those who have been born and bred members of other religious bodies, even if they have joined the Church of England, unless they are prepared to forswear membership of the Church of their upbringing, is directly contrary to the traditions of Anglicanism. In an appendix to *The Report of the Archbishops' Committee on Church and State*, published in 1917, details are given of the corresponding regulations of other Churches of the Anglican Communion. In the Church of Ireland the qualification for inclusion in

---

[1] A. L. Lilley, *Religion and Revelation*, p. 6.

what corresponds to the Electoral Roll is registered membership of the congregation for three months; in the Canadian Church a declaration of registration as a habitual worshipper in a congregation; in nearly all the Australian dioceses a written declaration of Church membership, though "in two cases at least" this must be supplemented by a declaration that the member belongs to no other denomination; in New Zealand a declaration of membership subject to registration for two months. In South Africa, on the other hand, a declaration that the applicant is not a member of any other religious body is demanded. By the insertion of the negative words in the Form of Application for Enrolment on the Church Electoral Roll, the Church of England has aligned itself with the South African Church and dissociated itself from the general position and tradition of the Anglican Communion. It was a retrogressive step, an innovation to be deplored by all who still conceive the Church of England as in ideal a National Church.

AUTHORITY

To the younger generation, the years 1914–1918 constitute a gulf separating the old from the new. The controversy which followed the publication of *Foundations*, hardly less than the more distant "Essays-and-Reviews" debate, is to many of those under forty years of age little more than an echo of

> faint, unhappy, far-off things
> And battles long ago.

This is unfortunate. For the formation of a sound judgement about present problems a sense of continuity is of value, and it is almost essential to a wise approach to the problems which the future will bring. It is the more unfortunate because the war turned men's minds to objects unrelated to the search for truth, while the early post-war period was character-ized by a rank growth of superstition which flour-ished side by side with widespread cynicism and disillusionment. Reconstruction became a "blessed word", and the Church, following the prevailing fashion, busied itself with organization. For some years machinery took precedence over theology.

Looking back over the ecclesiastical history of the past seventy-five years, there runs clearly through-out it, like a red thread, the question of authority. The authority of Scripture conceived as inerrant was smashed by the new scientific knowledge and the findings of Higher Criticism. The dread that this would happen accounts for the panic of 1864. Liddon's protest against *Lux Mundi* was the despairing cry of one who realized that it had happened. The tenacity of Gore's insistence on the authority of the Creeds literally interpreted, was the stubborn defence of a credal authority which should be a substitute for the authority of an inerrant Bible. The appeal to the Catholic Church, ambiguous though it be, is determined by the craving for an authority which shall serve as a final court of appeal.

Behind the question of authority lies that of the criterion of authority. On this point there has been a consistent post-Reformation tradition. How-ever august an authority may be, it must submit to judgement at the bar of reason.

> For men to be tied and led by authority, as it were with a kind of captivity of judgment, and though there be reason to the contrary not to listen unto it, but to follow like beasts the first in the herd, they know not nor care not whither, this were brutish. Again, that authority of men should prevail with men either against or above Reason, is no part of our belief. "Companies of learned men" be they never so great and reverend, are to yield unto Reason; the weight thereof is no whit prejudiced by the simplicity of his person which doth allege it, but being found to be sound and good, the bare opinion of

men to the contrary must of necessity stoop and give place.[1]

The condemnation of Galileo was the *reductio ad absurdum* of the claim of the Church to an inherent authority in all matters touching religion. If Galileo had reason on his side, neither Pope nor Inquisition nor, for that matter, any Church Council, however "great and reverend", had legitimate authority over him. The authority of Convocation on a matter of Biblical criticism is likewise invalid as against that of competent Biblical critics, unless it be assumed that the majority of those voting are more learned than those whom they judge. The condemnation by Convocation of *Essays and Reviews* was of no more intrinsic value than the condemnation of Galileo by the Holy Office. In the seventeenth century the Cambridge Platonists maintained Hooker's position. "To go against *Reason*", says Whichcote, "is to go against *God*: it is the self same thing, to do that which the Reason of the Case doth require; and that which God himself doth appoint: Reason is the *Divine* Governor of Man's Life; it is the very Voice of God." [2] Frederick Temple was in the line of the authentic Anglican tradition when he asserted the supremacy of Truth and Reason.

The same tradition asserts the rationality of the moral judgement. "The *Rule* of Right is the Reason of Things; the *Judgement* of Right is the Reason of our Minds, *perceiving* the Reason of Things." [3] When the moral judgement is based on mere feeling, the dissolution of morality has already begun to set in, and the first step has been taken along the road which leads to moral anarchism. There is, happily, such a thing as moral progress no less than progress

---

[1] Richard Hooker, *Laws of Ecclesiastical Polity*, Book II. chap. vii.

[2] Benjamin Whichcote, *Aphorisms*; E. T. Campagnac, *The Cambridge Platonists*, p. 67.

[3] *Ibid.* p. 66.

in knowledge. With changing conditions and growth in knowledge, the application of moral principles develops. As the moral consciousness of a century ago demanded the abolition of the slavery which the moral consciousness of the Middle Ages tolerated, so the moral consciousness of to-day demands a reform of marriage laws which were not only tolerable but sacrosanct to our fathers. The dictates of authority, whether of the present or the past, are, without any exception whatever, answerable at the bar of the enlightened moral judgement. Frederick Temple was justified in demanding loyalty not only to reason and truth, but also to conscience, "the supreme interpreter, whom it may be a duty to enlighten, but whom it can never be a duty to disobey".

The supremacy of the moral judgement within the sphere of doctrine, whatever be the weight of ecclesiastical authority, which may be alleged on the other side, was asserted uncompromisingly by Dean Rashdall. As the enlightened moral consciousness of the nineteenth century had challenged the ancient doctrine of Eternal Punishment, so Rashdall, on moral grounds, in his book on the Atonement,[1] published in 1919, challenged the doctrine of a propitiatory substitutionary sacrifice of Jesus on the Cross. He did not shirk the fact that behind the doctrine which he criticized lay an immense weight of authority. He frankly admitted, for example, that "there is no getting rid of the substitutionary element in the theology of St. Paul".[2]

The Catholic doctrine of the Sacrifice of the Mass and the Evangelical Plan of Salvation are alike bound up with the traditional doctrines of the Fall and the Propitiatory Sacrifice. Liberal Catholicism has found it possible to retain the cultus of the Mass,

---

[1] Hastings Rashdall, *The Idea of Atonement in Christian Theology.*
[2] *Op. cit.* p. 101.

while abandoning or radically modifying the doctrine which it was intended to express. It is a dangerous procedure, though it may claim a pragmatic justification. In practice the stress is laid on cultus, and when appeal is made to the multitude through cultus of a mediaeval type, eloquent of mediaeval ideas, though, in truth, these have been abandoned by Liberals, the rational and moral elements in religion are in danger of being submerged in the numinous mass-emotion which is induced. Cultus of this type is apt only too easily to breed superstition.

The Anglo-Catholic feels under a certain compulsion to maintain the tradition for which he stands, even if, in doing so, he is driven to practise an eclecticism impossible to justify on Catholic principles. The Evangelical also has behind him a tradition; but he is in a freer relationship with it. Though it was long before it became explicit, from the beginning the right of private judgement was implicit in Protestantism. The liberalizing of Evangelicalism, however, was not without pain. Equally with the Tractarians, the Evangelicals were distressed by the impact of the new science and the new Biblical scholarship on old beliefs. But, when once the Evangelical is convinced that reason and conscience demand an abandonment or modification of traditional belief, he is free to move forward untrammelled by allegiance to the authority of a tradition which, in principle, he has always been free to criticize.

There are to-day signs of the growth of an anti-rationalism which threatens the hard-won gains of Liberalism in all departments of life, social, political, and theological. A widely prevalent failure of nerve tempts men to abandon the ground won by their fathers. Voices which have the public ear summon them to seek security by retreat. The Church of England has ever bred sons who, inspired by loyalty to truth, reason, and conscience, have undertaken the adventure of the faithful pioneer. It is true that within the Church there is and has been a conflict of ideals; but the Liberal tradition has not been the exclusive monopoly of any one party. If, as is possible, religion in England is threatened by a resurgence of Fundamentalism, superstition, and obscurantism, it is certain that there will, as ever, be men who will make a firm stand against "captivity of judgement". But they will need the frank and courageous support, not of one party only, but of men of whatever party who acknowledge as their final authority the reason and the moral judgement which are "the very Voice of God".